MASTERS OF POLITICAL THOUGHT

VOLUME TWO

Machiavelli to Bentham

D0897142

MASTERS OF POLITICAL THOUGHT

Under the Editorship of
EDWARD McCHESNEY SAIT

✳

VOLUME ONE : *Plato to Machiavelli*
MICHAEL B. FOSTER
CHRIST CHURCH, OXFORD

VOLUME TWO : *Machiavelli to Bentham*
W. T. JONES
POMONA COLLEGE, CALIFORNIA

Under the Editorship of
W. T. JONES

✳

VOLUME THREE : *Hegel to Dewey*
LANE W. LANCASTER
UNIVERSITY OF NEBRASKA

MASTERS *of*
POLITICAL THOUGHT

VOLUME TWO

Machiavelli to Bentham

by W. T. JONES, B.Litt.(*Oxon*), Ph.D.(*Princeton*)
PROFESSOR OF PHILOSOPHY, POMONA COLLEGE

HARRAP   LONDON

First published in Great Britain 1947
by GEORGE G. HARRAP & CO. LTD
182 High Holborn, London WC1V 7AX
Reprinted: 1949; 1950; 1955; 1956; 1957; 1959; 1960; 1961; 1963;
1964; 1966; 1967; 1969; 1970; 1973; 1975; 1977; 1980

ISBN 0 245 56783 6

Printed in Great Britain by
Redwood Burn Limited
Trowbridge & Esher

Editor's Introduction

Masters of Political Thought marks a departure from current practice. For undergraduates the medium of instruction in political theory has too often been the comprehensive and encyclopedic text-book. The writers are catalogued and their doctrines summarized, sometimes upon the basis of other and more specialized summaries and not upon the basis of the original works. While the text-book may be indispensable for certain purposes, anything like exclusive dependence upon it inculcates superficiality.

The conventional text-book is more appropriate to som branches of Politics than to others. I believe, for example, that its use is necessary, or at any rate desirable, in the first approach to American government or to international relations, among other courses. Political theory, however, stands apart. It is peculiar in being tied, in the closest fashion, to the personality and genius of the individual thinker, and even to his literary form and his mode of argument. An epitome of Plato's *Republic* or of Hobbes's *Leviathan* can be little more adequate than a paraphrase of *Paradise Lost*. Two centuries ago a wise man warned us against treating books like members of the nobility; that is, against learning their titles and bragging afterwards of acquaintance with them. One cannot become acquainted with the *Republic* by reading what another man thought about it.

Ideally the original works should displace the text-book. There would be more intellectual profit in reading eight or ten such works than in committing to memory a tabulation that brought within its encyclopedic sweep all the political philosophers from Plato to Dewey. But the ideal must give way to the practicable. The undergraduate course, according to firmly established tradition in America, presents a systematic survey of the whole range of theory. Is there, then, no way of escape from the text-book method? Some measure of relief has been afforded by the supplementary use of the source book or book of readings, an anthology or golden treasury of extracts, which establishes a precious contact with the original sources, awakens in persons of discernment a desire to make that contact still more intimate, and so deserves our gratitude. But the source book, aside from the brevity and the arbitrary selection of quoted passages, does not meet all our needs. It does not, in scattered comment and interpretation, shed light upon obscurities as they arise, or emphasize points that otherwise might receive scant attention, or show the significance of environment in accounting for some vagary of doctrine. It does not weave together the various extracts and present the writer's doctrine as a whole—at least, in its major aspects.

The text-book supplemented by the source book is better than the text-book alone. But another possibility suggests itself and is embodied in the *Masters of Political Thought*. It brings us a stage nearer to familiarity with the most conspicuous theorists. It assigns to the text-book the purely subordinate role of filling interstices wherever teacher or student may wish to do so. That is the plan that has been adopted here. The plan calls for concentration upon a few great masters from Plato to the present and recourse to numerous and lengthy quotations, quotations that have been chosen judiciously and then elucidated and woven together by unobtrusive comment. Aquinas or Montesquieu speaks for himself, in his own words. Comment, instead of supplanting the original and disguising its flavour, is designed to clarify and interpret.

Concentration, though an essential feature of the plan, involves some difficulty. There are degrees of concentration. Shall the list of philosophers be confined to a few men of undisputed pre-eminence in the field of theory? Or shall we listen favourably to the claims of Dante and Marsiglio of Padua, Harrington and Paine, John Stuart Mill (along with Bentham) and Lenin (along with Marx)? Where shall the line be drawn between the great and the near-great? Opinion will differ as particular claims are advanced. This much is clear. The list would grow portentously in length and defeat the whole object of the plan unless each claim were subjected to rigid scrutiny. In designing the *Masters of Political Thought* a high standard of selection has been applied, the integrity of the plan protected. Teacher or student may feel that some philosopher who has been left out deserves a place among the masters. In such a case he can, as I have already pointed out, fill the vacuum partially by turning to one of the text-books in the library. But surely he will wish to have more than a formal bowing acquaintance with an authentic master and so will seek intimate friendship by reading the master's own works.

Politics, like many other branches of learning, has been subdivided for the purposes of specialization. An expert in international law may know very little about political parties or public administration; and, carrying subdivision still farther, an expert in theory may be reluctant to speak as an authority in matters that lie outside his chosen and limited field, which may embrace only one or two centuries. This will explain why *Masters of Political Thought* appears in three small volumes, each by a different author. The preparation of the first volume— Plato to Machiavelli—was entrusted to Dr Michael B. Foster, of the University of Oxford; of the second—Machiavelli to Bentham—to Dr W. T. Jones, of Pomona College; and of the third—Bentham to the Present—to Dr William M. McGovern, of North-western University. Both Dr Jones and Dr McGovern took degrees at Oxford, where much emphasis is laid upon political theory.

Each volume consists of extracts—which tend to preponderate— and interpretative comment. Extracts are distinguished from comment, not by any change in the size of the type, but by (1) indentation and (2) the appearance of a type ornament at the beginning of the quotation, and also at the beginning of each page on which quotations are continued.

EDWARD McCHESNEY SAIT

Acknowledgments

SINCE THE appearance of volume one the General Editor of this series, Edward McChesney Sait, has died. The novel idea, described in the preface to this volume, which has served as the principle on which the whole series is constructed, was his own, and to his energy, scholarship, and wisdom the series owes much. The author of the present volume in particular is indebted to Mr Sait, both as friend and mentor in ways too numerous to list in detail; he therefore wishes his first acknowledgment to record his gratitude and his sense of loss.

The extracts printed in this volume are derived from the following texts and translations:

MACHIAVELLI (*Discourses*). Translation by C. E. Detmold (London, 1882).

MACHIAVELLI (*The Prince*). Translation by Luigi Ricci, revised by E. H. P. Vincent.

BODIN (*Six Livres*). I have made my own translation.

HOBBES (*Leviathan*). Oxford University Press (London and New York).

LOCKE (*Treatise*). All quotations are from the 1727 edition.

MONTESQUIEU (*Spirit of Laws*). Translation by Thomas Nugent, revised by J. V. Prichard (Bell, 1878).

ROUSSEAU (*Œuvres Complètes*). I have made my own translation.

ROUSSEAU (*Social Contract*). I have made my own translation.

BURKE (*Writings and Speeches*). J. C. Nimmo (London, 1899).

BENTHAM (*Theory of Legislation*). Translated and edited from the French of E. Dumont by C. M. Atkinson (Oxford, 1914); quoted by permission of the Oxford University Press.

I have altered the translations in some places where I thought I could improve them, but such alterations are not extensive. I desire to express my gratitude to the Publishers mentioned who have granted me permission to use their copyright.

W. T. J.

PUBLISHER'S NOTE

THE PROPORTION of text and quoted material
has made necessary a special type arrangement.
The author's comments and the quotations are in
the same size type. Quoted passages are indented
slightly from the left and are further marked by
a type ornament at the beginning of the passage
and at the head of each page on which quotations
are continued.

Contents

Sovereignty is the absolute and perpetual power . . . of commanding in a state. It is necessary to define this term since no political philosopher or jurist has yet defined it, though the presence of sovereignty is the chief property which distinguishes a state from other organizations or societies of men.

BODIN

Force is physical power; I do not see that its effects can ever be moral. To yield to force is an act of necessity, not of will. . . . In what sense can that be a duty? . . . Let us agree that might never makes right, and that we have a duty to obey only legitimate powers.

ROUSSEAU

CHAPTER ONE

Introductory

In this volume we consider eight more writers, beginning with Machiavelli and ending with Bentham, who are said to be "masters of political thought." Why begin with Machiavelli? Why end with Bentham? Is there any defining characteristic which distinguishes these eight as a group? To begin with, of course, their lives all fall in a fairly well-defined period. They are separated on the one hand from the classical and mediæval writers considered in Dr Foster's volume by the tremendous break of the Renaissance, and from ourselves, on the other hand, by the Industrial Revolution, the Napoleonic wars, and the other events which shaped the course of the nineteenth century. But are these thinkers distinguished by anything more than chronology? Is there any set of problems peculiar to them which marks them off as a group from their predecessors? That there is we shall shortly see.[1] But before we consider what distinguishes them from other political thinkers it is reasonable to ask, What distinguishes political thought as such? What, indeed, is this political thought of which these writers, along with Plato and Aristotle and Hegel and Marx, are said to be 'masters'? It is easy to reply that by political thought we mean theory—but what, after all, is political theory?

Some people deny its existence, because they suppose it is an attempt to tell us about a fictitious realm of so-called 'Eternal Truths.' Others deny its utility, because they think of utility solely in terms of practice. No one would deny either the existence or the use of political science; but is there, indeed, such a thing as political philosophy, distinct from political science yet in its own way a real, meaningful, and useful inquiry? That there is the reader of the following chapters can see for himself. Here we may content ourselves with pointing out, in a general way, what political philosophy undertakes to tell us and what its uses are.

First, then, as regards the kind of inquiry political philosophy purports to be. Certainly, to some extent, political philosophers seem

---

[1] *Vide infra*, pp. 18*ff.*

concerned to offer advice to rulers and statesmen about specific matters of policy and procedure. Thus Machiavelli gives useful maxims for seizing and maintaining power, and Bodin discusses how a king ought to organize his privy council and what its rules of procedure ought to be. But if the philosophical reputations of the writers who appear in this volume depended on the soundness of the advice which they offer we would hardly need to devote so much attention to them. Certainly their advice is in some cases shrewd and still timely; but on the whole their procedure is not sufficiently empirical for us to repose much trust in it. And even where (as in the case of Machiavelli or Burke) the method is empirical it is not sufficiently objective. The studies whose consideration we are about to begin contain intuitive, rather than scientific, generalizations; they are based upon the personal experience of the author or on his reading of history; they are tinged with all his emotional and conative reactions to his own peculiar situation. If they do reach sound conclusions about the phenomena of politics it is, as it were, by accident rather than as the result of any careful and controlled methodology. Such a scientific study of politics, such a factual investigation of political phenomena, is doubtless possible; and such knowledge is doubtless useful and significant. But the controlled, experimental, objective method by which such knowledge is to be obtained is very different from the procedure of those thinkers whose work we have to examine here. And whatever use their work may have is clearly different from the immediate, practical use of political science.

As a matter of fact, however, our writers are not chiefly concerned with maxims derived from the facts of political behaviour. While they do not, and cannot, ignore concrete political facts their attention is rather concentrated on such abstract questions as the meaning of sovereignty or the right relation between sovereign and subject. They do not tell us who was actually sovereign in France in 1576, but they tell us who they believe ought to have been sovereign. They do not tell us what rights Englishmen actually had against their king in 1690; they tell us what rights they believe Englishmen ought to have. In other words, these writers seem chiefly to be concerned with two rather special kinds of questions—in the first place, questions about definition; in the second place, questions of appraisal. This should give us some insight into the kind of inquiry political philosophy is. Like any other philosophical enterprise it is concerned with facts, but its concern for facts is a special kind of concern. It is an attempt (1) to understand the facts by seeing them in relation to a larger whole and (2) to evaluate them in terms of this relation. It differs from science because the latter does not try to evaluate the facts, and because, though science certainly tries to understand the facts, its procedure is different. In a word, both philosophy and science are concerned with facts, but philosophy's concern is special and not always understood. This difference may be illustrated by an example. The chair I am now sitting on is a fact—what we may call a 'physical' fact. There is a sense in which I understand this fact when I look at it and feel it. We may call this the plain man's (or common-sense) knowledge of the chair. And this knowledge becomes scientific when, instead of merely looking at the chair, we measure it—instead of lifting it, we weigh it. Whether scientist or plain man, I am concerned to know the chair as a particular and, as it were, isolated fact. But I become a philosopher of chairs just so far as I relate this particular chair in thought to other types and styles of chairs—to Chippendale, Sheraton, Hepplewhite chairs, and so on. The further I carry this process of comparison the better I understand this particular chair. Its particularity is now illuminated by the various relations of similarity and contrast in which it stands to other chairs. This cognitive (or defining) process is accompanied by a process of appraisal. Indeed, we do not have two distinct processes at all; for as I determine this chair's nature through comparing it with other chairs I also determine its 'moral' status: whether it be good or bad of its kind, and whether its kind, as such, be good or bad. A political philosophy differs in no fundamental way from this furniture philosophy. The dual process of definition and evaluation is identical in both cases, but in the former case the facts being subjected to this process are political facts (e.g., the actual powers of the sovereign, the actual rights of the subject) instead of physical facts like tables and chairs.

Both the political philosopher and the political scientist, then, are concerned with the facts of political relationship, but they are not concerned with the facts in the same way. It is not the political philosopher's function to ascertain what the political facts are (though, of course, he may also occupy himself in this way[1]); it is his function to try to understand, interpret, and evaluate these facts by putting them

---

[1] Before the development of modern specialized, fact-finding techniques this was obviously much more the concern of the political philosopher than it is to-day. Thus Machiavelli, Bodin, Montesquieu, and the rest of our writers were not only political philosophers, they were also political fact-finders—though doubtless they were not so 'scientific' as our fact-finders are to-day.

in relation to other kinds of facts—the facts of man's moral, religious, and æsthetic experience, facts about man's ideals and about his conception of the universe in which he lives.

Another way of saying all this is to say that the philosophical question *par excellence* in the realm of politics is the question, *Why* does the state exist? What end or purpose does it serve? The state is one of the most omnipresent facts of human experience. It is an enormous structure of interrelated facts—forces, powers, institutions—of an almost unbelievably complex character. It is hardly surprising, therefore, that men should want to understand the state, to know how all of these complex interconnected facts are fitted together; and it is the business of the political scientist, so far as he can, to satisfy men on this point. It is natural also that men should ask themselves what justifies the existence of this complex of forces, powers, and institutions. After all, we are very much a part of the state: it intervenes either explicitly or implicitly in everything we do, it colours everything we think and feel. We can hardly fail to ask, about anything which is of such consequence to us, whether it is good for us. This is a question on which political science, as such, can throw no light. It is a question which requires a philosophical analysis, because the attempt to answer it inevitably takes us outside of the limited sphere of political facts and requires us to relate these facts to man's conception of himself and of his place in the world.

If the question, What justifies the state? is a perennial philosophical problem different philosophers have certainly given quite different answers to it. Some have thought that the state is justified because it enables men to attain a kind of happiness they could never hope to achieve in solitude; others, because it gives them security and protects their property; still others, because it is the instrument of God's design for man. Others, again, have maintained that the state serves no further purpose—that it is its own end. All of this diversity is natural and inevitable. Because men's ideals and purposes, because their conceptions of their place in the universe, are not always the same their estimates of the value of different types of political organization will also vary. There may, indeed, be a final and complete Truth-about-Politics. Some people, certainly, have supposed themselves to be giving us information about it. But we should do well if we set political philosophy a humbler and at the same time a more useful task—namely, that of making sense of the state to the various men who live in it. Hence there will be as many different political philosophies as there are different kinds of men. And we shall judge the relative soundness of these different philosophies, not by the amount they deviate from this ideal Truth-about-Politics, but by the degree with which they produce, for the men who conceive them, an understanding of politics in its relation to the total picture of the world as they conceive it to be. Thus different political theories have a common object, not in the sense that they all explore the same realm of 'eternal verities,' but rather in the sense that they are all engaged in the same task: the working out of a schema on which facts can be arranged and in terms of which otherwise chaotic and incoherent experience becomes intelligible and significant. The more facts to be made sense of, the more difficult the construction of a satisfactory schema; but the better the theory, the more facts does it succeed in making meaningful.

If political philosophy is an inquiry such as we have described, then in one sense we have answered already the question, What is its use? If understanding is useful; if it is good to have knowledge and bad to be ignorant; if it is pleasant to have ideas which are consistent, ordered, and systematic, and disagreeable to own a mind which is only a grab-bag of vague, confused, and disconnected items—then political philosophy is not idle or purposeless. This is perhaps all the defence that such an inquiry demands.

But there is another use of political philosophy which is too important not to be mentioned.

It is particularly important that citizens of democratic countries should think about what metaphysicians sometimes call 'first principles,' about the basic concepts on which political theory rests and which guide political practice. Of course, if the form of the state be imposed from above by an act of violence; if the sovereign be in no sense responsible to the ordinary men over whom he rules; if 'justification' be a meaningless term, because the possession of power justifies and explains all—in these circumstances, certainly, the study of political philosophy is either idle or dangerous. But if ordinary men have, or ought to have, some voice in determining what the state is like; if they have a right to expect the sovereign to justify his use of force upon them; if the state is somehow a nexus of mutual rights and duties—then we can hardly call political philosophy useless. On the contrary, it would be truer to say that democratic states can survive in the long run only if their citizens do ask themselves questions which are philosophical in character. In non-democratic states it does not matter whether the citizens understand the state. It is far better, indeed, that they should not. But democratic states cannot long endure if their citizens do not think about the state, or if they think about it only at the level of newspaper editorials and Fourth of July speeches. So far we have been speaking of political philosophy in general, but after all this book is not devoted to contemporary theories. Bentham died one hundred years ago; Machiavelli, four hundred. However successful their syntheses were in their own days, what possible use can they be to us now? We could reply (and it would be true) that they have an antiquarian interest and that it is at least as interesting to know what kinds of ideas people had in Renaissance Italy or in Georgian England as it is to know how they dressed or what they ate. This sort of purely historical interest is widespread, but it is not universal. If we want a really satisfactory answer to our question we must, therefore, take our stand on somewhat higher ground.

The fact is that though political philosophies change they do so very slowly. To study the theories of Machiavelli, Hobbes, or Locke is not to transport ourselves to a dusty and remote antiquity. The basic problems which these thinkers struggled with still face us; the experiences which seemed to them important and which required to be synthesized are still important for us, still await synthesis. Hence in learning to understand their problems and the meaning of their concepts we are not indulging in a merely academic or historical research.

Not all citizens, even under Utopian conditions, can be political philosophers; it would hardly be Utopian if they were. Fewer still can be *original* political philosophers in their own right. Few people, that is, could ever reach 'first principles' if left to their own devices. That this is the case determines the importance of the history of political theory. The study of the great theories of the past ought to sharpen our wits, clarify our thinking, help us to reach more coherent definitions and sounder moral appraisals than most of us could ever hope to do by ourselves. And this is especially the case if, as we have said, the problems considered by these thinkers are identical with our own.

It may be worth our while to consider briefly what are these basic problems shared by ourselves with all these political thinkers from Machiavelli to Bentham. All the questions considered important in the early modern period fall into two distinct, though closely connected, groups. One of these groups is focused on the concept of sovereignty. Now, sovereignty, as Bodin remarks, is a new concept in this period; he could not, he tells us, find anything in any of the Greek or mediæval thinkers about sovereignty. The reason is that certain conditions arose at the beginning of the early modern period which necessitated a new theoretical schema. The schema which was finally worked out is based on the notion of sovereignty, and, since the same conditions survive to-day, the notion of sovereignty is still of the first importance. These conditions are, of course, the emergence out of the feudal political system of the national territorial state. This kind of political organization had to come into being; or, rather, the modern world would not have developed as it has—into a lay, industrial, and capitalistic culture—had it not been for the creation of the national territorial state, which is at once an instrument and an effect of this development. In their theories Machiavelli, Bodin, Hobbes, and the others within our period only reflect their sensitivity to these economic and social changes, and their recognition of the political problem which these changes entail.

The full complexity of the problem was not at first grasped. Bodin and Hobbes see only the imperative need of a strong, central power, which can fuse the old divergent feudal forces into a real unity, which can control all the energies and aspirations unleashed by the new spirit. They see simply, but very clearly, that a supreme and absolutely powerful ruler—a sovereign—is an indispensable condition of the new order of things.

By the time Locke, Montesquieu, and Rousseau appear on the scene the social and political picture has developed sufficiently for the full complexity of the problem to emerge. There must be an absolute sovereign; yes, certainly. But this sovereign must be so conceived that the individual rights of private men are not imperilled, but rather implemented, by his existence. How can we have a sovereign who is powerful enough to maintain order and to keep all the intricate parts of the new complex working together efficiently, and yet at the same time not so powerful that he destroys individual liberty, initiative, and spontaneity? This raises a whole series of questions about legitimacy, about the mutual rights and duties of sovereign and subject, about the relation between government and sovereign, about the extent of powers which are still very much with us. These questions are still with us just because the antinomy between individual freedom and state control is even more frighteningly real to-day than when it was first formulated. The development towards complexity and mutual interdependence, which began in the sixteenth and seventeenth centuries, was enormously accelerated by the Industrial Revolution, so that it is more than ever necessary to-day to have a central authority to keep all the parts of the organism moving.[1] On the other hand, we still feel, just as these early modern thinkers did, the value and significance of human personality. Our problem, then, is precisely the same as that of, say, Locke—namely, how to reconcile this great Greek and mediæval humane tradition with the increasing complexity of modern life.

The other main group of problems which occupied all of these early modern thinkers results from the conception of the state as a natural organism. At the beginning of the modern period men began to look on the physical world in which they lived, not as a "vale of tears" designed by God as a punishment for man's sins, but as a neutral and independent entity, capable of objective, dispassionate study, and conforming to simple, non-teleological, mechanical laws. It was inevitable that everything else in the world should come, sooner or later, to be regarded in the same light, as a purely natural entity. Thus Machiavelli saw the state, not as God's voice on earth, but as a tension of human, all-too-human, forces—ambition, jealousy, fear. Both Bodin and Montesquieu long ago saw what modern social study has been patiently rediscovering—that the state is not only a product of human motives, but also of the physical environment—climate, soil, altitude. Hence, if one wanted to understand the state one no longer asked what God's plan for man is; one no longer asked what truth, goodness, and justice are aiming at. One asked, instead, how all these natural forces affect each other causally. In a word, these early modern thinkers were just as convinced as we are that the state has a natural history, as certainly as any animal or plant. Just as what the oak-tree grows to be depends on the various forces—sun, air, water—that play upon it, so the state is a natural product of certain physical factors.

But they also saw—perhaps more clearly than we do—that the state at the same time belongs to another order altogether—a moral order. That is, they saw that it is reasonable to ask not only *how* the

---

[1] To-day, indeed, the economic and social organism far transcends the limits of any one national territorial state; and we are faced, therefore, with the additional task of discovering a suitable international (or supra-national) political form. But this does not mean that the problem of sovereignty vanishes. It only means that it has become wider and more complex and requires to be transferred to a new and larger sphere.

state got to be the sort of thing it is, but whether what it is is good; and this meant for them, not merely whether individual men judge it to be good here and now because it satisfies their present desires and expectations, but whether it is *really* good. Our ancestors put the problem this way, of course, because they stood so near to the mediæval conception of natural laws promulgated by God for man. We perhaps would no longer talk to-day of God's commands; but, whatever the phrases we employ, it is not uncommon to-day to hold that people have rights even though no one recognizes them, that certain laws are unjust though on the statute book, that certain acts are wrong though permitted and encouraged by the sovereign. The difficulty is to reconcile the existence of this moral order with the natural order to which the state also belongs. The difficulty is to see how man, who is a part of this natural order and so conditioned by its processes, can also have rights and duties, obligations and responsibilities, which seem to take him out of it altogether. The attempt of all the early modern thinkers (with one exception) to effect this reconciliation can hardly be insignificant for those who are faced with the same problem. And the conclusions of Hobbes—who alone of them took his stand on the state as *merely* natural—are perhaps even more instructive negatively than are theirs positively.

For none of the thinkers whose work we are to study in this book can be said to have given a satisfactory solution of either of these problems. If he had there would be no need for us to study political philosophy and to reflect on political problems. All we should have to do would be to memorize the correct answer. It would be a serious mistake to suppose that we need only turn to these thinkers as to a gospel which will settle, once and for all, all our doubts. It is rather the case that their mistakes, confusions, inconsistencies, and downright failures may perhaps stimulate us to think a little—even if badly—for ourselves. It is in this kind of enterprise, rather than in learning the answers, that philosophy consists. It is in this life of the mind, in this free, intellectual life of the spirit, that the hope of democratic societies exists.

CHAPTER TWO

Niccolò Machiavelli

(1469–1527)

LIFE

BIOGRAPHERS of Machiavelli would do well to observe his own dictum that men are "neither utterly wicked nor perfectly good."[1] Even the simplest human character is complex. No man, not even a Iago (who is said, incidentally, to have been inspired by an Englishman's conception of Machiavelli)[2] or a Richard III, is completely a villain; and heroes, on the other hand, are in some respects base—and not alone to their valets. If we take Machiavelli as a completely selfish and unscrupulous schemer, intent on promoting his own interests by flattering the Medici, we find the last chapter of *The Prince*, with its fervent appeal to Italian nationalism, and the greater part of the *Discourses*, with their strong republicanism, completely unintelligible. On the other hand, Machiavelli's personality is just as much out of focus if we suppose him (as Rousseau did) to be an ardent republican, using his *Prince* in order to unmask and expose the wicked designs of tyrants.

The truth is that, like every one else in the world, Machiavelli is neither simply good nor simply bad. Like every one else his character is a compound of more or less contradictory motives forced into a relative and partial unity. There is his republicanism, on the one hand, and his advocacy of princedoms, on the other, somehow reconciled by his conviction that in these corrupt and degenerate times men are incapable of ruling themselves and so require a strong unified power

[1] *Discourses on the First Ten Books of Titus Livius, the Writings of Niccolò Machiavelli* (translated by Christian E. Detmold, 4 vols., 1882), Book I, chapter 27. This edition has been used in all subsequent extracts from the *Discourses*. Page references to it are given in parentheses. For *The Prince* I have used the translation by Luigi Ricci, revised by E. R. P. Vincent. This has been printed in the "Modern Library, 1940" (edited by Max Lerner) (to which page references are given) and in the "World's Classics" (Oxford, 1935).

[2] *Vide* introduction to "Modern Library" edition of *The Prince* and the *Discourses* by Max Lerner (1940), p. 39.

over them. And there is his consideration of his own interests and his concern for the well-being of his country, brought into a precarious union by the convenient belief that both his future and the future of Italy were dependent on the success and prosperity of the Medici family.

Machiavelli was born in 1469, when the Medici were at the height of their power. He was thus a young man when, after Lorenzo's death, they were overthrown and the republic was established; and he was only twenty-nine years old when he became an official in the new Government, as the secretary to the Second Chancery—a post he held for fourteen years. In this capacity he was at the centre of the political life of Florence; he saw what made it go, and he had a hand in making it go. His concern was not only the internal life of the city, but, since its very existence depended on maintaining a balance in the ever-shifting relationships between the city states of Italy and the great Powers beyond the Alps, he also had an important finger in the direction of foreign affairs.

In 1512 the republic came to an end, and with it Machiavelli's political career. Florence had made the mistake of siding with the loser in a contest between France and Julius II. When the French were driven from Italy the victorious Pope made the restoration of the Medici a condition of peace. Thereupon Machiavelli was arrested, tortured, and finally released to live in retirement on his farm in the country. He occupied himself, like many another outcast politician, with literary pursuits.

The man of affairs, however, could never be content with a life of solitary inactivity, and he saw a way, through his writings, of gaining the favour of the Medici and so securing another political post. In a letter to a friend he says:

To a prince, especially to a new one, [*The Prince*] should be welcome: therefore I dedicate it to his Magnificence Guiliano. Filippo Casavecchio has seen it; he will be able to tell you what is in it, and of the discourses I have had with him; it will be seen that during the fifteen years I have given to the study of statecraft I have neither slept nor idled; and men ought ever to desire to be served by one who has reaped experience at the expense of others. And of my loyalty none could doubt, because having always kept faith I could not now learn how to break it; for he who has been faithful and honest, as I have, cannot change his nature; and my poverty is a witness to my honesty.

These pious sentiments and optimistic expectations were of no avail. Nor were the *Discourses on Livy*, which occupied him up to 1518, any more successful. In both of these works Machiavelli draws on the two sources of information which he mentions in this letter: the past and the present. Thus, in the *Discourses* he tells us:[1]

¶ Wise men say, and not without reason, that whoever wishes to foresee the future must consult the past; for human events ever resemble those of preceding times. This arises from the fact that they are produced by men who have been, and ever will be, animated by the same passions, and thus they must necessarily have the same results. . . .

I have thought it proper [therefore] to write upon those books of Titus Livius that have come to us entire despite the malice of time; touching upon all those matters which, after a comparison between the ancient and modern events, may seem to me necessary to facilitate their proper understanding. In this way those who read my remarks may derive those advantages which should be the aim of all study of history. . . .

On the other hand, Machiavelli does not depend merely on the examples of history. Both *The Prince* and the *Discourses* are filled with detailed accounts of the stratagems and policies, the successes and mistakes, of such contemporaries as Cæsar Borgia, Julius II, and Louis XII. Thus Machiavelli's method is largely empirical. His aim, as he himself described it, was to embody in his book "all that long experience and assiduous research have taught me of the affairs of the world."[2] The conclusions that he reaches are naturally characteristic of the method he employs: they are a series of maxims for the successful conduct of a state. Machiavelli's position is thus like that of the physician. Just as the latter assumes, without concerning himself overmuch about it, that the end of his profession is the health of his patients; just as he does not ask himself whether such and such patients are fit to live or are better dead (which would involve raising questions about ethical standards), but devotes his whole attention to working out experimentally certain rules or prescriptions for the acquisition or for the maintenance of health; so Machiavelli tends to assume (at least in *The Prince*) that the end is the possession of *power*. He does not

---

[1] *Discourses*, III, 43 (422); I, Intro. (94).
[2] *Ibid.*, Dedication (92).

concern himself overmuch with what the power is to be used *for*, but concentrates his attention on the discovery of the steps by which power can be seized and retained.

Thus Machiavelli was not a philosopher in the strict sense of the word. He was rather a man of affairs who found the time, in a multitude of other interests, to write down his impressions of the world and of man, but who lacked the inclination or the ability to organize these impressions into a systematic account.[1] Machiavelli was simply too much concerned with improving his relations with the Medici to have the leisure which Aristotle describes as being a condition of philosophy. Although his *Discourses* failed to win him their favour he was at least commissioned by the Cardinal de Medici (later Pope Clement VII) to write a history of Florence. We may suppose that this was not so much a sign of approval as it was of a disposition to keep him out of mischief. If so the cardinal was but following a policy implied in one of Machiavelli's own maxims: "An able statesman out of work, like a huge whale, will endeavour to overthrow the ship unless he has an empty cask to play with." [2]

He finished the history in 1525, but it did him no good, since the fortunes of the Medici were once more on the decline. In 1527, when the imperial troops sacked Rome and the Pope had to flee, Florence rebelled, and a new republican government was set up. Machiavelli somewhat unreasonably hoped to get a post in it; but he had compromised himself with Clement, and his position was hopeless. He died a few days after he learned that his old post of secretary had been given to another, and that this final effort to re-enter the political arena had been one more failure.

The Man of the Renaissance

Even if Machiavelli is not a philosopher in the formal sense he is unable completely to dispense with theory—at least in the form of the unconscious assumption of certain basic and very general concepts. If we want to uncover these we cannot do better than to begin by making an analysis of Machiavelli's character. It was the man's own personality, more than anything else, which determined his attitude towards life, and thereby fixed those aspects of human nature and of conduct which seemed to him important and significant. Machiavelli

---

[1] This is also true of Burke. *Vide infra*, chapter 8.
[2] *Vide* H. Höffding, *History of Modern Philosophy* (2 vols., 1900), Vol. I, chapter 3.

was the child of Florence and of the Renaissance. All the qualities
which characterize his city and his age appear in his own personality.

The fifteenth century saw the flowering of a new attitude towards
man and his universe; it marked the growth of a whole new set of
values. It thus broke with much that the Middle Ages had regarded
as valuable and important. But the new institutions—social, political,
economic—within which the fresh forms of thought and feeling were
destined to flow, and whose development was to be the appearance
of the modern mind, were not yet worked out. The result was that
the century itself was inevitably individualistic, unrestrained, and
violent. As a matter of fact, Italy had to be content with producing
this heady new vintage. The irruption of foreign armies and the wars
which they brought destroyed the possibility that Italy herself might
also fashion the institutions in which it was to be bottled. These
—the national territorial state, protestantism, capitalism—had to be
developed north of the Alps and were brought to Italy, if at all, only
long after the new wine had ceased to effervesce.

In subsequent chapters we shall have to trace the story of this
bottling process, at least so far as it is reflected in the evolution of
modern political theory. But for the moment we must try to understand the character and flavour of the wine produced on Italy's sunny
slopes.

For the Middle Ages the centre from which all thought proceeded
and to which it returned was the conviction that there exists a God
who is perfect, infinite, and completely good, whose representative on
earth is the Pope in Rome, and whose heavenly kingdom finds an
earthly counterpart in the holy and apostolic catholic church. In
comparison with God, man is a worm, whose body, however, im-
prisons an immortal soul made in God's image. The world is a vale
of tears separating man from God, and 'things of the flesh' are
dangerous and sinful, because they distract man from his end in life:
the cultivation of a right relation between the soul and its God.
Thus, for the Middle Ages, the salvation of the soul is not merely
man's primary concern; it is his only concern. Everything else pales
into complete insignificance in comparison with its terrible and pressing importance; the value of everything else in the world is appraised
in terms simply of the degree to which it promotes or hinders the
soul's salvation. Music, painting, and the other arts, for instance, are
good so far as they induce piety; but, generally speaking, they are bad
because delight in colours or sounds for their own sakes is a snare and

delusion. Or, again, the whole problem of politics is conceived by St Thomas[1] as being simply the task of discovering that form of organization which will most facilitate the saving of souls.

For the Renaissance, on the other hand, man is more important than God, and man's relations to his fellows more important than his soul's relation to the Deity. Instead of the old supernatural ideal of divine perfection, man adopts an ideal which is natural and human. What matters are the things of this world, not of the next: the enrichment of the individual personality, the development of intellect and of the talents, the enjoyment of beauty in all its forms, and a life of rich and varied activity. And the world, so far from being a static mirror or symbol of God's plan for man, becomes a dynamic play of natural forces. In their competition we have actively to join if we are not to be thrust down and lost.

What the Renaissance and the Middle Ages judge to make for success in life differ at every point, not only because of the differences in the ends aimed at, but also because of the different conceptions of the world in which these ends are aimed at. According to the Renaissance success cannot be won by a life of piety, prayer, and good deeds. On the contrary, it requires determined self-assertion and ruthless disregard of conventional morality. A product of the Renaissance, such as Machiavelli, repudiates the old mediæval notion of an objective moral order, determined by God, and in accordance with whose prescriptions men live 'best.' On the contrary, for him that life is best which brings fame, distinction, honours, and reputation to a man. To attain these ends *power* is required; not only to bring one to, and maintain one in, a position of prominence, but also because power is good in itself, for the satisfaction it brings and for the self-assertion its possession affords. And power is essentially something which one owns in relation to other men and which is exercised through political institutions. Thus, for the Renaissance man, ethics and politics become fused together as much as they were for any Greek, though in a different way.

It is, therefore, a mistake to say, as many people do, that Machiavelli is unconcerned with ethical questions; he is very much concerned with ethical questions. What is meant (or, at any rate, what is true) is that he *assumed* his ethical standards, his definition of the good life, without any effort to prove them. Taking his end for granted, he was concerned simply to describe what he judged to be the means for achieving

[1] *Vide* Michael B. Foster, *Masters of Political Thought*, Vol. I (1942), chapter 7.

this end. In all of this, in his view of the end of life and in his conception of the world in which this end has to be won, Machiavelli was
very much a man of the Renaissance. In his works we find a brilliant
epitome of his period. But the value of the study of Machiavelli is not
merely historical. For better or for worse, we are, of course, the
children and the heirs of all our long past, but we stand in a peculiarly
close filial relation to the Renaissance. Many currents came to the
surface then, subsequently to merge with others surviving from the
past, and so to form from their union the character of the modern
mind: a new sense of the dignity and importance of man and of the
beauty and significance of Nature; an affirmation of individualism
which accepts no bounds to *any* man's advancement save the limits
set by his own capacities and ambition; a corresponding repudiation
of the old claims to predominance of birth and rank; a rationalism
which tries to see man and his world as they really are, undistorted by
religious dogma; an empiricism which goes back to the facts rather
than beginning from certain metaphysical and theological prejudices;
a nationalism which sees that man's destiny can best be realized in a
larger political unit than a city; a humaneness which puts away an
impossibly high, other-worldly ideal in favour of a human standard
of conduct and of manners.

Unfortunately these are not the only qualities of mind which we
share with the Renaissance, and with Machiavelli. To-day, as then,
there exists a widespread naturalism which denies the existence of an
objective moral order defining the right relations of men to each
other; a ruthless and determined egoism which rejects the claims of
others to equality and which sees in force alone the arbiter of men's
fate; and a cynicism which, so far from judging man to be a little
lower than the angels, takes him to be merely another animal—a little
more cunning, but just as bestial as any other. Never altogether dead,
this point of view (which has come to be called Machiavellianism [1])
has recently had a remarkable recrudescence; and we cannot read even
so much as a single page of *The Prince* without thinking of modern
examples of Machiavelli's principles.

Whether we like it or not, it seems more and more to be the case
that men are acting, so far as their abilities permit, like Machiavelli's
prince. And whatever we think of individual men, certainly the
relations of the 'Great Powers' to each other and to the small states have

[1] But not altogether fairly, since other and quite different elements are generally present
in Machiavelli's writings.

been Machiavellian. It would be idle, then, to deny that Machiavelli's conception of the state possesses any truth. What we have to do is to find out how true it is, and how true it *needs* to be.

POLITICAL PHILOSOPHY

View of Human Nature

Every account of politics has to begin from human nature—its possibilities and limitations. What we take man to be obviously determines both the kind of government which we think he deserves and the kind of which we think he is capable. We have already seen in a general way what the Renaissance view of human nature was. For his part, Machiavelli nowhere works out a detailed and formal psychological doctrine, as Hobbes, for instance, was later to do.[1] But over and over again in his comments on the conduct of the men of his own time we find that same black view of human nature which all of his contemporaries seemed to share, and for which, indeed, there was ample evidence in the lives of Cæsar Borgia and the other Italian princes whose careers Machiavelli had studied.

Let us begin by considering what Machiavelli takes to be the primary motives that determine men's actions. What sort of things do men want? What sort of things do they value? The answers to these questions determine not only the kind of state which is feasible, but the policy of the ruler who wishes to maintain himself in power.

Ideally, of course, men ought to be moved by a careful, objective, and dispassionate consideration of their own interests. Instead of leaping into the first course of action that suggests itself, instead of allowing some immediate interest to determine their conduct, they would do much better to make a cold-blooded appraisal of the whole situation in order to discover what best promotes their own private good on the whole and in the long run. "Before deciding upon any course, . . . men should well consider the objections and the dangers which it presents; and if its perils exceed its advantages they should avoid it, even though it had been in accordance with their previous determination. . . ."[2]

But it is not easy to tell exactly what is one's own best interest. Most men are stupid and irrational.[3]

---

[1] *Vide infra*, chapter 4.

[2] *Ibid.*, I, 53 (204); II, 22 (286).

[3] *Discourses*, I, 52 (203).

¶ ... The people often, deceived by an illusive good, desire their own ruin. . . . Those who have been present at any deliberative assemblies of men will have observed how erroneous their opinions often are; and in fact, unless they are directed by superior men, they are apt to be contrary to all reason. But as superior men in corrupt republics (especially in periods of peace and quiet) are generally hated, either from jealousy or the ambition of others, it follows that the preference is given to what common error approves, or to what is suggested by men who are more desirous of pleasing the masses than of promoting the general good. . . .

And even the shrewd and clever find a hedonic calculation difficult, since human affairs are "in a state of perpetual movement, always either ascending or declining." [1] Hence it is impossible to look far ahead. Men must adapt their actions to the changing times. [2]

¶ I have often reflected that the causes of the success or failure of men depend upon their manner of suiting their conduct to the times. . . . He errs least and will be most favoured by fortune who suits his proceedings to the times . . . and always follows the impulses of his nature. Every one knows how Fabius Maximus conducted the war against Hannibal with extreme caution and circumspection, and with an utter absence of all impetuosity or Roman audacity. It was his good fortune that this mode of proceeding accorded perfectly with the times and circumstances. . . .

In any case, finally, men's emotions colour and determine their conception of their interests and lead them often to behaviour which is quite unjustifiable from a strictly selfish point of view. There are, indeed, two primary motives which determine men's conduct. First, there is a [3]

¶ love of novelty, which manifests itself equally in those who are well off and in those who are not. For, as we have said elsewhere, and with truth, men get tired of prosperity, just as they are afflicted by the reverse. This love of change, then, so to speak, opens the way to every one who takes the lead in any innovation in any country. If he is a stranger they run after him, and if he is of the country

---

[1] *Discourses*, II, Introduction (224).   [2] *Ibid.*, III, 9 (353).
                                    [3] *Ibid.*, III, 21 (379).

¶ they surround him, increase his influence, and favour him in every way; so that, whatever his mode of proceeding and conduct may be, he will succeed in making rapid progress. In the second place, men are prompted in their actions by two main motives—namely, love and fear; so that he who makes himself beloved will have as much influence as he who makes himself feared, although generally he who makes himself feared will be more readily followed and obeyed than he who makes himself beloved.

Besides these love of wealth is a powerful motive,[1] as are fear and envy.[2] Ambition, too, is a passion[3]

¶ so powerful in the hearts of men that it never leaves them, no matter to what height they may rise. The reason of this is that nature has created men so that they desire everything, but are unable to attain it; desire being thus always greater than the faculty of acquiring, discontent with what they have and dissatisfaction with themselves result from it. This causes the changes in their fortunes; for as some men desire to have more, whilst others fear to lose what they have enmities and war are the consequences. . . .

Again, men desire *liberty*—that is, they desire to be independent of others.[4] They want to be free to lead their own lives, to follow their own inclinations, to find their own good, unrestricted in any way by others. And, since the only sure way to be independent oneself is to make all others dependent, this means that men wish to dominate. Even those who have no ambition other than to live their own lives thus necessarily come to seek dominion over others, if only to insure themselves of the means to this modest end. Thus strife between individual men and between states is inevitable.[5]

¶ Men rise from one ambition to another: first they seek to secure themselves against attack, and then they attack others. . . .

As Titus Livius has most judiciously given the causes that produced these, it seems to me proper to quote his own words, where

[1] Cf. *Discourses*, I, 27 (157).   [2] *Ibid.*, III, 21 (379).
[3] *Ibid.*, I, 37 (174).
[4] Some of the advantages, Machiavelli tells us, "that result to the mass of the people from a free government" are "to be able freely to enjoy one's own without apprehension, to have nothing to fear for the honour of one's wife and daughters, or for oneself" (*ibid.*, I, 16 (138)).
[5] *Ibid.*, I, 5 (109); I, 46 (192); II, Introduction (225).

¶ he says: "The pride of the people or of the nobles always increased as the opposite party was humbled. . . . And thus the desire of liberty caused one party to raise themselves in proportion as they oppressed the other. And it is the course of such movements that men, in attempting to avoid fear themselves, give others cause for fear; and the injuries which they ward off from themselves they inflict upon others, as though there were a necessity either to oppress or to be oppressed." . . .

The fear to lose stirs the same passions in men as the desire to gain, as men do not believe themselves sure of what they already possess except by acquiring still more; and, moreover, these new acquisitions are so many means of strength and power for abuses. . . .

As human desires are insatiable, (because their nature is to have and to do everything, whilst fortune limits their possessions and capacity of enjoyment,) this gives rise to a constant discontent in the human mind and a weariness of the things they possess; and it is this which makes them decry the present, praise the past, and desire the future, and all this without any reasonable motive.

This is certainly not a pretty picture. Nor is it much of a comfort to be told that men were not always thus. In the past, which Machiavelli looks back to with nostalgia, even the ordinary man was strong, stalwart, calm, and well poised. In classical antiquity men were capable, indeed, of ruling themselves, and did so.[1] Now, on the other hand, men have so far degenerated that republics are impossible, or, if they are attempted, turn out to be miserable failures. In this modern age the only really feasible government is a princedom, ruled by a single individual with an iron hand. In fact, a despotism is the only effective government for contemporary society.[2]

¶   The only way to establish any kind of order . . . is to found a monarchical government; for where the body of the people is so thoroughly corrupt that the laws are powerless for restraint, it becomes necessary to establish some superior power which, with a royal hand, and with full and absolute powers, may put a curb upon the excessive ambition and corruption of the powerful.

---

[1] Here we detect a strain of the same "romantic primitivism" which appears in Rousseau's thought. *Vide infra*, p. 258.
[2] *Discourses*, I, 55 (210–211).

Again and again in the *Discourses* Machiavelli returns to this theme of modern degeneracy as opposed to ancient virtue and probity, and to the thesis that the times and the customs require desperate measures.[1]

¶ It will be seen that Rome was from the first free and independent; and . . . that neither the fertility of the soil, nor the proximity of the sea, nor their many victories, nor the greatness of the Empire, could corrupt them during several centuries, and they maintained there more virtues than have ever been seen in any other republic. . . .

It is wonderful to think of the greatness which Athens attained within the space of a hundred years after having freed herself from the tyranny of Pisistratus; and still more wonderful is it to reflect upon the greatness which Rome achieved after she was rid of her kings. The cause of this is manifest, for it is not individual prosperity, but the general good, that makes cities great; and certainly the general good is regarded nowhere but in republics, because whatever they do is for the common benefit, and should it happen to prove an injury to one or more individuals, those for whose benefit the thing is done are so numerous that they can always carry the measure against the few that are injured by it. . . .

Only those cities and countries that are free can achieve greatness. Population is greater there because marriages are more free and offer more advantages to the citizen; for people will gladly have children when they know that they can support them, and that they will not be deprived of their patrimony, and where they know that their children not only are born free and not slaves, but, if they possess talents and virtue, can arrive at the highest dignities of the state. In free countries we also see wealth increase more rapidly, both that which results from the culture of the soil and that which is produced by industry and art; for everybody gladly multiplies those things, and seeks to acquire those goods the possession of which he can tranquilly enjoy. Thence men vie with each other to increase both private and public wealth, which consequently increase in an extraordinary manner.

Thus Machiavelli certainly cannot be described as a royalist or monarchist, if by these terms we mean to describe one who holds that the rule of a single individual is best. On the contrary, *ceteris paribus* the people as a whole rule better than a single individual.[2]

[1] *Discourses*, I, 1 (98); II, 2 (230–231, 234).   [2] *Ibid.*, I, 57 (216*ff.*).

¶   The character of the people is not to be blamed any more than that of princes, for both alike are liable to err when they are without any control. . . . I could adduce numerous [examples] from amongst the Roman Emperors and other tyrants and princes, who have displayed as much inconstancy and recklessness as any populace ever did. Contrary to the general opinion, then, which maintains that the people, when they govern, are inconsistent, unstable, and ungrateful, I conclude and affirm that these defects are not more natural to the people than they are to princes. To charge the people and princes equally with them may be the truth, but to except princes from them would be a great mistake. For a people that governs and is well regulated by laws will be stable, prudent, and grateful, as much so, and even more, according to my opinion, than a prince, although he be esteemed wise; and, on the other hand, a prince, freed from the restraints of the law, will be more ungrateful, inconstant, and imprudent than a people similarly situated. The difference in their conduct is not due to any difference in their nature (for that is the same, and if there be any difference for good, it is on the side of the people); but to the greater or less respect they have for the laws under which they respectively live. . . . But as regards prudence and stability, I say that the people are more prudent and stable, and have better judgment than a prince; and it is not without good reason that it is said, "The voice of the people is the voice of God"; for we see popular opinion prognosticate events in such a wonderful manner that it would almost seem as if the people had some occult virtue, which enables them to foresee the good and the evil. As to the people's capacity of judging of things, it is exceedingly rare that, when they hear two orators of equal talents advocate different measures, they do not decide in favour of the best of the two; which proves their ability to discern the truth of what they hear. And if occasionally they are misled in matters involving questions of courage or seeming utility (as has been said above), so is a prince also many times misled by his own passions, which are much greater than those of the people. We also see that in the election of their magistrates they make far better choice than princes; and no people will ever be persuaded to elect a man of infamous character and corrupt habits to any post of dignity, to which a prince is easily influenced in a thousand different ways. . . . We furthermore see the cities where the people are masters make the greatest progress in the least possible time, and

❡ much greater than such as have always been governed by princes; as was the case with Rome after the expulsion of the kings, and with Athens after they rid themselves of Pisistratus; and this can be attributed to no other cause than that the governments of the people are better than those of princes.

The modern reader will be curious to know why this extraordinary decline in human nature occurred. He will get no satisfactory answer from Machiavelli. The truth, of course, is that there is no such great change from ancient virtue to modern vice. Machiavelli has exaggerated ancient virtue because of his admiration for classical antiquity, and modern vice because of his proximity to it. Hence it is impossible for him to reveal the causes of a disintegration which did not in fact occur.

Machiavelli does, indeed, attempt to meet this difficulty. But the only explanation he offers is to put all the blame on the Church. Doubtless the Church was in considerable measure responsible for the evil condition of Italy in Machiavelli's day; but his attack is more significant as revealing the lay, anti-clerical bias of his modern mind, than it is in throwing light on the causes of contemporary troubles.[1]

❡ Reflecting now as to whence it came that in ancient times the people were more devoted to liberty than in the present, I believe that it resulted from this, that men were stronger in those days, which I believe to be attributable to the difference of education, founded upon the difference of their religion and ours. For, as our religion teaches us the truth and the true way of life, it causes us to attach less value to the honours and possessions of this world; whilst the Pagans, esteeming those things as the highest good, were more energetic and ferocious in their actions. We may observe this also in most of their institutions, beginning with the magnificence of their sacrifices as compared with the humility of ours, which are gentle solemnities rather than magnificent ones, and have nothing of energy or ferocity in them, whilst in theirs there was no lack of pomp and show, to which was superadded the ferocious and bloody nature of the sacrifice by the slaughter of many animals, and the familiarity with this terrible sight assimilated the nature of men to their sacrificial ceremonies. Besides this, the Pagan religion

[1] *Discourses*, II, 2 (232–233).

¶ deified only men who had achieved great glory, such as commanders of armies and chiefs of republics, whilst ours glorifies more the humble and contemplative men than the men of action. Our religion, moreover, places the supreme happiness in humility, lowliness, and a contempt for worldly objects, whilst the other, on the contrary, places the supreme good in grandeur of soul, strength of body, and all such other qualities as render men formidable; and if our religion claims of us fortitude of soul it is more to enable us to suffer than to achieve great deeds.

These principles seem to me to have made men feeble, and caused them to become an easy prey to evil-minded men, who can control them more securely, seeing that the great body of men, for the sake of gaining Paradise, are more disposed to endure injuries than to avenge them. . . .

The Condition of Italy makes a Republic Impracticable [1]

No change, however great or violent, could ever restore Milan and Naples to liberty, because the whole people of those states [are] thoroughly corrupt. This was seen after the death of Philip Visconti, when Milan attempted to recover her liberty, but knew not how, nor was she able to maintain it. . . .

It is vain to look for anything good from those countries which we see nowadays so corrupt, as is the case above all others with Italy. France and Spain also have their share of corruption, and if we do not see so many disorders and troubles in those countries as is the case daily in Italy, it is not so much owing to the goodness of their people, in which they are greatly deficient, as to the fact that they have each a king who keeps them united, not only by his virtue, but also by the institutions of those kingdoms, which are as yet preserved pure.

This is the basis of the ringing appeal to the Medici with which Machiavelli closes *The Prince*.[2]

¶   Having now considered all the things we have spoken of, and thought within myself whether at present the time was not propitious in Italy for a new prince, and if there was not a state of things

[1] *Discourses*, I, 17 (172); I, 55 (209).
[2] *The Prince*, chapter 26 (94–98).

¶ which offered an opportunity to a prudent and capable man to introduce a new system that would do honour to himself and good to the mass of the people, it seems to me that so many things concur to favour a new ruler that I do not know of any time more fitting for such an enterprise. . . .

Almost lifeless, [Italy] awaits one who may heal her wounds and put a stop to the pillaging of Lombardy, to the rapacity and extortion in the Kingdom of Naples and in Tuscany, and cure her of those sores which have long been festering. Behold how she prays God to send some one to redeem her from this barbarous cruelty and insolence. Behold her ready and willing to follow any standard if only there be some one to raise it. There is nothing now she can hope for but that your illustrious house may place itself at the head of this redemption, being by its power and fortune so exalted, and being favoured by God and the Church, of which it is now the ruler. . . .

This opportunity must not, therefore, be allowed to pass, so that Italy may at length find her liberator. I cannot express the love with which he would be received in all those provinces which have suffered under these foreign invasions, with what thirst for vengeance, with what steadfast faith, with what love, with what grateful tears. What doors would be closed against him? What people would refuse him obedience? What envy could oppose him? What Italian would withhold allegiance? This barbarous domination stinks in the nostrils of every one. May your illustrious house therefore assume this task with that courage and those hopes which are inspired by a just cause, so that under its banner our fatherland may be raised up, and under its auspices be verified that saying of Petrarch:

> Valour against fell wrath
> Will take up arms; and be the combat quickly sped!
> For, sure, the ancient worth,
> That in Italians stirs the heart, is not yet dead.

In appealing to the Medici Machiavelli doubtless had an eye to his personal advancement, which may have blinded him to Lorenzo's [1] unsuitability for the high mission for which he was being nominated. But the moral fervour is unmistakable. Machiavelli is really sincere in urging his prince to a programme which, as he believes, will be best

---

[1] Not the great Lorenzo, of course (who died in 1492), but a weak and incompetent younger member of the family.

for all Italians, and not merely for the house of Medici. Here, in the last chapter of *The Prince*, and often in the *Discourses*, Machiavelli is concerned to prescribe a policy for his prince which will be directed to the good of the people as a whole.

Though the rehabilitation of Italy initially requires the energetic and determined action of a single individual, there is no need for him to continue to rule despotically.[1]

¶   We must assume, as a general rule, that it never or rarely happens that a republic or monarchy is well constituted, or its old institutions entirely reformed, unless it is done by only one individual; it is even necessary that he whose mind has conceived such a constitution should be alone in carrying it into effect. A sagacious legislator of a republic, therefore, whose object is to promote the public good, and not his private interests, and who prefers his country to his own successors, should concentrate all authority in himself; and a wise mind will never censure any one for having employed any extraordinary means for the purpose of establishing a kingdom or constituting a republic. It is well that, when the act accuses him, the result should excuse him; and when the result is good, as in the case of Romulus, it will always absolve him from blame. For he is to be reprehended who commits violence for the purpose of destroying, and not he who employs it for beneficent purposes. The law-giver should, however, be sufficiently wise and virtuous not to leave this authority which he has assumed either to his heirs or to any one else; for mankind, being more prone to evil than to good, his successor might employ for evil purposes the power which he had used only for good ends. Besides, although one man alone should organize a government, yet it will not endure long if the administration of it remains on the shoulders of a single individual; it is well, then, to confide this to the charge of many, for thus it will be sustained by the many. . . .

This shows that Machiavelli did not exclude the possibility, even in contemporary Italy, of a government which would take the form of an enlightened monarchy, or even, eventually, of a republic. But he has no real hope of either. The people are too corrupt to be brought back to ancient ideals of virtue, and the rulers (or those likely to win the supreme place in a state) are too selfish to bring them back, even

---

[1] *Discourses*, I, 9 (120–121).

if it were possible. Being a man of his own time, the prince is only
too likely to be as selfish and as grasping as his subjects, unlike them
only in being strong enough to get and to hold on to what he
wants. And since his private interests conflict with theirs, it is probable that he will continue to rule despotically for his own personal
advantage.[1]

¶ A [prince's] private interests are generally in opposition to those
  of the city, whilst the measures taken for the benefit of the city are
  seldom deemed personally advantageous by the prince. This state of
  things soon leads to a tyranny, the least evil of which is to check the
  advance of the city in its career of prosperity, so that it grows neither
  in power nor wealth, but on the contrary rather retrogrades. And
  if fate should have it that the tyrant is enterprising, and by his
  courage and valour extends his dominions, it will never be for the
  benefit of the city, but only for his own; for he will never bestow
  honours and office upon the good and brave citizens over whom he
  tyrannizes, so that he may not have occasion to suspect and fear
  them. . . .

Thus it is unreasonable, Machiavelli thinks, to hope for the people
as a whole to get any particular benefits from a princely rule. They
may, of course, profit indirectly from the fact that a successful prince
will be able to maintain order and so prevent internal and external
disturbances—but this is all. They cannot expect security in the larger
sense of a freedom to live their lives in their own ways, which men
enjoyed in ancient republics. Despite his ardent republicanism,
Machiavelli does not appear to find these conclusions particularly
distressing. Here his cynical realism and prudent self-seeking come to
the top. A republican government might, indeed, be desirable; but
since it is impracticable, let us not press the matter. Let us rather hasten
to take the part of the winner.[2]
On this basis the art of politics boils down, for Machiavelli, to the
science of securing, and of maintaining oneself in, power, without
consideration of anything except one's own personal well-being. In
other words, what we have is simply a handbook on the art of ruling,

---

[1] *Discourses*, II, 2 (231).
[2] "Men in their conduct, and especially in their most prominent actions, should well
consider and conform to the times in which they live. And those who, from an evil choice
or from natural inclination, do not conform to the times in which they live, will in most
instances live unhappily, and their undertakings will come to a bad end; whilst, on the
contrary, success attends those who conform to the times" (*ibid.*, III, 8 (352)).

in which the end *for which* one rules is regarded as irrelevant. This attitude appears plainly in such a passage as the following:[1]

¶ He who desires to attempt to reform the government of a state, and wishes to have it accepted and capable of maintaining itself to the satisfaction of everybody, must at least retain the semblance of the old forms; so that it may seem to the people that there has been no change in the institutions, even though in fact they are entirely different from the old ones. For the great majority of mankind are satisfied with appearances, as though they were realities, and are often even more influenced by the things that seem than by those that are. . . . And this rule should be observed by all those who wish to abolish an existing system of government in any state, and introduce a new and more liberal one. For as all novelties excite the minds of men, it is important to retain in such innovations as much as possible the previously existing forms. . . . This, as I have said, should be observed by whoever desires to convert an absolute government either into a republic or a monarchy; but, on the contrary, he who wishes to establish an absolute power, such as ancient writers called a tyranny, must change everything, as we shall show in the following chapter.

When writing in this vein Machiavelli seems indifferent to the question of which form of government is preferable. He simply points out that if you want a republic you must do so and so, while if you want a despotism you must do something else again. Since in by far the larger part of *The Prince* and in many sections of the *Discourses* Machiavelli's whole emphasis is simply on the art of maintaining oneself in power, and since this is almost exclusively limited to the question how a *prince* can maintain himself in power (because, as we have seen, republics are impracticable), Machiavelli has come to be regarded as the tutor of tyrants.[2] There is, of course, the greatest possible difference between this view and the contention we have already examined, that in these troublous and contentious times a strong hand is needed to preserve the people's liberties for them. To see this difference clearly we have only to compare the passage just quoted with this emphatic condemnation of tyrannies.[3]

---

[1] *Discourses*, I, 25 (154-155).
[2] *The Prince* is far better known than the *Discourses*, so that Machiavelli's reputation is based almost entirely on the former work.
[3] *Discourses*, I, 10 (122-123).

¶ Of all men who have been eulogized, those deserve it most who have been the authors and founders of religions; next come such as have established republics or kingdoms. . . . All others—and their number is infinite—receive such share of praise as pertains to the exercise of their arts and professions. On the contrary, those are doomed to infamy and universal execration who have destroyed religions, who have overturned republics and kingdoms, who are enemies of virtue, of letters, and of every art that is useful and honourable to mankind. Such are the impious and violent, the ignorant, the idle, the vile and degraded. And there are none so foolish or so wise, so wicked or so good, that, in choosing between these two qualities, they do not praise what is praiseworthy and blame that which deserves blame. And yet nearly all men, deceived by a false good and a false glory, allow themselves voluntarily or ignorantly to be drawn towards those who deserve more blame than praise. Such as by the establishment of a republic or kingdom could earn eternal glory for themselves incline to tyranny, without perceiving how much glory, how much honour, security, satisfaction, and tranquillity of mind, they forfeit; and what infamy, disgrace, blame, danger, and disquietude they incur. . . .

It is true, of course, that precisely the same actions on the part of the prince might conceivably be advocated from both points of view. But there is all the difference in the world between *justifying* a ruthless programme of, say, suppression of opposition on the grounds that (1) such measures are necessary to maintain one's sovereignty and that (2) this is to the advantage of the citizens as a whole; and simply saying that a prince who wishes to maintain his position must brook no opposition. In the one case, a moral justification for the exercise of force is at least attempted. The argument may well be fallacious,[1] but at least it is contended by implication that a greater good (peace and public order) justifies a certain amount of evil (the suffering of the suppressed minority). In the other case, this moral justification drops out of the picture altogether. No effort is made to justify the use of force except on the purely selfish ground that it is to the sovereign's personal advantage to do so.

This same duality appears in Machiavelli's definition of 'virtue.'[2] In those passages which we have quoted so far in which Machiavelli talks about modern degeneracy and ancient virtue he means by

[1] *Vide infra*, pp. 125*ff*.   [2] *Cf.* Foster, *op. cit.*, pp. 276–281.

'virtue' about what those of us brought up in a Christian tradition would expect: he means courage, honesty, obedience to law, and all the rest—*i.e.*, those virtues of classical antiquity which were taken over by the Christian Church and which, coupled with the so-called 'theological' virtues—faith, hope, love—became a part of basic Christian teaching.[1]

On the other hand, when Machiavelli takes the point of view that power is itself the end his whole conception of virtue is altered.[2] Those acts are now regarded as virtuous which enable the prince to accomplish his end—*viz.*, the cunning, deceit, unscrupulousness, and ruthlessness which enable him to maintain himself in power.

Curiously enough, this conception of virtue is also traceable to Greek sources. The reason is that for Plato and Aristotle the virtue of anything is its excellence, or that which it does best. In other words, a thing is virtuous when it is fulfilling its function—an axe, for instance, is 'virtuous' when it is being used to chop down a tree, because that is what it has been designed to do; but it is vicious if it is used, say, to dig a ditch, because it does this badly and inefficiently. Plato and Aristotle derive their list of human virtues by considering man s function, which they take to be reason.[3] Hence for them a virtuous life for man consists in the proper exercise of his rational faculty in discipling the other, lower, parts of his soul. In the *Republic* the Sophist, Thrasymachus, reaches a different conclusion because he takes man's end, of function, to be no different from that of any other animal.[4] Man is not distinguished from other animals by being

---

[1] Machiavelli also adopts one classical virtue which was *not* taken over by the Church. Humility is an important Christian virtue—"Blessed are the meek," said Jesus in the Sermon on the Mount. But Aristotle thought that pride is "the crown of all the other virtues" (*Nicomachean Ethics*, 1123a 33*ff*.). For his part, Machiavelli says, "We often see that humility not only is of no service, but is actually hurtful, especially when employed towards insolent men, who from jealousy or some other motive have conceived a hatred against you. . . . And therefore no prince should ever forgo his rank, nor should he ever voluntarily give up anything (wishing to do so honourably) unless he is able or believes himself able to hold it. For it is almost always better (matters having come to the point that he cannot give it up in the above manner) to allow it to be taken from him by force, rather than by the apprehension of force. For if he yields it from fear it is for the purpose of avoiding war, and he will rarely escape from that; for he to whom he has from cowardice conceded the one thing will not be satisfied, but will want to take other things from him, and his arrogance will increase as his esteem for the prince is lessened. And on the other hand, the zeal of the prince's friends will be chilled on seeing him appear feeble or cowardly" (*Discourses*, II, 14 (260–261)).

[2] A striking example of this fluctuation in meaning is contained in Machiavelli's remark that "it is necessary for a prince, who wishes to maintain himself, to learn how not to be good. . . ." (*The Prince*, 15 (56)).

[3] *Cf.* Foster, *op. cit.*, pp. 26–27; 142*ff*.

[4] *Cf.* Foster, *op. cit.*, p. 37.

rational; on the contrary, being merely an animal, his end, like that of any other animal, is simply pleasure. For Thrasymachus, therefore, the virtues are those acts which get one pleasure; and, since this involves dominion over others, the virtues are cunning, deceit, and so on, just as they are for Machiavelli. In the nineteenth century Nietzsche reached the same conclusion. He adopted the Darwinian thesis that life is a struggle for survival, which Machiavelli anticipated in his view of life as a dynamic conflict of forces. If success in this competition is our end—and if we can survive only by fighting our way to the top—then deceit, cunning, and ruthlessness once again appear as virtues. If a prince wants to maintain his position he cannot afford to keep promises, fulfil treaties, or tell the truth. Therefore lying, faithlessness, and dishonesty are all virtues.[1]

¶ From this arises the question whether it is better to be loved more than feared, or feared more than loved. The reply is, that one ought to be both feared and loved, but as it is difficult for the two to go together, it is much safer to be feared than loved, if one of the two has to be wanting. For it may be said of men in general that they are ungrateful, voluble, dissemblers, anxious to avoid danger, and covetous of gain; as long as you benefit them, they are entirely yours; they offer you their blood, their goods, their life, and their children, as I have before said, when the necessity is remote; but when it approaches, they revolt. And the prince who has relied solely on their words, without making other preparations, is ruined; for the friendship which is gained by purchase and not through grandeur and nobility of spirit is bought but not secured, and at a pinch is not to be expended in your service. And men have less scruple in offending one who makes himself loved than one who makes himself feared; for love is held by a chain of obligation which, men being selfish, is broken whenever it serves their purpose; but fear is maintained by a dread of punishment which never fails. . . .

How laudable it is for a prince to keep good faith and live with integrity, and not with astuteness, every one knows. Still the experience of our times shows those princes to have done great things who have had little regard for good faith, and have been able by astuteness to confuse men's brains, and who have ultimately overcome those who have made loyalty their foundation.

[1] *The Prince*, 17–18 (61–65).

¶   You must know, then, that there are two methods of fighting, the one by law, the other by force: the first method is that of men, the second of beasts; but as the first method is often insufficient, one must have recourse to the second. It is therefore necessary for a prince to know well how to use both the beast and the man. . . .

A prince being thus obligated to know well how to act as a beast must imitate the fox and the lion, for the lion cannot protect himself from traps, and the fox cannot defend himself from wolves. One must therefore be a fox to recognize traps, and a lion to frighten wolves. Those that wish to be only lions do not understand this. Therefore, a prudent ruler ought not to keep faith when by so doing it would be against his interest, and when the reasons which made him bind himself no longer exist. If men were all good, this precept would not be a good one; but as they are bad, and would not observe their faith with you, so you are not bound to keep faith with them. Nor have legitimate grounds ever failed a prince who wished to show colourable excuse for the non-fulfilment of his promise. Of this one could furnish an infinite number of modern examples, and show how many times peace has been broken, and how many promises rendered worthless, by the faithlessness of princes, and those that have been best able to imitate the fox have succeeded best. But it is necessary to be able to disguise this character well, and to be a great feigner and dissembler; and men are so simple and so ready to obey present necessities, that one who deceives will always find those who allow themselves to be deceived.

I will mention only one modern instance. Alexander VI did nothing but deceive men, he thought of nothing else, and found the occasion for it; no man was ever more able to give assurances, or affirmed things with stronger oaths, and no man observed them less; however, he always succeeded in his deceptions, as he well knew this aspect of things. . . .

The Art of Ruling

So far we have been considering the qualities that make for princely virtue. Machiavelli formulates these as he does because he starts where Hobbes starts—with a black view of human nature.[1]   But while Hobbes remains at the level of abstract generalities and pro-

---

[1] *Vide infra*, pp. 96*ff.*

ceeds from this initial premise to deduce the various attributes
of sovereignty, Machiavelli is almost entirely uninterested in such
theoretical questions. He drops at once to the level of specific cases,
in order to show how the sovereign, using his knowledge of human
nature, can actually acquire the various powers which the more
legalistic Hobbes is content to 'assign' to him.

Machiavelli's maxims for would-be tyrants are always shrewd and
often singularly apposite to-day. One or two passages may be selected
to illustrate the general character of Machiavelli's recommendations.

(a) *Use force ruthlessly.* This is perhaps the most important rule
for the prince to observe, and it is particularly important in 'new
monarchies'—*i.e.*, in former republics whose free regimes have been
overthrown by one who hopes to rule despotically.[1]

¶   When those states which have been acquired are accustomed to
     live at liberty under their own laws, there are three ways of holding
     them. The first is to despoil them; the second is to go and live there
     in person; the third is to allow them to live under their own laws,
     taking tribute of them, and creating within the country a govern-
     ment composed of a few who will keep it friendly to you. Because
     this government, being created by the prince, knows that it cannot
     exist without his friendship and protection, and will do all it can
     to keep them. What is more, a city used to liberty can be more
     easily held by means of its citizens than in any other way, if you
     wish to preserve it. . . .

     [But] in truth there is no sure method of holding [such a city]
     except by despoiling [it]. And whoever becomes the ruler of a free
     city and does not destroy it, can expect to be destroyed by it, for
     it can always find a motive for rebellion in the name of liberty
     and of its ancient usages, which are forgotten neither by lapse of
     time nor by benefits received; and whatever one does or provides,
     so long as the inhabitants are not separated or dispersed, they do not
     forget that name and those usages, but appeal to them at once in
     every emergency, as did Pisa after being so many years held in
     servitude by the Florentines. . . .

     It is to be noted that in taking a state the conqueror must arrange
     to commit all his cruelties at once, so as not to have to recur to them
     every day, and so as to be able, by not making fresh changes, to
     reassure people and win them over by benefiting them. Whoever

[1] *The Prince*, 5 (18–19); 8 (35).

¶ acts otherwise, either through timidity or bad counsels, is always obliged to stand with knife in hand, and can never depend on his subjects, because they, owing to continually fresh injuries, are unable to depend upon him. For injuries should be done all together, so that being less tasted, they will give less offence. Benefits should be granted little by little, so that they may be better enjoyed. And above all, a prince must live with his subjects in such a way that no accident of good or evil fortune can deflect him from his course; for necessity arising in adverse times, you are not in time with severity, and the good that you do does not profit, as it is judged to be forced upon you, and you will derive no benefit whatever from it.

(b) *Use persuasion artfully.* The prudent prince will not, however, depend on force alone to maintain himself in power. In the long run, force is an expensive and inefficient instrument of government, for a reasonably contented population is much more easily ruled than one kept in order by the bayonet's point alone. Now, there exist many devices for lulling the people into peace and quiet, yet without making any real concessions to them. One of the most important of these 'propaganda' techniques, as we would call them to-day, is religion.

Machiavelli begins his discussion of religion by showing how Roman policy was furthered by skilfully playing upon the religious feelings of the people.[1]

¶   Numa, finding [the Romans] a very savage people, and wishing to reduce them to civil obedience by the arts of peace, had recourse to religion as the most necessary and assured support of any civil society; and he established it upon such foundations that for many centuries there was nowhere more fear of the gods than in that republic, which greatly facilitated all the enterprises which the Senate or its great men attempted. Whoever will examine the actions of the people of Rome as a body, or of many individual Romans, will see that these citizens feared much more to break an oath than the laws; like men who esteem the power of the gods more than that of men. . . . And . . . citizens, whom neither the love of country nor the laws could have kept in Italy, were retained there by an oath that had been forced upon them by compulsion; and the Tribune Pomponius disregarded the hatred which he bore to the

---

[1] *Discourses,* I, 11–14 (146–158).

¶ father, as well as the insult offered him by the son, for the sake of complying with his oath and preserving his honour; which can be ascribed to nothing else than the religious principles which Numa had instilled into the Romans. And whoever reads Roman history attentively will see in how great a degree religion served in the command of the armies, in uniting the people and keeping them well conducted, and in covering the wicked with shame. . . . In truth, there never was any remarkable lawgiver amongst any people who did not resort to divine authority, as otherwise his laws would not have been accepted by the people; for there are many good laws, the importance of which is known to the sagacious lawgiver, but the reasons for which are not sufficiently evident to enable him to persuade others to submit to them; and therefore do wise men, for the purpose of removing this difficulty, resort to divine authority. Thus did Lycurgus and Solon, and many others who aimed at the same thing. . . .

And therefore everything that tends to favour religion (even though it were believed to be false) should be received and availed of to strengthen it; and this should be done the more, the wiser the rulers are, and the better they understand the natural course of things. Such was, in fact, the practice observed by sagacious men; which has given rise to the belief in the miracles that are celebrated in religions, however false they may be. For the sagacious rulers have given these miracles increased importance, no matter whence or how they originated; and their authority afterwards gave them credence with the people. Rome had many such miracles; and one of the most remarkable was that which occurred when the Roman soldiers sacked the city of Veii; some of them entered the temple of Juno, and, placing themselves in front of her statue, said to her, "Will you come to Rome?" Some imagined that they observed the statue make a sign of assent, and others pretended to have heard her reply, "Yes." Now these men, being very religious, as reported by Titus Livius, and having entered the temple quietly, they were filled with devotion and reverence, and might really have believed that they had heard a reply to their question, such as perhaps they could have presupposed. But this opinion and belief was favoured and magnified by Camillus and the other Roman chiefs. . . .

It does not seem to me from my purpose to adduce here some examples to show how the Romans employed religion for the purpose of reorganizing their city, and to further their enterprises. . . .

¶   The system of auguries was . . . the cause of the prosperity of
the Roman republic. . . . Amongst other auspices the armies were
always accompanied by a certain class of soothsayers, termed Pollari
(guardians of the sacred fowls), and every time before giving battle
to the enemy, they required these Pollari to ascertain the auspices;
and if the fowls ate freely, then it was deemed a favourable augury,
and the soldiers fought confidently, but if the fowls refused to eat,
then they abstained from battle. Nevertheless, when they saw a
good reason why certain things should be done, they did them
anyhow, whether the auspices were favourable or not; but then
they turned and interpreted the auguries so artfully, and in such
manner, that seemingly no disrespect was shown to their religious
belief. . . . Nor had this system of consulting the auspices any other
object than to inspire the soldiers on the eve of battle with that
confidence which is the surest guaranty of victory. . . .

(c) *Act decisively.* The one sure way to destruction is to hesitate.
It is safer to make mistakes, so long as one moves firmly, promptly,
and decisively, than to lose the initiative by procrastination and
uncertainty.[1]

¶   All wise princes should . . . consider not only present but also
future discords and diligently guard against them; for being foreseen
they can easily be remedied, but if one waits till they are at hand,
the medicine is no longer in time, as the malady has become incur-
able; it happening with this as with those hectic fevers, as doctors
say, which at their beginning are easy to cure but difficult to recognize, but in course of time when they have not at first been recognized and treated, become easy to recognize and difficult to cure.
Thus it happens in matters of State; for knowing afar off (which it
is only given to a prudent man to do) the evils that are brewing,
they are easily cured. But when, for want of such knowledge, they
are allowed to grow so that every one can recognize them, there
is no longer any remedy to be found. Therefore, the Romans,
observing disorders while yet remote, were always able to find a
remedy, and never allowed them to increase in order to avoid a
war; for they knew that war is not to be avoided, and can be
deferred only to the advantage of the other side; they therefore
declared war against Philip and Antiochus in Greece, so as not to

---

[1] *The Prince,* 3 (10–11).

¶ have to fight them in Italy, though they might at the time have avoided either; this they did not choose to do, never caring to do that which is now every day to be heard in the mouths of our wise men—namely to enjoy the advantages of delay, but preferring to trust their own virtue and prudence; for time brings with it all things, and may produce indifferently either good or evil.

(d) *Maintain a strong national army.* It is obvious that a prince cannot act decisively without a strong army at his back. In urging the advantages of a 'regular' army, drawn from the citizenship of the state, Machiavelli speaks with his usual prevision.[1]

¶ The arms by which a prince defends his possessions are either his own, or else mercenaries, or auxiliaries, or mixed. The mercenaries and auxiliaries are useless and dangerous, and if anyone supports his state by the arms of mercenaries, he will never stand firm or sure, as they are disunited, ambitious, without discipline, faithless, bold among friends, cowardly among enemies. They have no fear of God, and keep no faith with men. Ruin is only deferred as long as assault is postponed; in peace you are despoiled by them, and in war by the enemy. The cause of this is that they have no love or other motive to keep them in the field beyond a trifling wage, which is not enough to make them ready to die for you. They are quite willing to be your soldiers so long as you do not make war, but when war comes, it is either fly or decamp altogether. I ought to have little trouble in proving this, since the ruin of Italy is now caused by nothing else but through her having relied for many years on mercenary arms. . . . Thus it came about that King Charles of France was allowed to take Italy without the slightest trouble, and those who said that it was owing to our sins, spoke the truth, but it was not the sins they meant but those that I have related. And as it was the sins of princes, they too have suffered the punishment.

[1] *The Prince*, 12 (44–45). The importance of this thesis has been recognized by later generations of Italians. After national union was finally achieved this was judged worthy of special note on the monument erected to his memory:

To Nicholas Machiavelli
The Intrepid and Prophetic Precursor of National Unity,
The First Institutor and Master of Her Own
In Place of Adventitious Armies,
United and Armed Italy Placed This Tablet,
On His Fourth Centenary, 3rd May, 1869.

(*Life of Machiavelli*, C. E. Detmold, *op. cit.*, I, 41.)

¶ I will explain more fully the defects of these arms. Mercenary captains are either very capable men or not; if they are, you cannot rely upon them, for they will always aspire to their own greatness, either by oppressing you, their master, or by oppressing others against your intentions; but if the captain is not an able man, he will generally ruin you. . . .

Machiavelli and Ourselves

We have already suggested that Machiavelli is an excellent epitome of his times.[1] In his cool, calculating cynicism, his frank and undisguised naturalism, his extreme individualism, his pragmatism, his devotion to classical antiquity, in his rejection of religion and of supernatural sanctions in favour of a 'here-and-now' philosophy and a hedonistic morality—in all these things he is characteristic of the Renaissance and, to a very considerable extent, of the modern mind.

All of this is obviously relevant to the study of culture and of the history of ideas, but it does not explain why a book on political theories includes a chapter on Machiavelli, or, more especially, why a study of *modern* political thought begins with Machiavelli. The reason is that Machiavelli, more than any other individual, and despite the fact that he is hardly a political *theorist*, is the father of modern political theory. He makes the first decisive break with the thought of the catholic Middle Ages on political problems. For Machiavelli the state is a *natural* entity. It rises out of, and exists in the midst of, a play of natural forces, which the ruler must understand and make use of if he and his state are to survive in the ruthless competition which is living. Here Machiavelli lays the foundation for Marx and those later theorists who reduce politics to the study of power-conflicts and their control.

It is true, of course, that there are great differences between Machiavelli and these later thinkers. Machiavelli had, for instance, no conception of the economic forces which Marx sees at the basis of all change, political, social, and intellectual. But for Machiavelli, as for Marx, there is no divine order of things designed by God in accordance with His plan for man and the universe. This comes out clearly in Machiavelli's repeated remarks on the instability of things and in his emphasis on the role of 'Fortune' in man's life, which is his way of repudiating divine, and asserting an amoral, non-human causality in the world. It is, he thinks, "an incontrovertible truth, proved by all

[1] *Vide supra*, pp. 25*ff.*

history, that men may second Fortune, but cannot oppose her; they may develop her designs, but cannot defeat them." [1]

Thus, despite all differences, a basic identity of point of view remains. Machiavelli's insight that the state can be understood only in terms of human lusts and appetites, and his supplementary recognition that the successful ruler must learn to control these forces, mark an epoch in political thinking and constitute the basis for the whole modern development.

Again, although, of course, he does not state it formally or definitively, Machiavelli is clearly looking forward to the concept of sovereignty and to the corresponding notion of the national territorial state. He completely rejects the feudal conception of a complex hierarchy of relatively autonomous entities, and for it substitutes an all-powerful central authority, who is supreme over all institutions within the region over which he has any jurisdiction at all. This concept is dominant in the thought of every one of the writers we have to consider in this book. Bodin and Hobbes, as we shall see, are primarily concerned with the definition of sovereignty; Locke and later thinkers with the problems which this definition entails. Indeed, sovereignty is *the* problem of modern politics. Nothing so clearly separates ancient from modern theory as the appearance on the scene of this concept, which at once reflects the nature of, and makes possible, the highly developed, industrial and capitalistic society in which we all live to-day.

There is a final reason for Machiavelli's importance in the history of political thought. Machiavelli was the first exponent, as he is one of the clearest, of power-politics. A little over one hundred years ago Lord Grey said that the policies of great states could not be governed by rules of morality. Lord Grey differs from most statesmen only by being more frank. Whatever may be the case about the conduct of *individual* men in their relations to other men (and Lord Grey said that no one 'admired' these moral principles more than himself), it is certainly true that states do behave towards each other very much in the ways in which Machiavelli describes. And refusal by optimistic and idealistic statesmen to recognize the facts has caused untold suffering to themselves and those they have ruled. We need not be cynical (as Machiavelli was inclined to be) in order to look at the world realistically. We may not like the world as it is; but we

---

[1] *Discourses*, II, 29 (309). We must not be misled by Machiavelli's anthropomorphic language to suppose that he really *personifies* fortune.

cannot improve it by closing our eyes to its deficiencies. Neville Chamberlain, for instance, would have learned a great deal about Hitler (and hence about how to deal with him) by studying Machiavelli; and if President Wilson had pondered *The Prince* the disaster of Versailles might never have occurred.

FOR FURTHER READING

Translations

See footnote, p. 22.

Commentaries and General Works

BURCKHARDT, JAKOB: *The Civilization of the Renaissance in Italy* (translated by S. G. C. Middlemore, 1898).
    Invaluable for the background of Machiavelli's thought.
CELLINI, BENVENUTO: *Autobiography* (translated by J. A. Symonds, 1899).
    The exciting and racy life of a near contemporary.
GILBERT, ALLAN H.: *Machiavelli's "Prince" and its Forerunners* (Duke University Publications, 1938).
    An attempt to show that *The Prince* is not a handbook for tyrants, but rather a far from unconventional treatise on governance.

CHAPTER THREE

Jean Bodin

(1530–96)

LIFE

BODIN is one of the least read, and yet one of the most frequently mentioned, of political theorists. He is often referred to because his theory of sovereignty is one of the prototypes of the modern view. He is seldom read because his *Six Books concerning the State* is one of the most verbose, repetitious, and contradictory of essays on a political subject.

The author of this important but long-winded treatise lived during the period of the French wars of religion, and his work reflects at every point the turmoil and the distress of those unhappy days. We cannot hope to understand Bodin (or any other writer on politics) unless we see the pressures under whose impact his views were formed and which they were intended to control. At the beginning of the century the French monarchy was, in the words of J. W. Allen, "an invasive and aspiring rather than a governing power." [1] Earlier kings had indeed begun the transformation of France from a collection of feudally independent territories into a national territorial state. But the process was far from completion.

"In every part of its territory the action of the central government was limited or obstructed by clerical, noble, provincial, and communal privileges or customs. . . . The centralized machinery of administration, so far as it existed, was at once extremely insufficient and very imperfectly controlled. Law varied from province to province and even from town to town. . . ." [2] With the religious quarrels later in the century this situation was aggravated. The religious dissenters, allied with others who wished to resist the government, formed the Huguenot party. In the civil wars which followed "centralized government practically disappeared and France all but broke up." [3]

---

[1] J. W. Allen, *A History of Political Thought in the Sixteenth Century* (Methuen, 1928), p. 212.   [2] *Ibid.*, p. 271.   [3] *Ibid.*, p. 272.

The extremely arid and intellectualistic tone of Bodin's writing should not lead us to suppose him an ivory-towered spectator of these events. Though his life began academically enough, as a legal theorist (an occupation which continued to mark his thinking), he was still young when he went to Paris to seek his fortune in more active pursuits. There he won the regard of the King and of his brother, the Duke d'Alençon, and gradually rose to a position of some prominence. He was a member of, and played a leading role in, the states-general which was convened at Blois in 1576.[1] Bodin's policy, as against the League and other extremists, was to support measures of toleration. For, whatever his personal religious views, he rightly saw that peace could not be lastingly established as long as either side—Catholic or Huguenot—insisted on trying to enforce its own doctrines on the other. He therefore opposed, and by his adroitness was able to defeat, a scheme of the League for forcing Catholicism on the whole population.

This and other activities cost him the King's favour, and he shortly afterwards retired to Laon, where he held an important magistracy. There he joined the League—an act for which he has subsequently been severely condemned. It is true that the views of the League were in most respects contrary to his own principles. But, as we shall see,[2] Bodin argues in his *State* that there comes a time when a policy of toleration has to give way to the use of force. It may well be that by 1589 he had come to the conclusion that the League was the only body in France capable of ruling, and that the salvation of the country required all men to end further turmoil by adhering to it.

In any case, his relations with his new associates were far from easy. In 1590 he was accused of heresy, his home was searched, and several 'suspect' books were discovered, including a genealogy of Henry of Navarre. This is symptomatic of the way in which his mind was moving: here was a prince shrewd enough to see the value of the policy of compromise which Bodin had long advocated, and powerful enough to have some chance of establishing himself on the throne. It is not surprising, therefore, to find Bodin shifting his position once more. In 1593 he broke with the League and openly declared himself for Henry. He died, however, in 1596 before he could see the new king crowned and his own policy triumph.

[1] This was also the year in which his *Six Books concerning the State* was published.
[2] *Infra*, p. 83.

POLITICAL PHILOSOPHY

The State defined

Bodin is rightly aware of the novelty of his conception of a state, or commonwealth. He puts a definition of it at the very start of his *Six Books concerning the State* and devotes the whole of the first book to its elucidation. He does this because, as he says, every one who has ever written about politics has either failed to define the state at all or has at least failed to see its essence. What, then, is a state?[1]

¶ A state is a lawful government of many families and of what is common to them, together with a supreme sovereignty. We put this definition at the beginning of our book because it is necessary always first to inquire what the chief end of a thing is and afterwards about the means of attaining it.

We may follow Bodin in this treatment of his subject. Let us begin therefore, with his analysis of each of the terms of this definition:

I. The Family [2]

¶ A commonwealth, we have said, is composed of a number of families. If each family be well governed and orderly, the state as a whole will be well and peaceably governed. . . . It is of the first importance, therefore, to see to it that family life is well-regulated. . . . There are four types of regulation involved: that of the husband in respect of his wife, a father in respect of his children, a master towards his servants, a lord towards his slaves.

Bodin rejects the fourth type of authority (slavery) as being both immoral and imprudent. He does not treat the third type in any detail. We may indicate briefly his conception of the kind of authority which a husband and father ought to exercise in a well-regulated family.[3]

(a) The Husband

¶ If the husband be neither slave nor son in his father's house, he has absolute authority over his wife. . . . Since neither slave nor son

---

[1] *Les Six Livres de la République* (1629), Book I, chapter I. This is my own translation from the French text of 1629. An English translation was made by R. Knollers and published in 1606. Reference to its paging is given in parentheses.
[2] *Ibid.*, I, 2 (14).   [3] *Ibid.*, I, 3–4 (15–28).

¶ has authority over himself, neither, obviously, can have authority over some one else. For a family is like a state: there can be but one ruler, one master, one lord. If there were several persons in authority, they might issue contrary orders, and the family would be in continual turmoil. . . . If, then, we except the father's (or master's) power over his son (or slave), we may say that all laws, both divine and human, agree that the wife must obey her husband's commands—unless, of course, these commands themselves are contrary to divine law.

(b) *The Father*

¶   A father . . . is the true image of God, our sovereign Lord, the Father of all things. . . . A father is obliged by nature to support his children while they are still weak and helpless, and to bring them up in honourable and virtuous ways. On the other hand, a child is obliged, but far more stringently, to love, reverence, serve, and support his father; to execute his commands in loyal obedience; to shield his infirmities; and never to spare his own life or property in order to save the life of him to whom he owes his own. . . .

Examples from the practice of the Romans and other early people demonstrate that a well-ordered state requires parents to have over their children the power of life and death, which both the law of God and that of nature assigns to them. . . . Unless this power is restored to parents, we can never hope to see revived the good customs, honour, virtue, and splendour of ancient states. . . .

It is necessary for parents to have this power because the public courts cannot have any real jurisdiction over such private matters as the education and discipline of children. . . . If, therefore, authority be taken away from parents, it is altogether lacking; and children, having no fear of their parents and still less of God, grow up without any discipline, public or private. . . .

It may be objected that violent or wicked fathers will abuse this power. . . . I reply that most fathers and mothers have so much affection and love for their children that they aim at nothing but the children's honour and profit. . . . It is true, of course, that occasionally a parent may abuse his power. But a wise legislator will not leave a good law unmade merely because it will inconvenience a few persons. What law, however natural, just, and necessary, is not subject to some inconveniences? He who would

¶ rescind a law because it involves some few absurdities would not leave a single law standing. . . .

II. *Lawful Government* [1]

¶   We have said that a state is a *lawful* government, in order to distinguish it from a gang of robbers or of pirates. . . . However much such a gang may seem to form a society, and its members to live in amity among themselves, we ought not to call it a "society" or "state" . . . , because it lacks the principal mark of a peaceful society, namely, a lawful government according to the laws of nature.

III. *Sovereignty* [2]

¶   Sovereignty is the absolute and perpetual power . . . of commanding in a state. It is necessary to define this term since no political philosopher or jurist has yet defined it, though the presence of sovereignty is the chief property which distinguishes a state from other organizations or societies of men. . . . So far we have said only that a state is a lawful government of many families and of what is common to them, together with a supreme sovereignty. Now it remains to say exactly what sovereignty is. To begin with, then, it is a *perpetual* power. For, if power be held only for a certain time (it does not matter how long a time), it is not sovereign power, and he who holds it for that time is not a sovereign prince, but only a trustee or custodian of that power so long as it pleases the real prince (or the people) not to revoke it. . . .

We may now go on to the other part of our definition, and explain what *absolute* power is. For the people or the nobles of a state can give the sovereign and perpetual power to anyone they choose. They can give this power simply and completely to dispose of their goods, their lives, and the whole state at the sovereign's pleasure, and to be left as he chooses, simply and completely, without any other reason than his liberality. This power is given to the prince without any charges or conditions attached (except, of course, those set by the law of God or nature), for power given with restrictions is neither absolute power nor, properly speaking, sovereignty. . . .

[1] *Six Books*, I, 1 (3).   [2] *Ibid.*, I, 8 and 10 (84 *ff.*, 156*ff.*).

¶ Since there is nothing on earth greater than a sovereign prince, save God alone, and since sovereigns are established by God as His lieutenants to rule over men, we must take care that their majesty be reverenced and respected and that they be always spoken of with honour. For he who is contemptuous of his sovereign prince scorns God Himself, of whom the prince is the earthly image. . . .

In order to give him the respect that is his due we must therefore know how to distinguish the true sovereign from all other men. What, then, are the marks of sovereignty? . . .

I say that the first mark of a sovereign prince is the power of giving laws to all the people in general or to each one in particular . . . without consent of any besides himself. . . . It may be said that custom is as powerful as law and that if the prince be the source of law it is ordinary men who are the source of custom. To this I reply that custom acquires its force little by little and after many years by the common consent of all or at least the greater part. A law, on the other hand, is made in a moment and derives its strength from him who owns the supreme power. Customs steal in softly and unnoticed; laws are commanded and published by authority and often against the wishes of the subjects. . . . Moreover, the law can put an end to a custom, but custom cannot derogate a law. . . . In brief, custom has force only on suffrance and so long as it pleases the sovereign prince to allow it. . . . Hence we see that the real authority of law and of custom alike rests on the power of the sovereign prince.

This power of being the source of law is incommunicable. The sovereign may, of course, give to certain persons the right to make laws, which will then have the same authority as if made by the sovereign himself. Thus, for instance, the people of Athens gave this power to Solon, and those of Sparta to Lycurgus. Nevertheless those laws were the laws of the people of Athens and of Sparta, not of Solon and of Lycurgus, who were only the commissioners and agents of the people who had charged them to make the laws in question.

Under this power of giving and abrogating laws are included all the other rights and marks of sovereignty. Indeed, if one is to speak precisely, there is but this one mark of sovereignty. All the various specific rights of a sovereign prince are only aspects of, or derivatives from, this primary right of giving laws. . . . Since, however,

❡ the word 'law' is so general, it will be expedient to name specifically the additional rights included in sovereignty, as, for instance, the right of declaring war and of making peace, the right of being the court of last resort from the judgment of all magistrates, the right of instituting and of removing even the most important officers and ministers, the right of imposing charges and subsidies on subjects and of exempting them from such charges, the right of increasing or depreciating the value of money, the right of requiring an oath of allegiance from all subjects and liegemen without exception. . . .

Sovereignty, it is important to see, involves supreme and absolute power, but not any and every exercise of supreme power is an act of sovereignty. A large gang of robbers or of pirates may, for instance, have a considerable formal organization. Order may be maintained, discipline preserved. But the leader of such a gang is not a sovereign, in Bodin's sense, even though he owes obedience to no one else, while a habit of obedience on the part of his subordinates exists.

The fact that he is not a sovereign results from Bodin's conception of law as distinguished from mere order. There are, Bodin believes, natural laws, found out by reason, which are just and which ought, therefore, to govern men's relations to one another. They are just and ought to command us, because they are God's decrees. They do not do so, because, since Adam's fall, we are weak and sinful. It is, indeed, precisely because of this difference between what most men's conduct is and what it ought to be that they require a sovereign over them. His function is to enforce upon them the natural laws which ought to govern their relations. The sovereign has to have supreme power because sinful men will follow this right rule only if they are compelled to do so. They are too much slaves of passion and desire to follow God's law spontaneously. Where their sovereign differs from them is precisely in this: he has learned, as they have not, how to subject appetite to the rule of reason. An actual ruler is fit to rule only if he rules, not in the interest of private or selfish desire, but as God's lieutenant—that is, according to the dictates of reason and justice. Hence Bodin draws a sharp distinction between the ruler as he only too often actually is and the ruler as he always ought to be: both types of ruler may wield supreme power and control many men's lives, but he only is truly sovereign who does so in the interests of justice.

This is one of the principal points in Bodin's theory. It effectively distinguishes him from Hobbes, who in other respects maintains a theory of sovereignty very close to Bodin's, and from Machiavelli—both of whom defend a more purely naturalistic theory of the state. Increasingly nineteenth-century and contemporary writers have followed in their footsteps. For them the state and its fabric of laws and institutions is supreme—supreme in the sense, that is, that there is no higher, *moral* law in terms of which the state and all its institutions are criticized. In modern theory our national territorial state may be only an element in a larger whole, and, if so, its laws may be subject to revision by that superior body. But, still, the final laws in terms of which revision is undertaken are always held to be man-made. Bodin, it is true, points in the direction of this modern type of theory when he makes his sovereign the source of law. But in spite of this he is still close to the great mediæval tradition, which sees the state and its laws as only the more or less inadequate reflection of that perfect justice, goodness, and truth which are expressed in God's moral order. The earthly sovereign—whether king, parliament, or people—may, therefore, be supreme in the sense that no other earthly power can question its decrees. It may be the source of law in the sense that its decisions are commands for all those who live within its territorial jurisdiction. But above all earthly power is God's power. And the sovereign's authority is, in the ultimate analysis, conditioned by this fact. Sovereignty is not identical with dominion, because the exercise of force, to be lawful, legitimate, and right, must be in accord with an independent and absolutely valid moral order, the 'laws of nature' decreed by God.

The chief problem which Bodin's view has to face results from the difficulty of determining what these laws of nature are. Bodin himself did not feel the seriousness of this problem, because he thought the laws of nature were clear and certain.[1] The whole question for him, therefore, turned on getting a good man, rather than a bad man, as ruler. This is, indeed, a problem. But it seems also to be the case that the laws of nature are not so easily or so universally recognized as Bodin optimistically believed. And even if there be widespread agreement on certain very general principles, like truthfulness, honesty, and justice for all, there is the greatest possible difference of opinion about how these principles ought to be applied in the concrete alter-

---

[1] Thus, for instance, Bodin says that a good king "obeys the laws of nature—that is, he governs his subjects and guides their actions in accordance with natural justice, which he sees and recognizes clearly and distinctly, like the brilliance of the sun" (*Six Books*, II, 2).

natives of conduct.[1] In fact, if we take any principle in a sense sufficiently general to secure for it widespread acceptance it is almost
inevitably too abstract to have much relevance to actual conduct.
Thus almost every one will agree that telling the truth and acting
justly are good. But on specific questions, whether it is right to tell
the truth to so and so at such and such a time, whether it is just to hang
this man or imprison that one, men always reach different conclusions,
even with the best will in the world, because their decisions are
coloured by all sorts of private desires, prejudices, and biases.

Hence we are not very likely to have the kind of unanimity which
Bodin expected, about whether a given ruler is, or is not, ruling in
accordance with the laws of nature. The ruler may believe himself
to be executing God's commands on earth, while his subjects may
judge him to be the worst kind of tyrant. This situation is likely to
result in exactly the sort of civil strife which Bodin's supreme sovereign is designed to avert. One exit from the difficulty would be to
say, as Hobbes later was to do, that the sovereign alone knows what
the natural laws are. This would effectively silence disputes about
them. But while apparently leaving God's laws supreme, this solution
really denies them any significance. For to say that divine law is
whatever the sovereign says it is, is in effect to deny the real existence
of an eternal, objective moral law, over sovereign and subject alike.
Hobbes could do this easily enough, because he did not, as we shall see,
take divine law seriously. But since a belief in the real existence of
natural law is basic to Bodin's whole position, he could not possibly
accept the Hobbesian answer.

Locke, like Bodin, believes also in the supremacy of natural law.
His solution of the problem is to limit the sovereign's supremacy to
the realm of public law. There, indeed, he is supreme, but he has no
jurisdiction over religious and moral matters. In this realm he is on
the same footing with the meanest of his subjects. This solution, exactly
the opposite of Hobbes's, is no more open to Bodin. He was too close
to the furious religious dissensions of his own time not to feel that civil
control of religion was essential to the peace and safety of the state.

Hence Bodin is in the paradoxical position of wanting both to give
his sovereign authority over moral and religious matters and to exclude
them from his control. This is because the concept of the supremacy
of natural law conceived of as having a divine source and the concept
of the supremacy of the human ruler of the territorial state are rival

---

[1] *Vide infra*, pp. 360-361.

principles intertwined, but not reconciled, in his thought. The former rises from his deeply moral and religious nature and binds him to the great mediæval tradition; the latter issues from a consideration of the condition of his own country and makes him a precursor of the modern development.

On the one hand, he saw France torn asunder by hopeless civil and religious conflict and judged that the only cure for such a chaotic state of affairs was the creation of a central authority powerful enough to hold together the various elements in society. What was needed, he felt, was a power sufficiently strong to enforce order, put down disturbances, and maintain the peace. Here Bodin was merely sensitive to the actual current of events: the monarchy had already long since begun its development as a central authority in opposition to the diversive forces of feudalism. It was certainly the institution in the state best suited to the role Bodin assigned to it. It was natural for him to want to strengthen the monarchy, seeing, as he did, the bitter fruits of its weakness.[1]

On the other hand, he saw just as clearly that there is a certain absolute order at which human conduct ought to aim and in terms of which it can be judged. Might does not, he thought, make right. Robbers and gangsters are not real sovereigns, however powerful they may be, because their rule is merely tyrannical and brutal regulation from above. Hence Bodin does not make his sovereign supreme in the Hobbesian sense that whatever he does is right simply because he wills it. Rather, in the ultimate analysis, the supreme sovereign's decisions are not absolutely final, since they are subject to divine law. But how this restriction is to be effective or who is to recognize it and put it into operation, Bodin does not tell us.

Hence he does not effect a harmonious reconciliation of his two principles. Failing to see their antithetical character with sufficient

---

[1] The legal picture, he saw, was hopelessly complicated, confused, and full of exceptions. All sorts of ancient privileges and rights existed or were claimed by different persons and magistrates which hedged the monarchy in or prevented an efficient exercise of executive power. Bodin discusses innumerable examples of this sort of thing, of which the following may serve as an illustration.

"Notwithstanding the ordinance of Louis XII, the chapter of the church at Rouen claims to have the right of granting pardon in honour of its patron, St Romain. Before the feast of that saint the chapter forbids the judges to execute any condemned persons, as I myself saw when I served on the commission for the reform of Normandy. Now, on one such occasion the courts had a condemned prisoner executed despite the wishes of the chapter" (*Six Books*, II, 10 (173)). The chapter complained to the king, and, "having for its head one of the princes of the blood," was able to make great trouble for the magistrates. This kind of situation, of which to-day one can have no real conception, was hopelessly inefficient. Bodin's argument against it is just that.

clarity, he does little more than state the problem which must inevitably arise for any political theorist who admits a higher law than force. It remained for later philosophers, like Locke and Rousseau, to wrestle with the problem's solution. But, as we shall find, even they do not altogether adequately explain how the necessary existence of force is to be restrained in the interest of a higher moral law.

The State's End

So far Bodin has given only a detailed analysis of his definition of the state. In the course of this we have seen, in a general way, what the state's end is. It is, so far as this is possible, to let God's will be done on earth, to reproduce amongst men the kind of relations which hold in heaven. But can we say more specifically what the state should aim at achieving for each individual man? [1]

¶ Ancient writers have called a state "a society of men assembled together in order to live virtuously and happily." This definition is faulty. It contains at once too little and too much. Too little because it omits mention of three characteristics of states already described; too much because the word 'happily,' as the ancients understand it, is unnecessary. . . . A state can be well governed and nevertheless be unhappy, in the ordinary sense of the word. That is, despite its good government, it may be afflicted with poverty, deserted by its friends, besieged by its enemies, and overwhelmed by all sorts of calamities. . . . On the other hand, a state may have a fertile situation and abound in riches, strength, and glory. Yet, for all that, it may overflow with vice and wickedness of all kinds. In fact, it is certain that virtue has no greater enemy than that kind of success which men call happiness, so difficult it is to combine things as contrary as are virtue and happiness. Hence let us exclude happiness from our description of the state's end. Let us aim higher, so that we can attain, or at least approach, good government. We do not mean, however, to aim so high that we describe merely an ideal state, without real counterpart, like those of Plato and Thomas More, Chancellor of England, have imagined. For our part, we shall limit ourselves to the sort of state which will be possible.

Let us say, then, that the highest end, the true happiness, of the individual man and state alike, consists in intellectual virtue, or

[1] *Six Books*, I, 1 (4*ff.*).

¶ contemplation. All of the deepest thinkers have agreed that man enjoys his highest good when he contemplates things natural, human, and divine, tying all together in praise of Almighty God. If this be the chief end of the truly happy man, it must be admitted that it is also the end and happiness of the state.

Nevertheless, material well-being cannot be ignored. Man has a double nature. He is composed of diverse things and hence has a double happiness. If the virtue of his highest part, his soul, consists in the contemplation of God's handiwork, his body also has its specific virtue, which is health, strength, happiness, and the beauty of well-proportioned limbs. Similarly, reasoning from the lesser to the greater, we may say that the state, too, has a secondary happiness. Besides seeking virtue, it ought to have a territory sufficiently large to support its population, a fertile soil, beasts and cattle sufficient to feed and clothe its citizens, temperate climate, abundance of water and of materials suitable for constructing houses and fortifications. . . .

Moreover, though contemplation is the higher end, neither man nor the state can survive unless the lesser end is assured. A state cannot be well ordered if such ordinary matters as the guard and defence of the subjects, the administration of justice, and the procurement of necessary provisions be not seen to, just as a man cannot survive very long if his soul is so ravished in contemplation that he forgets to eat and drink.

It is clear from this how far less modern Bodin is than either Machiavelli or Hobbes. Though most of the *Six Books* is concerned with devices for ensuring material well-being, we must never forget that, for Bodin, all of this is of secondary importance. The primary end is to make men religious by leading them to a contemplation of the beauty and grandeur of nature.

¶ When a man's mind is clear and free from the vices and passions which trouble the soul he begins to attend to the diversity of human affairs, to the different ages of men, the contrary humours which possess them, the success of some and the failure of others, and to the changes of states, seeking always for the causes of these effects. Then, turning from things human to the beauty of nature, he finds satisfaction in the variety of animals, of plants, and of minerals, considering the form, quality, and essence of each, their affinities

¶and antagonisms, and the succession of necessary causal relations involved in all natural phenomena. Next, leaving this elementary region, he takes flight on the wings of contemplation, in order to see the splendour, beauty, and power of the celestial orbs, their movement, size, and distance, and the melodious harmony of the whole universe. Then he is ravished by a noble pleasure, accompanied by an unending desire to find the first Cause and Author of so beautiful a masterpiece. Here his contemplation finally rests, seeing that this Cause is infinite and incomprehensible in essence, in magnitude, in power, in wisdom, and in goodness. Thus, by means of contemplation, wise men and good have fashioned a noble demonstration of the existence of one eternal and infinite God, and from this they draw a conclusion of human happiness.

Monarchy

Having considered what sovereignty is, Bodin now passes on to examine the various possible types of sovereignty—*i.e.*, the various forms under which this absolute power can manifest itself, in order to determine which is most likely to achieve the state's end.[1]

¶ The place in which sovereignty resides determines what sort of state we have. If sovereignty resides in a single prince we call the state a monarchy; if the people have a share in the sovereign power we call it a popular state; if only a part of the people have the supreme power we call it an aristocracy. . . . It is important to observe these distinctions because we cannot expect to have exactly the same laws in all three types. Different states require different laws and ordinances. . . .

We have already said that monarchy is that kind of state in which absolute sovereignty rests in the hands of a single man. We must now explain this definition. . . .

But before we do so we must draw attention to another distinction, which is of the first importance, though never observed before. This is the distinction between sovereignty and government. A state can be monarchical in form and yet be governed popularly. It is a monarchy if it has one man for sovereign; but it has a popular government if this sovereign distributes the offices, magistracies, and other places equally to all men, without having a

[1] *Six Books*, II, 1–2 (179*ff*.).

¶ special regard to nobility of birth, to wealth, or to virtue. Obviously, also, monarchy may have an aristocratic government. It does so, if the sovereign prince gives the magistracies and benefices only to the nobility, or if he limits them in some other way, say, to the virtuous. Similarly, an aristocracy may govern either popularly or aristocratically, depending on how the sovereign (in this case, the few, rather than the one or many) distributes the magistracies. . . .

Now, monarchy itself is divided into three sub-types, for it may be lordly,[1] royal, or tyrannical. In a legitimate, or royal, monarchy, the subjects are obedient to their prince's laws, while he in turn obeys the laws of nature. In this kind of monarchy the subjects enjoy their natural liberty and the possession of their property. Monarchy is tyrannical when the prince scorns the laws of nature and treats his free subjects as if they were mere slaves and their property as if it were his own. The same difference can be found in both the aristocratic and popular forms of state: both may be either legitimate or tyrannical, depending on how well the laws of nature be adhered to by the sovereign. . . .

It is then a true mark of a royal monarchy that the prince himself is just as obedient to the laws of nature as he desires his subject to be to him. Further marks of royal monarchy are that the prince fears God above all, that he is pitiful towards the afflicted, prudent in business, brave in exploits, modest in prosperity, constant in adversity, faithful to his promises, wise in council, helpful to his friends, terrible to his enemies, charitable to men of goodwill, dreadful to evil-doers, and just to all. . . .

If the subjects obey their king's law, and he obeys the laws of nature, then it is really the laws that rule . . . and pleasant, sweet harmony will exist throughout the whole state. If such conditions exist we call the state a royal monarchy however the kingdom may have been acquired, whether it be the prince's by right of inheritance . . . or his by law . . . or by election . . . or by gift. . . . A royal monarchy may even be acquired by force of arms . . . or by fraud. It is royal and legitimate so long as the conqueror governs equitably. . . .

In order, next, to ascertain the true nature of tyranny let us compare the two extreme cases—a good and just king with the most detestable of tyrants. In this way the differences will be more

---

[1] Bodin's discussion of this type has been omitted. It differs from tyranny chiefly in having been acquired by a 'just' war.

¶ marked. Of course, when I say, "a good and just king," I am speaking popularly. I do not mean the possessor of heroic virtues or a paragon of wisdom, justice, and piety. . . . These perfections are too rare to consider. I call that king just and good who strives with all his might towards such ideal virtues and who spends his fortune, his blood, and his life for the good of his people. . . . The greatest difference between such a king and a tyrant is simply this: the king conforms to the laws of nature, the tyrant tramples them under foot. The one respects piety, justice, and faith; the other knows neither God, nor faith, nor law. The one thinks only of the public good and the well-being of his subjects; the other does nothing except for his private profit, for vengeance, or for pleasure. The one seeks to enrich his subjects; the other builds his house on the ruin of those of other men. The one punishes public wrongs, while pardoning those done to himself; the other punishes those who injure him and lets all others go free. The one protects the honour of modest women; the other triumphs in their shame. . . . The one is concerned to maintain the peace and union of his subjects; the other endeavours to sow seeds of discord among them, for he gains by their disorders. The one delights to show himself to his loyal subjects; the other hides from them as from his enemies. The one founds his state on his subjects' love; the other on their fear. The one is honoured during his life and missed when he has passed away; the other is defamed while still alive and reviled after his death. . . .

These are the most noteworthy differences between a king and a tyrant. They are easy to recognize in the extreme cases we have taken; but it is more difficult if, as is sometimes the case, the good king has to take upon himself something of the tyrant. In fact, the circumstances—the times, the places, and the persons—often constrain a prince to practices which seem as tyrannical to some of his subjects as they are praiseworthy to others. We have already remarked that lawful governments must vary among different peoples. We must mention this point again here in order to show that tyranny should not be identified with the severity to which even the best of princes is sometimes compelled. A state which is corrupt and diseased requires a vigorous treatment from its physician. The prince who cures it is not a tyrant though he has to kill some and banish others. He is rather called one of the wisest and most virtuous princes of his day. In a word, good government

¶ requires on occasion the use of force, and states are often ruined by the prince's mildness, while others are saved by cruelty.

To summarize all this we may say that a ruler should not be judged to be a tyrant by his severity but by his violation of the laws of God and of nature. This point being now sufficiently clear, let us see whether it is right to take the life of a tyrant.

A tyrant, once more, is he who has taken sovereignty upon himself on his own authority, without election, inheritance, lot, just war, or the special calling of God. Both the laws and the writings of the ancients agree that such a one should be slain and that the greatest rewards—titles of nobility and knighthood and the property of the tyrant—should be given to tyrannicides as the liberators of their country. . . .

So much for the tyrant. But what if a legitimate prince—one who has come to his estate by inheritance or election or lot or just war or divine vocation—become cruel, exacting, and beyond all measure wicked? May he be killed like a tyrant? Some learned doctors and theologians have maintained that there is no distinction between such a wicked prince and a tyrant. But we maintain that there is an important difference, the overlooking of which has led to the ruin of many fair states. . . . There is also a difference between a foreigner and a subject. It is one thing to say that a cruel and wicked king may be killed by a foreign prince and quite another to claim that he may be killed by one of his own subjects. The former is not only permissible, but glorious and noble. The latter is not. . . . For, if the prince be really sovereign, as are the true monarchs of France, Spain, England, Scotland, Ethiopia, Turkey, Persia and Muscovy . . . , then it is not lawful either for one subject or for all in general to make an attempt upon the life or honour of their sovereign, neither by way of fact nor by way of justice. To take the latter alternative first: it is obviously impossible for a subject to proceed against his king by way of justice, that is, by way of the courts. For the courts are the king's, and the subject can have no jurisdiction in them over his prince who is the source of whatever authority the laws and the courts possess. . . . And if it be not lawful for subjects to proceed against their prince by way of justice, how should they proceed against him by way of fact? It is not a question here which is the stronger, king or subject, but of what is right and lawful. . . . Now not only is that subject guilty of treason in the highest degree who kills his king, but so also are those who

¶ attempt it or counsel it or desire it; so also, even those who so much as think of it.

An enormous number of authorities from Moses to Martin Luther are cited in support of this contention. Instead of trying to evaluate Bodin's conclusion it will be more profitable to consider why he reached it. If it seems strange in view of his liberal attitude towards tyrannicide, we must see that, like so many paradoxes in Bodin's thought, it results from a difficulty already discussed. If a king have (legally) supreme power it is obviously illegal to remove him. But the question is, exactly, does a bad king have a legal position? Obviously yes, if we are thinking in terms of a sovereign who is the supreme and final source of all law. Then we argue with Hobbes that removing or destroying a king, however wicked, is untenable. In fact, from this point of view, his wickedness is quite irrelevant. But, on the other hand, obviously no, if we are thinking in terms of a sovereign who is merely God's lieutenant on earth. From this point of view, his wickedness is the deciding factor, for the bad ruler is not God's lieutenant and so not sovereign. In other words, whether the ruler's position is legal or not depends on what we take law to be. Obviously his position is legal if by law we mean his own commands. Obviously it is not legal if we limit law to what corresponds to God's commands. Bodin wants the two to be identical, and, ideally, they doubtless are. But in the case of a bad king they must be different, and, for reasons which we need not repeat here, Bodin cannot make up his mind which meaning of law to adopt.

One more point in this connexion requires notice. While a writer like Locke draws as sharp a distinction as ever Bodin does between the law of force and the law of justice, Locke reaches a different conclusion about the subject's relation to his king. This is because they read the content of natural law differently. Bodin's view of natural law is coloured by a somewhat legalistic approach: for him natural law merely gives sanctity and authority to legally (rather than morally) established relations, in this case to the relation which the law decrees to exist between king and subject. For Locke the basic natural law is not juridical, but moral. And this moral law is to a certain very considerable extent determined by utilitarian factors. Hence on Locke's view the subject does have a right under natural law to rebel, because the wicked king has violated that law by his immoral conduct. Neither Locke nor Bodin is interested in what the latter calls "the way of fact"—that is, neither is concerned with the question whether the king or subject is in fact stronger. They agree also in their calculation of where the utility resides, as is shown by Bodin's assertion that foreigners may kill wicked kings. In such circumstances, utility can determine policy, because, of course, the king has no legal position *vis à vis* a foreigner, who is not his subject.

So far we have reached the conclusion that monarchy is the best form of state. It remains to be inquired what form of government is best.

Though a popular state is likely to be no better than a detestable tyranny, popular government is often successful. In fact, "the combination of a monarchy with a popular government constitutes the most assured monarchy that it is possible to have."[1] In any case, however the magistracies be filled by him, the sovereign will be well advised to let his ministers govern. Whatever the form of the state, fundamental laws should be decided on and a government established in such a way and of such a form that subsequently the business of the state is dealt with in a regular and systematic manner, according to law, rather than by the arbitrary and changeable will of the sovereign himself or of anyone appointed by him. The state should in fact be like a machine which is designed so as not to require constant tinkering and adjustment by an engineer.

¶ The question is whether kings should act as judges over their subjects. To many this may seem a foregone conclusion, for all the ancients agree that kings exist for no other end than to judge their subjects. . . . And this may seem to follow from what we ourselves have said about the king being the source of all law and the protector of his subjects' lives and property. . . . Doubtless there is much to be said in favour of the king's ruling directly, but weighty reasons on the other side prevail over these advantages. . . .

Kings do not always have the requisite learning to act as judges; but, passing that over, let us suppose the king to have all the wisdom, knowledge, prudence, discretion, patience, and other virtues required of a good judge. I still say that there are grave difficulties in the way of his acting as judge. For the safest maxim that a prince can follow is this: to be loved by all and hated by none. Now this means that the king must stand above all disputes and all decisions about punishments, leaving all this to his judges, who will then incur the odium which inevitably accompanies all acts of punishment,

<hr />

[1] *Six Books*, II, 7 (249).

¶ and reserving to himself, on the other hand, the distribution of pensions, honours, benefices, privileges, and other awards. . . . For if a prince act as judge, he will be hated by those he has condemned, it being immaterial whether he has judged well or ill. Yet he ought to be loved by all his subjects and looked up to by all as a high and sure fortress. Thus there are difficulties in a prince's acting as judge even if he has not the slightest personal interest in the decision. How much more ought he to avoid participating in the judgment if he is interested in one of the parties to the suit. . . .[1]

The inconvenience of having the prince directly administer justice is even better seen in the case of a popular state where the whole people is sovereign, for who can surmount the difficulties involved in bringing the people together or in getting them to decide reasonably when they assembled? But the fact is that in any state, whether monarchical, aristocratic, or popular, nothing is so ruinous as to strip the council and magistrates of their ordinary and legitimate powers and to place all these subordinate powers in the hands of those who have the supreme sovereign power. For the less power the sovereign has (I am not talking, of course, about the special marks of sovereignty), the more assured it is. This was remarked by Theopompus, King of Sparta. After he had increased the powers of his council and set up five tribunes to represent the people, his wife reproached him for having, as she thought, so much diminished his power. He replied that he had not diminished it but assured it for the future. A building that is too tall, he said, will not long stand. . . .

The state cannot fail to prosper when the sovereign holds to what pertains to his majesty, when the council guards its authority, when the magistrates execute their authority, and when justice takes its regular course. How otherwise it is when he who is sovereign appropriates to himself the functions of his council or magistrates. Then the whole state is likely to be ruined and the sovereign to lose his power. Those, therefore, do their sovereign great harm who think to enhance his power by urging him to show his claws or who tell him that his very gesture or glance is as good as a law or edict, so that there is not one of his subjects who can initiate any policy without having it changed or reversed by the sovereign.

[1] All of these arguments hold against any other special activities which the sovereign might think to perform in his own right, such as negotiating with foreign states or exercising the functions of the various magistracies.

The king is not, of course, the only element in the state who may cause its destruction by appropriating functions that are not properly his. It is just as dangerous if the ordinary citizens, the plain people, try to usurp the place of the magistrates.[1]

¶ Let us remember what an ancient writer once said. Speaking to the rebellious plebeians, a Roman senator said, "Should the feet complain against the eyes because they do not occupy so high a place?" If citizens all insist on being equal and having equal rights and privileges, how many disturbances and civil wars we will see.... It is important, therefore, to remember that it is not equality of rights that makes men equally citizens. . . . A citizen is a free subject under the sovereignty of another. In olden days there were no citizens, no cities, no form of state amongst men. The head of each family was, as it were, a sovereign in his own house . . . ; and when violence, ambition, avarice, and lust for revenge set them one against the other, the issue of war gave victory to some and made others slaves to the victors. Thus, for the full and complete freedom they had once enjoyed, they exchanged pure and complete servitude. . . .

But neither is a slave a citizen. I said that a citizen is a free subject, just because I wished to distinguish him from a slave. A slave has no rights: he counts for nothing. . . . But a citizen, on the one hand, is free because he has certain rights and privileges, and, on the other subject because his liberty is diminished by the majesty of him to whom he owes obedience.

How much the citizen's liberty is diminished is a matter of wide variation. Hence we have to leave our definition general without trying to specify what rights and privileges belong to the citizen. These vary from state to state and, indeed, among the different groups in the same state. Plutarch is correct when he says that the right of citizenship is to have some part in the rights and privileges of a city. He means that the extent of any man's part varies according to his condition and quality: all are citizens, but nobles have the rights and privileges of nobles, commoners the rights and privileges of commoners, and so on, depending on the age, sex, condition, and merits of each person. . . . Every citizen, even the meanest, has some rights. Every citizen, even the noblest, has some duties. There is not a state anywhere in which those with the greatest

---

[1] *Six Books*, I, 6 (46*ff.*).

¶ rights and privileges are not also subject in some respects. Thus, with us, the nobility are exempted from taxes but are bound to take up arms for the defence of the state, upon pain of losing their property and lives. . . .

Thus, once more, it is not equality of rights that makes men citizens. It is a mutual obligation of sovereign and subject: for the good faith and obedience which the one receives, he owes justice, counsel, comfort, aid, and protection to the other.

Here, in the notion of citizen, the concepts of law and of sovereignty come together. The citizen is distinguished both from the stateless man who is completely free to do whatever he wants (and can) and from the slave of some despot, who has no freedom at all. The citizen's freedom is restricted, but it is restricted by law. And, since it is law that restricts, the sovereign, too, is not completely free. Command is not conterminous with the power to command. It involves duties which are as real as those of the most insignificant citizen. Thus, though Bodin's state is in some respects the opposite of equalitarian, though there are the greatest possible differences in rank, there is one sense in which all are equal. Every one, from the lowest to the highest, has a station which entails certain corresponding duties and responsibilities. The good state is simply one in which every one from the king down knows his station and lives up to its duties; and the essence of good government consists in finding the means for maintaining this structure. Exactly how seriously Bodin takes this idea of the state as an ordered hierarchy and the precision with which he thinks the various levels can be distinguished and ranked, appear in his list of the orders of citizenship.[1]

¶ Next to the king himself should follow the holy order of the clergy. After the clergy come the king's council; then the military, and amongst them first the general of the army, or great constable, next the dukes, counts, marquesses, governors of provinces . . . , captains of castles, vassals, and other soldiers. After the military come the civil officers of the kingdom—magistrates, judges, lawyers, pleaders, advocates, attorneys, proctors, scribes, registers, notaries, sergeants, trumpeters, jailers, and all other legal officers. Next follow the physicians, surgeons, and apothecaries. Next those who instruct the youth and the professors of divine law‘

[1] *Six Books*, III, 7 (402-403).

❡ physics, natural philosophy, mathematics, logic, rhetoric, history, poetry, and grammar. After the teachers I put the merchants, collectors of custom, bankers, those who are appointed to bring the corn into the city and all other essential food products, such as butchers, bakers, and fishmongers. Let us add to these the farmers and shepherds. Next I put all sorts of handicraft men. The more important ones, like carpenters, armourers, masons, and metal-workers, should be put first. Next in this group come goldsmiths, glass-makers, blacksmiths . . . , and all kinds of weavers and spinners —those who spin silk, wool, animal hair, flax, hemp, cotton, and so on. Next I put . . . tailors and shoemakers. With those I also put the printers. Indeed, though printing cannot be compared with them as regards antiquity, its importance makes it worthy to be put first in this group. As for painters and sculptors, the makers and sellers of paintings of women, minstrels, actors, dancers, tumblers, and jesters—in my opinion they ought either to be driven out altogether or put in the lowest place of all, so that even bath-keepers, barbers, sailors, ostlers, coachmen, carters, grave-diggers, and hangmen should be placed above them. The reason is these latter serve a function in the state, being necessary for carrying away filth from the city and maintaining the health and sanitation of the citizens. Those others, however, with their base trades, are but the ministers of foul and vain pleasures, and so not only corrupt the citizens' manners but even overthrow the city itself.

Revolutions : Their Causes and Their Cure [1]

❡   However states be established—whether by the violent act of some strong man or by the consent of all, subjecting themselves freely to a sovereign—and however long they endure, none lasts for ever, so changeable and uncertain are human affairs. Some states rise slowly to a great height and then fall all at once of their own weight; others are destroyed by the attack of enemies from without when they think themselves safest; still others by interior maladies. . . . Hence there is great need that this whole matter be studied and that we come to some conclusion about what exactly are the causes of the change and overthrow of states. Let me say first that by a change of state, I mean a change of the seat of sovereignty. . . . Anything else, such as a change of laws, of customs, or of religion,

[1] *Six Books*, IV, 1 (406–407).

❡ is but an alteration. . . . Changes are most frequently involuntary, though they may be voluntary, as when one sovereign prince willingly submits to the sovereignty of an overlord. . . . Whether voluntary or involuntary, changes may be either natural or violent. Just as the death of the human body can be natural or violent, so the change of a state may be either so slow and gradual that one scarcely notices it, a kind of growing old, or it may happen all at once, as a consequence of a sudden, violent blow. . . .

It is this last type of change, of course, which interests Bodin most. He deals in exhaustive detail with the causes of revolution in each of the three types of state (though monarchy naturally receives the most attention), and with specific means for preventing it in each type. We cannot follow Bodin through the whole discussion, but we may single out two or three representative maxims to illustrate his point of view and procedure.

Astrology [1]

❡   All the theologians and philosophers are agreed that nothing in this world happens by chance or accident. We can, therefore, confidently set down this maxim for our start: the causes of the changes of state are either human or natural or divine. That is to say things happen as a result of the direct judgment of God, without any intermediate operations; or by ordinary, natural causality; or by man's own will, which the theologians acknowledge to be free, at least as far as concerns civil actions. Now, as a matter of fact, men's wills are so changeable and uncertain that it is quite impossible to base any prediction about the course of politics on human conduct. And as regards direct, divine causality, God's ways are so inscrutable that we cannot make predictions from this basis, either, unless He chooses to reveal His will to us as He did to His inspired prophets. Hence any knowledge we may hope to have about politics, any predictions we may hope to make about the changes that overtake them, must rest on our knowledge of natural causality.

At this point we might reasonably expect an analysis of the various social, economic, and physical factors which contribute to the stability and instability of states. Bodin does indeed discuss these matters

[1] *Six Books*, IV, 2 (436ff.).

elsewhere,[1] but here, curiously enough to our modern ears, he is thinking of the stars in their courses.

¶ When I say "natural causes" I do not mean the events which immediately precede and determine the effects, but rather the more remote, celestial causes of these occurrences. Let no one suppose that study of the stars and of their secret powers diminishes in any degree the greatness and might of God. On the contrary, it is even more noble and more beautiful to have such things produced by His creatures than it would be for Him to have made them Himself directly and without any means. No one of sane and sober judgment denies the marvellous effects which the celestial bodies have throughout all nature. . . . Many indeed have tried to predict the course of states by the celestial movements. This is reasonable, since, leaving aside the ultimate causality of God, they do depend entirely on the heavens. But the difficulty is much greater in the case of states than in the case of predictions about the lives of individual men, for men, unlike states, are born at a particular moment of time and it is possible, therefore, to determine more easily what the positions of the planets are on that occasion. . . .

This does not mean, however, that astrological science cannot be applied to the growth and decay of states. It can be made to yield certain and useful results for politics if we take care to study the matter scientifically. We must know the conjunctions of the major planets for the last 1570 years, and the conjunctions and eclipses of the lesser planets and of the fixed stars; we must know their aspects on the occasions of the major conjunctions, and, finally, we must be able to relate all of this astrological knowledge to the truths of history. . . .

Thus, for instance, take the case of the conjunctions of the major planets in Scorpio. Four or five years before one such conjunction the Roman republic was changed to a monarchy under the power of Cæsar, and all of Europe was in arms. The same conjunction occurred again in the year 630, when the Arabs enunciated the doctrine of Mahomet, revolted against the Byzantine empire, and altered the political structure, the language, the customs, and the religion of the Near East. . . . Once again we had this conjunction

---

[1] *Vide infra*, "Climate," pp. 78–81. Bodin also discusses at great length, and with remarkable perception, various economic and financial matters which have a bearing on the state's health. Vide *Six Books*, V and VI.

¶ in Scorpio in the year 1464, after which there were numerous rebellions and civil wars throughout Europe, Asia, and Africa. Zadamach, king of Tartary, was forced to flee by his subjects; Henry V,[1] king of England, was captured and killed by one of his subjects, later King Edward IV; Frederick III, the Emperor, was driven from Hungary by Matthias Corvinus[2]...; Louis XI, king of France, was besieged in his capital city by his princes and vassals, and almost reduced to the extremity of losing his state. At the same time Scanderbeg, a slave of the Turkish sultan, revolted and stole two provinces from him.[3] This conjunction in Scorpio has greater effects than any other, since Scorpio is a martial sign; and this is especially true if Mars be one of the conjoined planets. . . . We note also a great conjunction in the sign of the Archer 74 years after Christ, when all of Palestine was pillaged, Jerusalem razed and given over to fire and the sword, and 110,000 persons killed. At the same time there were civil wars in Europe and no less than four emperors suffered violent deaths within the space of a single year. . . .

Few people to-day are likely to take to heart Bodin's recommendations in this respect. Nevertheless it is important to see that the spirit behind Bodin's enthusiasm for astrology is entirely modern. For him it is an empirical study, calculated to assist us in translating our abstract, general political rules into maxims serviceable in the changing circumstances of daily life. The statesman is like the physician: since states vary among themselves just as much as individual men do, it is folly to try to apply the same rules identically in all illnesses. Hence the wise statesman will study astrology just as the wise physician studies physiology: each attempts to recognize the particular causes of a given disease in some particular case, to predict the course it will take in these circumstances, and to adjust his treatment to this knowledge. Bodin does not, for a moment, deny the existence of proximate causes (among them, physical, economic, and social factors); indeed, he insists on them. But the statesman who frames his policies in accordance with them alone is in the same position as the physician who is content to treat symptoms only. In each case it is necessary to

[1] It was King Henry VI, not his father, whom Bodin has in mind. He certainly died a violent death, but it was not until 1471.

[2] Matthias I, King of Hungary.

[3] Scanderbeg was hardly a slave of the sultans. Bodin probably refers to a temporary truce in 1461, as a result of which Mohammed II acknowledged him lord of Albania and Epirus.

get below the surface pattern of proximate causes to the real underlying events which produce these observed changes. We do not differ
from Bodin in all this; we differ from him only in not believing, as
he did, that these underlying events are the stars in their courses.

Nor does Bodin hold that the course of history is completely
determined, so that men can only sit by, helpless to alter the course
of events.[1] There is doubtless a certain regular order in the way in
which a disease attacks the human body, but the physician who understands the science of pathology may be able to slow down the course
of the disease or even to interrupt it altogether. Just so, the wise
statesman, understanding the pathology of states, and therefore
"foreseeing the maladies which overtake them, can prevent their
ruin by good laws and other convenient remedies."

Climate

The stars do not, of course, determine events here on earth directly,
but rather by means of proximate causes. Among these is climate.[2]

¶ So far we have discussed only what concerns states in general.
Let us now turn from the abstract to the particular in order to point
out those characteristics which result from differences in men and
which require that the form of the state be accommodated to the
nature of its situation. Many writers neglect this matter altogether
and try to force nature to comply with their statutes, instead of
realizing that man-made laws must be accommodated to the laws
of nature. Many great states have been destroyed because of the
failure to see that, since states differ just as animals do, the same laws
cannot hold everywhere. Not only do we see a great number of
species in every animal genus, but we also observe that these species
vary with the animals' habitat. We can say the same of men.
Their natures and dispositions vary with the climate of the region
in which they live. Western peoples differ markedly from those
living in the East; northerners are not like southerners. And, even
if the climate and the latitude and longitude be the same, differences
of altitude affect men's dispositions, so that those living in lowland

---

[1] Bodin is careful to point out that his view does not conflict with Christian doctrine by
committing us to a blind fatalism. He avoids this difficulty by assuming that it is God
who has adjusted the relationship between the movements of the planets and the course of
events on earth.
[2] *Six Books*, V, 1 (545*ff.*).

¶ plains will not be like those living in mountainous country. Indeed, even in the same city differences of altitude can be observed to be reflected in differences of disposition and custom.

For this reason the study of climate is of the first importance to statesmen. The most secure foundation for a state consists in having its form adjusted to the nature and disposition of its people, its laws and ordinances suitable to the places, the men, and the times. . . . The form of a state, in a word, must vary with its situation, just as the character of a building is adjusted by a good architect to the nature of the soil on which it is to rest. . . .

If we observe their natures closely, we shall see that men of the northern, southern, and middle regions are like young men, old men, and the middle aged, respectively, and that they have the various qualities, virtues, and vices attributed to each age group. In northern lands states are governed by force, in the middle by justice, and in the south by religion. Thus Tacitus says of the Germans that their magistrates have no authority except at the point of a sword, and Cæsar reports that the Germans have no religion and care about nothing save war and the chase. . . . We also find that combats and trials by arms had their origin in the North. The laws of all northern peoples, like the Salians, the Franks, and the English are full of regulations governing such contests. Many princes and popes have tried to alter these warlike customs and uniformly failed, not realizing that northerners are different from southerners and so require different laws and customs.

Peoples of the middle region are more reasonable than the superstitious southerners and less violent than the northerners. Hence they have recourse to reason, to judges, and to legal processes in the settlement of their disputes. It is certain that the laws and forms of pleading before a court have come down to us from these middle peoples, as from Asia Minor (where orators and rhetoricians were in such repute), Greece, Italy, and France. . . . Very nearly all of the great orators, legislators, jurists, historians, poets, story-tellers, and any others who entice men's hearts with sweet discourse and fair words have come from the middle regions. . . .

The southerners, for their part, rely on craft and subtlety like foxes, or on religion. The discourse of reason, the legal opinions and arguments of the rhetoricians, who balance one piece of evidence against another, are at once too refined for the dull wits of

¶ the northerners and too lowly for the southerners, who prefer absolutely certain demonstrations or divine oracles, surpassing anything that human reason is capable of. . . .

It is obvious that men who differ so much cannot be expected to live under exactly the same kind of government. Northerners, for instance, and those who live in mountains, are bold and warlike. Suitable to them, therefore, are popular states or, at the most, elective monarchies. They will suffer themselves to be commanded only by brave men, and they expel any leader who attempts to tyrannize over them. . . . Hence it would be a serious mistake to try to change the popular state of a people like the Swiss into a monarchy. For even though a monarchy is much the best in itself, it is not so fit for these mountaineers.

On the other hand, it is equally important to observe that laws, customs, and education can alter human nature just as well as man's physical environment. Thus not so long ago the English were reputed so fractious and ungovernable that it was necessary to separate English merchants from those of other nationalities. The city of Anvers, for instance, was obliged to set aside a special establishment for their use, though all the other foreigners dwelt together amicably in one house. Now, however, that the English have made treaties of peace with Scotland and France, and are governed by a sweet and peaceable queen, they have grown tame, while the French, who once yielded to none in courtesy and humanity, have radically altered their nature since their civil wars commenced and have become like wild beasts. Thus war renders men warlike and peace makes them gentle, courteous, and tractable. . . .

It must be understood, therefore, that by 'climate' I mean a variety of factors: water, soil, altitude, laws, customs, and the forms of states. All of these factors enter into, and so help to constitute, the natural inclination of a people; and a knowledge of them is therefore of the greatest consequence to the legislator.

Certainly much of what Bodin says about the influence of climate is nonsense, and all of it is based upon too hasty and unscientific generalization. But, once again, Bodin's outlook is far more important than what he actually says. He is looking forward to the development of an empirical theory of the state, a development which is, perhaps, the chief distinction of political thought in the nineteenth and twentieth centuries. He is pointing along the road towards a modern type of social study—towards the recognition that man is not only a political animal, but a social animal, and towards the recognition that this social nature is not something innate, which is identical in all men everywhere, but that it is a product of a complex set of factors, among which physical environment plays a prominent part. Like Aristotle before him and like Montesquieu after him, Bodin was acutely aware that completely abstract reasoning in politics is sterile. Like them he felt the need for empirical study of all the multiplicity and variety in human nature; like them, he recognized the need of taking these differences into account in the actual structure of the state: what is sauce for the goose may not be sauce for the gander.

On the basis of this kind of empirical study, Bodin proceeds to work out a large number of maxims, often as shrewd and detailed as any of Machiavelli's, for the prudent ruler to follow. These vary all the way from a recommendation that the king's privy council be prohibited from meeting after dinner, when its members might be in their cups, to a detailed discussion of how to handle religious dissension. We may illustrate Bodin's procedure by some extracts from this latter discussion.

The Dangers of Religious Disputation

When we recall the times Bodin lived in it is easy to understand why he should have thought that one of the sovereign's primary concerns was the religion of his subjects. Depending on his policy towards it, and the maxims which he follows, it can be either a support to him or a constant source of trouble.[1]

❡ It is obvious that factions or parties (religious or otherwise) are dangerous and pernicious in any kind of state. It is best, therefore, to take counsel to prevent their formation; or if this be impossible, to prevent any dangerous developments by employing any medicines which will cure them. . . . When I say 'faction' I do not mean every little handful or society of subjects whatever. I mean a good-sized group banded together against some other group in the state. For if the numbers be small, the sovereign can usually bring them to reason by putting their differences in the hands of impartial and dispassionate judges for settlement. But if the groups be large and violent, or if they be not appeased by justice and judgment, the

---

[1] *Six Books*, IV, 7 (520*ff.*).

¶ sovereign must not delay until they grow still stronger. He must act promptly, employing force to extinguish the faction utterly, a thing which he can accomplish at that stage by punishing a few of the ring-leaders. It will be understood that I am speaking here of rival factions within the state. Of course, if the faction be directed against the sovereign himself, instead of against another group of subjects, that is treason, which no prudent prince will for a moment endure. . . .

Among the many causes for internal faction is religion. Changes in the religion of a state, as we have seen in the German empire, Sweden, England, and other countries, are always accompanied by extreme violence and bloodshed. Therefore the maxims just asserted should be followed with respect to religion. In the first place, then, if a state be so fortunate as to have a religion universally followed by all the inhabitants, the greatest care should be taken to prevent its being questioned or brought into dispute. For anything much argued about is rendered doubtful, and it is certainly a rank impiety to make men uncertain about their religion—a thing above all else about which they ought to be assured. And it does not matter how clear and true the thing be in itself, it can be obscured and shaken by disputation, especially when its truth is not a matter of demonstration and reasoning, but of faith.

But what if there exist several religions in the state? This is unfortunate, but not necessarily fatal. For we have many examples from history of wise kings who ruled successfully and peacefully over subjects divided into many distinct sects. Theodosius the Great, for instance, found many of the Arian sect in the Roman Empire. . . . Although he was opposed to their beliefs, he did not wish to force them to accept his or to punish them for being Arians. On the contrary, he rescinded previous edicts against them, permitted them to live in liberty of their conscience, to worship according to their own rites, and to bring up their children in their faith. Nevertheless, he succeeded in considerably reducing the number of Arians in Europe. . . .

I will not here try to determine which religion is the best and truest (though there can be but one truth, one divine law, issuing from the mouth of God). But if a prince be well assured of his possession of the true religion and if he wish, therefore, to draw his subjects to it, he should not, in my opinion, use force. For the more one tries to force men's wills, the more unwilling and stubborn

¶ they become. He will be better able to turn their minds and hearts to his religion if he himself adheres to it without pretence or dissimulation, without using force or violence to advocate it, humbly following its tenets. In this way he will not only avoid commotions, troubles, and civil war, but he will also have the satisfaction of leading his straying subjects to their salvation. . . .

Except, therefore, where a dissenting sect becomes seditious, a good prince will not try to destroy it.[1] For those who have been forbidden their own religion and who are disgusted with all other kinds, become atheists and, after having lost their fear of God, they know no restraint, and commit all manner of crimes and impieties, which it is impossible to correct by any human laws or other devices. The prudent prince, therefore, will remember that just as the worst tyranny is less miserable than anarchy . . . , so the worst superstition is far less detestable than no religion at all. . . . For in the reverent fear which religion awakes, there lies a mighty power for controlling a tumultuous people. . . . Indeed, even atheists themselves agree that nothing is so useful in maintaining a state than is religion and that it is the chief support on which the power of kings and princes rests. Religion assists in securing execution of the laws, obedience of the subjects, and reverence for their superiors by inculcating a fear of wrong-doing, and a mutual love of all for one another. . . .

If history were only as logical as the Hegelians would have us believe, this chapter and the preceding one would be reversed. Bodin represents the beginning of modern political thought much better than does Machiavelli (whatever their respective chronological positions), just because he is on the threshold of the new era, while Machiavelli has already got as far as the drawing-room, where he occupies a prominent place on the hearth-rug. People do not read Bodin any more, because he is verbose and repetitious, because none of his novelties is any longer new, and because everything of importance in his theories has been better and more briefly said by some one else. But for the historian of ideas there could hardly be a more fascinating object of study. Standing as he does between two worlds, Bodin looks in both directions. Thus it is symbolic that he should at one and the same time lay the foundation for empirical social study

---

[1] And then, presumably, it is to be put down because it is seditious, not because it is a dissenting sect. Bodin's position here is really very close to Locke's. *Vide infra*, pp. 201 *ff*.

with his theory of climate and also urge upon his ruler the study of astrology and other mediæval lore; that he should point ahead to the completely lay notion of sovereignty as a centre of force for administrating the state, and back to the conception of the ruler as God's vicar, deputized to implement divine law on earth.

Thus, again, Bodin does not solve the problem of sovereignty. But in a sense it is precisely this failure which makes his theory interesting and illuminating. For the difficulty Bodin is wrestling with is not peculiar to himself: it is one of the great and crucial problems of political thought. Put in modern terms, it is the problem of reconciling the exercise of force (necessary for the efficient conduct of affairs) with the freedom and spontaneity of the individual member of the state. It is the problem of reconciling order with liberty. It is the problem of justifying in a moral world the existence of a natural instrument like the state or, conversely, of finding a place in a world of physical, natural forces (of which the state is one) for the moral purposes of men. It is true, of course, that the problem did not appear to Bodin in this form; indeed, he did not see the problem very clearly in any form. Nevertheless, when everything is said and done, there are two things Bodin sees very clearly: one, that the state, whether conceived as the will of one man or many, is a natural instrument; second, that there is a rational order in the universe superior to any man's will, to which therefore that will ought to correspond.

For Further Reading

Translations

See footnote, p. 55.

Commentaries and General Works

ALLEN, J. W.: *A History of Political Thought in the Sixteenth Century* (Methuen, 1928).
> The chapter on Bodin is excellent, and the whole book will be found useful for other figures in the century.

FIGGIS, J. N.: *The Divine Right of Kings* (Cambridge University Press, Second edition, 1922).
> A useful account of a theory which has some affinities with Bodin's.

CHAPTER FOUR

Thomas Hobbes

(1588–1679)

LIFE

IF ever a man set for all time the opening sentence of every subsequent account of his life, it was Hobbes. In the year of the Spanish Armada, he tells us in his own autobiography, his mother gave birth to twins —himself and fear. It is questionable whether this is not better rhetoric than it is historical truth. Certainly Hobbes's conduct in life did not show him to be as fearsome as he would have us (because it corresponded with his theory of human nature) believe him to be. Although it is true that he fled England when the clouds of civil war began to gather, this was rather the act of the prudent man than of the coward, for the reputation which his early writings had made for him was scarcely calculated to endear him to the Parliamentarians. And, on the other hand, in his solitary and determined, if completely wrong-headed, stand against the authority of the Oxford mathematical faculty and of the Royal Society, in his open and savage attacks on the Roman Church in particular, and in his only partially disguised and equally savage assaults on religion in general—in these and a hundred other ways he showed himself anything but fearsome in the defence of his intellectual convictions.

Of infinitely more consequence in moulding Hobbes's character and career than any alleged prenatal influences that resulted from the threatening invasion were the events and circumstances of his youth and early manhood. After receiving his early education at Malmesbury, in Wiltshire, where he was born, Hobbes was sent up to Oxford, which he entered before he was fifteen years of age. Like so many of her most brilliant sons, Hobbes found the university's teaching barren and profitless. He must have had in mind the scholastic logic and the Aristotelian science to which he was then subjected when, years later, in the *Leviathan*, he condemned universities for what he called their "frequency of insignificant speech." [1] It may well be, however, that Hobbes minimized his debt to his university. A recent writer [2] has attempted to show that Hobbes was more of an Aristotelian than he himself believed or anyone else has suspected. And, whatever his contempt for mediæval philosophy and all its works, Hobbes somewhere acquired both a perfect mastery of logic as an instrument and a trust in the power of rational thought so sublime that it would have done justice to a St Thomas. Indeed, against the empiricism and anti-rationalism of the new age, [3] and especially against its great English exponent, Bacon, Hobbes stands firmly on the side of that earlier age which he scorned.

On leaving Oxford, Hobbes became tutor to the son and heir of William Cavendish, later Earl of Devonshire. His life-long connexion with this powerful and distinguished family was certainly one of the greatest influences on his subsequent career; it is difficult indeed not to conclude that, without the stimulus and the opportunities which this connexion gave him, Hobbes would have died another "mute, inglorious Milton." It was the Cavendishes who introduced him to the many distinguished Englishmen—Ben Jonson, Bacon himself, and, later, Clarendon—whom it was his good fortune to know. Through them, again, he first became acquainted with the philosophical and scientific thought of the Continent, and so learned that the mediæval physics still taught at Oxford was outmoded and that a whole new world of explanation lay open before him.

Finally, it is surely not far-fetched to suppose that his intimacy with, and friendship for, the Cavendishes encouraged the aristocratic, anti-democratic tenor of his thought. But here we must not go too far; for, though Hobbes was a thorough-going monarchist, he was not at all a 'royalist,' as seventeenth-century England understood this term. He moved for a time, it is true, in royalist circles, and he was even, though only briefly, mathematical tutor to the Prince of Wales while the latter was in exile in France. But Hobbes's 'atheistical' attitude towards religion was too much for the Stuart entourage; and, when his *Leviathian* appeared, the opposition among the exiled

[1] *Leviathan, or The Matter, Forme, and Power of a Commonwealth Ecclesiasticall and Civill*, Part I, chapter 1. In these extracts the original spelling and punctuation have been preserved (*vide* reprint of 1909). But for the convenience of the reader the paging of the Molesworth edition is given in parentheses (vide *The English Works of Thomas Hobbes*, edited by Sir William Molesworth (11 vols., 1839-45)).

[2] Leo Strauss, *The Political Philosophy of Hobbes* (Oxford University Press, 1936).

[3] On the anti-rationalism of early seventeenth-century science, see A. N. Whitehead, *Science and the Modern World* (Cambridge University Press, 1925), pp. 12*ff*.

Englishmen, as well as at the French court, was such that he felt obliged to flee once more, this time returning to England. The fact is that Hobbes was a monarchist *in theory*, and not out of sentimental loyalty to the memory of the 'martyred' king. He was a monarchist because he thought a king would be most likely to give his country the strong and absolutely sovereign government which he believed it needed. When, therefore, on returning to England after his dismissal by Charles Stuart, he found, somewhat to his surprise, that the Protectorate was precisely the type of government he desired he easily became reconciled to it.

All of this, naturally, brought down charges of disloyalty upon his head at the time of the Restoration. Hobbes, however, replied to his critics; and so successfully that the king, who liked his wit ("Here comes the bear to be baited," he used to say, when Hobbes appeared), not only took him back into favour, but gave him a handsome pension.

When Hobbes died in 1679, at the age of ninety-one, he left a great, if not altogether enviable,[1] reputation and a tremendous body of literary works ranging all the way from an early translation of Thucydides, through a vast series of treatises on circle-squaring, to a poetical translation of the *Iliad* and the *Odyssey*, undertaken when he was eighty-five, "because," as he said, "I had nothing else to do. Why publish it? Because I thought it might take off my adversaries from showing their folly upon my more serious writings, and set them upon my verses to show their wisdom." [2]

By far the most distinguished of all Hobbes's numerous works, and one of the greatest books ever written by any Englishman, is his treatise on political theory, the *Leviathan* (printed in 1651). Let us begin our examination of it by noticing briefly two crucial occurrences of the first half of the seventeenth century which must have impressed every observant and thinking European, but which left their stamp in an unusually striking manner on Hobbes's thought— especially on his thought about political questions.

The first of these was the development on the Continent by Galileo and others of a new physical science, which was transforming the old dramatic and qualitative conception of the physical world into

---

[1] The name 'Hobbes' had come, even before his death, to be almost synonymous with 'atheist' and everything else objectionable, so that it was used with about the same connotation that the term 'communist' has to-day for some people. For some interesting references to Hobbes in contemporary literature, see John Laird, *Hobbes* (Benn, 1934), pp. 247*ff*., and Sir Leslie Stephen, *Hobbes* (Macmillan, 1904), pp. 68–69.
[2] Quoted by Laird, *op. cit.*, p. 27.

the abstract, purely quantitative conception of colourless, soundless particles moving with mathematical precision in accordance with simple, determinable mechanical laws. Hobbes was one of the earliest adherents of the new science. It is unlikely that he ever knew Galileo, but during his self-imposed exile in Paris he became the intimate of Father Mersenne, the rival—at least in his own estimation—of Descartes, the friend of Gassendi, Campanella, and other members of the Cartesian circle. Although we can hardly credit Hobbes, despite his own claims, with having much advanced any specific frontiers of the new physics,[1] it is impossible to exaggerate the originality and the magnificence of scope of the philosophic generalization which resulted from his various and prolonged investigations in this field. He conceived of Galileo's principle of mathematical explanation as serving not only to describe and to predict the behaviour of gross bodies on this planet, but of all phenomena everywhere, from the infinite reaches of the starry heavens to the most minute and subtle movements of the human mind. The vast scheme which Hobbes conceived and whose execution he commenced was thus truly philosophic, since it was universal in its scope. Beginning with those abstract and fundamental propositions about the nature of space, in which Euclidean geometry consists, it was his intention to pass, by certain and self-evident stages, first to the study of the spatial properties of bodies, and thence to those of moving particles in varying and increasing degrees of complication.

In order to make this undertaking feasible it was necessary to assume that everything which exists is *body*—that is, that everything which exists consists of particles moving in accordance with deterministic mechanical laws. There is no difference in principle, on this view, between the behaviour of billiard-balls colliding and rebounding on a billiard-table, and the behaviour of plants, of animals, or, indeed, of men. Everywhere we are confronted, according to Hobbes, with the same fundamental laws of behaviour. It is simply the case that the motions which these laws describe become more complicated in each succeeding case, because of the increasing number of particles involved. Everywhere we have completely determined behaviour every change in the state of affairs, whether it be the self-conscious and apparently spontaneous act of a man or the reaction of billiard-balls in a collision, is entirely determined by antecedent events in time and may be predicted (theoretically at least) with the same certainty.

[1] Except, perhaps, in the field of optics.

Though man is doubtless the most complex single mechanism in the universe, Hobbes did not intend his grand scheme of explanation to end with what to-day we should call physiological psychology, any more than physics itself ends with the explanation of the behaviour of a single moving particle. Just as the behaviour of a single billiard-ball is altered and complicated when other balls are moving on the table with it, so the behaviour of a man is altered and complicated when he is in contact—as all men always are—with other men. It follows that societies, conceived of as groups of individual men reacting upon one another in a purely mechanical way, like billiard-balls, require to be subjected to the same mode of analysis and explanation used in the case of less complicated objects. In a word, the explanation of human conduct is not complete until the individual human being is seen to be a complicated machine which has a definite and completely determined part in the functioning of a larger and vastly more complicated machine, the state. Thus, in Hobbes's view, the whole world lies open before the expectant eyes of the scientist; it is through and through capable of precisely identical treatment because it is equally subject in all its parts to the same simple and fundamental laws of motion, from the simplest movement of an isolated particle to the whole complex of human society. It is hardly necessary to add that this audacious undertaking was not carried to a successful conclusion. In particular Hobbes utterly failed to deduce either his psychological theory or his sociological theory from the laws of motion as he proposed to do; and he had, therefore, as we shall see, to find another basis for both. Nevertheless, as even the most casual reader can see, this ideal of explanation in terms of physics deeply marked his thought on social questions.

The second powerful influence on Hobbes's thought was constituted by the violence, the brutality, and the appalling waste of life and property which the Civil War in England occasioned. Hobbes's own observation of human nature—in himself, as he frankly admits, but also, surely, as he saw it revealed in those dreadful years of revolutionary disturbance—led him to the conclusion that man is an animal who is moved by two, and only two, considerations: fear and self-interest. Every other motive which may at first sight seem to distinguish man from the other animals is reduced by Hobbes to one or the other of these basic tendencies. A sense of humour might, for instance, be taken to be a distinctly human trait and laughter a sign of friendliness, good nature, and good fellowship. Not so, according to

Hobbes. On the contrary, it is occasioned in men "either by some sudden act of their own, that pleaseth them; or by the apprehension of some deformed thing in another, by comparison whereof they suddenly applaud themselves. [Moreover,] it is incident most to them, that are conscious of the fewest abilities in themselves; who are forced to keep themselves in their own favour, by observing the imperfections of other men." [1]

The only attribute which distinguishes man is his capacity for rational thought; but the possession of reason, though an important function, does not really alter the picture, since it is conceived by Hobbes as purely instrumental: it enables the animal who possesses it to avoid many of the things which he fears and to secure many selfish gratifications whose enjoyment he would otherwise have to forgo. Moreover, the fact that fear and self-interest are the sole motives which affect human behaviour means, obviously enough, that life is hard and cruel. The very nature of the animals—human as well as brute—determines them to violent and continual conflict, to what two centuries later was to be called a struggle for survival. For where a direct opposition of interests does not issue in bitter strife, mutual fear certainly will do so.

We may call this view 'naturalism.' It consists in a denial of any real or fundamental difference between man and the rest of nature. It will be observed that both of the factors we have been discussing led Hobbes, though by different routes, to this conclusion, since the presuppositions of his physical theory as well as the alleged facts of introspection involve the denial of any distinctly *human* properties, any uniquely human character, such as that which Hesiod long ago affirmed when he asserted that there exists a law of justice, "which the son of Cronos set up for men. To fish and beasts and birds he allotted that they should devour one another; but there is no justice in them; but to man he gave justice, which is for the best." [2] The naturalist and, as we may call his opponent, the 'humanist' take issue on this fundamental question; it is agreed by both parties that among animals life is a struggle in which only successful survival and those qualities which make for survival have any significance. Among

---

[1] *Leviathan*, Part I, chapter 6 (46).

[2] The same thought has been expressed in almost identical words by Emerson:

There are two laws discrete
Not reconciled—
Law for man, and law for thing;
The last builds town and fleet,
But it runs wild,
And doth the man unking.

animals the only qualities that count are cunning, strength, force. As Hesiod puts it, justice among animals "lies in the fist." That is to say, the concept of real justice is simply meaningless in the animal kingdom. Now, is there or is there not a moral order, a law of justice, fundamentally different from *any* law of physics, which exists for men, which doubtless they do not often obey, but which, nevertheless, they *ought* to obey? The humanist asserts that there is such a moral order, and that it is precisely this which distinguishes men from all the rest of creation; the naturalist, on the other hand, believing that man is merely animal, denies that a moral order holds for men any more than for the other animals. Among men, as well as among animals, might makes right. It follows that the only conceivable instrument for achieving any sort of order out of the chaotic conflict of human wills is force, for force alone makes any appeal to animals who are dominated by fear and by selfish desire. It is this conception of human nature which is the basis of the theory of government developed in accordance with a cold and ruthless logic in the *Leviathan*. In that theory, to the details of which we must now turn our attention, we have, therefore, not only the first *scientific* social theory—one which, incidentally, antedates Comte's positivism by two hundred years; we have also one of the most thorough-going and far-reaching applications ever made of a completely frank and clear-sighted naturalism to the field of politics.

POLITICAL PHILOSOPHY

Hobbes's Method

Political theory, then, is to rest firmly on a knowledge of the strengths and weaknesses, the capacities and limitations of human nature; but, as we have seen, Hobbes has two different methods for ascertaining this essential information about man. One is the repeatedly enunciated, but never completely executed, programme of a physiological psychology, based upon the laws of motion. The other cuts away this basis in physics, though retaining the assumptions of complete determinism and of scientific objectivity and precision which that basis naturally involved, and begins from the alleged facts of introspection. Signs of both of these methods of approach can be observed in the short Introduction with which the *Leviathan* opens.[1]

---

[1] *Leviathan*, Intro. (9ff.).

¶   Nature . . . is by the *Art* of man, as in many other things, so in
this also imitated, that it can make an Artificial Animal. For seeing
life is but a motion of Limbs, the beginning whereof is in some
principall part within; why may we not say, that all *Automata*
(Engines that move themselves by springs and wheeles as doth a
watch) have an artificiall life? For what is the *Heart*, but a *Spring*;
and the *Nerves*, but so many *Strings*; and the *Joynts*, but so many
Wheeles, giving motion to the whole Body, such as was intended
by the Artificer? *Art* goes yet further, imitating that Rationall and
most excellent worke of Nature, *Man*. For by Art is created that
great LEVIATHAN called a COMMON-WEALTH, or STATE,
(in latine CIVITAS) which is but an Artificiall Man; though of
greater stature and strength than the Naturall, for whose protection
and defence it was intended. . . .

    . . . there is a saying much usurped of late, That *Wisedome* is
acquired, not by reading of *Books*, but of *Men*. Consequently
whereunto, those persons, that for the most part can give no other
proof of being wise, take great delight to shew what they think
they have read in men, by uncharitable censures of one another
behind their backs. But there is another saying not of late understood, by which they might learn truly to read one another, if they
would take the pains; and that is, *Nosce teipsum*, *Read thy self*: which
was not meant, as it is now used, to countenance, either the barbarous
state of men in power, towards their inferiors; or to encourage men
of low degree, to a sawcie behaviour towards their betters; But to
teach us, that for the similitude of the thoughts, and Passions of
one man, to the thoughts, and Passions of another, whosoever
looketh into himself, and considereth what he doth, when he does
think, opine, reason, hope, feare, etc., and upon what grounds; he
shall thereby read and know, what are the thoughts, and Passions
of all other men, upon the like occasions. . . . And though by men's
actions wee do discover their designe sometimes; yet to do it
without comparing them with our own, and distinguishing all
circumstances, by which the case may come to be altered, is to
decypher without a key, and be for the most part deceived, by
too much trust, or by too much diffidence; as he that reads, is
himself a good or evil man.

    But let one man read another by his actions never so perfectly,
it serves him onely with his acquaintance, which are but few. He
that is to govern a whole Nation, must read in himself, not this,

¶ or that particular man; but Man-kind: which though it be hard to do, harder than to learn any Language, or Science; yet, when I shall have set down my own reading orderly, and perspicuously, the pains left another, will be onely to consider, if he also find not the same in himself. For this kind of Doctrine, admitteth no other Demonstration.

Conception of Human Nature

In accordance with this dual programme of psychological investigation, the first book of the *Leviathan* is devoted entirely to an examination of man, who, as Hobbes says, is the matter as well as he is the artificer of that artificial man, the State. In the early chapters a theory of cognition is developed from a completely mechanistic doctrine of sensation—*i.e.*, from the assumption that sensation must consist in the movements of particles, since only body and its motions are real.[1]

¶ The cause of Sense, is the Externall Body, or Object, which presseth the organ proper to each Sense, either immediately, as in the Tast and Touch; or mediately, as in Seeing, Hearing, and Smelling: which pressure, by the mediation of Nerves, and other strings, and membranes of the body, continued inwards to the Brain, and Heart, causeth there a resistance, or counter-pressure, or endeavour of the heart, to deliver it self: which endeavour because *Outward*, seemeth to be some matter without. And this *seeming*, or *fancy*, is that which men call Sense. . . . All which qualities called *Sensible*, are in the object that causeth them, but so many several motions of the matter, by which it presseth our organs diversely. Neither in us that are pressed, are they any thing else but divers motions; (for motion, produceth nothing but motion).

Thus the diverse and qualitatively distinct phenomena of sensation, like the various phenomena which fall within the field of physics proper, can be exhaustively described and precisely explained in accordance with the fundamental laws of motion. On this basis, and with great ingenuity, Hobbes proceeds to work out an account of the various cognitive powers of man—perception, imagination, even reason itself—in which one by one they are all reduced to sensation and so become simply a matter of the motion of particles.

[1] *Leviathan*, Part I, chapter 1 (1–2).

(a) Determinism

From cognition, Hobbes passes to what is of more importance for his political theory, the emotio-conative side of man's nature. As we could expect, Hobbes conceives of the will as completely determined. Volition is a motion and is distinguished from other motions in no way except that it happens to be preceded or accompanied by the thought of the subsequent motion of which it is the cause.[1]

¶ There be in Animals, two sorts of *Motions* peculiar to them: One called *Vitall*; begun in generation, and continued without interruption through their whole life; such as are the *course* of the *Bloud*, the *Pulse*, the *Breathing*, the *Concoction*, *Nutrition*, *Excretion*, etc.; to which Motions there needs no help of Imagination. The other is *Animall motion*, otherwise called *Voluntary motion*; as to *go*, to *speak*, to *move* any of our limbes, in such manner as is first fancied in our minds. . . . And because *going*, *speaking*, and the like Voluntary motions, depend alwayes upon a precedent thought of *whither*, *which way*, and *what*; it is evident, that the Imagination is the first internall beginning of all Voluntary Motion. . . . These small beginnings of Motion, within the body of Man, before they appear in walking, speaking, striking, and other visible actions, are commonly called ENDEAVOUR.

This Endeavour, when it is towards something which causes it, is called APPETITE, or DESIRE; the later, being the generall name; and the other, often-times restrayned to signifie the Desire of Food, namely *Hunger* and *Thirst*. And when the Endeavour is fromward something, it is generally called AVERSION. . . .

Of Appetites, and Aversions, some are born with men; as Appetite of food, Appetite of excretion, and exoneration, . . . and some other Appetites, not many. The rest, which are Appetites of particular things, proceed from Experience, and triall of their effects upon themselves, or other men. . . .

But whatsoever is the object of any man's Appetite or Desire; that is it, which he for his part calleth *Good*: And the object of his Hate, and Aversion, *Evill*; And of his Contempt, *Vile* and *Inconsiderable*. For these words of Good, Evill, and Contemptible, are ever used with relation to the person that useth them. . . .

As, in Sense, that which is really within us, is (as I have sayd

---

[1] *Leviathan*, Part I, chapter 6 (38*ff.*).

¶ before) onely Motion, caused by the action of externall objects . . . , so, when the action of the same object is continued from the Eyes, Eares, and other organs to the Heart; the reall effect there is nothing but Motion, or Endeavour, which consisteth in   Appetite, or Aversion, to, or from the object moving.

(b) Subjectivity of Value

Here Hobbes asserts not only the complete determinism of human conduct, so that what we call free and spontaneous choice is an illusion, and it is possible to predict from the antecedent states of a man's body and environment what his subsequent behaviour will be. He also asserts the complete subjectivity of value. No man's judgment of value, therefore, can be mistaken, since his judgment "This is good" or "This is bad" is simply an expression of the motion of his body towards or away from the object about which he makes the judgment. It is not the case that we desire the objects which we do desire because we judge them to be good. On the contrary, 'good' is the name we give to those objects which attract us (*i.e.*, towards which we move). Another way of putting this is to say that the goodness we assert of the object is not in it; it is a feeling *in us*, produced by the motion of the particles which form our body, in exactly the same way as the heat or colour which we feel or perceive is really in us, though it seems to be *there* in the object.

Hence there is no more disputing about values than there is about tastes. We can expect people, of course, to disagree about which particular objects they find good and which bad; but this is the case only because, their bodies being different, different motions are, or may be, set up in them in the presence of the same object. And these differences, when they occur, can (theoretically at least) be predicted in advance, so that if we know enough about the bodies of Peter and of Paul we can predict that Peter will desire chocolate ice-cream and call it good, while Paul will be averse to it and call it bad.

Finally, it follows not only that good and bad are subjective, but that they are private—that is, that the things which we call good are the things which attract *us*. However much I may believe that I sometimes sacrifice my own private good for some one else's, this is a mistake and illusion. Such a choice between a course of action leading to my own good and one which would be good for some one else (except where my own good is also attained in the long run) is a meaningless and impossible alternative, for that only which is good for me attracts me. We are all always necessarily selfish and never really altruistic, because the good for each of us is simply that thing which happens to be the object of our own appetite. This will become clearer as we proceed. In the meantime Hobbes enumerates the various different kinds of objects which men desire, and shows how the desire for these objects tends to promote or to discourage harmonious social relationships among men.[1]

(c) The Causes of Dissension

¶   Nature hath made men so equall, in the faculties of body, and mind; as that though there bee found one man sometimes manifestly stronger in body, or of quicker mind then another; yet when all is reckoned together, the difference between man, and man, is not so considerable, as that one man can thereupon claim to himselfe any benefit, to which another may not pretend, as well as he. For as to the strength of body, the weakest has strength enough to kill the strongest, either by secret machination, or by confederacy with others, that are in the same danger with himselfe.

And as to the faculties of the mind, . . . I find yet a greater equality amongst men, than that of strength. . . .

From this equality of ability, ariseth equality of hope in the attaining of our Ends. And therefore if any two men desire the same thing, which neverthelesse they cannot both enjoy, they become enemies; and in the way to their End, (which is principally their owne conservation, and sometimes their delectation only,) endeavour to destroy, or subdue one an other. . . .

And from this diffidence of one another, there is no way for any man to secure himselfe, so reasonable, as Anticipation; that is, by force, or wiles, to master the persons of all men he can, so long, till he see no other power great enough to endanger him. . . .

Againe, men have no pleasure, (but on the contrary a great deale of griefe) in keeping company, where there is no power able to over-awe them all. For every man looketh that his companion should value him, at the same rate he sets upon himselfe: And upon all signes of contempt, or undervaluing, naturally endeavours, as far as he dares (which amongst them that have no common power to keep them in quiet, is far enough to make them destroy each other,)

[1] *Leviathan*, Part I, chapter 13 (110*ff*.).

¶ to extort a greater value from his contemners, by dommage; and from others, by the example.

So that in the nature of man, we find three principall causes of quarrell. First, Competition; Secondly, Diffidence; Thirdly, Glory.

The first, maketh men invade for Gain; the second, for Safety; and the third, for Reputation. The first use Violence, to make themselves Masters of other mens persons, wives, children, and cattell; the second, to defend them; the third, for trifles, as a word, a smile, a different opinion, and any other signe of undervalue, either direct in their Persons, or by reflexion in their Kindred, their Friends, their Nation, their Profession, or their Name.

It is true, of course, that there is another side to the picture. Certain human desires lead not to strife, but to peace and harmony.[1]

¶ Desire of Ease, and sensual Delight, disposeth men to obey a common Power: Because by such Desires, a man doth abandon the protection might be hoped for from his own Industry, and labour. Fear of Death, and Wounds, disposeth to the same; and for the same reason. . . .

Desire of Knowledge, and Arts of Peace, enclineth men to obey a common Power: For such Desire, containeth a desire of leasure; and consequently protection from some other Power than their own.

But there is no doubt, at least in Hobbes's view, that most of man's native desires and inclinations tend to result in struggle with his fellows. For the fact is that, though "all men agree on this, that peace is good,"[2] man's basic and fundamental selfishness causes in him a desire for power which conflicts with his desire for peace and security.[3]

¶ In the first place, I put for a generall inclination of all mankind, a perpetuall and restlesse desire of Power after power, that ceaseth onely in Death. And the cause of this, is not always that a man hopes for a more intensive delight, than he has already attained to; or that he cannot be content with a moderate power: but because he cannot assure the power and means to live well, which he hath present, without the acquisition of more.

[1] *Leviathan*, Part I, chapter 11 (86–87).   [2] *Ibid.*, Part I, chapter 15 (146).
[3] *Ibid.*, Part I, chapter 11 (85–86).

It is important to see that this "perpetuall and restlesse desire for power" is not confined merely to the ambitious few, but exists necessarily in every one, even in those who desire only to hold to what they already have. Hence everything else which might, conceivably, be desired for the pleasure it brought—knowledge, art, leisure, ease— everything is subordinated to the requirement of power and judged solely on the grounds of its ability to make its possessor powerful.[1]

¶ The POWER *of a Man*, (to take it Universally,) is his present means, to obtain some future apparent Good. And is either *Originall*, or *Instrumentall*.

Naturall Power, is the eminence of the Faculties of Body, or Mind: as extraordinary Strength, Forme, Prudence, Arts, Eloquence, Liberality, Nobility. *Instrumentall* are those Powers, which acquired by these, or by fortune, are means and Instruments to acquire more: as Riches, Reputation, Friends, and the secret working of God, which men call Good Luck. For the nature of Power, is in this point, like to Fame, increasing as it proceeds; or like the motion of heavy bodies, which the further they go, make still the more hast. . . .

The *Value*, or WORTH of a man, is as of all other things, his Price; that is to say, so much as would be given for the use of his Power: and therefore is not absolute; but a thing dependant on the need and judgment of another. An able conductor of Souldiers, is of great Price in time of War present, or imminent; but in Peace not so. A learned and uncorrupt Judge, is much Worth in time of Peace; but not so much in War. And as in other things, so in men, not the seller, but the buyer determines the Price. For let a man (as most men do,) rate themselves at the highest Value they can; yet their true Value is no more than it is esteemed by others.

The manifestation of the Value we set on one another, is that which is commonly called Honouring, and Dishonouring. To Value a man at a high rate, is to *Honour* him; at a low rate, is to *Dishonour* him. But high, and low, in this case, is to be understood by comparison to the rate that each man setteth on himselfe. . . .

Nor does it alter the case of Honour, whether an action (so it be great and difficult, and consequently a signe of much power,) be just or unjust: for Honour consisteth onely in the opinion of Power.

[1] *Leviathan*, Part I, chapter 10 (74*ff.*).

The State of Nature

If such be the nature of man what must his life be where these natural instincts, tendencies, and inclinations are not held in check, but are allowed free and unrestricted play?[1]

⁋ Hereby it is manifest, that during the time men live without a common Power to keep them all in awe, they are in that condition which is called Warre; and such a warre, as is of every man, against every man. . . .

Whatsoever therefore is consequent to a time of warre, where every man is Enemy to every man; the same is consequent to the time, wherein men live without other security, than what their own strength, and their own invention shall furnish them withall. In such condition, there is no place for Industry; because the fruit thereof is uncertain: and consequently no Culture of the Earth; no Navigation, nor use of the commodities that may be imported by Sea; no commodious Building; no Instruments of moving, and removing such things as require much force; no Knowledge of the face of the Earth; no account of Time; no Arts; no Letters; no Society; and which is worst of all, continuall feare, and danger of violent death; And the life of man, solitary, poore, nasty, brutish, and short.

Before we can go any further we must ask what Hobbes meant by this state of nature which he has just described and which is supposed to be men's condition when they have no sovereign over them. Did he mean to assert that men have ever actually lived in such a condition without any form of government or society? If, as many people think, he did mean this he is obviously altogether mistaken, since as far back as we go in human history we find evidence of social and communal living.

However, the facts seem rather to be that Hobbes expressed himself very loosely on this point because he was not much interested in the question of the actual historicity of the state of nature. He would not, therefore, be much perturbed by the strictures of his critics, since the question whether men have actually lived without a sovereign is irrelevant to the question what life *would be* like *if* they had no sovereign, just as the question whether or not I have ever actually been ill

[1] *Leviathan*, Part I, chapter 13 (112–113).

is irrelevant to the question what my disposition would be like if ever I were ill. The fact, supposing it to be a fact, that men had never so lived, could not disprove the Hobbesian thesis that men's life would be "solitary, poore, nasty, brutish, and short" without a sovereign over them, and similarly, the fact, if it could be ascertained, that men *had* so lived would be simply additional evidence, where none was really needed, to support Hobbes's view. For, to Hobbes's way of thinking, there is no want of evidence that life without an all-powerful sovereign would be miserable. Since all the evidence goes to show that the weaker the sovereign, the unhappier the lot of his subjects, he holds it reasonable to assume that in the extreme case, where there was no sovereign at all, life would be very unhappy indeed.[1] And this supposition is entirely confirmed when we consider the case of the relations of nations, over whom, by definition, there is no super-sovereign. Just because there exists no sovereign with power to keep them in order they are constantly at war with one another; and the life of a nation, therefore, unless it be strong and powerful, is poor and short.[2]

¶   Though there had never been any time, wherein particular men were in a condition of warre one against another; yet in all times Kings, and Persons of Soveraigne authority, because of their Independency, are in continuall jealousies, and in the state and posture of Gladiators; having their weapons pointing, and their eyes fixed on one another; that is, their Forts, Garrisons, and Guns upon the Frontiers of their Kingdoms; and continuall Spyes upon their neighbours; which is a posture of War.

Thus the state of nature, as Hobbes conceives it, *is* actual; for, though the extreme case has perhaps never occurred, every society or nation which has ever existed has had more or less of the character of a state of nature, just so far as its actual sovereign lacked absolute power to command perfect obedience from all his subjects. And in any case, the whole question about the historicity of the state of nature is really irrelevant to Hobbes's main contention, which is that human nature is such that without a supremely powerful sovereign

---

[1] Thus Hobbes points out that "the savage people in many places of America" are an example of men living in a state of nature, because, "except the government of small Families," they "have no government at all." And it is not unfair to describe them as living "in that brutish manner, as I said before."

[2] *Leviathan*, Part I, chapter 13 (115).

men's lives would be miserable and not worth living. Hobbes may be mistaken, but he cannot be proved to be mistaken by denying the existence of a state of nature.[1]

In a word, Hobbes's main contention here is simply this, that, though man doubtless wants peace, his fear of others, his anxiety to maintain what he already has, his selfish and grasping desire for still more—these basic appetites and aversions lead him to continuous strife with his neighbours. Nothing but consideration of his own private interests can, as we have already seen, move him; and even if his reason shows him the short-sightedness of this competition, even if he recognizes that his own private interest would best be served by co-operation with his fellows, he is helpless. For reason, after all, is but the slave and tool of the passions. Being dependent upon them, its only function is to serve their interests by seeking out objects which would satisfy them. If, therefore, a man uses his reason it is merely in order to get the better of other men, even though he knows that in doing so he will plunge himself and them into painful struggle and unrest.

One thing, and one thing only, will hold the passions in check. This is not reason, but something which the passions can understand —force. If we want to appeal to the passions we must speak to them in their own language—in the language of fear and of self-interest. If we wish to put an end to the strife and competition which result from diffidence and selfish desire we must appeal to diffidence and selfish desire themselves, not to reason, good sense, kindliness, benevolence, or any other alleged, but unreal, human motive. We must, in a word, make it worth men's while, either through fear of punishment or desire for gain, to give up competition and live in harmony with one another. This means that we must, somehow or other, institute a strong and powerful government which will be capable of inspiring fear in those who disobey its laws and of offering attractive rewards to those who do conform. Put thus generally, Hobbes's reasoning seems both powerful and convincing. On a closer examination, however, it reveals serious flaws.

The Laws of Nature

There are two stages in Hobbes's argument which we must clearly distinguish from each other. The first is the contention that, by

[1] For a discussion of what the state of nature meant for Locke, *vide infra*, pp. 163 *ff.*

following certain rules (which Hobbes chooses to call the "laws of nature"), we could live together in peace and harmony; the second is that, since we are too intemperate and short-sighted to follow these rules of our own volition, we require an all-powerful sovereign authority to enforce them on us. These two stages in the argument are logically distinct, although in Hobbes's presentation of it they are not clearly separated. Either could be true and the other false, but the Hobbesian conclusion, that we require an absolutely powerful sovereign, does not follow, it must be observed, unless *both* are true. As a matter of fact, we shall see that neither is true in the sense in which Hobbes understands it and that, therefore, his conclusion does not follow. This is the case even if we accept his estimate of human nature; it is still more obviously the case if this account of man's character and motives is rejected as being one-sided and exaggerated.[1]

¶   The RIGHT OF NATURE, which Writers commonly call *Jus Naturale*, is the Liberty each man hath, to use his own power, as he will himselfe, for the preservation of his own Nature; that is to say, of his own Life; and consequently, of doing any thing, which in his own Judgment, and Reason, hee shall conceive to be the aptest means thereunto. . . .

A LAW OF NATURE (*Lex Naturalis*) is a Precept, or generall Rule, found out by Reason, by which a man is forbidden to do that which is destructive of his life, or taketh away the means of preserving the same; and to omit that by which he thinketh it may be best preserved. For though they that speak of this subject, use to confound *Jus*, and *Lex*, *Right* and *Law*; yet they ought to be distinguished; because RIGHT, consisteth in liberty to do, or to forbeare; Whereas LAW, determineth, and bindeth to one of them: so that Law, and Right, differ as much, as Obligation, and Liberty; which in one and the same matter are inconsistent.

And because the condition of Man, (as hath been declared in the precedent Chapter) is a condition of Warre of every one against every one; in which case every one is governed by his own Reason; and there is nothing he can make use of, that may not be a help unto him, in preserving his life against his enemyes; It followeth, that in such a condition, every man has a Right to every thing; even to one anothers body. And therefore, as long as this naturall Right of every man to every thing endureth, there can be no security to

<hr>

[1] *Leviathan*, Part I, chapter 14-15 (116ff.).

¶ any man, (how strong or wise soever he be,) of living out the time, which Nature ordinarily alloweth men to live. And consequently it is a precept, or generall rule of Reason, *That every man, ought to endeavour Peace, as farre as he has hope of obtaining it; and when he cannot obtain it, that he may seek, and use, all helps, and advantages of Warre.* The first branch of which Rule, containeth the first, and Fundamentall Law of Nature; which is, *to seek Peace, and follow it.* The Second, the summe of the Right of Nature; which is, *By all means we can, to defend our selves.*

From this Fundamentall Law of Nature, by which men are commanded to endeavour Peace, is derived this second Law; *That a man be willing, when others are so too, as farre-forth, as for Peace, and defence of himselfe he shall think it necessary, to lay down this right to all things; and be contented with so much liberty against other men, as he would allow other men against himselfe.* For as long as every man holdeth this Right, of doing any thing he liketh; so long are all men in the condition of Warre. But if other men will not lay down their Right, as well as he; then there is no Reason for any one, to devest himselfe of his: For that were to expose himselfe to Prey, (which no man is bound to) rather than to dispose himselfe to Peace. This is that Law of the Gospell; *Whatsoever you require that others should do to you, that do ye to them.* And that Law of all men, *Quod tibi fieri non vis, alteri ne feceris.* . . .

Right is layd aside, either by simply Renouncing it; or by Transferring it to another. By *Simply* RENOUNCING; when he cares not to whom the benefit thereof redoundeth. By TRANSFERRING; when he intendeth the benefit thereof to some certain person, or persons. And when a man hath in either manner abandoned, or granted away his Right; then is he said to be OBLIGED, or BOUND, not to hinder those, to whom such Right is granted, or abandoned, from the benefit of it: and that he *Ought*, and it is his DUTY, not to make voyd that voluntary act of his own: and that such hindrance is INJUSTICE, and INJURY, as being *Sine Iure*; the Right being before renounced, or transferred. So that *Injury*, or *Injustice*, in the controversies of the world, is somewhat like to that, which in the disputations of Scholers is called *Absurdity.* For as it is there called an Absurdity, to contradict what one maintained in the Beginning: so in the world, it is called Injustice, and Injury, voluntarily to undo that, which from the beginning he had voluntarily done. . . .

❡   Whensoever a man Transferreth his Right, or Renounceth it; it is either in consideration of some Right reciprocally transferred to himselfe; or for some other good he hopeth for thereby. For it is a voluntary act: and of the voluntary acts of every man, the object is some *Good to himselfe*. And therefore there be some Rights, which no man can be understood by any words, or other signes, to have abandoned, or transferred. As first a man cannot lay down the right of resisting them, that assault him by force, to take away his life; because he cannot be understood to ayme thereby, at any Good to himselfe. The same may be sayd of Wounds, and Chayns, and Imprisonment; both because there is no benefit consequent to such patience; as there is to the patience of suffering another to be wounded, or imprisoned: as also because a man cannot tell, when he seeth men proceed against him by violence, whether they intend his death or not. And lastly the motive, and end for which this renouncing, and transferring of Right is introduced, is nothing else but the security of a mans person, in his life, and in the means of so preserving life, as not to be weary of it. And therefore if a man by words, or other signes, seem to despoyle himselfe of the End, for which those signes were intended; he is not to be understood as if he meant it, or that it was his will; but that he was ignorant of how such words and actions were to be interpreted.

The mutuall transferring of Right, is that which men call CONTRACT. . . .

When the transferring of Right, is not mutuall; but one of the parties transferreth, in hope to gain thereby friendship, or service from another, or from his friends; or in hope to gain the reputation of Charity, or Magnanimity; or to deliver his mind from the pain of compassion; or in hope of reward in heaven; This is not Contract, but GIFT, FREE-GIFT, GRACE: which words signifie one and the same thing.

Signes of Contract, are either *Expresse*, or *by Inference*. Expresse, are words spoken with understanding of what they signifie: And such words are either of the time *Present*, or *Past*; as, *I Give, I Grant, I have Given, I have Granted, I will that this be yours*: Or of the future; as, *I will Give, I will Grant*: which words of the future, are called PROMISE. . . .

The force of Words, being . . . too weak to hold men to the performance of their Covenants; there are in mans nature, but two imaginable helps to strengthen it. And those are either a Feare of

¶ the consequence of breaking their word; or a Glory, or Pride in appearing not to need to breake it. This later is a Generosity too rarely found to be presumed on, especially in the pursuers of Wealth, Command, or sensuall Pleasure; which are the greatest part of Mankind. The Passion to be reckoned upon, is Fear; whereof there be two very generall Objects: one, The Power of Spirits Invisible; the other, The Power of those men they shall therein Offend. Of these two, though the former be the greater Power, yet the feare of the later is commonly the greater Feare. The Feare of the former is in every man, his own Religion: which hath place in the nature of man before Civill Society. The later hath not so; at least not place enough, to keep men to their promises; because in the condition of meer Nature, the inequality of Power is not discerned, but by the event of Battell. So that before the time of Civill Society, or in the interruption thereof by Warre, there is nothing can strengthen a Covenant of Peace agreed on, against the temptations of Avarice, Ambition, Lust, or other strong desire, but the feare of that Invisible Power, which they every one Worship as God; and Feare as a Revenger of their perfidy. All therefore that can be done between two men not subject to Civill Power, is to put one another to swear by the God he feareth: Which *Swearing,* or OATH, is a *Forme of Speech, added to a Promise; by which he that promiseth, signifieth, that unlesse he performe, he renounceth the mercy of his God, or calleth to him for vengeance on himselfe.* Such was the Heathen Forme, *Let* Jupiter *kill me else, as I kill this Beast.* So is our Forme, *I shall do thus, and thus, so help me God.* And this, with the Rites and Ceremonies, which every one useth in his own Religion, that the feare of breaking faith might be the greater.

By this it appears, that an Oath taken according to any other Forme, or Rite, then his, that sweareth, is in vain; and no Oath: And that there is no Swearing by any thing which the Swearer thinks not God. For though men have sometimes used to swear by their Kings, for feare, or flattery; yet they would have it thereby understood, they attributed to them Divine honour. And that Swearing unnecessarily by God, is but prophaning of his name: and Swearing by other things, as men do in common discourse, is not Swearing, but an impious Custome, gotten by too much vehemence of talking.

It appears also, that the Oath addes nothing to the Obligation. For a Covenant, if lawfull, binds in the sight of God, without the

¶ Oath, as much as with it: if unlawfull, bindeth not at all; though it be confirmed with an Oath. . . .

From that law of Nature, by which we are obliged to transferre to another, such Rights, as being retained, hinder the peace of Mankind, there followeth a Third; which is this, *That men performe their Covenants made*: without which, Covenants are in vain, and but Empty words; and the Right of all men to all things remaining, wee are still in the condition of Warre.

And in this law of Nature, consisteth the Fountain and Originall of JUSTICE. For where no Covenant hath preceded, there hath no Right been transferred, and every man has right to every thing; and consequently, no action can be Unjust. But when a Covenant is made, then to break it is *Unjust*: And the definition of INJUSTICE, is no other than *the not Performance of Covenant.* And whatsoever is not Unjust, is *Just.* . . .

Therefore before the names of Just, and Unjust can have place, there must be some coercive Power, to compell men equally to the performance of their Covenants, by the terrour of some punishment, greater than the benefit they expect by the breach of their Covenant. . . .

The Foole hath sayd in his heart, there is no such thing as Justice; and sometimes also with his tongue; seriously alleaging, that every man's conservation, and contentment, being committed to his own care, there could be no reason, why every man might not do what he thought conduced thereunto: and therefore also to make, or not make; keep, or not keep Covenants, was not against Reason, when it conduced to ones benefit. . . . This specious reasoning is . . . false.

For the question is not of promises mutuall, where there is no security of performance on either side; as when there is no Civill Power erected over the parties promising; for such promises are no Covenants: But either where one of the parties has performed already; or where there is a Power to make him performe; there is the question whether it be against reason, that is, against the benefit of the other to performe, or not. And I say it is not against reason. For the manifestation whereof, we are to consider; First, that when a man doth a thing, which notwithstanding any thing can be foreseen, and reckoned on, tendeth to his own destruction, howsoever some accident which he could not expect, arriving may turne it to his benefit; yet such events do not make it reasonably or wisely

¶ done. Secondly, that in a condition of Warre, wherein every man to every man, for want of a common Power to keep them all in awe, is an Enemy, there is no man can hope by his own strength, or wit, to defend himselfe from destruction, without the help of Confederates; where every one expects the same defence by the Confederation, that any one else does: and therefore he which declares he thinks it reason to deceive those that help him, can in reason expect no other means of safety, than what can be had from his own single Power. He therefore that breaketh his Covenant, and consequently declareth that he thinks he may with reason do so, cannot be received into any Society, that unite themselves for Peace and Defence, but by the errour of them that receive him; nor when he is received, be retayned in it, without seeing the danger of their errour; which errours a man cannot reasonably reckon upon as the means of his security: and therefore if he be left, or cast out of Society, he perisheth; and if he live in Society, it is by the errours of other men, which he could not foresee, nor reckon upon; and consequently against the reason of his preservation; and so, as all men that contribute not to his destruction, forbear him onely out of ignorance of what is good for themselves. . . .

Justice therefore, that is to say, Keeping of Covenant, is a Rule of Reason, by which we are forbidden to do any thing destructive to our life; and consequently a Law of Nature. . . .

The names of Just, and Injust, when they are attributed to Men, signifie one thing: and when they are attributed to Actions, another. When they are attributed to Men, they signifie Conformity, or Inconformity of Manners, to Reason. But when they are attributed to Actions, they signifie the Conformity or Inconformity to Reason, not of Manners, or manner of life, but of particular Actions. A Just man therefore, is he that taketh all the care he can, that his Actions may be all Just: and an Unjust man, is he that neglecteth it. And such men are more often in our Language stiled by the names of Righteous, and Unrighteous; than Just, and Unjust; though the meaning be the same. Therefore a Righteous man, does not lose that Title, by one, or a few unjust Actions, that proceed from sudden Passion, or mistake of Things, or Persons: nor does an Unrighteous man, lose his character, for such Actions, as he does, or forbeares to do, for feare: because his Will is not framed by the Justice, but by the apparent benefit of what he is to do. That which gives to humane Actions the relish of Justice, is a certain Noblenesse

¶ or Gallantnesse of courage (rarely found), by which a man scorns to be beholding for the contentment of his life, to fraud, or breach of promise. This Justice of the Manners, is that which is meant, where Justice is called a Vertue; and Injustice a Vice. . . .

As Justice dependeth on Antecedent Covenant; so does GRATI-TUDE depend on Antecedent Grace; that is to say, Antecedent Free-gift: and is the fourth Law of Nature; which may be conceived in this Forme, *That a man which receiveth Benefit from another of meer Grace, Endeavour that he which giveth it, have no reasonable cause to repent him of his goodwill.* For no man giveth, but with intention of Good to himselfe; because Gift is Voluntary; and of all Voluntary Acts, the Object is to every man his own Good; of which if men see they shall be frustrated, there will be no beginning of benevolence, or trust; nor consequently of mutuall help; nor of reconciliation of one man to another; and therefore they are to remain still in the condition of *War*; which is contrary to the first and Fundamentall Law of Nature, which commandeth men to *Seek Peace.* The breach of this Law, is called *Ingratitude*; and hath the same relation to Grace, that Injustice hath to Obligation by Covenant.

A fifth Law of Nature, is COMPLEASANCE; that is to say, *That every man strive to accomodate himselfe to the rest.* . . .

A sixth Law of Nature, is this, *That upon caution of the Future time, a man ought to pardon the offences past of them that repenting, desire it.* For PARDON, is nothing but granting of Peace; which though granted to them that persevere in their hostility, be not Peace, but Feare; yet not granted to them that give caution of the Future time, is signe of an aversion to Peace; and therefore contrary to the Law of Nature.

A seventh is, *That in Revenges* (that is, retribution of Evil for Evil,) *Men look not at the greatnesse of the evill past, but the greatnesse of the good to follow.* Whereby we are forbidden to inflict punishment with any other designe, than for correction of the offender, or direction of others. For this Law is consequent to the next before it, that commandeth Pardon, upon security of the Future time . . . to hurt without reason, tendeth to the introduction of Warre; which is against the Law of Nature; and is commonly stiled by the name of *Cruelty*.

And because all signes of hatred, or contempt, provoke to fight; insomuch as most men choose rather to hazard their life, than not to

¶ be revenged; we may in the eighth place, for a Law of Nature, set down this Precept, *That no man by deed, word, countenance, or gesture, declare Hatred, or Contempt of another.* The breach of which Law, is commonly called *Contumely.* . . .

If Nature . . . have made men equall, that equalitie is to be acknowledged: or if Nature have made men unequall; yet because men that think themselves equall, will not enter into conditions of Peace, but upon Equall termes, such equalitie must be admitted. And therefore for the ninth law of Nature, I put this, *That every man acknowledge other for his Equall by Nature.* The breach of this Precept is *Pride.*

On this law, dependeth another, *That at the entrance into conditions of Peace, no man require to reserve to himselfe any Right, which he is not content should be reserved to every one of the rest.* As it is necessary for all men that seek peace, to lay down certaine Rights of Nature; that is to say, not to have libertie to do all they list; so is it necessarie for man's life, to retaine some; as right to governe their owne bodies; enjoy aire, water, motion, waies to go from place to place; and all things else without which a man cannot live, or not live well. If in this case, at the making of Peace, men require for themselves, that which they would not have to be granted to others, they do contrary to the precedent law, that commandeth the acknowledgement of naturall equalitie, and therefore also against the law of Nature. The observers of this law, are those we call *Modest,* and the breakers *Arrogant* men. The Greeks call the violation of this law πρεονεξία; that is, a desire of more than their share.

Also if *a man be trusted to judge between man and man,* it is a precept of the Law of Nature, *that he deale Equally between them.* For without that, the Controversies of men cannot be determined but by Warre. He therefore that is partiall in judgment, doth what in him lies, to deterre men from the use of Judges, and Arbitrators; and consequently, (against the fundamentall Lawe of Nature) is the cause of Warre. . . .

And from this followeth another law, *That such things as cannot be divided, be enjoyed in Common, if it can be; and if the quantity of the thing permit, without Stint; otherwise Proportionably to the number of them that have Right.* For otherwise the distribution is Unequall, and contrary to Equitie.

But some things there be, that can neither be divided, nor enjoyed in common. Then, The Law of Nature, which prescribeth Equity,

¶ requireth, *That the Entire Right; or else, (making the use alternate,) the First Possession, be determined by Lot.* For equall distribution, is of the Law of Nature; and other means of equall distribution cannot be imagined.

Of *Lots* there be two sorts, *Arbitrary,* and *Naturall.* Arbitrary, is that which is agreed on by the Competitors: Naturall, is either *Primogeniture* (which the Greek calls κρησονομία, which signifies, 'Given by Lot'); or *First Seisure.*

And therefore those things which cannot be enjoyed in common, nor divided, ought to be adjudged to the First Possessor; and in some cases to the First-Borne, as acquired by Lot.

It is also a Law of Nature, *That all men that mediate Peace, be allowed safe Conduct.* For the Law that commandeth Peace, as the *End,* commandeth Intercession, as the *Means*; and to Intercession the Means is safe Conduct.

And because, though men be never so willing to observe these Lawes, there may neverthelesse arise questions concerning a man's action; First, whether it were done, or not done; Secondly (if done) whether against the Law, or not against the Law; the former whereof, is called a question *Of Fact*; the later a question *Of Right*; therefore unlesse the parties to the question, Covenant mutually to stand to the sentence of another, they are as farre from Peace as ever. This other, to whose Sentence they submit, is called an ARBITRATOR. And therefore it is of the Law of Nature, *That they that are at controversie, submit their Right to the judgment of an Arbitrator.*

And seeing every man is presumed to do all things in order to his own benefit, no man is a fit Arbitrator in his own cause: and if he were never so fit; yet Equity allowing to each party equall benefit, if one be admitted to be Judge, the other is to be admitted also; and so the controversie, that is, the cause of War, remains, against the Law of Nature.

For the same reason no man in any Cause ought to be received for Arbitrator, to whom greater profit, or honour, or pleasure apparently ariseth out of the victory of one party, than of the other: for hee hath taken (though an unavoydable bribe, yet) a bribe; and no man can be obliged to trust him. And thus also the controversie, and the condition of War remaineth, contrary to the Law of Nature.

And in a controversie of *Fact*, the Judge being to give no more

¶ credit to one, than to the other, (if there be no other Arguments) must give credit to a third; or to a third and fourth; or more: For else the question is undecided, and left to force, contrary to the Law of Nature.

These are the Lawes of Nature, dictating Peace, for a means of the conservation of men in multitudes; and which onely concern the doctrine of Civill Society. There be other things tending to the destruction of particular men; as Drunkenness, and all other parts of Intemperance; which may therefore also be reckoned amongst those things which the Law of Nature hath forbidden; but are not necessary to be mentioned, nor are pertinent enough to this place.

And though this may seem too subtile a deduction of the Lawes of Nature, to be taken notice of by all men; whereof the most part are too busie in getting food, and the rest too negligent to understand; yet to leave all men unexcusable, they have been contracted into one easie sum, intelligible, even to the meanest capacity; and that is, *Do not that to another, which thou wouldest not have done to thy selfe*; which sheweth him, that he has no more to do in learning the Lawes of Nature, but, when weighing the actions of other men with his own, they seem too heavy, to put them into the other part of the ballance, and his own into their place, that his own passions, and selfe-love, may adde nothing to the weight; and then there is none of these Lawes of Nature that will not appear unto him very reasonable. . . .

These dictates of Reason, men use to call by the name of Lawes; but improperly: for they are but Conclusions, or Theoremes concerning what conduceth to the conservation and defence of themselves.

The two basic conceptions here are 'natural right' and 'natural law.' It is important to see that Hobbes uses them in a very special and quite unique way. We may, to put a difficult and complicated matter very briefly, say that philosophers of what we have called the humanistic tradition have generally understood these terms as involving at once certain privileges and certain restrictions which the fact of personality, the fact of being human instead of being merely animal, entails. The privileges which I have, for instance, imply certain corresponding limitations on your freedom to do whatever you please, just as your privileges mean that there are things which I may not do. And these privileges and restrictions, being rooted in human nature itself, have a totally different kind of status from the various privileges which the law may from time to time allow me and from the restrictions it may on occasion set up. The American Declaration of Independence, for example, is in the humanistic tradition when it declares that men possess certain inalienable rights—life, liberty, and the pursuit of happiness. The authors of this document did not, of course, mean to assert that these rights are always actually recognized; as a matter of fact, they were protesting against what they believed was a failure to recognize them. Since, unhappily, it is only too often the case that human rights are ignored or trampled on, what the humanist means by saying that these, or other, rights are 'inalienable' is simply that there exists a moral obligation to recognize them. And by saying that the rights are 'natural' he means that they are original, not derived. Obviously, the existence of rights, if they be admitted, implies the existence of a moral order—a set of principles—to which men's conduct ought to conform, so as to make these rights not merely ideals but actualities. Thus, in the humanistic tradition, natural law is the correlative of natural right. Natural rights are those privileges which natural law allows us; natural law is that order within which natural rights are set up and legitimated. Actual law *ought* to correspond to natural law; that it does not entirely do so simply means that human nature is not perfect. But the existence of this ideal of human rights gives us at once an objective and independent standard for criticizing all existing laws in the various states and a goal to aim at in all subsequent legislation.

The only similarity between this and Hobbes's conception is the name; and Hobbes must have had his tongue in his cheek when he chose to designate brute force as 'natural right' and a merely prudential calculation as 'natural law.' Natural right for Hobbes is, in fact, simply the state of nature as he conceives man's nature to be. When he says that man has a natural right to everything which he can obtain, Hobbes really means that there are no *moral* rights at all, and that, therefore, the world is one in which force is the sole determining principle of conduct. To say that man has a right to what he can get and hold on to means merely, for Hobbes, that he gets it by force, that he holds on to it by force, and that by force alone can it be taken away from him. It means, in a word, that, since there is no moral law, the only criterion by which conduct can be judged is by its success or failure in attaining whatever it has set out to attain.

Similarly, the various natural laws which Hobbes lists are nothing but what Kant was later to distinguish from the moral law as being merely "counsels of prudence." In the case of each law the argument follows the same pattern: Human nature being what it is, it will be best in the long run and for your own purely selfish and private interest for you to adhere to the following rules: to keep contracts, be complaisant, be modest, make a return for gifts received, *etc., etc.* The reason is that by doing so you will receive benefits which will more than make up for pain which such restriction of your natural appetites and tendencies inevitably produces. If you really want the peace and security which a stable government alone can bring, you must be prepared to surrender certain advantages which result from complete freedom, for the sake of ridding yourself of the far greater disadvantages which this freedom entails in the way of danger, uncertainty, and disquiet. Just as you should eat fresh vegetables, take plenty of exercise, and have eight hours of sleep nightly if you want to be healthy, so you should follow the rules which are here listed if you want a stable government and its advantages. In the former case the means to your end are determined by studying medicine or physiology and so ascertaining the factors which produce health; in the latter case the means to your end are ascertained by studying psychology or, if you cannot do that, by reading Mr Hobbes's *Leviathan*, where the rules are listed for your convenience. This analysis of human nature shows, for instance, that arrogance irritates people and that modesty pleases them; that men expect something in return for their gifts to us, even if these were unsolicited, and that they are therefore disappointed if we fail to reciprocate, and so on to the number of nineteen rules. On this basis we know how we should act in order to live comfortably in peace and security with our fellows. But, since we also know that we shall not be able to follow these rules freely, we must proceed to institute a sovereign who will make us do so.

Hence, postponing for the present a consideration of the last stages in this argument, we may say that in Hobbes's view natural law is simply the statement of a causal connexion which is found out by observation and rational thought, and which defines a process either for getting something we want or for avoiding something which displeases us. Hobbes's language sometimes disguises this; and some of his critics have supposed (as perhaps he intended them to) that he introduces a moral sanction. They have, for instance, supposed him to argue that with the institution of the state real justice is somehow miraculously introduced and that, therefore, we *ought* to obey the state's laws. These critics have then impressively pointed out that Hobbes has no business introducing such a moral sanction and have complained of his inconsistency in doing so. The fact is, however, that here at least Hobbes is entirely consistent. He never really appeals to anything but utility. We ought to be 'just,' to obey the law, and to keep contracts, not because we have a moral duty to do so, but merely because it is to our own advantage to do so. In a word, we ought to be just, in precisely the same sense as we ought to take plenty of exercise—because in each case there is something we want, to which this is a means, and which is sufficiently valuable to make it worth while doing something disagreeable like taking exercise or fulfilling a contract.

If Hobbes cannot be fairly criticized for inconsistently appealing to a moral sanction it is not unfair to remark that his sense of logic seems more developed than his moral sense. If the admission of a moral sanction is inconsistent with Hobbes's position, so much the worse, we might say, for that position. For it does seem to be the case that men have certain rights which it is our *duty* to recognize, quite irre- spectively of whether or not it is to our interest in the long run to do so. Most people would perhaps acknowledge the existence of this fundamental distinction between duty and interest—between what I ought to do as such, and what I ought to do only if I want something else to which it is a means. But even those who identify duty and interest [1] maintain that our duty is to aim at the interest of all, not, as Hobbes says, at our own private interest.

Even if we pass over this difficulty there remains another serious objection *in principle* to his position. It is true that at first sight little objection can be made to the detailed utilitarian arguments by which he attempts to show that it is to our advantage to conform to his various laws of nature. Hobbes has, in fact, listed a rather surprisingly diverse collection of rules for communal living, ranging all the way from matters of fundamental importance for the very existence of political and economic institutions, like contracts and equity, to the relatively trivial concerns of ordinary social intercourse. Thus no one would deny that it is to our interest, because we get on better with our fellows by doing so, to be modest and complaisant rather than arrogant and proud. But it seems hardly necessary to exalt such simple and obvious rules to the position of natural laws.

The difficulty with all of these utilitarian arguments arises when we

---

[1] For instance, J. S. Mill. See his *Utilitarianism*, especially chapter 5.

attempt to apply them universally. They are on the whole valid, we may agree, for the average man, but they do not hold for the exceptional man. Though it may be to the interest of most of us to obey the laws of the state and to fulfil contracts, etc., because otherwise social institutions would break down, it clearly would be still more to our interest if every one else obeyed the law and kept contracts, while we alone did not. And if we were sufficiently shrewd and cunning, this is precisely what we would do, since we could violate the law without incurring any penalties. Hence the really clever man who acts solely on utilitarian considerations will decide not to follow any of Hobbes's rules, but, instead, merely to give the appearance of doing so. It is because Hobbes realizes this that he thinks only the exercise of force by a superior power will make us follow the rules he has laid down. He suspects, in a word, that every man will think himself cleverer than his fellows, and hence that every man will decide on strictly utilitarian (though doubtless mistaken) calculations that it is to his advantage to break the rules. Hence, if life is not to be poor, short, and brutish, men must be compelled by force to conform to these rules.

So far we have considered the argument that men could live together in peace and security if they followed certain rules which Hobbes has drawn up as a result of his study of psychology, and which he calls the laws of nature. Throughout this argument he rests his case on the original assumption that men are fundamentally fearsome and selfish, and he attempts to appeal to what alone, on this basis, would attract them—*i.e.*, their own self-interest. The argument is therefore utilitarian in character: it will be to every man's interest in the long run to follow these rules, because by doing so he will get the peace and security which he desires—the security which will relieve his fear and the peace which will enable him to satisfy his various desires. This argument is, as we have seen, quite unsatisfactory. It is just because Hobbes recognizes its breakdown and because he knows no other consideration which would lead men to be obedient and amenable to social discipline that he has to appeal, over and above utilitarian calculations, to force as the factor which will produce and maintain order.

The Foundation of States

We have thus reached the second main stage in Hobbes's argument. Put briefly, it runs as follows. Since a simple utilitarian calculation of

THOMAS HOBBES

to) does not end decisively in favour of conformity to the 'laws of
nature,' the situation must be weighed artificially in their favour.
That is, a system of sanctions, of rewards and penalties, must be introduced so that a utilitarian calculation will show that the relative
advantages of conformity far outweigh the advantages of non-
conformity. That is to say, since the utilitarian argument alone breaks
down, it follows that men will not keep themselves in order and that
they therefore require a sovereign to rule over them. Moreover, if
this sovereign is to maintain peace and security permanently and
efficiently he must be supreme and all-powerful. This argument,
however, is complicated by the fact that Hobbes recognizes two
different ways by which a suitable sovereign may be established.[1]

¶ The attaining to this Soveraign Power, is by two wayes. One,
by Naturall force; as when a man maketh his children, to submit
themselves, and their children to his government, as being able to
destroy them if they refuse; or by Warre subdueth his enemies to
his will, giving them their lives on that condition. The other, is
when men agree amongst themselves, to submit to some Man,
or Assembly of men, voluntarily, on confidence to be protected
by him against all others. This later, may be called a Politicall
Common-wealth, or Common-wealth by *Institution*; and the
former, a Common-wealth by *Acquisition*.

Little needs be said about the latter of these two types.[2]

¶ A *Common-wealth by Acquisition*, is that, where the Soveraign
Power is acquired by Force; And it is acquired by force, when men
singly, or many together by plurality of voyces, for fear of death,
or bonds, do authorize all the actions of that Man, or Assembly,
that hath their lives and liberty in his Power.

And this kind of Dominion, or Soveraignty, differeth from
Soveraignty by Institution, onely in this, That men who choose
their Soveraign, do it for fear of one another, and not of him whom
they Institute: But in this case, they subject themselves, to him they
are afraid of. In both cases they do it for fear: which is to be noted
by them, that hold all such Covenants, as proceed from fear of

---

[1] *Leviathan*, Part II, chapter 17 (158-159).
[2] *Ibid.*, Part I, chapter 20 (185).

¶ death, or violence, voyd: which if it were true, no man, in any kind of Common-wealth, could be obliged to Obedience.

The Nature of Sovereignty by Institution

The institution of commonwealths is a more complicated matter. We have seen how man's nature inclines him to continual strife. On the other hand, the very same appetites and aversions which set man at odds with his fellows lead him, if he ever stops to consider the matter from a long-run point of view, to wish to live with them in peace and harmony, for the sake of the advantages peace brings.[1]

(a) The Contract

¶ The Passions that encline men to Peace, are Feare of Death; Desire of such things as are necessary to commodious living; and a Hope by their Industry to obtain them. And Reason suggesteth convenient Articles of Peace, upon which men may be drawn to agreement. . . .

The finall Cause, End, or Designe of men, (who naturally love Liberty, and Dominion over others,) in the introduction of that restraint upon themselves, (in which wee see them live in Common-wealths,) is the foresight of their own preservation, and of a more contented life thereby; that is to say, of getting themselves out from that miserable condition of Warre, which is necessarily consequent (as hath been shewn) to the naturall Passions of men, when there is no visible Power to keep them in awe. . . .

The only way to erect such a Common Power, as may be able to defend them from the invasion of Forraigners, and the injuries of one another, and thereby to secure them in such sort, as that by their owne industrie, and by the fruites of the Earth, they may nourish themselves and live contentedly; is, to conferre all their power and strength upon one Man, or upon one Assembly of men, that may reduce all their Wills, by plurality of voices, unto one Will: . . . made by Covenant of every man with every man, in such manner, as if every man should say to every man, *I Authorize and give up my Right of Governing my selfe, to this Man, or to this Assembly of men, on this condition, that thou give up thy Right to him, and Authorize all his Actions in like manner.* This done, the Multitude

[1] *Leviathan*, Part I, chapter 13 (116); Part I, chapter 17 (153ff.); Part I, chapter 18 (159).

¶ so united in one Person, is called a COMMON-WEALTH, in latine *Civitas*. This is the Generation of that great LEVIATHAN . . . to which wee owe . . . our peace and defence. . . .

A *Common-wealth* is said to be *Instituted*, when a *Multitude* of men do Agree, and *Covenant*, *every one*, *with every one*, that to whatsoever *Man*, or *Assembly of Men*, shall be given by the major part, the *Right* to *Present* the Person of them all, (that is to say, to be their *Representative*;) every one, as well he that *Voted for it*, as he that *Voted against it*, shall *Authorize* all the Actions and Judgements, of that Man, or Assembly of men, in the same manner, as if they were his own, to the end, to live peaceably amongst themselves, and be protected against other men.

It is perfectly clear that Hobbes here assumes, as the basis of their agreement to institute a sovereign, that it is to all men's interest in the long run to keep contracts, to be just and equitable, and to conform to all the other 'laws of nature,' and it is also perfectly clear that this directly contradicts what has been said earlier in criticism of Hobbes's utilitarian line of argument. It is obvious that this causes a serious difficulty for his conception of sovereignty by institution. However, before we consider this, we may complete this stage of Hobbes's argument by showing what powers he attributes to the sovereign, by whatever means he be established.

When men institute a sovereign, they do so for the sole reason that they desire peace and security. Therefore the sovereign whom they institute must have resources sufficient to achieve this end. This means, Hobbes contends, that the sovereign must be absolutely supreme and all-powerful.[1]

¶   By this Authoritie, given him by every particular man in the Common-wealth, he hath the use of so much Power and Strength conferred on him, that by terror thereof, he is inabled to forme the wills of them all, to Peace at home, and mutuall ayd against their enemies abroad. And in him consisteth the Essence of the Common-wealth; which (to define it,) is *One Person, of whose Acts a great Multitude, by mutuall Covenants one with another, have made themselves every one the Author, to the end he may use the strength and means of them all, as he shall think expedient, for their Peace and Common Defence.* . . .

[1] *Leviathan*, Part II, chapter 17 (158); Part II, chapter 18 (159*ff*.).

¶ From this Institution of a Common-wealth are derived all the *Rights*, and *Facultyes* of him, or them, on whom the Soveraign Power is conferred by the consent of the People assembled.

First, because they Covenant, it is to be understood, they are not obliged by former Covenant to any thing repugnant hereunto. And Consequently they that have already Instituted a Commonwealth, being thereby bound by Covenant, to own the Actions, and Judgments of one, cannot lawfully make a new Covenant, amongst themselves, to be obedient to any other, in any thing whatsoever, without his permission. . . . They have also every man given the Soveraignty to him that beareth their Person; and therefore if they depose him, they take from him that which is his own, and so again it is injustice. . . . And whereas some men have pretended for their disobedience to their Soveraign, a new Covenant, made, not with men, but with God; this also is unjust: for there is no Covenant with God, but by mediation of some body that representeth Gods Person; which none doth but Gods Lieutenant, who hath the Soveraignty under God. . . .

Secondly, Because the Right of bearing the Person of them all, is given to him they make Soveraign, by Covenant onely of one to another, and not of him to any of them; there can happen no breach of Covenant on the part of the Soveraign; and consequently none of his Subjects, by any pretence of forfeiture, can be freed from his Subjection. . . . If any one, or more of them, pretend a breach of the Covenant made by the Soveraign at his Institution; and others, or one other of his Subjects, or himselfe alone, pretend there was no such breach, there is in this case, no Judge to decide the controversie: it returns therefore to the Sword again; and every man recovereth the right of Protecting himselfe by his own strength, contrary to the designe they had in the Institution. It is therefore in vain to grant Soveraignty by way of precedent Covenant. . . .

Thirdly, because the major part hath by consenting voices declared a Soveraign; he that dissented must now consent with the rest; that is, be contented to avow all the actions he shall do, or else justly be destroyed by the rest. For if he voluntarily entered into the Congregation of them that were assembled, he sufficiently declared thereby his will (and therefore tacitely covenanted) to stand to what the major part should ordayne: and therefore if he refuse to stand thereto, or make Protestation against any of their Decrees, he does contrary to his Covenant, and therefore unjustly. . . .

¶   Fourthly, . . . whatsoever he doth, it can be no injury to any of his Subjects; nor ought he to be by any of them accused of Injustice. For he that doth any thing by authority from another, doth therein no injury to him by whose authority he acteth. . . . It is true that they that have Soveraign Power, may commit Iniquity; but not Injustice, or Injury in the proper signification.

Fifthly, and consequently to that which was sayd last, no man that hath Soveraign Power can justly be put to death, or otherwise in any manner by his Subjects punished. . . .

Because the End of this Institution, is the Peace and Defence of them all; and whosoever has right to the End, has right to the Means; it belongeth of Right, to whatsoever Man, or Assembly that hath the Soveraignty, to be Judge both of the meanes of Peace and Defence; and also of the hindrances, and disturbances of the same; and to do whatsoever he shall think necessary to be done, both before hand, for the preservation of Peace and Security, by prevention of Discord at home, and Hostility from abroad; and, when Peace and Security are lost, for the recovery of the same. And therefore,

Sixthly, it is annexed to the Soveraignty, to be Judge of what Opinions and Doctrines are averse, and what conducing to Peace; and consequently, on what occasions, how farre, and what, men are to be trusted withall, in speaking to Multitudes of people; and who shall examine the Doctrines of all bookes before they be published. For the Actions of men proceed from their Opinions; and in the wel governing of Opinions, consisteth the well governing of mens Actions, in order to their Peace, and Concord. And though in matter of Doctrine, nothing ought to be regarded but the Truth; yet this is not repugnant to regulating of the same by Peace. For Doctrine repugnant to Peace, can no more be True, than Peace and Concord can be against the Law of Nature. It is true, that in a Common-wealth, where by the negligence, or unskilfullnesse of Governours, and Teachers, false Doctrines are by time generally received; the contrary Truths may be generally offensive: Yet the most sudden, and rough busling in of a new Truth, that can be, does never breake the Peace, but only somtimes awake the Warre. For those men that are so remissely governed, that they dare take up Armes, to defend, or introduce an Opinion, are still in Warre; and their condition not Peace, but only a Cessation of Armes for feare of one another; and they live as it were, in the procincts of

¶ battaile continually. It belongeth therefore to him that hath the Soveraign Power, to be Judge, or constitute all Judges of Opinions and Doctrines, as a thing necessary to Peace; therby to prevent Discord and Civill Warre.

Seventhly, is annexed to the Soveraignty, the whole power of pre-scribing the Rules, whereby every man may know, what Goods he may enjoy, and what Actions he may doe, without being molested by any of his fellow Subjects: And this is it men call *Propriety*. For before constitution of Soveraign Power (as hath already been shewn) all men had right to all things; which necessarily causeth Warre: and therefore this Proprietie, being necessary to Peace, and depending on Soveraign Power, is the Act of that Power, in order to the publique peace. . . .

Eighthly, is annexed to the Soveraignty, the Right of Judica-ture; that is to say, of hearing and deciding all Controversies. . . . For without the decision of Controversies, there is no protection of one Subject, against the injuries of another; . . . and to every man remaineth . . . the right of protecting himselfe by his private strength, which is the condition of Warre; and contrary to the end for which every Common-wealth is instituted.

Ninthly, . . . the Right of making Warre, and Peace with other Nations, and Common-wealths; that is to say, of Judging when it is for the publique good, and how great forces are to be assembled, armed, and payd for that end; and to levy mony upon the Subjects, to defray the expences thereof. . . .

Tenthly, . . . the choosing of all Counsellours, Ministers, Magis-trates, and Officers, both in Peace, and War. For seeing the Sove-raign is charged with the End, which is the common Peace and Defence; he is understood to have Power to use such Means, as he shall think most fit for his discharge. . . .

These are the Rights, which make the Essence of Soveraignty; and which are the markes, whereby a man may discern in what Man, or Assembly of men, the Soveraign Power is placed, and resideth. For these are incommunicable, and inseparable. . . . If he transferre the *Militia*, he retains the Judicature in vain, for want of execution of the Lawes: Or if he grant away the Power of raising Mony; the *Militia* is in vain: or if he give away the government of Doctrines, men will be frighted into rebellion with the feare of Spirits. And so if we consider any one of the said Rights, we shall presently see, that the holding of all the rest, will produce no effect,

¶in the conservation of Peace and Justice, the end for which all Common-wealths are Instituted. And this division is it, whereof it is said, *a Kingdome divided in it selfe cannot stand*: For unlesse this division precede, division into opposite Armies can never happen. If there had not first been an opinion received of the greatest part of *England*, that these Powers were divided between the King, and the Lords, and the House of Commons, the people had never been divided, and fallen into this Civill Warre; first between those that disagreed in Politiques; and after between the Dissenters about the liberty of Religion; which have so instructed men in this point of Soveraign Right, that there be few now (in *England*,) that do not see, that these Rights are inseparable, and will be so generally acknowledged, at the next return of Peace; and so continue, till their miseries are forgotten; and no longer, except the vulgar be better taught than they have hitherto been. . . .

But a man may here object, that the Condition of Subjects is very miserable; as being obnoxious to the lusts, and other irregular passions of him, or them that have so unlimited a Power in their hands. And commonly they that live under a Monarch, think it the fault of Monarchy; and they that live under the government of Democracy, or other Soveraign Assembly, attribute all the inconvenience to that forme of Common-wealth; whereas the Power in all formes, if they be perfect enough to protect them, is the same; not considering that the estate of Man can never be without some incommodity or other; and that the greatest, that in any forme of Government can possibly happen to the people in generall, is scarce sensible, in respect of the miseries, and horrible calamities, that accompany a Civill Warre; or that dissolute condition of masterlesse men, without subjection to Lawes, and a coercive Power to tye their hands from rapine, and revenge: nor considering that the greatest pressure of Soveraign Governours, proceedeth not from any delight, or profit they can expect in the dammage, or weakening of their Subjects, in whose vigour, consisteth their own strength and glory; but in the restiveness of themselves, that unwillingly contributing to their own defence, make it necessary for their Governours to draw from them what they can in time of Peace, that they may have means on any emergent occasion, or sudden need, to resist, or take advantage on their Enemies. For all men are by nature provided of notable multiplying glasses, (that is their Passions and Selfe-love,) through which, every little payment appeareth a

¶ great grievance; but are destitute of those prospective glasses (namely Morall and Civill Science), to see a farre off the miseries that hang over them, and cannot without such payments be avoyded.

(b) The Right to Rebel

The conclusion of this argument is that the sovereign's power is, and must be, absolutely unlimited. This, of course, is Hobbes's usual position, but in at least one important passage he allows one exception to, one restriction of, the absolute power of the sovereign. This is the subject's 'liberty' (as Hobbes calls it) to defend his own life even against his sovereign. It is necessary for us to pause a moment to consider this point, since, on the one hand, the logic of his whole argument forces him to make this admission, while, on the other hand, it leads him, in its turn, into a paradoxical, not to say completely inconsistent, position. To begin with, it should be obvious why logic requires Hobbes to allow that every man has a right to disobey if his sovereign command him "to kill, wound, or mayme himselfe; or not to resist those that assault him; or to abstain from the use of food, ayre, medicine, or any other thing, without which he cannot live. . . ." [1] The reason is that, since men contract together to institute a sovereign only in order to save their lives, it cannot be maintained that they grant to the sovereign whom they thus set up the right to take their lives. It would be hopelessly inconsistent to claim that in the compact which they make together they contract away that for the sake of which they have made the compact. This would be a case of adopting as the means to a certain end something which rendered the end itself impossible.

Moreover, the right to protect one's life against one's sovereign applies, clearly enough, not only in the case of a subject against whom criminal proceedings are threatened, but whenever *any* act of the sovereign endangers the life of one of his subjects. Thus a subject has a right to refuse to serve when he "is commanded as a Souldier to fight against the enemy." [2] And this question of obedience is, of course, not limited to service in time of war. In fact, since "the end of Obedience is Protection," it follows that "the Obligation of Subjects to the Soveraign, is understood to last as long, and no longer, than the power lasteth, by which he is able to protect them." [3]

[1] *Leviathan*, Part II, chapter 21 (204).   [2] *Ibid.*, Part II, chapter 21 (205).
[3] *Ibid.*, Part II, chapter 21 (208).

We may begin by asking whether the 'liberty' Hobbes talks of here is to be understood in the normal Hobbesian sense of 'right'—*i.e.*, a power or capacity, or in some other sense as a *moral* right. The former, of course, is what, logically, Hobbes should mean, and that it is what he means is suggested by his conclusion that the criminal has a right to his life only *if he can* preserve it, while the sovereign, on the contrary, has a right to punish the criminal only *if he can* catch him. This does, indeed, remove the contradiction between the theses (1) that every one has a right to protect his life, and (2) that, since the threat of punishment is the most effective instrument of government, the sovereign must have the right to punish all his subjects. But though the contradiction is thus resolved, the position is hardly satisfactory. For, if the sovereign has sufficient actual power to govern the state as Hobbes thinks it requires to be governed, it is clear that the subject's right (*i.e.*, power) is non-existent. And, on the other hand, if the sovereign be sufficiently weak for the subject to have a genuine right (*i.e.*, power), he is too weak to be an efficient instrument of governance. In other words, either the right which Hobbes assigns the subject is insignificant and meaningless or the relation between sovereign and subject will result in chaos and anarchy.

That this is the case will be still clearer if we consider the right to refuse military service and the general right to revolution. It is clear either that Hobbes can mean nothing by these rights or else that he has reached a position in effect indistinguishable from that of Locke and utterly at variance with what he maintains everywhere else. Locke himself decided (probably rightly) that Hobbes did not mean that these are real (moral) rights. Hence he quite correctly points out that, if the subject's right to rebel is only a capacity, the right exists only when the sovereign's actual power (and right) has vanished.[1] But when the sovereign's power has been destroyed by the action of either internal or external enemies, according to Hobbes's own thesis, anarchy ensues until a new sovereign is established with sufficient power to control the various forces in the state. And in such a chaotic situation, to say that the single individual has a right to protect himself means simply that he would have to fend for himself in circumstances in which he obviously has small chance of success. Thus, if right means power (as it should, logically, for Hobbes) the subject has no right, in either case, whether the sovereign be strong or weak. If the sovereign be strong the subject clearly has no

---

[1] *Vide infra*, p. 199.

power to rebel. On the other hand, if he be weak he is, in effect, no sovereign, and society has lapsed into a state of nature, in which no one has much chance of protecting his life.

If we do not like this conclusion, we can try the other alternative and ask what the result would be if Hobbes had meant that men have a real right to disobey their sovereign when their lives are endangered. Unfortunately for Hobbes, the consequences are no more satisfactory. It is not merely the case that this admission would contradict the very basis of the Hobbesian system or that the existence of real rights is unthinkable if Hobbes's account of human nature be correct. For, passing over all this, the admission of this right could lead only to confusion. A right is not real unless the decision as to its existence rests with him who claims the right. Thus my right to rebel if my life be endangered implies that I, and I alone, decide whether my life is, or is not, endangered. Hence, in effect, I decide in every particular case whether I choose to obey the sovereign. This means a government of the most extreme democratic form—a state of affairs which, on Hobbes's view of human nature, would be hopelessly chaotic and anarchistic. But it is unnecessary to continue this line of criticism any further. The position is clear. Either the subject has a right against his sovereign or he has not. If he has not Hobbes certainly should not say that he has this right. On the other hand, if he does have the right Hobbes's major thesis—that the sovereign's power is, and must be, absolute— is false. Hobbes cannot have it both ways at once. If the sovereign's power is absolute it cannot be conditioned in *any* way; and if there is any sort of restriction or limitation on his power it is not absolute.

(c) The Absolute Sovereign

Although, as we have just seen, the logic of Hobbes's position requires him to admit at least one restriction on the sovereign's power, this admission involves him, as we have also seen, in such difficulties that, for the most part, he ignores the whole question and argues that the sovereign's powers may not be restricted in any way, either at the time of institution or afterwards, because any restriction defeats the purposes of the institution. That this position, too, is quite unsatisfactory may easily be shown.

In the case of every particular right which he assigns to his sovereign, Hobbes's argument has the same utilitarian form: human nature being what it is, unless this right is assigned to the sovereign, he will not be able to control men's native tendencies and dispositions in the interest of general peace and security. In reply to the criticism that in raising up this great power we only destroy ourselves, since we cannot be sure that the sovereign will not use it for his own selfish interests instead of using it for the interests of his subjects, Hobbes can only reply that this is a chance we must take. He has to admit of course that the sovereign is not bound in any way by a contract or any moral obligation to serve our interests. That this is so, follows simply from the fact that might makes right and the sovereign is all-powerful. Since obligation is only meaningful where it can be enforced, it is clear that a supreme sovereign cannot be obliged. But it is not only the case that the sovereign has no duty towards us; it is also obvious —since he too is a man and thus subject like ourselves to his human nature—that he considers, and can consider, only his own selfish interests, and will take ours into account only if in doing so he serves his own. Thus our life under such a sovereign is by no means a happy prospect; but the human condition is so miserable and wretched that it is better to live even under the most vicious and tyrannical of autocrats than to attempt to get on without any sovereign or with a sovereign who is less than all-powerful.

So far we have considered only the rights and powers which Hobbes assigns to an instituted sovereign. But a sovereign who has acquired his position must be allowed, Hobbes thinks, to own the same unlimited authority.[1]

❡ The Rights, and Consequences of Soveraignty, are the same in both. His Power cannot, without his consent, be Transferred to another: He cannot Forfeit it: He cannot be Accused by any of his Subjects, of Injury: He cannot be Punished by them: He is Judge of what is necessary for Peace; and Judge of Doctrines: He is Sole Legislator; and Supreme Judge of Controversies; and of the Times, and Occasions of Warre, and Peace: to him it belongeth to choose Magistrates, Counsellours, Commanders, and all other Officers, and Ministers; and to determine of Rewards, and Punishments, Honour, and Order. The reasons whereof, are the same which are alledged in the precedent Chapter, for the same Rights, and Consequences of Soveraignty by Institution.

We have two things to consider here: first, whether sovereignty is established in the two ways which Hobbes describes and, second,

[1] *Leviathan*, Part I, chapter 20 (186).

whether the argument is correct which asserts that the sovereign, however established, should be supremely powerful.

There are no difficulties about sovereignty by acquisition on either of these points. To begin with, it is unfortunately only too true that sovereigns have established themselves by the exercise of force. Many, perhaps most, states have been set up in this way—the history, for instance, of ancient Greece, or of Italy in the Middle Ages and in the Renaissance, is the story of city-states whose sovereigns, whether tyrants, oligarchs, or the masses, acquired their position and maintained themselves in it by force and violence. And this plain record of history is not in any way altered by the fact that often the actual seizure of power has been more or less effectively disguised by the use of legal forms, as was the case on the occasion of Hitler's 'acquisition' of Czechoslovakia.

Again, as regards sovereignty by acquisition, the question, How powerful *should* the sovereign be? is really meaningless. We have no choice in the matter: since his position has been acquired not with our consent, but by the use of force, he is just as powerful as he wishes to be. In a word, since power is obviously required in order to secure the sovereignty, a tyrant who has the resources and the means to seize the first place in a state presumably will have sense enough and ability enough to keep it firmly in his hands regardless of the wishes of those over whom he rules.

The case is obviously different when we consider the position of a sovereign who is established by the free consent of those over whom he is to rule, since at the time of the institution they presumably can, if they like, set certain restrictions on his exercise of authority. The fact that he claims that men can agree to establish a supreme sovereign for their common protection and advantage involves Hobbes in an insoluble problem. There is no difficulty, of course, about the historicity of the establishment of states by institution—the foundation of the United States is an example. On the contrary, the whole difficulty arises from the impossibility of making the historical fact of institution plausible on the basis of the account of human nature which Hobbes has already given. In this connexion we have to ask whether it is actually to men's interest to establish a supreme sovereign; whether they will reach this conclusion themselves; and finally whether, if they do, they will act on it. In every case Hobbes's argument has to be a utilitarian calculation: Hobbes has to argue both that it is to men's interest to be ruled by such a sovereign and that they will see that this is to their interest. Unfortunately, if Hobbes's psychological theory is correct, it is not to men's interest to be subject to such a sovereign, nor will they conclude that it is to their interest, nor, finally, is it possible, even if they did reach this conclusion, that they will act on it.

We can take the first two of these points together. It is clear, since men are moved only by fear and by a desire for gain, that the only way of their ever agreeing to institute a sovereign, or, indeed, of their ever agreeing about anything at all, would be for each of them to convince himself that it was to his own advantage to do so. Unfortunately, as we have seen, the appeal to private interest breaks down, since, in the first place, it is not to every man's interest that a sovereign be established, and, in the second place, even in cases where it actually is to the interest of all to institute a sovereign, men judge otherwise. And it is just because Hobbes himself recognized this weakness in the utilitarian argument that he holds men to need an absolute sovereign. Hence the position he takes here is hopeless. The very argument which he uses to show that we require such a sovereign makes it impossible for him to claim that men would ever conclude that it is to their advantage to have one.

We have, in fact, to distinguish the assertion that men actually do need such a sovereign from the assertion that men will severally conclude that they need him. The first assertion *may* be true, and, if Hobbes's account of human nature be accepted, it probably is true. The second is certainly false—even if (or, indeed, especially if) we accept that account of human nature. For (as Hobbes was careful to point out) men overestimate their own cleverness and shrewdness and hence conclude that it is rather to their own interest to be free to take advantage of their less clever fellows.

Thus Hobbes's argument requires him to maintain the following mutually contradictory propositions: men conclude (whether rightly or not) that it is to their interest to be independent of all authority; men institute a sovereign because they see it is to their advantage to do so. If, as Hobbes contends, men are moved solely by consideration of their own interests, it is obvious that we cannot hold that a consideration of these interests leads them both to institute and to refuse to institute a sovereign. Unfortunately Hobbes cannot dispense with either one of these conflicting propositions. He cannot abandon the admission that the utilitarian argument fails, for then he could not claim men need an absolute and supreme sovereign. If men concluded that their own several interests are best served by mutual help and co-operation, they would co-operate and would not need an authority to force them to do so. On the other hand, since Hobbes wants to maintain that sovereigns exist not only by force of their arms, but by the choice of free men, and, since he also maintains that no one is ever moved by any consideration except his own profit, he is obliged to say not only that it is after all to men's interest to have a sovereign, but that they themselves recognize this need. We can put all of this more shortly by saying that if, as Hobbes himself allows, the utilitarian argument breaks down when we attempt to prove the desirability of sovereignty in general, it follows *a fortiori* that this same argument can not be used to justify the institution of absolute sovereignty.

The other main difficulty with Hobbes's reasoning here is even more serious. It amounts to this. Let us suppose for the sake of argument that it is to men's interest to submit to a supremely power-ful sovereign and that they severally reach this conclusion. The difficulty is to see how, if Hobbes's account of human nature be correct, men would (or could) act in accordance with this judg-ment.

It is not just the case that the relative roles which we have seen assigned to the passions and to reason (and which must be assigned to them if solitary life is to be as "poore, nasty, brutish, and short" as Hobbes must have it appear) make it utterly impossible that men could ever deliberate coolly and calmly about their mutual best interest. Even if we suppose that men somehow overcome their fears and suspicions of each other sufficiently to sit down together; even if we suppose that some (or indeed all) of them have sufficient foresight to conceive articles of confederation which would, were they established, get them out of the miserable condition in which they find themselves, it is still impossible that human beings, as Hobbes judges them to be, could ever actually confederate on the lines that reason suggested to them. The fact is that Hobbes is con-fronted by a dilemma all the more serious because he seems not to have recognized it himself. Either men are merely animals or they are not. If they are they cannot institute states. If they are not force is not the only law of their nature. If, on the one hand, men are sufficiently reasonable and foresighted to institute a state, they do not require a completely absolute and ruthless sovereign. On the other hand, if they are so much the slaves of their passions as to require such a sovereign to keep them in order, they are not capable of instituting it by free and deliberate agreement among themselves. In a word, Hobbes cannot have his cake and eat it too. He cannot make man out to be a savage beast who recognizes only the authority of force and at the same time endow him with the prudence, the sympathy, and the fellow-feeling which the contract theory presupposes.

This difficulty is fatal, for Hobbes can abandon neither one of the two propositions whose conflict we are observing. If he denies establishment by institution he flies in the face of historical fact; if he moderates the dark colours of his portrait of human nature he destroys his argument for a supremely powerful sovereign, since his only means of justifying his insistence on such a sovereign is to make human nature so hopelessly bad and weak that it is incapable of taking even the first steps in self-government. Between these two positions Hobbes can turn as much as he likes, but from their mutual contradiction he cannot extricate himself without a major revision of the theory. If men can, on one occasion, sit down together to debate, and to decide on, questions of their common advantage, why can they not do so as well on other occasions? Why can they not remain what they are, a free democratic assembly, instead of choosing, in this one moment of freedom, to submit themselves for ever afterwards into the hands of an absolutely powerful sovereign? Hobbes's position becomes plausible (if indeed it does so then) only if we conceive all men to be like the confirmed drunkard or drug addict who, rousing from his insane dreams to a brief moment of sanity, may commit himself to the authority of a keeper, because he realizes that he will inevitably fall again into the state from which he is momentarily released. This is admittedly not a pretty picture of human nature; it is, surely, also a false one.

If the picture be false and overdrawn, we must ask why Hobbes held to it. Was it because he saw it was his only way of justifying the absolute sovereign he was determined to have? This may be the case, but it is more likely unfair to him. It is probable that he wanted to have an absolute sovereign only because his observation of human nature had convinced him that men are so hopelessly bad and weak as to require one. And the times Hobbes lived in surely to some extent justify this gloomy conclusion. Where he went wrong was in seeing only one side of human nature. He did not see that even the most vicious men can be, and sometimes are, generous, sympathetic, kind, and self-sacrificing. He did not see that war, besides bringing out man's natural brutality and savagery, brings out his nobility and courage—his willingness to suffer and even to die for something he believes in.

Equally important is Hobbes's failure to see that, besides these unselfish, altruistic tendencies (which he ignores) and rational self-interest (which he here inconsistently admits), there are still other factors in human nature which lead men to communal and social living. In an amusing passage Hobbes points out various differences between men and certain creatures, such as bees and ants, which make it possible for the latter, and impossible for the former, to "live in society without any coercive power." [1] If Hobbes had considered a pack of wolves or other wild animals instead of the more gentle bees, he might have had more difficulty with his argument, for wolves, surely, are no less savage and violent than men. Do wolves and other wild animals 'herd' together simply because one wolf has 'acquired' a sovereignty which the other wolves acknowledge on account of his superior power? Or is there not also what some modern psychologists call a 'herd instinct'—a natural tendency which brings these animals together, which causes them to seek out and to enjoy the company of their fellows? Hobbes, indeed, pays his brief respects to this tendency towards communal living when he says of the bees and ants that "the agreement of these creatures is Naturall; that of men, is by Covenant only, which is Artificiall: and therefore it is no wonder if there be somwhat else required (besides Covenant) to make their Agreement constant and lasting; which is a Common Power, to keep them in awe, and to direct their actions to the Common Benefit." [2] But why is agreement 'natural' only among bees and ants? Why not also among the other animals and, indeed, among men themselves? If Hobbes had studied more carefully the much-scorned Aristotle, whom he is here attacking, he would have read that man, too, is "by nature a political animal"; [3] that is, that men naturally live together in families, tribes, or other social groups, and that they do this, as it were, instinctively, and not as the result of a process of ratiocination which brings originally isolated individuals together because each perceives it is to his individual advantage to join with the others in a social group. Such a process of ratiocination may, of course, occur subsequently and so reinforce this native

[1] *Leviathan*, Part II, chapter 17 (156).
[2] *Ibid.*, Part II, chapter 17 (157).
[3] *Politics* (translated by B. Jowett), I, 2 (1253a 3).

tendency to sociability; and this reinforcement may be inportant on occasions when the native tendency is opposed by an impulse to satisfy some selfish desire at the expense of social cohesion. But the process of ratiocination could never, of itself, produce that cohesion.

Many philosophers tend to exaggerate the role of reason in the determination of human conduct. They talk as if they believed men could detach their minds completely from their bodies, so as to be able to do whatever is ' reasonable,' unswayed by any irrelevant and extraneous feelings or desires. In the eighteenth century, for instance, philosophers maintained that men always act in accordance with enlightened self-interest—that they can " sit down in a cool hour," determine what is the reasonable course of action, and proceed to act in accordance with it. Hobbes never made this mistake of supposing that man is merely a thinking machine. He realized, as we have seen, that men are moved by all sorts of passions and desires which prevent perfect and passionless rationality, and, so far from exaggerating the role of reason, he tended on the whole to minimize its part in human behaviour.

Unfortunately, however, because he ignores all appetites and tendencies which might bring men together, and admits only the self-regarding ones which separate them, he has no other way of explaining the obvious fact of social and communal living save on the basis of the elements he has left at his disposal—namely, reason and the self-regarding appetites. Since he will not allow himself to say that men unite either from mutual sympathy and pleasure in each other's company or from an instinctive tendency to join together, the only course open to him (save in cases where men are brought together by a show of force) is to say that they combine as a result of an elaborate calculation by each of them of his own best interests in the long run. This means that Hobbes ends, despite his earlier and better insight, in attributing to man a degree of calm prudence and foresight which might have given pause even to the "Age of Reason," and which is, as we have already seen, ludicrously out of harmony with his original account of human nature.

We may conclude this long discussion by drawing together the various threads of the argument against Hobbes.

It might be the case, if men were as completely unscrupulous as Hobbes believes them to be, that only the brutal and ruthless exercise of force could keep them in order. However, in point of fact, most men do possess *some* scruples, do believe (even though they may be only suffering from a delusion) [1] that they have a duty to respect the rights of others. And besides being scrupulous, most men are kind-hearted, generous, and sympathetic—so that, for instance, they often make gifts to other men, not because they believe it to be to their interest to do so, but because they like them; and, frequently, men are modest because to be so is their nature, not because they judge they will get on better by an appearance of being so. This does not mean, of course, that men are always and inevitably socially minded. There are self-regarding tendencies in men which move them to anti-social conduct in the ways which Hobbes so powerfully described. Certainly, therefore, the exercise of force is on occasion required. No one would care to deny the need of assigning police powers to the sovereign, for there will always, presumably, be men who are unscrupulous and who apparently lack any particle of sympathy or fellow-feeling. However, because Hobbes does not see that such men are exceptions, because, in fact, he assumes that all men are at heart criminals and outlaws, he does not stop with police power, but assigns *unlimited* power to the sovereign. But the existence of the great democratic states, and their survival even in a world at war, is evidence that Hobbes is mistaken and that most men conform to law for reasons—whether these be a sense of duty, altruistic sentiments, social feelings, or only habit and inertia—other than because they are compelled to do so.

Finally, since Hobbes admitted the phenomenon of sovereignty by institution—*i.e.*, by the free choice of the subjects—we had to ask not only whether men in fact require to be ruled by force, but also whether they could and would establish a supremely powerful sovereign. We saw that a completely selfish calculation of their own private interests would hardly lead men to the conclusion that they require such a sovereign and that, in any case, even if reason led them to this conclusion, being creatures of passion rather than purely rational beings, they could not in fact bring themselves so to surrender themselves to authority.

So far we have considered merely whether men need an absolute sovereign and, if so, whether they will institute him. We must now

---

[1] It is important to see that this criticism of Hobbes is valid independently of whether or not there actually are rights which it is our duty to respect. Even if no such rights really exist it is an obvious fact that many men believe them to, and that their conduct is influenced by this consideration. The point here simply is that men's behaviour is influenced by all sorts of factors (of which a sense of duty is one) other than selfish calculations of interest, on which alone Hobbes insists to the exclusion of everything else.

consider a somewhat different question: whether such a sovereign as Hobbes conceives him to be could actually perform the functions which men require of him. In other words, even if men need some one to keep them in order the question still remains whether this can be done successfully by the Hobbesian sovereign, who rules by the exercise of force and force alone. It may be doubted whether, if Hobbes's account of human nature is correct, even the ruthless exercise of unlimited power could ever produce socially cohesive conduct —at least over any considerable period. In point of fact, the exercise of force succeeds, where it does succeed, only because there are other factors in human nature than fear and desire for private gain, which of themselves tend to social cohesion. And actual sovereigns have always maintained themselves in power by appealing to, or playing upon, these tendencies, besides making use of force.

In the formal account of his sovereign Hobbes seems to imply that terror, or the threat of terror, which his unlimited power inspires, is a sufficient instrument in the hands of a sovereign. But in actual practice he admits not only that some sovereigns are much more efficient than others, quite apart from their use of terror, but also that sovereigns have at their disposal many other means, of which one of the chief is religion and religious superstitions, for maintaining order among their subjects and themselves in power. We may now consider briefly what Hobbes has to say on both of these points.

Types of Sovereign

Hobbes admits only three types of sovereignty, and of these he thinks, and argues at length, that monarchy is by far the most efficient.[1]

¶ The difference of Common-wealths, consisteth in the difference of the Soveraign, or the Person representative of all and every one of the Multitude. And . . . it is manifest, there can be but Three kinds of Common-wealth. For the Representative must needs be One man, or More: and if more, then it is the Assembly of All, or but of a Part. When the Representative is One man, then is the Common-wealth a MONARCHY: when an Assembly of All that will come together, then it is a DEMOCRACY, or Popular Common-wealth: when an Assembly of a Part onely, then it is called an ARISTOCRACY. Other kind of Common-wealth

[1] *Leviathan*, Part II, chapter 19 (171*ff.*).

¶ there can be none: for either One, or More, or All, must have the Soveraign Power (which I have shewn to be indivisible) entire.

There be other names of Government, in the Histories, and books of Policy; as *Tyranny*, and *Oligarchy*: But they are not the names of other Formes of Government, but of the same Formes misliked. For they that are discontented under *Monarchy*, call it *Tyranny*; and they that are displeased with *Aristocracy*, called it *Oligarchy*: So also, they which find themselves grieved under a *Democracy*, call it *Anarchy* (which signifies want of Government); and yet I think no man believes, that want of Government, is any new kind of Government: nor by the same reason ought they to believe, that the Government is of one kind, when they like it, and another, when they mislike it, or are oppressed by the Governours. . . .

. . . where there is already a Soveraign Power, there can be no other Representative of the same people, but onely to certain particular ends, by the Soveraign limited. For that were to erect two Soveraigns; and every man to have his person represented by two Actors, that by opposing one another, must needs divide that Power, which (if men will live in Peace) is indivisible; and thereby reduce the Multitude into the condition of Warre, contrary to the end for which all Soveraignty is instituted. And therefore as it is absurd, to think that a Soveraign Assembly, inviting the People of their Dominion, to send up their Deputies, with power to make known their Advise, or Desires, should therefore hold such Deputies, rather than themselves, for the absolute Representative of the people: so it is absurd also, to think the same in a Monarchy. And I know not how this so manifest a truth, should of late be so little observed; that in a Monarchy, he that had the Soveraignty from a descent of 600 years, was alone called Soveraign, had the title of Majesty from every one of his Subjects, and was unquestionably taken by them for their King, was notwithstanding never considered as their Representative; that name without contradiction passing for the title of those men, which at his command were sent up by the people to carry their Petitions, and give him (if he permitted it) their advise. Which may serve as an admonition, for those that are the true, and absolute Representative of a People, to instruct men in the nature of that Office, and to take heed how they admit of any other generall Representation upon any occasion whatsoever, if they mean to discharge the trust committed to them.

¶   The difference between these three kindes of Common-wealth, consisteth not in the difference of Power; but in the difference of Convenience, or Aptitude to produce the Peace, and Security of the people; for which end they were instituted. And to compare Monarchy with the other two, we may observe; First, that who-soever beareth the Person of the people, or is one of that Assembly that bears it, beareth also his own naturall Person. And though he be carefull in his politique Person to procure the common interest; yet he is more, or no lesse carefull to procure the private good of himselfe, his family, kindred and friends; and for the most part, if the publique interest chance to crosse the private, he preferrs the private: for the Passions of men, are commonly more potent than their Reason. From whence it follows, that where the publique and private interest are most closely united, there is the publique most advanced. Now in Monarchy, the private interest is the same with the publique. The riches, power, and honour of a Monarch arise onely from the riches, strength and reputation of his Subiects. For no King can be rich, nor glorious, nor secure; whose Subjects are either poore, or contemptible, or too weak through want, or dissention, to maintain a war against their enemies: Whereas in a Democracy, or Aristocracy, the publique prosperity conferres not so much to the private fortune of one that is corrupt, or ambitious, as doth many times a perfidious advice, a treacherous action, or a Civill warre.

Secondly, that a Monarch receiveth counsell of whom, when, and where he pleaseth; and consequently may heare the opinion of men versed in the matter about which he deliberates, of what rank or quality soever, and as long before the time of action, and with as much secrecy, as he will. But when a Soveraigne Assembly has need of Counsell, none are admitted but such as have a Right thereto from the beginning; which for the most part are of those who have beene versed more in the acquisition of Wealth than of Knowledge; and are to give their advice in long discourses, which may, and do commonly excite men to action, but not governe them in it. . . .

Thirdly, that the Resolutions of a Monarch, are subject to no other Inconstancy, than that of Humane Nature; but in Assem-blies, besides that of Nature, there ariseth an Inconstancy from the Number. For the absence of a few, that would have the Resolution once taken, continue firme (which may happen by security, negli-gence, or private impediments), or the diligent appearance of a

¶ few of the contrary opinion, undoes to-day, all that was concluded yesterday.

Fourthly, that a Monarch cannot disagree with himselfe, out of envy, or interest; but an Assembly may; and that to such a height, as may produce a Civill Warre.

Fifthly, that in Monarchy there is this inconvenience; that any Subject, by the power of one man, for the enriching of a favourite or flatterer, may be deprived of all he possesseth; which I confesse is a great and inevitable inconvenience. But the same may as well happen, where the Soveraign Power is in an Assembly: For their power is the same; and they are as subject to evill Counsell, and to be seduced by Orators, as a Monarch by Flatterers; and becoming one another's Flatterers, serve one anothers Covetousnesse and Ambition by turnes. And whereas the Favourites of Monarchs, are few, and they have none els to advance but their owne Kindred; the Favourites of an Assembly, are many; and the Kindred much more numerous, than of any Monarch. ... .

Of all these Formes of Government, the matter being mortall, so that not onely Monarchs, but also whole Assemblies dy, it is necessary for the conservation of the peace of men, that as there was order taken for an Artificiall Man, so there be order also taken, for an Artificiall Eternity of life; without which, men that are governed by an Assembly, should return into the condition of Warre in every age; and they that are governed by One man, as soon as their Governour dyeth. This Artificiall Eternity, is that which men call the Right of *Succession*.

There is no perfect forme of Government, where the disposing of the Succession is not in the present Soveraign. For if it be in any other particular Man, or private Assembly, it is in a person subject, and may be assumed by the Soveraign at his pleasure; and consequently the Right is in himselfe. And if it be in no particular man, but left to a new choyce; then is the Common-wealth dissolved; and the Right is in him that can get it; contrary to the intention of them that did Institute the Common-wealth, for their perpetuall, and not temporary security.

In a Democracy, the whole Assembly cannot faile, unlesse the Multitude that are to be governed faile. And therefore questions of the right of Succession, have in that forme of Government no place at all.

In an Aristocracy, when any of the Assembly dyeth, the election

¶ of another into his room belongeth to the Assembly, as the Sove-raign, to whom belongeth the choosing of all Counsellours, and Officers. . . .

The greatest difficultie about the right of Succession, is in Mon-archy: And the difficulty ariseth from this, that at first sight, it is not manifest who is to appoint the Successor; nor many times, who it is whom he hath appointed. . . . As to the question, who shall appoint the Successor, of a Monarch that hath the Soveraign Authority; that is to say, who shall determine of the right of Inheritance, . . . we are to consider, that either he that is in posses-sion, has right to dispose of the Succession, or else that right is again in the dissolved Multitude. For the death of him that hath the Soveraign power in propriety, leaves the Multitude without any Soveraign at all; that is, without any Representative in whom they should be united, and be capable of doing any one action at all: And therefore they are incapable of Election of any new Monarch; every man having equall right to submit himselfe to such as he thinks best able to protect him; or if he can, protect himselfe by his owne sword, which is a returne to Confusion, and to the condition of a War of every man against every man, contrary to the end for which Monarchy had its first Institution. Therefore it is mani-fest, that by the Institution of Monarchy, the disposing of the Suc-cessor, is alwaies left to the Judgment and Will of the present Possessor. . . .

But where Testament, and expresse Words are wanting, other naturall signes of the Will are to be followed: whereof the one is Custome. And therefore where the Custome is, that the next of Kindred absolutely succeedeth, there also the next of Kindred hath right to the Succession; for that, if the will of him that was in possession had been otherwise, he might easily have declared the same in his life time.

Little need be said in criticism of the argument that monarchy is the most efficient form of sovereignty. If we allow Hobbes's premises about human nature, it is undoubtedly the case that sove-reignty in the hands of one man is the best, or, more precisely, that it is the least evil, alternative. It is perfectly clear that, if Hobbes's psychological theory is correct, the sovereignty of all would be anarchy. As we have seen, the whole basis for the argument in favour of any coercive power, and especially that in favour of absolute power, depends on men being incapable of ruling themselves. But to say that sovereignty is in the hands of all is simply another way of saying that men rule themselves.[1] Hobbes must surely have realized this and presumably included democracy as a possible alternative—despite its obvious impossibility on his theory—only because it would have looked bad to have omitted it altogether. Thus the question really is whether a tyranny or an oligarchy is better. Of these two, it certainly seems to be the case that men would live somewhat less wretchedly under the former if they were fortunate enough to have a choice in the matter, which, of course, in actual practice they would not have.

But, though Hobbes is convincing on the fact that monarchy is the lesser of two evils, he is hardly successful in maintaining, as he tries to do here, that men have a reasonable expectation of happiness under the rule of a king. The fact is that if Hobbes's account of human nature is correct man is so vile that happiness is not his lot. The very conditions of human nature make its attainment altogether impossible. Hobbes himself realized this.[2]

¶   Felicity of this life, consisteth not in the repose of a mind satisfied. For there is no such *Finis ultimus*, (utmost ayme,) nor *Summum Bonum*, (greatest Good,) as is spoken of in the Books of the old Morall Philosophers. Nor can a man any more live, whose Desires are at an end, than he, whose Senses and Imaginations are at a stand. Felicity is a continuall progresse of the desire, from one object to another; the attaining of the former, being still but the way to the later.

It is important to bear this in mind in criticizing Hobbes's argument. Of course, his account of human nature is exaggerated, as we have tried to suggest; but, if it be accepted provisionally for the sake of argument, much in his position that seems ridiculously far-fetched becomes not only plausible but simply plain good sense. For when a

[1] Of course, *if* sovereignty could be maintained in the hands of all, and not relapse into the hands of a majority which then exercised its authority in its own interest, no objection could be taken to the existence of an absolute sovereign. We should, in fact, then have what in theory a modern democratic power is: an institution in which supreme and un-limited power (unlimited except by the laws of nature and the law of God) resides in the people as a whole. It was precisely this problem of how to maintain sovereignty effectively in the hands of all with which, as we shall see, Rousseau was preoccupied (*vide infra*, pp. 308*ff.*).

[2] *Leviathan*, Part I, chapter 11 (85).

man is hopelessly ill his physician is justified in taking desperate measures. These will be unpleasant, even acutely painful, in their application; and even if they are successful we cannot, of course, hope for complete recovery: the patient will be fortunate to have a partial use of his limbs and may look forward to a severely limited and restricted mode of life. On the other hand, it is worth while using desperate remedies because the patient's life is at stake; and if they fail he will be no worse off than he would have been had nothing at all been done for him. In other words, we must not hope to do very much for a man who is lying between life and death. We must be content with redeeming his life for a little while, even if afterwards we have to hold it in pawn; and he should be grateful to us for that, since neither he nor we should expect miracles to occur for a man in his situation.

The Uses of Religion

Hobbes's chief argument in favour of monarchy comes to this, that in order to rule effectively the sovereign must be capable of vigorous, determined, and unified action. With sufficient power behind him, such a sovereign can, he thinks, survive internal as well as external opposition. But it is obviously more satisfactory for the sovereign if, instead of having constantly to use force against a dissident population, he is able to prevent his subjects from feeling that kind of dissatisfaction with their lot which leads to revolt. One way, of course, of accomplishing this would be actually to make them satisfied—i.e., to rule in their interest. And Hobbes does argue (if somewhat sophistically) that a king is more likely to rule in this way since his own private interest and the public interest do in fact coincide. Another way of accomplishing this is to give the appearance of ruling in the interest of one's subjects. One can, for instance, by making use of the Press and other modes of communication, educate the expectations of the public. This is why Hobbes emphasizes the importance, for the sovereign, of maintaining a close control over "opinions and doctrines." [1] He knows that contentment is relative to expectations and that a prudent and judicious moulding of public opinion could not only inculcate ideals of obedience and discipline, but also create a happy and satisfied attitude of mind in the public. Thus the mediæval peasant, the American Negro before the Civil War, or the

[1] *Leviathan*, Part II, chapter 18 (*cf. supra*, p. 120).

modern industrial labourer was on the whole content even with his poor lot, because society had educated him to look upon it as his due and to expect nothing more. The lower classes (and in the Hobbesian state this includes every one except the monarch himself) only become discontent when the sovereign is too weak, thoughtless, or otherwise incompetent to prevent a small minority of 'reformers' with advanced ideas from setting before the masses the ideals of a higher standard of living and of greater privileges than he is prepared or able to grant to them.

The only one of the great variety of instruments of education and of propaganda which Hobbes thoroughly investigates in the *Leviathan* is religion. The reasons for this predominance are probably chiefly historical. Hobbes felt that one of the principal causes of the civil war was religious in origin. He was not at all concerned with whether the papists, the Anglicans, or the presbyterians had the right of the matter. He probably regarded them all as equally deluded: being himself completely lacking in any religious feeling, he was utterly indifferent to all the doctrinal and dogmatic questions over which the men of his country had become so enraged that they were tearing each other to pieces in bloody civil strife. Looking at the matter with complete objectivity, he thought he could discern the difficulty. It was that the sovereign had allowed the sects a dangerous independence. In fact, the very existence of *sects*, of differences of opinion on religious questions, was itself evidence of the weakness and incompetence of the sovereign. Religious superstition (as Hobbes regarded it) is so powerful a drug that it constitutes an appalling menace to the very fabric of society unless its administration is carefully and scrupulously supervised. If religion, in the hands of a prudent sovereign, is a powerful instrument for social cohesion, it is an equally powerful divisive force when it passes out of his control. The condition of Europe in the preceding century, the long and bloody religious war which had disrupted the kingdom of France and the equally grievous disturbances which were even then rending his own country apart, were all evidence of what could happen when this force was permitted to play freely and without control upon the human heart or when, still worse, it fell into the hands of rival aspirants to the sovereignty and was used by them to further their own rebellious ends. This historical accident explains the severity, as it does the untoward length, of Hobbes's strictures on religion. He was, of course, entirely aware of the advantages to the sovereign himself of playing upon the religious feelings of his subjects, but, because in his own day he had witnessed the abuse of religion, he was content for the most part to warn his sovereign against its disadvantages by emphasizing its destructive power.

Hobbes begins with an account of the origins of religion in which he undertakes to trace its roots, not to conscience or some other *sui generis* faculty, but to the fear and egotism which for Hobbes together constitute the basic drives in human nature. Men fear many different sorts of things: snakes, water, the dark, death. The objects vary; the fear is the same. The only thing, therefore, which distinguishes religion from any other fear is the object which religious men fear. "*Feare* of power invisible, feigned by the mind, or imagined from tales publiquely allowed, [is] RELIGION; not allowed, SUPERSTITION."[1] It is true that, as a sop to the theologians, Hobbes adds, "And when the power imagined, is truly such as we imagine, TRUE RELIGION." After all a prudent man does not say in so many words all that he thinks, though Hobbes makes it plain in what follows, as we shall see, that "true religion" is in fact precisely whatever the sovereign decides it is—nothing more, nothing less. Thus Hobbes reveals his own attitude much more clearly when, a little later, he says that this "Feare of things invisible, is the naturall Seed of that, which every one in himself calleth Religion; and in them that worship, or feare that Power otherwise than they do, Superstition."[2]

Why is it that, although all living things are fearsome, religion, which is the fear of invisible things, should be peculiar, as it is, to men? Hobbes thinks an answer to this question will show in more detail what the origin (or as he calls it the "seeds") of religion are.[3]

¶ Seeing there are no signes, nor fruit of *Religion*, but in Man onely; there is no cause to doubt, but that the seed of *Religion* is also onely in Man; and consisteth in some peculiar quality, or at least in some eminent degree thereof, not to be found in other Living creatures.

And first, it is peculiar to the nature of Man, to be inquisitive into the Causes of the Events they see, some more, some lesse; but all men so much, as to be curious in the search of the causes of their own good and evill fortune.

Secondly, upon the sight of any thing that hath a Beginning, to

---

[1] *Leviathan*, Part I, chapter 6 (45).   [2] *Ibid.*, Part I, chapter 11 (93).
[3] *Ibid.*, Part I, chapter 12 (94 *ff.*).

¶think also it had a cause, which determined the same to begin, then when it did, rather than sooner or later.

Thirdly, . . . Man observeth how one Event hath been produced by another; and remembreth in them Antecedence and Consequence; And when he cannot assure himselfe of the true causes of things, (for the causes of good and evill fortune for the most part are invisible,) he supposes causes of them, either such as his own fancy suggesteth; or trusteth to the Authority of other men, such as he thinks to be his friends, and wiser than himselfe.

The two first, make Anxiety. For being assured that there be causes of all things that have arrived hitherto, or shall arrive hereafter; it is impossible for a man, who continually endeavoureth to secure himselfe against the evill he feares, and procure the good he desireth, not to be in a perpetuall solicitude of the time to come. . . . So that man, which looks too far before him, in the care of future time, hath his heart all the day long, gnawed on by feare of death, poverty, or other calamity; and has no repose, nor pause of his anxiety, but in sleep.

This perpetuall feare, always accompanying mankind in the ignorance of causes, as it were in the Dark, must needs have for object something. And therefore when there is nothing to be seen, there is nothing to accuse, either of their good, or evill fortune, but some *Power*, or Agent *Invisible*. . . .

. . . the worship which naturally men exhibite to Powers invisible, . . . can be no other, but such expressions of their reverence, as they would use towards men; Gifts, Petitions, Thanks, Submission of Body, Considerate Addresses, sober Behaviour, premeditated Words, Swearing (that is, assuring one another of their promises,) by invoking them. . . .

And in these . . . things . . . consisteth the Naturall seed of *Religion*; which by reason of the different Fancies, Judgments, and Passions of severall men, hath grown up into ceremonies so different, that those which are used by one man, are for the most part ridiculous to another.

For these seeds have received culture from two sorts of men. One sort have been they, that have nourished, and ordered them, according to their own invention. The other, have done it, by Gods commandement,[1] and direction; but both sorts have done it,

---

[1] This should be taken as another effort on Hobbes's part to appease the theologians, rather than as a serious assertion of his own view.

¶ with a purpose to make those men that relyed on them, the more apt to Obedience, Lawes, Peace, Charity, and civill Society. . . .

And therefore the first Founders, and Legislators of Commonwealths . . . , whose ends were only to keep the people in obedience, and peace, have in all places taken care; First, to imprint in their minds a beliefe, that those precepts which they gave concerning Religion, might not be thought to proceed from their own device, but from the dictates of some God, or other Spirit; or else that they themselves were of a higher nature than mere mortalls, that their Lawes might the more easily be received. . . . Secondly, they have had a care, to make it believed, that the same things were displeasing to the Gods, which were forbidden by the Lawes. Thirdly, to prescribe Ceremonies, Supplications, Sacrifices, and Festivalls, by which they were to believe, the anger of the Gods might be appeased; and that ill success in War, great contagions of Sicknesse, Earthquakes, and each mans private Misery, came from the Anger of the Gods; and their Anger from the Neglect of their Worship, or the forgetting, or mistaking some point of the Ceremonies required. . . .

And by these, and such other Institutions, they obtayned in order to their end, (which was the peace of the Commonwealth,) that the common people in their misfortunes, laying the fault on neglect, or errour in their Ceremonies, or on their own disobedience to the lawes, were the lesse apt to mutiny against their Governors. And being entertained with the pomp, and pastime of Festivalls, and publike Games, made in honour of the Gods, needed nothing else but bread, to keep them from discontent, murmuring, and commotion against the State. . . .

From the propagation of Religion, it is not hard to understand the causes of the resolution of the same into its first seeds, or principles; which are only an opinion of a Deity, and Powers invisible, and supernaturall; that can never be so abolished out of humane nature, but that new Religions may againe be made to spring out of them, by the culture of such men, as for such purpose are in reputation.

For seeing all formed Religion, is founded at first, upon the faith which a multitude hath in some one person, whom they believe not only to be a wise man, and to labour to procure their happiness, but also to be a holy man, to whom God himselfe vouchsafeth to declare his will supernaturally; It followeth neces-

¶ sarily, when they that have the Government of Religion, shall come to have either the wisedome of those men, their sincerity, or their love suspected; or that they shall be unable to shew any probable token of Divine Revelation; that the Religion which they desire to uphold, must be suspected likewise; and (without the feare of the Civill Sword) contradicted and rejected.

That which taketh away the reputation of Wisedome in him that formeth a Religion, or addeth to it when it is allready formed, is the enjoyning of a beliefe of contradictories: For both parts of a contradiction cannot possibly be true: and therefore to enjoyne the beliefe of them, is an argument of ignorance; which detects the Author in that; and discredits him in all things else he shall propound. . . .

That which taketh away the reputation of Sincerity, is the doing, or saying of such things, as appeare to be signes, that what they require other men to believe, is not believed by themselves; all which doings, or sayings are therefore called Scandalous, because they be stumbling blocks, that make men to fall in the way of Religion: as Injustice, Cruelty, Prophanesse, Avarice, and Luxury. For who can believe, that he that doth ordinarily such actions, as proceed from any of these rootes, believeth there is any such Invisible Power to be feared, as he affrighteth other men withall, for lesser faults?

That which taketh away the reputation of Love, is the being detected of private ends: as when the beliefe they require of others, conduceth or seemeth to conduce to the acquiring of Dominion, Riches, Dignity, or secure Pleasure, to themselves onely, or specially. For that which men reap benefit by to themselves, they are thought to do for their own sakes, and not for love of others.

Here, quite obviously, we have Hobbes's analysis of the causes of the Protestant Reformation. This turning away of a large part of Europe from Catholicism is only one example of the way in which the sovereign (who is, of course, also supreme head of the state religion) can lose control of the religious feelings of his people. He must, so far as possible, restrain discussion of the religious doctrines which he has promulgated, since (presumably) even the most carefully drawn up set of dogmas may reveal contradictions if open discussion of it is permitted. Indeed, "it is with the mysteries of our Religion, as with wholsome pills for the sick, which swallowed whole, have the vertue to cure; but chewed, are for the most part cast up again without effect." [1] For the same reason the sovereign will be well-advised to regard as a criminal offence any attempt, from within or without, to change the established religion or to introduce a new religion. In a word, any form of proselytism or of foreign mission is much too dangerous to the foundations of the state for the prudent sovereign to tolerate it. [2]

¶ If a man come from the *Indies* hither, and perswade men here to receive a new Religion, or teach them any thing that tendeth to disobedience of the Lawes of this Country, though he be never so well perswaded of the truth of what he teacheth, he commits a Crime, and may be justly punished for the same, not onely because his doctrine is false, but also because he does that which he would not approve in another, namely, that comming from hence, he should endeavour to alter the Religion there.

Finally, Hobbes is not content merely to point out the utilitarian advantages of rigorous control of religion by the sovereign. With an exegetical skill which would put most theologians to shame, he argues that Scripture itself supports this contention. [3]

¶ Where God saith to *Abraham*, *In thee shall all Nations of the earth be blessed: For I know thou wilt command thy children, and thy house after thee to keep the way of the Lord, and to observe Righteousnesse and Iudgment*, it is manifest, the obedience of his Family, who had no Revelation, depended on their former obligation to obey their Soveraign. At Mount Sinai *Moses* only went up to God; the people were forbidden to approach on paine of death; yet were they bound to obey all that *Moses* declared to them for Gods Law. Upon what ground, but on this submission of their own, *Speak thou to us, and we will heare thee: but let not God speak to us, lest we dye?* By which two places it sufficiently appeareth, that in a Common-wealth, a subject that has no certain and assured Revelation particularly to himself concerning the Will of God, is to obey for such the Command of the Common-wealth: for if men were at liberty, to take for Gods Commandements, their own dreams, and fancies, or the dreams and fancies of private men; scarce two men would agree upon

---

[1] *Leviathan*, Part III, chapter 32 (360).   [2] *Ibid.*, Part II, chapter 27 (279–280).
[3] *Ibid.*, Part II, chapter 26 (274–275).

¶ what is Gods Commandement; and yet in respect of them, every man would despise the Commandements of the Commonwealth.

One-sidedness of Hobbes's Psychological Theory

Whether Hobbes's whole political theory stands or falls depends (as is the case with every political theory) on whether the account he gives of human nature is essentially correct. Of course, this is by no means the only difficulty which a theory of politics has to encounter. We may have to reject some theory because of other flaws even if its psychological basis seems correct; but *no* political theory can possibly be valid unless that basis be true to human nature.

We have already said enough in criticism of Hobbes's psychology. It is not that what he says about human nature is false: man is an animal; he is selfish and fearsome. But, if man is an animal, he is a *human* animal, capable also of sympathy, generosity, kindness, and fellow-feeling. Hobbes goes wrong, not in what he affirms, but in what he denies. In exaggerating and over-emphasizing the weaknesses of man Hobbes gives a cynical picture of human nature, just as a writer like Rousseau, who tends to regard men as fundamentally and basically good, gives an idealistic picture of human nature, which errs almost as much in the other direction. Neither cynicism nor idealism furnishes a suitable basis for a political theory or for anything else; what we need is a more realistic account of human nature, like that of Aristotle, which, instead of over-simplifying in some one direction, shows man as the complex, complicated, and often contradictory creature that he really is.

All of the objections which we have had to raise against Hobbes have their origin in the one-sided view of human nature on which he insists. As long as he holds this position the political problem, as he understands it, is incapable of solution. For that problem is not merely how to maintain order (whether by the exercise of force or by other means), but how to make men happy and contented. Hobbes in effect has to admit this failure himself; for, although he thinks that order can be maintained by the exercise of force, he holds out no real hope that men can be made happy by even the most thorough and efficient exercise of force.

The truth is that there is a very profound contradiction in Hobbes's thought: the spirit in which Hobbes conceives the state's purpose really runs counter to the extreme naturalism of the position from which he begins. This appears in many ways. For instance, the concept of a contract implies (though Hobbes himself did not see this and therefore created many difficulties for himself) a humanistic rather than a naturalistic notion of human nature. In the first place, it means that Hobbes departs from the pure naturalistic thesis that might is right. In the long run, force does not justify itself for Hobbes, since, as we have seen, he tries (even though unsuccessfully) to justify the use of force by means of a utilitarian argument which purports to show that it is to our own best interest to submit to it. Moreover, the concept of a contract really involves the belief that there do exist certain rights and corresponding duties which belong to man as such; that we are on occasion capable both of recognizing these rights and duties and of attempting to implement the former and to carry out the latter. For Hobbes to say that a contract is *possible* means, as we have seen, that men are not merely the creatures of blind and completely selfish passion, but that they are capable of reasonable conduct: of enlightened self-interest and of an altruistic point of view. Again, for Hobbes to urge that a contract is *desirable* means that the end in view is a common end, the peace of *all*. In a word, if we press the implications of Hobbes's insistence on a social contract we get a view of human nature fundamentally opposed to the one he formally adopts. We see man as being not merely passionate, but reasonable. We see him not as a ruthless egoist, thinking only of himself and standing only in temporary, artificial, and external relations to other men; but as a social animal, taking delight in the society of his fellows, finding pleasure and happiness in intercourse with them, and realizing his own good, also, in promoting theirs.

This does not mean, certainly, that the political problem is solved the moment we correct Hobbes's one-sided psychology and substitute a free contract for the exercise of brute force. On the contrary, the problem still exists and still admits of a variety of solutions, two of which we shall examine presently in the writings of Locke and of Rousseau. What it means is that, if our various criticisms are valid, this rigorous and thorough-going attempt to develop a naturalistic political theory has failed. We certainly cannot infer from this that every naturalistic theory must equally fail, for naturalism is not committed to maintaining that there are but two basic drives and that these are fear and selfishness. But we can infer that a consistent naturalism must lead inevitably to the concept of a totalitarian state—*i.e.*, to the concept of a state whose end and *raison d'être* is not the well-being of all the individuals who constitute it, but the private happiness of their rulers.

We should not identify this totalitarian state with one in which there exists a strong, central authority possessing supreme power. It is true, of course, that such an authority exists in the totalitarian state, but the converse proposition does not hold: a strong sovereign is not necessarily totalitarian. Hobbes's insistence on the supremacy of the sovereign is only the echo of the *Zeitgeist's* footsteps passing through the corridors of his observant mind. It was almost inevitable that a seventeenth-century political writer should emphasize this aspect of sovereignty. For this was the period in which the foundations of the modern national and territorial state were hewn out in blood and tears, and Hobbes only assigns to the sovereign powers sufficient for it to achieve the destiny already marked out for it.

A theory is not totalitarian because of the range of powers assigned to the sovereign (or else *every* modern theory would be totalitarian), but because of the nature of the sovereign to whom these powers are given and the end for which he is given them. Hobbes begins where every naturalist begins: with a low, black view of human nature. But he refuses to end altogether where the naturalist logically must end: in the view that force is the supreme and final arbiter of men's fate and that justice is the interest of the stronger. This inconsistency is doubtless a credit to Hobbes's much-abused moral sense; but what is more important is the example and the warning which it constitutes for us. What makes the study of Hobbes so instructive to-day is precisely the fact that we cannot read him without seeing dramatically before us the consequences of maintaining that man is *merely* an animal—a lesson which is all the more striking when we also observe that even Hobbes found these consequences too serious and too costly for him to be able to remain consistently a naturalist until the end.

FOR FURTHER READING

Texts

See footnote, p. 86.

Commentaries and General Works

LAIRD, J.: *Hobbes* (Benn, 1934).
    A sound and readable discussion of Hobbes's philosophy.
STEPHEN, L.: *Hobbes* (Macmillan, 1904).

STRAUSS, L.: *The Political Philosophy of Hobbes* (Oxford University Press, 1936).

>An interesting attempt to show the roots of Hobbes's theory—partly in his reading, partly in his character.

Other Contemporary Theories

GOOCH, G. P.: *The History of English Democratic Ideas in the Seventeenth Century* (Cambridge University Press, 1927).

>A useful book on the century as a whole.

MILTON, JOHN: *Areopagitica* and *The Doctrine and Discipline of Divorce*.

SPINOZA, BENEDICTUS DE : *Tractatus Politicus*, in *Chief Works of Spinoza* (translated by R. H. M. Elwes, Bohn, Second edition, 1887).

>An interesting view, in many ways parallel to that of Hobbes.

CHAPTER FIVE

John Locke

(1632–1704)

LIFE

DURING the period covered in this volume England produced but two political theorists of the first rank. And during this period the gentle meanderings of English political life, the still pools of English social institutions, were but twice broken by the violent eddies and whirlpools of revolution. Each of these occasions (as if to emphasize the intimate dependence in which even the most speculative of philosophies always stands to the changing world of events) marks the emergence of one of these two political thinkers.[1] The careers of Hobbes and Locke are, indeed, in more ways than one curiously parallel. It is not only the case that each of them lived through a period of civil disturbance and revolution. Each of them, also, although he had to flee his country and take refuge on the Continent because of his political beliefs, managed to end his days at home in peaceful sympathy with the government in power; and each of them, again, composed a great work on the nature of politics which seems to us to have grown largely out of reflection on his experiences in revolution. Thus the analogies are striking. Nevertheless, the doctrines which were thus produced by the Civil War and the Glorious Revolution are so different as to furnish to the detractors of political theory one of their favourite arguments for demonstrating the relativity and, thereby, the supposed uselessness, of philosophy. But, although political thought naturally does not develop in a vacuum, and although it would certainly be useless if it did so, we must observe that the influence of environment in moulding the character of a given theory is

---

[1] When the Revolution across the Channel in France seemed likely to have serious repercussions in England there appeared another thinker on political subjects. But Burke can no more be ranked with Hobbes and Locke than can the political events in England at the end of the eighteenth century be classed with the momentous occurrences at the middle and at the end of the seventeenth century. *Vide infra*, chapter 8.

by no means so simple or so direct as some people would like to believe.

Thus, if we believe that we can find the sources of Hobbes's theory simply in his experiences in revolution, we could logically expect Locke, since he lived through two revolutions, to take an even blacker view of human nature than did Hobbes. For the evil years before the bloodless revolution which dethroned James cost Locke his patron and his place, and for a time exiled him from his home, while his experiences as a child in the Civil War were probably far unhappier than those of Hobbes, who spent his time pleasantly and comfortably among the *savants* of Paris. Locke's father, for his part, sided actively with Parliament against the King; and since the West Country, where the Lockes lived, was mainly Royalist, the family suffered considerably before the cause that they supported was finally victorious.[1]

On the other hand, if we look for the origins of a theorist's conception of human nature in his own temperament, we should expect to find that Locke, even more than Hobbes, took selfish fear as a primary human motive. For Locke shows himself to have been, if anything, more fearsome and cautious than Hobbes. Thus, for instance, when Monmouth's rebellion failed in 1685 Locke was accused (probably without justification) of having supported him against James II; and, although at that time Locke was safe in friendly Holland, he took extraordinary precautions for his protection, even going to the length of adopting an assumed name. But here, again, the facts do not support what is *prima facie* an equally plausible thesis. For, instead of adopting the cynical, Hobbesian view of human nature, Locke held that men are basically decent, orderly, socially minded, and quite capable of ruling themselves.

The problem of accounting for this, in terms of Locke's life and surroundings, is, therefore, by no means a simple one. We can, however, put first in time, if not in importance, the influence exercised by his father. In the second *Treatise of Government*,[2] as we shall

[1] According to Lady Masham, who ought to have known, Locke's father was a "private sufferer" by the "public calamities" of the war. *Vide* the account in *The Life of John Locke*, by H. R. Fox Bourne (Harper, 2 vols., 1876), I, 6*ff.*

[2] Locke wrote two essays on the nature of government which were published together under the general title, *Two Treatises of Government. In the Former, The false Principles and Foundations of Sir Robert Filmer, and his Followers, are Detected and Overthrown. The Latter, is an Essay Concerning the True Original, Extent, and End of Civil Government.* The interest of the former is slight, since the arguments of Sir Robert Filmer and his followers are remembered to-day only because Locke thought they warranted attack. All of our extracts, therefore, are drawn from the second of the treatises. The version given here follows

see,[1] as well as elsewhere, Locke's accounts of family life show better than almost anything else could, the essential humaneness of his view of human nature. We cannot doubt that this conception is based on his own experience with his father. In her account of his life, his friend, Lady Masham, wrote that he "never mentioned [his father] but with great respect and affection. His father used a conduct towards him when young that he often spoke of afterwards with great approbation. It was the being severe to him by keeping him in much awe and at a distance when he was a boy, but relaxing, still by degrees, of that severity as he grew up to be a man, till, he being capable of it, he lived perfectly with him as a friend. And I remember he has told me that his father, after he was a man, solemnly asked his pardon for having struck him once in a passion when he was a boy." [2]

Next we must speak of Locke's friends. It is true, of course, that Locke must have had the kind of disposition which made people love him; but what is effect can also be cause. There is no doubt that the existence of this wide circle of warm and enduring friendships must itself in turn have contributed to his sympathetic view of human nature. Everywhere he went he made friends—at Westminster School; at Christ Church, Oxford, where he was educated and where he subsequently held a studentship; [3] in his long career in the service of the Earl of Shaftesbury, who looked upon him as friend and confidant, rather than as a paid employee; [4] in Holland, where he spent the years of his exile; [5] at Oates, the Masham place, where he passed the

(except for the correction of a few obvious typographical errors) the text printed in the third edition of Locke's *Works* (3 vols., 1727). References in the footnotes are to chapters and paragraphs, however, instead of to the paging of this edition.

[1] *Vide infra*, pp. 157*ff.*

[2] Quoted in Fox Bourne, I, 13.

[3] Locke held this position until he was removed from it by order of Charles II, in 1684, because the King objected to his political views.

[4] According to the third Earl, "Mr Locke grew so much in esteem with my grandfather that, as great a man as he experienced him in physic, he looked upon this as but his least part. He encouraged him to turn his thoughts another way; nor would he suffer him to practise physic except in his own family, and as a kindness to some particular friend. He put him upon the study of the religious and civil affairs of the nation, with whatsoever related to the business of a Minister of State, in which he was so successful that my grandfather soon began to use him as a friend, and consult with him on all occasions of that kind." (Quoted in Fox Bourne, I, 198.)

[5] In the excitement of leaving Holland to return to England in the party of the Princess Mary, who was about to ascend the throne with her husband, William of Orange, Locke nevertheless found time to write to a Dutch friend: "In going away I feel as though I were leaving my own country and my own kinsfolk: for everything that belongs to kinship, goodwill, love, kindness—everything that binds men together with ties stronger than the ties of blood—I have found among you in abundance. I leave behind me friends whom I can never forget and I shall never cease to wish for an opportunity of coming back to enjoy once more the genuine fellowship of men who have been such friends that, while

last years of his life happily and peacefully, surrounded by a circle of devoted friends. Nothing expresses the character of this life better than Locke's manner of leaving it. One of the last tasks with which he busied himself was the planning of elaborate celebrations in honour of the marriage of his nephew. And a month later, on October 28, after he had drunk the health of his friends, and Lady Masham had read to him from the Psalms, he closed his eyes and passed quietly away. No more fitting epitaph for him could be found than that contained in a letter by Lady Masham. "His death," she wrote, "was like his life, truly pious, yet natural, easy and unaffected; nor can time, I think, ever produce a more eminent example of reason and religion than he was, living and dying." [1]

Thus Locke had ample opportunity in his youth [2] to see the raw and vicious aspects of human nature and, in his age, to have this impression confirmed during the years of distress which followed Shaftesbury's fall from favour, as well as in the political career which both preceded and followed the interval of exile. Again, the ill health which pursued him throughout his life might have excused an embittered attitude towards life. Nevertheless he managed, through all this, to see enough native goodness and kindness in his fellow-men not to turn on them the jaundiced and cynical eyes of a Hobbes. This is all-important, because his political theory—his conception of the kind of government which men need and require—was naturally inevitably based upon his notion of what men are like.

And this conception of what men are like was, it must have seemed to Locke, completely confirmed and vindicated by the events of the year 1688. In this year the people, in effect, dismissed one sovereign for incompetence and, with a minimum of disturbance, elected another who, as they believed, would perform his proper functions efficiently and whom they could trust to recognize the rights and privileges which they claimed for themselves. The accession of William and Mary was thus a triumph for democracy and for the thesis that sovereigns rule by the consent and for the benefit of their

far away from all my own connexions, while suffering in every other way, I have never felt sick at heart. As for you, best, dearest, and most worthy of men, when I think of your learning, your wisdom, your kindness and candour and gentleness, I seem to have found in your friendship alone enough to make me always rejoice that I was forced to pass so many years amongst you." (Quoted in R. I. Aaron, *John Locke* (Oxford University Press, 1937), pp. 25–26.)

[1] Quoted in Fox Bourne, II, 560.

[2] At Westminster School Locke was only just around the corner from the place of the King's execution and may well have witnessed that momentous act.

subjects. It seemed to Locke to vindicate his belief in the ability of the people to rule themselves. It completely disproved Hobbes's conception of man as blindly irrational and utterly and narrowly selfish. It showed men to be possessed of a social sense which naturally brings them together, so that the pressure of force is not required to keep them from each other's throats. It was concrete evidence of the fact that men are sufficiently reasonable to see that their best interest lies in mutual and peaceful co-operation and of the fact that they have a sufficiently rational will to act in accordance with what they see to be good. This, at least, is the conclusion Locke drew from the Glorious Revolution, and thus, though in a sense it is true to say that the second *Treatise* was intended to 'justify' the Revolution,[1] it is even truer to say that the Revolution justifies the *Treatise*.

POLITICAL PHILOSOPHY

As we have just seen, Locke's political theory, like that of Hobbes, rests on a certain conception of human nature. This not only determines, at the moral level, the end or purpose for which the state exists, but also, at the psychological level, the means (*i.e.*, the precise form of state organization recommended in the theory) for attaining this end. Locke and Hobbes agree about the end for the sake of which a state exists: it is the peace, security, and well-being of its individual members; but they disagree fundamentally about the way in which this end can best be attained, because their conceptions of human motivation differ so profoundly.

Let us consider each of these points briefly. We can re-state the first by saying that Locke agrees with Hobbes in presenting a *teleological* account of the state. The state serves a purpose, is directed towards an end. Actually, each of them argues that, at least on occasion, this end is before men as a self-conscious and deliberate plan, whose execution they undertake by co-operative action together. But there is no reason why a teleological conception of the state need involve the notion of an explicit contract. Aristotle is a case in point. Political organization may be conceived to be a natural growth and at the same

---

[1] In the preface to the *Two Treatises of Government* Locke makes it clear that his aim in writing them is to help to "establish the Throne of our great Restorer, our present King *William* . . . and to justify to the World the People of England, whose love of their just and natural Rights, with their resolution to preserve them, saved the Nation when it was on the very Brink of Slavery and Ruin."

time be regarded as subserving a purpose. In such a case teleology appears only as the sense that the existence of states, however naturally they came into being *in fact*, requires a *moral* justification. The teleological theorist, in other words, distinguishes between what is the case and what ought to be the case. He starts from the assumption that every individual has certain rights, even if these rights are not in fact recognized. He starts, in Aristotelian language, from the position that there is for every individual an ideal end which he may not in fact have realized, but which he has it in him to realize if his environment permits it. However naturally and inevitably states may come into being without being planned by anybody, it is nevertheless the case, objectively considered, that their existence is morally justifiable only if, and so far as, they create the kind of environment in which men can realize their end, only if they implement the rights which men own and so permit them to live a good life. This is the position of Locke and of Hobbes, just as much as it is that of Aristotle.

We have seen that a basic contradiction occurs in Hobbes's thought because he attempts to combine this essentially moral, or humanistic, attitude with a pure, straightforward naturalism in human psychology. Locke's theory, on the other hand, avoids this contradiction because his psychological theory is humanistic in character. That is to say, instead of maintaining that man is merely an animal—a centre of blind passions which are entirely self-regarding and which recognize only the law of force—Locke holds that man is a moral and a social animal.

Conception of Human Nature

This psychological theory is never set out formally and explicitly as Hobbes set out his in Book I of *The Leviathan*, but we can easily collect Locke's conception of human nature from numerous passages in the second *Treatise*. For instance, his account of what he calls "paternal power"—*i.e.*, of the right relationship between parents and children—shows clearly his conception of human nature as it is and as it ought to be. To begin with we must observe that all men are born equal.[1]

¶ All Men are naturally in . . . a *State* . . . of *Equality*, wherein all the Power and Jurisdiction is reciprocal, no one having more than

[1] *Of Civil Government* (*vide supra*, p. 152, note 2), II, 4; IV, 21.

¶another; there being nothing more evident than that Creatures of the same Species and Rank, promiscuously born to all the same Advantages of Nature, and the Use of the same Faculties, should also be equal one amongst another without Subordination or Subjection. . . . The *Natural Liberty* of Man is to be free from any superior Power on Earth, and not to be under the Will or Legislative Authority of Man, but to have only the Law of Nature for his Rule.

Such statements do not mean, as similar ones meant for Hobbes, that men's physical and mental powers are pretty much equal. They mean that every individual counts as one and is therefore, morally, the equal of every other; that he has rights which belong to him simply as a human being and not because of his pre-eminence in strength, wealth, or position, and which all other individuals ought to recognize, just as he ought to recognize theirs. What Locke is stating is, in a word, the view which Kant formulated at the end of the eighteenth century in his "categorical imperative":

¶ Rational beings . . . are called *persons*, because their very nature points them out as ends in themselves, that is as something which must not be used merely as means. . . . These, therefore, are not merely subjective ends whose existence has a worth *for us* as an effect of our action, but *objective ends*, that is things whose existence is an end in itself. . . . Accordingly the [categorical] imperative will be as follows: *So act as to treat humanity, whether in thine own person or in that of any other, in every case as an end withal, never as means only.*[1]

Thus men's physical powers and capacities, as well as their actual status and conditions, have nothing whatever to do with their moral equality: they *ought* to be equal even if *in fact* they are not. In a word, men are morally equal if, and just as soon as, reason in them, which makes them persons, is sufficiently developed for them to recognize those natural laws which define their rights and duties. This means that children occupy a very special place in Locke's state. Not yet possessed of fully developed reason, they cannot be said to have the rights and duties of citizens. For, coming into the world [2]

[1] *Grundlegung zur Metaphysik der Sitten* (translated by T. K. Abbott, *Kant's Theory of Ethics*, Longmans, 1927, pp. 46–47).
[2] *Of Civil Government*, VI, 57 and 59.

¶ignorant and without the Use of *Reason*, they [are] not presently *under that* [*i.e.*, the natural] *Law*; for no body can be under a Law which is not promulgated to him; and this Law being promulgated or made known by *Reason* only, he that is not come to the Use of his *Reason* cannot be said to be *under this* Law [and so is] not presently *free*. For *Law*, in its true Notion, *is* not so much the Limitation as *the Direction of a free and intelligent Agent* to his proper Interest, and prescribes no farther than is for the general Good of those under that Law: Could they be happier without it, the *Law*, as an useless Thing, would of it self vanish; and that ill deserves the Name of Confinement which hedges us in only from Bogs and Precipices. So that, however it may be mistaken, *the End of Law is* not to abolish or restrain, but to *preserve and enlarge Freedom*. For in all the States of created Beings capable of Laws, *where there is no Law there is no Freedom*. For *Liberty* is to be free from Restraint and Violence from others, which cannot be, where there is no Law: But Freedom is not, as we are told, *A Liberty for every Man to do what he lists*. . . . But a *Liberty* to dispose and order as he lists his Person, Actions, Possessions, and his whole Property within the Allowance of those Laws under which he is, and therein not to be subject to the arbitrary Will of another, but freely follow his own. . . .

This holds in all the Laws a Man is under, whether Natural or Civil. Is a Man under the Law of Nature? *What made him free* of that Law? What gave him a free disposing of his Property, according to his own Will, within the Compass of that Law? I answer, a State of Maturity, wherein he might be supposed capable to know that Law, that so he might keep his Actions within the Bounds of it. When he has acquired that State, he is presum'd to know how far that Law is to be his Guide, and how far he may make use of his *Freedom*, and so comes to have it; till then, some body else must guide him, who is presum'd to know how far the Law allows a Liberty.

If, therefore, children are not born *in* a state of freedom and equality, because their rational powers are not fully developed, they are born *to* such a state, because these powers will be developed. Hence they are obviously not—any more than are grown men—merely animals, which it is right and proper to compel by force. They have, indeed, to be ruled, since they cannot yet rule themselves; but, if they are ruled, it is not by the threat of terror exercised by an arbitrary sovereign, but by the kindness of a loving parent.[1]

¶ Though I have said above, *Chapter 2, That all Men by Nature are equal*, I cannot be supposed to understand all sorts of *Equality*. *Age* or *Virtue* may give Men a just Precedency. *Excellency of Parts* and *Merit* may place others above the common Level. *Birth* may subject some, and *Alliance* or *Benefits* others to pay an Observance to those to whom Nature, Gratitude, or other Respects may have made it due; and yet all this consists with the *Equality* which all Men are in, in respect of Jurisdiction or Dominion one over another, which was the *Equality* I there spoke of as proper to the Business in Hand, being that *equal Right*, that every Man hath, *to his natural Freedom*, without being subjected to the Will or Authority of any other Man.

Children, I confess, are not born in this full State of *Equality*, though they are born to it. Their Parents have a sort of Rule and Jurisdiction over them when they come into the World, and for some time after, but 'tis but a temporary one. The Bonds of this Subjection are like the Swadling-Cloaths they are wrapt up in, and supported by in the Weakness of their Infancy: Age and Reason, as they grow up, loosen them, till at length they drop quite off, and leave a Man at his own free Disposal.

... To supply the Defects of this imperfect State, till the Improvement of Growth and Age had removed them, ... all *Parents* [are] by the Law of Nature, *under an Obligation to preserve, nourish, and educate the Children* they [have] begotten, not as their own Workmanship, but the Workmanship of their own Maker the Almighty, to whom they were to be accountable for them. ...

The *Power* then *that Parents have* over their Children, arises from that Duty which is incumbent on them, to take Care of their Offspring, during the imperfect State of Childhood. To inform the Mind, and govern the Actions of their yet ignorant Nonage, till Reason shall take its Place, and ease them of that Trouble, is what the Children want, and the Parents are bound to. ...

[1] *Of Civil Government*, VI, 54–56, 58, 60, 61, 63–64, 66–67.
What is said here about children applies *mutatis mutandis*, as the nineteenth century was quick to find out, to savages and to less-developed peoples generally. As exploration and discovery increasingly gave place to colonization and expansion, the great imperial powers had to justify to themselves their dominion over other peoples. Thus Kipling's sense of "the white man's burden," the notion in America of the Indians as the "wards of the nation," and the League theory of mandates are nothing but logical extensions of Locke's idea.

¶   But if, through Defects that may happen out of the ordinary Course of Nature, any one comes not to such a Degree of Reason, wherein he might be supposed capable of knowing the Law, and so living within the Rules of it, he is *never capable of being a Freeman*, he is never let loose to the Disposure of his own Will, (because he knows no Bounds to it, has not Understanding, its proper Guide) but is continued under the Tuition and Government of others, all the Time his own Understanding is uncapable of that Charge. And so *Lunaticks* and *Ideots* are never set free from the Government of their Parents. . . . All which seems no more than that Duty which God and Nature has laid on Man, as well as other Creatures, to preserve their Offspring, till they can be able to shift for themselves, and will scarce amount to an Instance or Proof of *Parents* Regal Authority.[1]

Thus we are *born free*, as we are born rational; not that we have actually the Exercise of either: Age that brings one, brings with it the other too. And thus we see how *natural Freedom and Subjection to Parents* may consist together, and are both founded on the same Principle. . . .

The *Freedom* then of Man, and Liberty of acting according to his own Will, is *grounded on* his having *Reason*, which is able to instruct him in that Law he is to govern himself by, and make him know how far he is left to the Freedom of his own Will. To turn him loose to an unrestrain'd Liberty before he has Reason to guide him, is not the allowing him the Privilege of his Nature to be free; but to thrust him out amongst Brutes, and abandon him to a State as wretched, and as much beneath that of a Man, as theirs. This is that which puts the *Authority* into the *Parents* Hands to govern the *Minority* of their Children. . . .

But what Reason can hence advance this Care of the *Parents* due to their Offspring into an *absolute arbitrary Dominion* of the Father, whose Power reaches no farther, than by such a Discipline, as he finds most effectual, to give such Strength and Health to their Bodies, such Vigour and Rectitude to their Minds, as may best fit his Children to be most useful to themselves and others. . . .

But though there be a Time when a *Child* comes to be . . . *free* from Subjection to the Will and Command of his Father . . . , and they are each under no other Restraint, but that which is common to them both, whether it be the Law of Nature, or municipal Law of

---

[1] By "regal" authority Locke means an absolute and unlimited exercise of power.

¶ their Country: Yet this Freedom exempts not a Son from that *Honour* which he ought, by the Law of God and Nature, *to* pay his *Parents.* God having made the Parents Instruments in his great Design of continuing the Race of Mankind, and the Occasions of Life to their Children; as he hath laid on them an Obligation to nourish, preserve, and bring up their Offspring, so he has laid on the Children a perpetual Obligation of *honouring their Parents,* which containing in it an inward *Esteem* and Reverence to be shewn by all outward Expressions, ties up the Child from any thing that may ever injure or affront, disturb or endanger the Happiness or Life of those from whom he received his; and engages him in all Actions of Defence, Relief, Assistance and Comfort of those, by whose Means he entered into Being, and has been made capable of any Enjoyment of Life. From this Obligation no State, no Freedom can absolve Children. But this is very far from giving Parents a Power of Command over their Children, or an Authority to make Laws and dispose, as they please, of their Lives or Liberties. 'Tis one thing to owe Honour and Respect, Gratitude and Assistance; another to require an absolute Obedience and Submission. . . .

The want of distinguishing these two Powers, *viz.,* That which the Father hath in the Right of *Tuition* during Minority, and the Right of *Honour* all his Life, may perhaps have caused a great part of the Mistakes about this Matter. For to speak properly of them, the first of these is rather the Privilege of Children, and Duty of Parents, than any Prerogative of Paternal Power. The Nourishment and Education of their Children is a Charge so incumbent on Parents for their Childrens Good, that nothing can absolve them from taking Care of it. And tho' the *Power of Commanding and Chastising* them go along with it, yet God hath woven into the Principles of human Nature such a Tenderness for their Offspring, that there is little Fear that Parents should use their Power with too much rigour. The Excess is seldom on the severe Side, the strong Byass of Nature drawing the other Way. And therefore God Almighty when he would express his gentle Dealing with the *Israelites,* he tells them, that tho' he chasten'd them, *he chasten'd them as a Man chastens his Son,* Deut. 8. 5.—*i.e.*, with Tenderness and Affection, and kept them under no severer Discipline than what was absolutely best for them, and had been less Kindness to have slacken'd. . . .

Thus the relations between parent and child, between child and parent and, for that matter, between every man and every other man, are *humane*. This means, to begin with, that there is a moral order in which men participate and to which, therefore, their lives ought to correspond. It also means that, being rational, they are capable of recognizing the existence of this order and of their duty to conform to it. It means, finally, that men are moved by sympathy, love, and tenderness to perform such socially cohesive acts, even when and if they do not recognize that they have a duty to do so. In a word, man, as Locke conceives him, differs from man, as Hobbes conceives him, in the first place simply in this, that for Hobbes man is merely an animal and a creature of nature, while for Locke he is also a member of a moral order and subject to a moral (and in this sense, natural) law. Doubtless this moral law is only an 'ought': it states not the way in which men do behave, but the way in which they *ought* to behave. Locke was certainly realist enough to see that men do not always, or even very often, do what they ought. But this in itself is enough to distinguish man from the other animals: in their case an 'ought' is meaningless; being irrational, the moral law simply does not apply to them. Moreover, the fact that Locke's man is thus subject to a moral order also distinguishes him from Hobbes's man at the merely psychological level. For, while Hobbes's man is moved solely by animal considerations of bodily comfort, Locke's man hears, and sometimes, at least, heeds, the voice of duty; and, while Hobbes's man is always utterly selfish, Locke's is sometimes really altruistic.

It is obvious that, from such a basis as this, Locke must develop a conception of the state very different from that of Hobbes. Since men are naturally humane, since it is natural for them to live in relative peace and harmony with their fellows, Locke conceives of life without a state as being by no means intolerable. It follows that, if political life is to appeal, if the formation of a state is to be justified, it must produce considerable positive benefits. Since, for Hobbes, life without the state is nasty, poor, short and brutish, any state, however bad, is better than no state. Therefore the sovereign does not have to justify himself to those over whom he rules. For Locke, on the other hand, since we can easily get on without a state, since we establish it, not because we require it, but because we expect "certain conveniences" from it, we need not continue in it unless it actually produces the results which we anticipate in setting it up. Thus, though both Hobbes and Locke use a strictly utilitarian argument to justify their respective state organizations, they reach radically different conclusions about the kind of organization which utilitarian considerations can justify. Hobbes thinks that they justify (and indeed make expedient) an absolute and unlimited monarch. Locke thinks that utility can justify only a sovereign whose conduct is limited by the same moral order in which his subjects share, whose sole *raison d'être* is to produce the various conveniences which those subjects desire, and whose continuance as sovereign is conditional upon his willingness and ability to perform this function.

The Foundation of States based upon Right and Justice

Before, however, we can consider in detail the form of political organization which Locke recommends, we must ask what he means by the *state of nature* which he describes as preceding that organization and the *contract* which he says creates it. This analysis will lead, on the one hand, to the notion of an ideal moral order to which political organizations ought to correspond, and, on the other hand, to the concept of the *consent* of every individual member of the state as being that which makes its particular organization right and just.

Much ink has been wasted in efforts to determine whether or not the various contract theorists (among them, Hobbes, Locke, and Rousseau) thought that the state of nature and the contract which they write about are, or were, actual and historical occurrences. If this question has seemed much more difficult to answer than it actually is the contract theorists are themselves at least partially to blame, for they, like their critics, have failed to see that the question as stated is ambiguous and really involves several quite separate problems.

It is clear, of course, that what Locke has to say about the contract is closely related to what he says about the state of nature; but it is important, if we wish to understand his discussion, to keep the two subjects clearly separated.

(a) The State of Nature

In the first place, although the contract theorists may well have believed in the historicity of the state of nature, they are on the whole not so much interested in describing an historical fact as they are in asserting the existence of a moral fact. To-day we mean by natural law, or the law of nature, a generalized and abstract set of formulæ which describe the behaviour of various parts of the physical world —we call the law of gravity a natural law because it describes the ways in which particles actually do move. On the other hand, Locke means by the natural law, as we have seen, a rule for human behaviour only, and one which is not a description of how men do behave, but a statement of how they ought to behave. Hence by his state of nature, paradoxically enough, Locke primarily means something which is *not* natural or historical.[1] By saying, for instance, that in a state of nature men are free and equal he does not merely mean that there was a time in the past when men were in fact free and equal; he means rather to assert that they ought to be free and equal.

In the second place, however, the state of nature is not merely a general description of how men should behave: it is a description of how men should behave *if* there were not, as in fact there is to-day, political authority. Thus the obligations which men have in the state of nature differ in some respects from the obligations which men have in an organized political state. For instance, in a state of nature and in a political state alike murder is wrong, and a murderer ought, therefore, to be punished. In the state of nature, where no constituted political authority exists, this is the duty of the individual man; but in a political state this duty devolves upon the political authority, which should execute justice, the individual's duty being merely to help that authority in the exercise of its function.[2]

¶   Though this [*i.e.*, the state of nature] be *a State of Liberty*, yet *it is not a State of License*; though Man in that State have an uncontroulable Liberty to dispose of his Person or Possessions, yet he has not Liberty to destroy himself, or so much as any Creature in his Possession, but where some nobler Use than its bare Preservation calls for it. The *State of Nature* has a Law of Nature to govern it, which obliges every one: And Reason, which is that Law, teaches

---

[1] To say that Locke's interest in the historicity of the state of nature and of the contract is secondary to his interest in the moral relation which he thought ought to exist between men, does not mean, of course, that he did not also hold that they were historical. When we come to consider the nature of the contract we shall see Locke specifically asserting its occurrence. But even here his chief interest is not to show that there was an original union of primitive men ages ago by means of a contract, but to point out that states have been founded by contracts in historical times. In other words, his chief interest is not, as his critics suppose it to be, to assert a ridiculous original contract. It is rather to show that the Hobbesian position (which denies that men are sufficiently rational to organize themselves into states) is proven false by historical facts. *Vide infra*, pp. 173–174, and passages quoted there.

[2] *Of Civil Government*, II, 6–8, 10–13.

¶ all Mankind, who will but consult it, that being all *equal and independent*, no one ought to harm another in his Life, Health, Liberty, or Possessions. For Men being all the Workmanship of one Omnipotent and infinitely wise Maker . . . and being furnished with like Faculties, sharing all in one Community of Nature, there cannot be supposed any such *Subordination* among us, that may authorize us to destroy one another, as if we were made for one another's Uses, as the inferior Ranks of Creatures are for ours. . . .

And that all Men may be restrained from invading others' Rights, and from doing hurt to one another, and the Law of Nature be observed, which willeth the Peace and *Preservation of all Mankind*, the *Execution* of the Law of Nature is in that State put into every Man's Hand, whereby every one has a Right to punish the Transgressors of that Law to such a Degree as may hinder its violation. . . .

And thus in the State of Nature, *one Man comes by a Power over another*; but yet no absolute or arbitrary Power, to use a Criminal, when he has got him in his Hands, according to the passionate Heats or boundless Extravagancy of his own Will; but only to retribute to him, so far as calm Reason and Conscience dictate, what is proportionate to his Transgression, which is so much as may serve for *Reparation and Restraint*. For these two are the only Reasons, why one Man may lawfully do harm to another, which is that we call *Punishment*. In transgressing the Law of Nature, the Offender declares himself to live by another Rule than that of common Reason and Equity, which is that Measure God has set to the Actions of Men for their mutual Security; and so he becomes dangerous to Mankind, the Tie, which is to secure them from Injury and Violence, being slighted and broken by him. . . .

Besides the Crime which consists in violating the Law, and varying from the right Rule of Reason, whereby a Man so far becomes degenerate, and declares himself to quit the Principles of human Nature, and to be a noxious Creature, there is commonly *Injury* done some Person or other, some other Man receives Damage by his Transgression; in which case he who hath received any Damage, has besides the right of Punishment common to him with other Men, a particular Right to seek *Reparation* from him that has done it. And any other Person who finds it just, may also join with him that is injur'd, and assist him in recovering from the Offender so much as may make Satisfaction for the harm he has suffered.

¶ . . . And thus it is, that every Man in the State of Nature, has a Power to kill a Murderer, both *to deter* others from doing the like Injury, . . . and also to secure Men from the attempts of a Criminal, who having renounced Reason, the common Rule and Measure God hath given to Mankind, hath by the unjust Violence and Slaughter he hath committed upon one, declared War against all Mankind, and therefore may be destroyed as a *Lion* or a *Tyger*, one of those wild savage Beasts, with whom Men can have no Society nor Security: And upon this is grounded that great Law of Nature, *whoso sheddeth Man's Blood, by Man shall his Blood be shed.* . . .

By the same Reason, may a Man in the State of Nature *punish the lesser Breaches* of that Law. It will perhaps be demanded, With Death? I answer, each Transgression may be *punished* to that *degree*, and with so much *Severity*, as will suffice to make it an ill Bargain to the Offender, give him cause to repent, and terrify others from doing the like. Every Offence that can be committed in the State of Nature, may in the State of Nature be also punished equally, and as far forth as it may in a Commonwealth. For though it would be beside my present Purpose, to enter here into the Particulars of the Law of Nature, or its *Measures of Punishment*; yet it is certain there is such a Law, and that too as intelligible and plain to a rational Creature, and a Studier of that Law, as the positive Laws of Commonwealths; nay possibly plainer; as much as Reason is easier to be understood, than the Fancies and intricate Contrivances of Men, following contrary and hidden Interests, put into Words; for so truly are a great part of the *municipal Laws* of Countries, which are only so far right, as they are founded on the Law of Nature, by which they are to be regulated and interpreted.

. . . I doubt not but it will be objected, that it is unreasonable for Men to be Judges in their own Cases, that Self-love will make Men partial to themselves and their Friends: And on the other side, that ill Nature, Passion and Revenge will carry them too far in punishing others; and hence nothing but Confusion and Disorder will follow; and that therefore God hath certainly appointed Government to restrain the Partiality and Violence of Men. I easily grant, that *Civil Government* is the proper Remedy for the Inconveniencies of the State of Nature, which must certainly be great, where Men may be Judges in their own Case, since 'tis easie to be imagined, that he who was so unjust as to do his Brother an

¶Injury, will scarce be so just as to condemn himself for it: But I shall desire those who make this Objection, to remember, that *absolute Monarchs* are but Men; and if Government is to be the Remedy of those Evils which necessarily follow from Men's being Judges in their own Cases, and the State of Nature is therefore not to be endured, I desire to know what kind of Government that is, and how much better it is than the State of Nature, where one Man commanding a Multitude, has the Liberty to be Judge in his own Case, and may do to all his Subjects whatever he pleases, without the least question or controll of those who execute his Pleasure? And in whatsoever he doth, whether led by Reason, Mistake or Passion, must be submitted to? Which Men in the State of Nature are not bound to do one to another: And if he that judges, judges amiss in his own or any other Case, he is answerable for it to the rest of Mankind.

Although what Locke means by the state of nature is thus an ideal moral order, the question may still be raised, of course, whether this moral order does in fact exist, or ever has existed; just as we may both assert that I have a duty to keep my promise to so-and-so and ask whether I have in fact done so. Now, in a number of passages Locke clearly claims that this state of nature has existed, and this seems hopelessly unhistorical unless we see that Locke does not mean to claim that there was once a time when all men did their duties and when they lived in perfect peace and harmony with their neighbours. It is rightly pointed out by Locke's critics that the conception of a Golden Age is mistaken, and that, if we have to choose between them, Hobbes's notion of a war of all against all is nearer to the truth. Unfortunately, however, for his critics, Locke did not mean anything of the sort. What he meant to assert (though it must be confessed that he did not say so very plainly) was something quite different—that there have been periods in which men have not lived under *political* institutions. Defining 'political' as Locke does, this assertion is obviously true and cannot be for a moment denied.

¶   Political power [he says [1]] I take to be a Right of making Laws with Penalties of Death, and consequently all less Penalties, for the regulating and preserving of Property, and of employing the Force of the Community in the Execution of such Laws, and in

[1] *Of Civil Government*, I, 3.

¶ the Defence of the Commonwealth from Foreign Injury, and all this only for the Publick Good.

Indeed, when political power is defined in this way it is clear that men, so far from having never lived in a state of nature, have actually been in a state of nature much oftener than in a political state. Locke does not for a moment mean to claim that men have ever lived alone, separate and isolated existences. He insists just as much as ever Aristotle did on the fact that man is naturally gregarious. We are told, for instance,[1]

¶ God having made Man such a Creature, that in his own Judgment it was not good for him to be alone, put him under strong Obligations of Necessity, Convenience, and Inclination, to drive him into *Society*, as well as fitted him with Understanding and Language to continue and enjoy it. The *first Society* was between Man and Wife, which gave beginning to that between Parents and Children; to which in time, that between Master and Servant came to be added: And though all these might, and commonly did meet together, and make up but one Family, wherein the Master or Mistress of it had some Sort of Rule proper to a Family; each of these, or all together, came short of *Political Society*. . . .

No more, again, does Locke mean to deny that the societies or communities in which men have always lived have at all times been divided into those who rule and those who are ruled. What he asserts is merely the obvious truth that those who rule have not always governed with the consent of their subjects nor in their interest.

Thus what Locke means by saying that even in his own day nations, if not individual men, still live in a state of nature is simply that no institutions exist of which the various states are members and to whose authority they are subordinate. This does not mean that they do not have duties towards each other (whether they actually conform to their duties is, of course, another matter); they do have such duties, but these are the duties of autonomous and independent individual states over whom there is no law except the law of nature and no magistrate save their own consciences.[2]

---

[1] *Of Civil Government*, VII, 77.
[2] *Ibid.*, II, 14.
Hobbes makes precisely the same point: "But though there had never been any time, wherein particular men were in a [state of nature]; yet in all times, Kings, and Persons of

¶ 'Tis often asked as a mighty Objection, *where are*, or ever were, there any *Men in such a State of Nature*? To which it may suffice as an Answer at present: That since all Princes and Rulers of *Independent* Governments all through the World are in a State of Nature, 'tis plain the World never was, nor ever will be, without Numbers of Men in that State. I have named all Governors of *Independent Communities*, whether they are, or are not, in League with others. For 'tis not every Compact that puts an end to the state of Nature between Men, but only this one of agreeing together mutually to enter into one Community, and make one *Body Politick*; other Promises and Compacts Men may make one with another, and yet still be in the State of Nature. The Promises and Bargains for Truck, etc. between the two Men in the desert Island, . . . or between a *Swiss* and an *Indian* in the woods of *America*, are binding to them, though they are perfectly in a State of Nature in Reference to one another. For Truth, and keeping of Faith, belong to Men as Men, and not as Members of Society.

To those that say, There were never any men in the State of Nature, I will . . . affirm, That all Men are naturally in that State, and remain so, till by their own Consents they make themselves Members of some politick Society. . . .

(b) The Contract

This brings us to the contract by means of which, according to Locke, men pass out of a state of nature into a political state.[1]

¶ Man being born, as has been proved, with a Title to perfect Freedom, and an uncontrolled Enjoyment of all the Rights and Privileges of the Law of Nature, equally with any other Man or Number of Men in the World, hath by Nature a Power, not only to preserve his Property, that is, his Life, Liberty, and Estate, against the Injuries and Attempts of other Men; but to judge of, and punish the Breaches of that Law in others. . . . But . . . there,

Soveraigne authority, because of their Independency, are in continuall jealousies, and in the state and posture of Gladiators; having their weapons pointing, and their eyes fixed on one another; that is, their Forts, Garrisons, and Guns upon the Frontiers of their Kingdoms; and continuall Spyes upon their neighbours; which is a posture of War" (*Leviathan*, Part I, chapter 13 (115)). It should, of course, not be forgotten that the state of nature which Hobbes thus demonstrates is "a condition of war," not, as it is for Locke, a state of relative peace and goodwill.

[1] *Of Civil Government*, VII, 87 and 89.

¶ and there only is *Political Society*, where every one of the Members hath quitted this natural Power, resign'd it up into the Hands of the Community in all Cases that exclude him not from appealing for Protection to the Law established by it. And thus all private Judgment of every particular Member being excluded, the Community comes to be Umpire . . . and . . . decides all the Differences that may happen between any Members of that Society concerning any Matter of Right; and punishes those Offences which any Member hath committed against the Society, with such Penalties as the Law has established. . . .

Wherever therefore any Number of Men are so united into one Society, as to quit every one his executive Power of the Law of Nature, and to resign it to the Publick, there and there only is a *Political or Civil Society*. And this is done wherever any number of Men in the State of Nature, enter into Society to make one People, one Body Politick, under one supreme Government; or else when any one joins himself to, and incorporates with any Government already made. For hereby he authorises the Society, or which is all one, the Legislative thereof, to make Laws for him as the publick Good of the Society shall require; to the Execution whereof, his own Assistance . . . is due. And this *puts Men* out of a State of *Nature into* that of a *Commonwealth*, by setting up a Judge on Earth, with Authority to determine all the Controversies, and redress the Injuries that may happen to any Member of the Commonwealth; which Judge is the Legislative, or Magistrate appointed by it. And wherever there are any number of Men, however associated, that have no such decisive Power to appeal to, there they are still in *the State of Nature*.

It follows from this that there is but one way that political societies may be founded: by consent.[1]

¶　Men being, as has been said, by Nature all free, equal, and independent, no one can be put out of this Estate, and subjected to the political Power of another, without his own Consent. The only Way whereby any one divests himself of his natural Liberty, and puts on the *Bonds of civil Society*, is by agreeing with other Men to join and unite into a Community, for their comfortable, safe, and peaceable living one amongst another, in a secure Enjoyment

[1] *Of Civil Government*, VIII, 95–99.

¶ of their Properties, and a greater Security against any that are not of it. This any Number of Men may do, because it injures not the Freedom of the rest; they are left as they were in the Liberty of the State of Nature. When any Number of Men have so *consented to make one Community or Government*, they are thereby presently incorporated, and make one *Body Politick*, wherein the *Majority* have a Right to act and conclude [for] the rest.

For when any Number of Men have, by the Consent of every Individual, made a *Community*, they have thereby made that *Community* one Body, with a Power to act as one Body, which is only by the Will and Determination of the *Majority*. For that which acts any Community, being only the Consent of the Individuals of it, and it being necessary to that which is one Body to move one Way, it is necessary the Body should move that Way whither the greater Force carries it, which is the *Consent of the Majority*: Or else it is impossible it should act or continue one Body, *one Community*. . . .

And thus every Man, by consenting with others to make one Body Politick under one Government, puts himself under an Obligation to every one of that Society, to submit to the Determination of the *Majority*, and to be concluded by it; or else this *original Compact*, whereby he with others incorporates into *one Society*, would signify nothing, and be no Compact, if he be left free, and under no other Ties, than he was in before in the State of Nature. . . .

For if *the Consent of the Majority* shall not, in Reason, be receiv'd, as *the Act of the Whole*, and conclude every Individual; nothing but the Consent of every Individual can make any Thing to be the Act of the Whole: But such a Consent is next to impossible ever to be had, if we consider the Infirmities of Health, and Avocations of Business, which in a Number, though much less than that of a Commonwealth, will necessarily keep many away from the publick Assembly. To which, if we add the variety of Opinions, and contrariety of Interest, which unavoidably happen in all Collections of Men, the coming into Society upon such Terms would be only like *Cato's* coming into the Theatre, only to go out again. . . .

Whosoever therefore out of a State of Nature unite into a *Community* must be understood to give up all the Power necessary to the Ends for which they unite into Society, to the *Majority* of the Community, unless they expressly agreed in any Number greater than the *Majority*.

In this passage Locke deals rather too facilely, and almost in passing, with one of the most serious problems which democratic societies have to face. A democracy is supposed, theoretically, to be the rule of all. It seems to be implied, therefore, that in a democracy every citizen shall consent to, and approve of, the acts which the community as a whole does. But, if a democracy has to wait upon the free consent of every one of its members, it is no democracy or indeed any government at all: it simply lapses into anarchy. On the other hand, if democracy be the rule of a majority, many men no longer rule themselves; and this kind of government is quite compatible with the most brutal and cruel of tyrannies. Since the solution of this problem was one of the chief undertakings of Rousseau, we may profitably postpone a detailed consideration of it until we consider his theory. But we may observe that Locke adduces two arguments in support of his thesis that consent means, not acceptance individually of each measure proposed, but consent to the will of the majority. The first argument is purely legalistic. Men have made a contract to form a political society. A society in which every one does precisely what he pleases is no different from the state of nature out of which they have wished to contract. Therefore, if they really wanted to leave the state of nature and to enter a political society we may assume that they must have meant to give up their liberty to do whatever they please; and this may be held to be tacitly implied in their original contract. The second argument is more simple: unless the whole community abides by the decision of the majority, even when it disapproves of that decision, the state will disintegrate. Since, in a word, we can never or only very rarely achieve unanimity, if the state is to act at all, it must conform to the will of the majority.

Neither of these arguments is very satisfactory, but what is interesting about them is the importance which we can infer that consent had for Locke. Why is Locke so anxious to prove that the citizen really is consenting, even when the government, acting in accordance with the decision of the majority, does something which he personally disapproves of? It is because he thinks no society is a political society unless it is founded upon the consent of its members. According to his view, only democratic societies are founded upon consent; but, even here, the objection might be raised that in democracies, just as much as in other societies, minorities are compelled. Hence, unless Locke wishes to admit the surprising conclusion that there are no political societies (since there are no societies all of whose acts are unanimously consented to), he has to show that minorities in democratic societies really are not compelled, since every individual tacitly agreed in the original contract to accept the decision of the majority in all cases. But this is hardly satisfactory, for the fact that men may have made an agreement (tacitly or otherwise) to accept the decision of the majority does not, unfortunately, ensure that they shall never find themselves compelled by the majority.

Locke does not deal with this question satisfactorily, because, although he recognizes the crucial importance of consent, he does not see the problems which it entails. The objection which he seems to feel most important and from which he is most anxious to defend himself is simply the criticism, which might be made from Hobbesian grounds, that the conception of consent is vague and utopian and that no societies founded on consent, in the sense defined, have ever existed. Now, whatever Locke may have held about the historicity of an original state of nature,[1] he definitely affirms that states have been founded by contract.

To the objection [2]

¶ that there are no Instances to be found in Story, of a Company of Men Independent, and equal one amongst another, that met together, and in this Way began and set up a Government, . . . there is this to answer, That it is not at all to be wonder'd, that *History* gives us but a very little *Account of Men that lived together in the State of Nature.* The Inconveniences of that Condition, and the love and want of Society, no sooner brought any Number of them together, but they presently united, and incorporated, if they design'd to continue together. And if we may not suppose *Men* ever to have been *in the State of Nature,* because we hear not much of them in such a State, we may as well suppose the Armies of *Salmanasser,* or *Xerxes* were never Children, because we hear little of them till they were Men, and embodied in Armies. Government is every where antecedent to Records, and Letters seldom come in amongst a People, till a long continuation of Civil Society has, by other more necessary Arts, provided for their Safety, Ease, and Plenty. And then begin to look after the History of their Founders, and search into their *Original,* when they have out-liv'd the Memory of it. For 'tis with Commonwealths as with particular Persons, they are commonly *ignorant of their own Birth and Infancies.* . . .

[1] *Vide supra,* pp. 163*ff.*   [2] *Of Civil Government,* VIII, 100–104.

¶ He must shew a strange Inclination to deny evident Matter of Fact, when it agrees not with his Hypothesis, who will not allow, that the *Beginning* of *Rome* and *Venice* were by the uniting together of several Men free and independent one of the other, amongst whom there was no natural Superiority or Subjection. And if *Josephus Acosta's* Word may be taken, he tells us, that in many Parts of *America*, there was no Government at all. . . . So that their *Politick Societies* all *began* from a voluntary Union, and the mutual Agreement of Men freely acting in the Choice of their Governors, and Forms of Government.

And I hope those who went away from *Sparta* with *Palantus*, mention'd by *Justin*, I. 3. c. 4. will be allow'd to have been *Freemen, Independent* one of another, and to have set up a Government over themselves, by their own Consent. Thus I have given several Examples out of History, of *People Free and in the State of Nature*, that being met together incorporated and *began a Commonwealth*. . . .

But to conclude, Reason being plainly on our Side that Men are naturally Free, and the Examples of History shewing, that the *Governments* of the World, that were begun in Peace, had their Beginning laid on that Foundation, and were *made by the Consent of the People*; there can be little Room for Doubt, either where the Right is, or what has been the Opinion or Practice of Mankind, about the *first erecting of Governments*.

Although some of Locke's examples are, to say the least, dubious, no one is likely to contest the truth of his claim that there are and have been societies founded on consent in the sense in which he understands it. The objection that is much more likely to be made is rather that most political societies have been founded and maintained by force, and that Locke simply ignores this fact. Or the same objection may be put by asking why it is that Locke defines political society in such a way as to exclude most societies which men ordinarily would call political. Unless Locke's position is to appear hopelessly absurd we must see that he was fully aware of the facts on which this objection rests. But they are simply irrelevant from his point of view. For, once again, Locke is drawing a distinction between what is and what ought to be, and, again, he is talking about what he thinks ought to be.

Thus Locke would not for a moment deny that most societies do, as a matter of fact, rest on force, not on consent. "I will not deny, that if we look back as far as History will direct us, towards the

Original of Commonwealths, we shall generally find them under the Government and Administration of one Man." [1] And this man, more often than not, is an absolute sovereign. But this simply means that things are not often as they ought to be. Might never makes right. No matter how long or how completely one man actually exercises power over others he is never morally justified in doing so unless they consent to his authority. Since a political society is a moral society, we simply cannot call such a society political.[2]

¶ Hence it is evident, that *Absolute Monarchy*, which by some Men is counted the only Government in the World, is indeed *inconsistent with Civil Society*, and so can be no Form of Civil Government at all.[3] For the *End of Civil Society*, being to avoid and remedy those Inconveniences of the State of Nature, which necessarily follow from every Man's being Judge in his own Case, by setting up a known Authority, to which every one of that Society may appeal upon any Injury received, or Controversy that may arise, and which every one of the Society ought to obey; wherever any Persons are, who have not such an Authority to appeal to, for the Decision of any Difference between them, there those persons are still *in the State of Nature*. And so is every *absolute Prince*, in respect of those who are under his *Dominion*.

[In fact a man's condition is far worse in an absolute monarchy than it is in the state of nature, for] whereas, in the ordinary State of Nature, he has a Liberty [4] to judge of his Right, and according to the best of his Power, to maintain it; now whenever his Property is invaded by the Will and Order of his Monarch, he has not only no Appeal, as those in the Society ought to have, but as if he were degraded from the common state of Rational Creatures, is denied a Liberty to judge of, or to defend his Right: and so is exposed to all the Misery and Inconveniences, that a Man can fear from one,

---

[1] *Of Civil Government*, VIII, 105.
Societies which are not 'bodies politic' may be founded by conquest, usurpation, or tyranny. For a discussion of these forms, *vide infra*, p. 184*ff*.
[2] *Of Civil Government*, VII, 90–93.
[3] This, of course, is directed against Hobbes. Absolute monarchy is inconsistent with civil society because the former is a rule of force, the latter a rule of right, founded upon consent.
[4] Here Locke distinguishes between 'right,' which is a moral claim, and 'liberty,' which is the actual state of affairs which implements this 'right.' His point is that while the right, of course, is the same in both cases, the state of affairs in the case of an absolute monarchy is such that men have less liberty to exercise their right than they would have in any other form of social organization.

¶ who being in the unrestrained state of Nature, is yet corrupted with Flattery, and armed with Power.

For he that thinks *absolute Power purifies Men's Bloods*, and corrects the Baseness of human Nature,[1] need read but the History of this, or any other Age to be convinced of the contrary. He that would have been insolent and injurious in the Woods of *America*, would not probably be much better in a Throne; where perhaps Learning and Religion shall be found out to justify all that he shall do to his Subjects, and the Sword presently silence all those that dare question it. . . .

In Absolute Monarchies indeed, as well as other Governments of the World, the Subjects have an Appeal to the Law, and Judges to decide any Controversies, and restrain any Violence that may happen betwixt the Subjects themselves, one amongst another. This every one thinks necessary. . . . But whether this be from a true Love of Mankind and Society, and such a Charity as we owe all one to another, there is Reason to doubt. For this is no more, than that every Man who loves his own Power, Profit, or Greatness, may and naturally must do, keep those Animals from hurting or destroying one another, who labour and drudge only for his Pleasure and Advantage; and so are taken care of, not out of any Love the Master has for them, but Love of himself, and the Profit they bring him. For if it be asked, what Security, *what Fence* is there, in such a State, *against the Violence and Oppression of this absolute Ruler*? The very Question can scarce be born. They are ready to tell you, that it deserves Death only to ask after Safety. Betwixt Subject and Subject, they will grant there must be Measures, Laws and Judges, for their mutual Peace and Security: But as for the Ruler, he ought to be *absolute*, and is above all such Circumstances; because he has Power to do more Hurt and Wrong, 'tis right when he does it. To ask how you may be guarded from Harm or Injury, on that side where the strongest Hand is to do it, is presently the Voice of Faction and Rebellion. As if when Men quitting the State of Nature enter'd into Society, they agreed that all of them but one should be under the Restraint of Laws, but that he should still retain all the Liberty of the State of Nature, increased

---

[1] Hobbes, against whom this argument is apparently directed, never maintained this. As we have seen (*supra*, pp. 125–126), Hobbes had no expectation that the monarch's native human baseness would be 'purified,' but he contended that even the basest monarch is better than the sovereign, however well intended, who lacks absolute power. Whether this argument is satisfactory is, of course, another question.

¶with Power, and made licentious by Impunity. This is to think that Men are so foolish that they take care to avoid what Mischiefs may be done them by *Pole-cats* or *Foxes*, but are content, nay, think it Safety, to be devoured by *Lions*.

There are, in a word, certain fundamental human rights. They belong to men just because, and in so far as, they are rational beings; and a society can be called a *civil* society, a body politic, only if its organization and institutions recognize and implement those rights. This means that the argument by which Locke justifies the existence of the state differs profoundly from that which Hobbes used. Locke criticizes Hobbes, in the passage we have just quoted, on the grounds that an absolute monarchy is not the kind of social organization which is likely to secure even the physical well-being of the community. But it is clear that the 'peace and security' which it is the state's end to produce has a deeper and more profound meaning for Locke than it has for Hobbes. Hobbes thinks of it chiefly in terms of relief from the constant fear of death and physical suffering which is our lot where there is no authority to keep us in order. But, for Locke, 'peace and security' means more than merely continued survival. It means the possession of certain 'conveniences' which we have a natural right to and which it is the function of the state's institutions to produce and maintain for us. Of these the chief is the enjoyment of the property which is fruit of our labour.[1]

Property

¶ Whether we consider natural *Reason* . . . or *Revelation* . . . , 'tis very clear that God, as King *David* says, *Psal.* 115. 16. *has given the Earth to the Children of Men*; given it to Mankind in common. But this being supposed, it seems to some a very great Difficulty, how any one should ever come to have a *Property* in any thing. . . .

God, who hath given the World to Men in common, hath also given them Reason to make use of it to the best Advantage of Life and Convenience. The Earth, and all that is therein, is given to Men for the Support and Comfort of their Being. And . . . all the Fruits it naturally produces, and Beasts it feeds, belong to Mankind in common, as they are produced by the spontaneous Hand of Nature; and no Body has originally a private Dominion, exclusive

[1] *Of Civil Government*, V, 25-29, 31-33, 40, 46-47.

¶ of the rest of Mankind, in any of them, as they are thus in their natural State. . . .

Though the Earth and all inferior Creatures be common to all Men, yet every Man has a *Property* in his own *Person*: This no Body has any Right to but himself. The *Labour* of his Body, and the *Work* of his Hands, we may say, are properly his. Whatsoever then he removes out of the State that Nature hath provided and left it in, he hath mixed his *Labour* with, and joined to it something that is his own, and thereby makes it his *Property*. It being by him removed from the common State Nature hath placed it in, it hath by this *Labour* something annexed to it, that excludes the common Right of other Men. For this *Labour* being the unquestionable Property of the Labourer, no Man but he can have a Right to what that is once joined to, at least where there is enough, and as good left in common for others.

He that is nourished by the Acorns he pick'd up under an Oak, or the Apples he gathered from the Trees in the Wood, has certainly appropriated them to himself. No Body can deny but the Nourishment is his. I ask then, When did they begin to be his? When he digested? Or when he eat? Or when he boiled? Or when he brought them home? Or when he pick'd them up? And 'tis plain, if the first Gathering made them not his, nothing else could. That *Labour* put a Distinction between them and common: That added something to them more than Nature, the common Mother of all, had done, and so they became his private Right. . . . The *Labour* that was mine, removing them out of that common State they were in, hath *fixed* my *Property* in them.

. . . Tho' the Water running in the Fountain be every ones, yet who can doubt, but that in the Pitcher is his only who drew it out? His *Labour* hath taken it out of the Hands of Nature, where it was common, and belong'd equally to all her Children, and *hath* thereby *appropriated* it to himself. . . .

It will perhaps be objected to this, That if gathering the Acorns, or other Fruits of the Earth, etc. makes a Right to them, then any one may *ingross* as much as he will. To which I answer, Not so. The same Law of Nature that does by this Means give us Property, does also *bound* that *Property* too. *God, who giveth us richly all things to enjoy* [I Tim. vi, 17[1]], is the Voice of Reason confirmed by Inspiration. But how far has he given it us? *To enjoy.* As much as any one can

---

[1] Locke gives this, incorrectly, as II Tim. vi, 12.

¶ make use of to any Advantage of Life before it spoils, so much he may by his Labour fix a Property in: Whatever is beyond this, is more than his Share, and belongs to others. Nothing was made by God for Man to spoil or destroy. And thus considering the Plenty of natural Provisions there was a long Time in the World, and the few Spenders, and to how small a Part of that Provision the Industry of one Man could extend it self, and ingross it to the Prejudice of others; especially keeping within the *Bounds* set by Reason, *of* what might serve for his *Use*; there could be then little Room for Quarrels or Contentions about Property so establish'd.

But the *chief Matter of Property* being now not the Fruits of the Earth, and the Beasts that subsist on it, but *the Earth it self*; as that which takes in, and carries with it all the rest; I think it is plain, that *Property* in that too is acquir'd as the former. *As much Land* as a Man tills, plants, improves, cultivates, and can use the Product of, so much is his *Property*. He by his Labour does, as it were, inclose it from the Common. . . .

Nor was this *Appropriation* of any Parcel of *Land*, by improving it, any Prejudice to any other Man, since there was still enough, and as good left, and more than the yet unprovided could use. So that in effect, there was never the less left for others because of his Inclosure for himself. For he that leaves as much as another can make use of, does as good as take nothing at all. No Body could think himself injur'd by the drinking of another Man, though he took a good Draught, who had a whole River of the same Water left him to quench his Thirst: And the Case of Land and Water, where there is enough of both, is perfectly the same. . . .

Nor is it so strange, as perhaps before Consideration it may appear, that the *Property of Labour* should be able to over-balance the Community of Land. For 'tis *Labour* indeed that *puts the Difference of Value* on every thing; and let any one consider what the Difference is between an Acre of Land planted with Tobacco or Sugar, sown with Wheat or Barley; and an Acre of the same Land lying in Common without any Husbandry upon it, and he will find that the Improvement of *Labour makes* the far greater Part of the Value. . . .

The greatest Part of *Things really useful* to the Life of Man, . . . *are* generally Things of *short Duration*; such as if they are not consumed by Use, will decay and perish of themselves: Gold, Silver and Diamonds, are Things that Fancy or Agreement hath put the

¶Value on, more than real Use, and the necessary Support of Life. Now of those good Things which Nature hath provided in Common, every one had a Right (as hath been said) to as much as he could use, and *Property* in all he could effect with his Labour; all that his Industry could extend to, to alter from the State Nature had put it in, was his. He that *gathered* a hundred Bushels of Acorns or Apples, had thereby a *Property* in them, they were his Goods as soon as gathered. He was only to look, that he used them before they spoiled, else he took more than his Share, and robb'd others. And indeed it was a foolish thing, as well as dishonest, to hoard up more than he could make use of. If he gave away a Part to any body else, so that it perished not uselessly in his Possession, these he also made use of. And if he also bartered away Plumbs, that would have rotted in a Week, for Nuts that would last good for his eating a whole Year, he did no Injury; he wasted not the common Stock; he destroy'd no Part of the Portion of Goods that belonged to others, so long as nothing perished uselesly in his Hands. Again, if he would give his Nuts for a Piece of Metal pleased with its Colour; or exchange his Sheep for Shells, or Wool for a sparkling Pebble or a Diamond, and keep those by him all his Life, he invaded not the Right of others, he might heap up as much of these durable Things as he pleased; the *exceeding of the Bounds of* his *just Property* not lying in the Largeness of his Possession, but the perishing of any thing uselesly in it.

And thus *came in the Use of Money*, some lasting thing that Men might keep without spoiling, and that by mutual Consent Men would take in exchange for the truly useful but perishable Supports of Life.

We can only admire the ingenuity with which Locke manages to justify an unequal distribution of the world's goods despite his original premise of perfect human equality, even if the case in the end turns out to be far more complicated than he seems to have realized. Locke can maintain his position with considerable success so long as he conceives of private property as justified only so far as it is the product of every man's own labour and is limited to what he can use; for, as Locke points out, with these restrictions no one will have a right to very much property and there will be ample for every one. But obviously, while such a definition of property is suitable for some simple, agrarian society, it would satisfy no one in the England of

Locke's day. Therefore, unless he wished to be merely utopian, it was necessary for him considerably to expand the definition he started out from. He does this by introducing the concept of money, which he says gives men a way of storing up property without wastage and thereby removes the difficulty involved in owning more than one can use oneself. In the laws by which they establish and regulate a currency, "governments," he says, have "found out a Way how a Man may fairly possess more . . . than he himself can [make use of] by receiving . . . Gold and Silver, which may be hoarded up without Injury to any one; these Metals not spoiling or decaying in the Hands of the Possessor." [1] Certainly it is true that gold does not decay as, say, grain does, and that, therefore, the man who takes gold for his surplus grain does not injure others as does the man who simply lets his surplus rot away in his barns. But wastage of their surplus goods is surely by no means the only way in which men can injure others. It is not obviously self-evident that men who build up great fortunes do not, in doing so, whether deliberately or not, prevent others from exercising their full rights. Since many economists, on the contrary, maintain that precisely this is the case, Locke's argument is, therefore, incomplete until he can show that they are mistaken.

Without considering any further Locke's analysis of property, we may pass on to the argument by which he attempts to justify the existence of the state on the ground that it maintains men in their rights to their property.[2]

¶ If Man in the State of Nature be so free, as has been said; if he be absolute Lord of his Own Person and Possessions, equal to the greatest and subject to no Body, why will he part with his Freedom? Why will he give up this Empire, and subject himself to the Dominion and Controul of any other Power? To which 'tis obvious to answer, that though in the State of Nature he hath such a Right, yet the Enjoyment of it is very uncertain, and constantly exposed to the Invasions of others. For all being Kings as much as he, every Man his equal, and the greater Part no strict Observers of Equity and Justice, the Enjoyment of the Property he has in this State, is very unsafe, very unsecure. This makes him willing to quit this Condition, which however free, is full of Fears and continual Dangers; and 'tis not without Reason, that he seeks out, and is willing to join in Society with others, who are already united, or

[1] *Of Civil Government*, V, 50.   [2] *Ibid.*, IX, 123-131.

¶ have a mind to unite, for the mutual *Preservation* of their Lives, Liberties, and Estates, which I call by the general Name, *Property*.

The great and *chief End* therefore, of Men's uniting into Commonwealths, and putting themselves under Government, *is the Preservation of their Property*. To which in the State of Nature there are many Things wanting.

First, There wants an *establish'd*, settled, known *Law*, received and allow'd by common Consent to be the Standard of Right and Wrong, and the common Measure to decide all Controversies between them. For though the Law of Nature be plain and intelligible to all rational Creatures; yet Men being biassed by their Interest, as well as ignorant for want of Study of it, are not apt to allow of it as a Law binding to them in the Application of it to their particular Cases.

Secondly, In the State of Nature there wants *a known and indifferent Judge*, with Authority to determine all Differences according to the establish'd Law. For every one in that State, being both Judge and Executioner of the Law of Nature, Men being partial to themselves, Passion and Revenge is very apt to carry them too far, and with too much Heat in their own Cases; as well as Negligence and Unconcernedness, to make them too remiss in other Men's.

Thirdly, In the State of Nature there often wants *Power* to back and support the Sentence when Right, and to *give* it due *Execution*. They who by any Injustice offend, will seldom fail, where they are able, by Force to make good their Injustice; such Resistance many times makes the Punishment dangerous, and frequently destructive to those who attempt it.

Thus Mankind, notwithstanding all the Privileges of the state of Nature, being but in an ill Condition, while they remain in it, are quickly driven into Society. Hence it comes to pass, that we seldom find any Number of Men live any time together in this State. The Inconveniencies that they are therein exposed to, by the irregular, and uncertain Exercise of the Power every Man has of punishing the Transgressions of others, make them take Sanctuary under the establish'd Laws of Government, and therein seek *the Preservation of their Property*. 'Tis this makes them so willingly give up every one his single Power of punishing, to be exercised by such alone, as shall be appointed to it amongst them; and by such Rules as the Community, or those authorized by them to that Purpose, shall agree on. And in this we have the original *Right and*

¶ *Rise of both the legislative and executive Power*, as well as of the Governments and Societies themselves.

For in the State of Nature, to omit the Liberty he has of innocent Delights, a Man has two Powers:

The first is to do whatsoever he thinks fit for the Preservation of himself and others, within the Permission of the *Law of Nature*; by which Law, common to them all, he and all the rest of *Mankind are of one Community*, make up one Society, distinct from all other Creatures. . . .

The other Power a Man has in the State of Nature, is the *Power to punish the Crimes* committed against that Law. Both these he gives up, when he joins in a private, if I may so call it, or particular political Society, and incorporates into any Common-wealth, separate from the rest of Mankind.

The first *Power*, . . . *he gives up* to be regulated by Laws made by the Society, so far forth as the Preservation of himself, and the rest of that Society shall require; which Laws of the Society in many Things confine the Liberty he had by the Law of Nature.

Secondly, The *Power of punishing he wholly gives up*, and engages his natural Force, (which he might before employ in the Execution of the Law of Nature, by his own single Authority, as he thought fit) to assist the executive Power of the Society, as the Law thereof shall require. For being now in a new State, wherein he is to enjoy many Conveniencies, from the Labour, Assistance, and Society of others in the same Community, as well as Protection from its whole Strength; he is to part also with as much of his natural Liberty in providing for himself, as the Good, Prosperity, and Safety of the Society shall require; which is not only necessary, but just; since the other Members of the Society do the like.

But though Men when they enter into Society, give up the Equality, Liberty, and executive Power they had in the State of Nature, into the Hands of the Society, . . . yet it being only with an Intention in every one the better to preserve himself his Liberty and Property; (For no rational Creature can be supposed to change his Condition with an Intention to be worse) the Power of the Society, or *Legislative* constituted by them, can *never be suppos'd to extend farther than the common Good*; but is obliged to secure every ones Property, by providing against those three Defects abovemention'd, that made the State of Nature so unsafe and uneasie. And so whoever has the Legislative or supreme Power of any

¶ Common-wealth, is bound to govern by establish'd *standing Laws*, promulgated and known to the People, and not by extemporary Decrees; by *indifferent* and upright *Judges*, who are to decide Controversies by those Laws; and to employ the Force of the Community at Home, *only in the Execution of such Laws*, or Abroad to prevent or redress foreign Injuries, and secure the Community from Inroads and Invasion. And all this to be directed to no other *End*, but the *Peace*, *Safety*, and *publick Good* of the People.

Societies not founded on Consent

It is important to see, and it is therefore worth repeating, that Locke did not mean to claim that all governments are established by a contract of the form he has been describing. If it is true, he thinks, that "all peaceful beginnings of government have been laid in the consent of the people," it is also unfortunately true that many, if not most, societies have been founded in other ways. Locke describes three such ways: conquest, usurpation, and tyranny.[1]

¶   Though Governments can originally have no other Rise than that before-mention'd, nor *Polities* be *founded on* any thing but the *Consent of the People*; yet such has been the Disorders Ambition has filled the World with, that in the Noise of War, which makes so great a Part of the History of Mankind, *this Consent* is little taken Notice of: And therefore many have mistaken the Force of Arms, for the Consent of the People; and reckon Conquest as one of the Originals of Government. But *Conquest* is as far from setting up any Government, as demolishing an House is from building a new one in the Place. Indeed it often makes way for a new Frame of a Commonwealth, by destroying the former; but without Consent of the People, can never erect a new one.

That the *Aggressor*, who puts himself into the State of War with another, and unjustly invades another Man's Right, *can* by such an unjust War, *never* come to *have a Right over the Conquered*, will be easily agreed by all Men, who will not think that Robbers and Pyrates have a Right of Empire over whomsoever they have Force enough to master; or that Men are bound by Promises, which unlawful Force extorts from them. Should a Robber break into my House, and with a Dagger at my Throat, make me seal Deeds

---

[1] *Of Civil Government*, XVI, 175-176, 186-187, 195; XVII, 197; XVIII, 199 and 201.

¶ to convey my Estate to him, would this give him any Title? Just such a Title by his Sword, has an *unjust Conqueror*, who forces me into Submission. The Injury and the Crime are equal, whether committed by the Wearer of a Crown, or some petty Villain. The Title of the Offender, and the Number of his Followers make no Difference in the Offence, unless it be to aggravate it. The only Difference is, great Robbers punish little ones, to keep them in their Obedience; but the great ones are rewarded with Laurels and Triumphs, because they are too big for the weak Hands of Justice in this World, and have the Power in their own Possession, which should punish Offenders. . . .

The Conqueror, 'tis true, usually by the Force he has over them, compels them with a Sword at their Breasts, to stoop to his Conditions, and submit to such a Government as he pleases to afford them; but the Enquiry is, What Right he has to do so? If it be said, they submit by their own Consent, then this allows their own *Consent* to be *necessary to give the Conqueror a Title to rule* over them. It remains only to be considered, whether *Promises extorted by Force* without Right, can be thought Consent, and *how far they bind*. To which I shall say, they *bind not at all*; because whatsoever another gets from me by Force, I still retain the Right of, and he is obliged presently to restore. . . . For the Law of Nature laying an Obligation on me only by the Rule she prescribes, cannot oblige me by the Violation of her Rules: Such is the extorting any thing from me by Force. . . .

From all which it follows, that the *Government of a Conqueror*, imposed by Force on the Subdued, against whom he had no Right . . . *has no Obligation* upon them.

I will not dispute now, whether Princes are exempt from the Laws of their Country; but this I am sure, they owe Subjection to the Laws of God and Nature. No Body, no Power can exempt them from the Obligations of that eternal Law. Those are so great, and so strong in the Case of *Promises*, that Omnipotency it self can be tied by them. *Grants*, *Promises* and *Oaths*, are *Bonds* that *hold the Almighty*; whatever some Flatterers say to Princes of the World, who all together with all their People joined to them, are in Comparison of the great God, but as a Drop of the Bucket, or a Dust on the Balance, inconsiderable, nothing. . . .

As Conquest may be called a foreign Usurpation, so Usurpation is a Kind of domestick Conquest; with this Difference, that an

¶ Usurper can never have Right on his Side, it being no Usurpation, but where one is got into the *Possession of what another has a Right to*. This, so far as it is *Usurpation*, is a Change only of Persons, but not of the Forms and Rules of the Government: For if the Usurper extend his Power beyond what of Right belonged to the lawful Princes or Governors of the Commonwealth, 'tis *Tyranny* added to *Usurpation*. . . .

As Usurpation is the Exercise of Power, which another hath a Right to; so *Tyranny is the Exercise of Power beyond Right*, which no Body can have a Right to. And this is making use of the Power any one has in his Hands, not for the Good of those who are under it, but for his own private separate Advantage: When the Governor, however entituled, makes not the Law, but his Will the Rule; and his Command and Actions are not directed to the Preservation of the Properties of his People, but the Satisfaction of his own Ambition, Revenge, Covetousness, or any other irregular Passion. . . .

'Tis a Mistake to think this Fault is proper only to Monarchies; other Forms of Government are liable to it as well as that. For wherever the Power, that is put in any Hands for the Government of the People, and the Preservation of their Properties, is applied to other Ends, and made use of to impoverish, harass, or subdue them to the arbitrary irregular Commands of those that have it; there it presently becomes *Tyranny*, whether those that thus use it are one or many. Thus we read of the Thirty Tyrants at *Athens*, as well as one at *Syracuse*; and the intolerable Dominion of the *Decemviri* at *Rome* was nothing better.

The Justification of the Existence of Political Societies

But, in any case, the questions whether the contract is an historical fact and whether Locke thought that it was, are both really irrelevant considerations. For, as we have seen, what Locke is really concerned to set forth in his doctrine of the contract is *not* the occurrence of certain historical facts but the existence of certain moral facts. And he talks about a *contract* only because he sees that these moral facts require the free *consent* of all men to the government under which they live, if that government is to be the kind of government which ought to exist. In other words, since all men are *naturally* equal (since, that is, they ought or have a right to be equal), and since in political societies they cannot all be equal (for some must rule and some be ruled), it

follows that no political society is moral unless men have freely consented to this inequality.

No one understands Locke's position until he sees that Locke means
to assert, not that every state has come into being through a contract
made by its members, but that no state has a right to exist which
exists without the consent of its members. Now it might be claimed
that Hobbes could say the same of his position, since, according to him,
the subjects have consented in an original contract to the rule of their
sovereign. But this is not the case. In the first place, for Hobbes any
state which exists *eo ipso* has a right to exist. This follows because
might makes right, and a state which exists is obviously strong enough
to exist. In the second place, the state to which Hobbes's subjects
consent is one to which they are ever afterwards committed,[1] while
for Locke, as we shall see shortly, the consent of the citizens is conditional on the good behaviour of the sovereign. In the third place,
according to Hobbes, men consent to the formation of a state as
drowning men clutch at a straw: it is a desperate last measure whose
success is doubtful and which is undertaken only because no other
alternative is open. In other words, Hobbes justifies the existence of
the state by arguing that it produces a greater surplus of pleasure over
pain, or rather, that it produces less pain and unhappiness than any of
its alternatives.

On the other hand, in Locke's view, the state is justified, and men
give their consent to it, only if it maintains and preserves "their
Lives, Liberties, and Estates, which I call by the general Name,
Property." They consent to it and give up their absolute and complete freedom in it, only so long as it, in its turn, implements others
of their rights which they prize still more highly.[2] This is what the
'justification' of the state really means: it is justified, in the first place,
by the fact that it gives men something they want—the enjoyment
of property—for the sake of which they are prepared to give up something else, which, though good, is less good—complete freedom and
independence of conduct. So far, the justification is purely utilitarian:
the state is justified because it is to men's advantage that it should
exist. But, so far, the state would be justified, supposing it really were
to men's advantage for it to exist, even if men, not knowing this,
did not choose it; and this would be quite compatible with the

[1] For a discussion of this point, *vide supra*, pp. 123*ff*.
[2] That is, absolute and complete, within the limitations of the laws of nature. Nobody,
of course, has a right to do *anything* he pleases, but everybody has a right to do whatever
the laws of nature permit. Vide *Of Civil Government*, XVI, 195.

institution of the state by force. Thus Hitler claimed that the Nazi state served the best interests of the German people, but that, since many Germans were too stubborn or stupid to realize this, it was right to maintain it by force. Locke would deny this. Men of course have a right to their property, and it ought, therefore, to be protected for them; but men also have a right to freedom and equality. No one can take away one of these rights *for* them, even if, by doing so, the other is preserved. Or rather, though the right may be denied, trampled on, and forgotten, it still exists: it ought to be recognized and implemented. There is, in fact, only one way in which a right can be abrogated—that is, by the free consent of the person who abandons it; and that man or government which denies his right without his consent, even supposing it be really in his best interest, is acting immorally: his act, its procedure, is not justified.

Thus, in the second place, the state is justified for Locke by the fact that it sustains and supports the system of human rights; that its institutions serve, as it were, to mirror in the actual structure of this world that ideal realm of moral obligation which Locke has described. Doubtless this, too, is in the end a utilitarian argument, since it is clearly to men's advantage that their rights should be implemented. But it should not be overlooked that the advantage which the state serves is not merely the bodily advantage of peace and security. It also serves the further and different advantage of recognizing, and helping men to realize, their nature as moral beings.

This will doubtless, as Locke says, "seem a strange Doctrine, it being so quite contrary to the Practice of the World; there being nothing more familiar in speaking of the Dominion of Countries, than to say such an one conquer'd it. As if Conquest, without any more ado, convey'd a Right of Possession. But when we consider, that the Practice of the strong and powerful, how universal soever it may be, is seldom the Rule of Right,[1] however it be one part of the Subjection of the conquered, not to argue against the Conditions, cut out to them by the conquering Sword."[2] "Conquerors," in a word, "seldom trouble themselves to make the Distinction" which Locke has drawn between what is and what ought to be, but no refusal to recognize this distinction can remove it. And what ought to be (and what alone is morally justified in existing) is a government which recognizes that

---

[1] Seldom, that is, because the strong and powerful do not often wait for consent before they take the power and begin their rule.
[2] *Of Civil Government*, XVI, 180.

there are certain rights inherent in human nature, that one of these is the right freely to determine its own character as a government, and that, finally, men give their consent only when, and so long as, they believe that the government's existence serves their best interest.

The Nature of the Morally Justified State

What now are the characteristics in more detail of this ideal, moral type of state which Locke thinks ought to exist? In the first place we can say briefly that its precise form does not matter so long as it serves its function of implementing and maintaining the fabric of human ights.[1]

¶ The Majority having, as has been shew'd, upon Men's first uniting into Society, the whole Power of the Community naturally in them, may employ all that Power in making Laws for the Community from time to time, and executing those Laws by Officers of their own appointing; and then the *Form* of the Government is a perfect *Democracy*: Or else may put the Power of making Laws into the Hands of a few select Men, and their Heirs or Successors; and then it is an *Oligarchy*: Or else into the Hands of one Man, and then it is a *Monarchy*: If to him and his Heirs, it is an *Hereditary Monarchy*: If to him only for Life, but upon his Death the Power only of nominating a Successor to return to them, an *Elective Monarchy*. And so accordingly of these, the Community may make compounded and mixt Forms of Government, as they think good.

It will be noticed that, whatever the specific form of the government, the real and final power—*i.e.*, the sovereignty—remains in the hands of the community as a whole, or rather, in the hands of the majority, whose agent only the actual government is. This leads us to ask what the right and duties of that government are, *vis-à-vis* the community which it represents and whose interest it has to promote.[2]

(a) Legislature

¶ Though the Legislative, whether placed in one or more, whether it be always in being, or only by Intervals, tho' it be the *supreme* Power in every Commonwealth; yet,

[1] *Of Civil Government*, X, 132.   [2] *Ibid.*, XI, 135–138, 140–142.

¶ *First*, It is *not*, nor can possibly be absolutely *Arbitrary* over the Lives and Fortunes of the People. For it being but the joint Power of every Member of the Society given up to that Person, or Assembly, which is Legislator; it can be no more than those Persons had in a State of Nature before they entered into Society, and gave up to the community. . . . Their Power in the utmost Bounds of it, *is limited to the publick good* of the Society. It is a Power, that hath no other End but Preservation, and therefore can never have a Right to destroy, enslave, or designedly to impoverish the Subjects. The Obligations of the Law of Nature, cease not in Society, but only in many Cases are drawn closer, and have by human Laws known Penalties annexed to them, to inforce their Observation. Thus the Law of Nature stands as an eternal Rule to all Men, *Legislators* as well as others, the *Rules* that they make for other Men's Actions, must, as well as their own and other Men's Actions, be conformable to the Law of Nature, *i.e.*, to the Will of God, of which that is a Declaration; and the *fundamental Law of Nature being the Preservation of Mankind*, no human Sanction can be good or valid against it.

Secondly, the *Legislative*, or supreme Authority, cannot assume to it self a Power to Rule by extemporary arbitrary Decrees, but *is bound to dispense Justice*, and decide the Rights of the Subject, *by promulgated standing Laws, and known authoriz'd Judges*. For the Law of Nature being unwritten, and so no where to be found but in the Minds of Men, they who through Passion or Interest shall mis-cite, or misapply it, cannot so easily be convinced of their Mistake, where there is no establish'd Judge. . . .

Absolute arbitrary Power, or governing without *settled standing Laws*, can neither of them consist with the Ends of Society and Government, which Men would not quit the Freedom of the State of Nature for, and tie themselves up under, were it not to preserve their Lives, Liberties and Fortunes; and by *stated Rules* of Right and Property to secure their Peace and Quiet. It cannot be supposed that they should intend, had they a Power so to do, to give to any one or more, an *absolute arbitrary Power* over their Persons and Estates, and put a Force into the Magistrate's Hand to execute his unlimited Will arbitrarily upon them. This were to put themselves into a worse Condition than the State of Nature. . . . He being in a much worse Condition, who is exposed to the arbitrary Power of one Man who has the Command of 100,000, than he that is

¶exposed to the arbitrary Power of 100,000 single Men; no body being secure that his Will, who hath such a Command, is better than that of other Men, tho' his Force be 100,000 times stronger. And therefore whatever Form the Commonwealth is under, the ruling Power ought to govern by *declared* and *received Laws*, and not by extemporary Dictates and undetermin'd Resolutions. . . .

Thirdly, The *supreme Power cannot take* from any Man any Part of his *Property* without his own Consent. For the Preservation of Property being the End of Government, and that for which Men enter into Society, it necessarily supposes and requires, that the People should *have Property*, without which they must be supposed to lose that by entering into Society, which was the End for which they enter'd into it; too gross an Absurdity for any Man to own. . . . Hence it is a Mistake to think, that the *supreme or legislative Power* of any Commonwealth can do what it will, and dispose of the Estates of the Subjects *arbitrarily*, or take any Part of them at Pleasure. This is not much to be fear'd in Governments, where the *Legislative* consists wholly or in Part, in Assemblies which are variable. . . . But in Governments where the *Legislative* is in one lasting Assembly always in being, or in one Man, as in absolute Monarchies, there is Danger still, that they will think themselves to have a distinct Interest from the rest of the Community; and so will be apt to increase their own Riches and Power, by taking what they think fit from the People. . . .

'Tis true, Governments cannot be supported without great Charge, and 'tis fit every one who enjoys a Share of the Protection, should pay out of his Estate his Proportion for the Maintenance of it. But still it must be with his own Consent, *i.e.*, the Consent of the Majority, giving it either by themselves, or their Representatives chosen by them. For if any one shall claim a *Power to lay* and levy *Taxes* on the People by his own Authority, and without such Consent of the People, he thereby invades the *fundamental Law of Property*, and subverts the End of Government. For what Property have I in that which another may by Right take when he pleases to himself?

Fourthly, The *Legislative cannot transfer the Power of making Laws* to any other Hands. For it being but a delegative Power from the People, they who have it, cannot pass it over to others. The People alone can appoint the Form of the Commonwealth, which is by constituting the Legislative, and appointing in whose Hands that

¶shall be. And when the People have said, we will submit to Rules, and be govern'd by *Laws* made by such Men, and in such Forms, no Body else can say other Men shall make *Laws* for them; nor can the People be bound by any *Laws*, but such as are enacted by those whom they have chosen, and authorized to make *Laws* for them. The Power of the *Legislative* being derived from the People by a positive voluntary Grant and Institution, can be no other, than what that positive Grant convey'd, which being only to make *Laws*, and not to make *Legislators*, the *Legislative* can have no Power to transfer their Authority of making Laws, and place it in other Hands.

These are the *Bounds* which the Trust that is put in them by the Society, and the Law of God and Nature have *set to the Legislative* Power of every Commonwealth, in all Forms of Government.

(b) Executive

Although the legislature—however constituted—is always the supreme power in a state, the well-organized state requires an executive [1] which is separated from it.[2]

¶   The *Legislative* Power is that which has a Right *to direct how the Force of the Commonwealth* shall be employ'd for preserving the Community and the Members of it. But because those Laws . . . may be made in a little time; therefore there is no need, that the *Legislative* should be always in Being, not having always Business to do. And because it may be too great a Temptation to human Frailty, apt to grasp at Power, for the same Persons who have the Power of making Laws, to have also in their Hands the Power to execute them, whereby they exempt themselves from Obedience to the Laws they make, and suit the Law . . . to their own private Advantage . . . , contrary to the End of Society and Government; Therefore, in well-order'd Commonwealths, where the Good of the whole is so consider'd as it ought, the *Legislative* Power is put into the Hands of divers Persons, who duly assembled, have . . . a Power to make Laws, which when they have done, being separated again, they are themselves subject to the Laws they have made;

---

[1] Locke also distinguishes a third power, the "federative," which is concerned solely with foreign affairs. Though it and the executive power are "really distinct in themselves, yet they are hardly to be separated, and placed at the same Time in the Hands of distinct Persons" (XII, 148). Locke does not distinguish the judiciary as a separate power.

[2] *Of Civil Government*, XII, 143-144; XIII, 151-152.

¶ which is a new, and near Tie upon them to take Care that they make them for the publick Good.

But because the Laws that are at once and in a short time made, have a constant and lasting Force and need a *perpetual Execution* or an Attendance thereunto: Therefore it is necessary there should be a *Power always in Being*, which should see to the *Execution* of the Laws that are made, and remain in Force. And thus the *Legislative* and *Executive Power* come often to be separated. . . .

In some Commonwealths where the *Legislative* is not always in Being, and the *Executive* is vested in a single Person, who has also a Share in the Legislative; there that single Person in a very tolerable Sense may also be called *Supreme*; not that he has in himself all the supreme Power, which is that of Law-making, but because he has in him the *supreme Execution*, from whom all inferior Magistrates derive all their several subordinate Powers, or at least the greatest Part of them. . . . But yet it is to be observed, that though *Oaths of Allegiance* and Fealty are taken to him, . . . he has no Right to Obedience, nor can claim it otherwise than as the publick Person vested with the Power of the Law, and so is to be consider'd as the Image, Phantom, or Representative of the Commonwealth, acted by the Will of the Society, declared in its Laws; and thus he has no Will, no Power, but that of the Law. But when he quits this Representation, this publick Will, and acts by his own private Will, he degrades himself, and is but a single private Person without Power, and without Will, that has not any Right to *Obedience*; the Members owing no *Obedience* but to the publick Will of the Society. . . .

Of other *ministerial and subordinate Powers* in a Commonwealth we need not speak, they being so multiply'd with infinite Variety, in the different Customs and Constitutions of distinct Commonwealths, that it is impossible to give a particular account of them all. Only thus much, which is necessary to our present Purpose, we may take Notice of concerning them, that they have no manner of Authority any of them, beyond what is by positive Grant and Commission delegated to them, and are all of them accountable to some other Power in the Commonwealth.

(c) *Prerogative*

The two principal spheres of authority may seem to be rigidly defined and distinguished when we say that the executive administers

the law which the legislature determines on; but it is as impossible as
it is unwise to fix everything arbitrarily and in advance by statute. As
Locke points out,[1]

¶   Where the Legislative and Executive Power are in distinct Hands,
(as they are in all moderated Monarchies and well-framed Governments) there the Good of the Society requires, that several Things
should be left to the Discretion of him that has the executive Power.
For the Legislators not being able to foresee and provide by Laws,
for all that may be useful to the Community, the Executor of the
Laws . . . has by the common Law of Nature a Right to make use
of [his power] for the Good of the Society in many Cases, where the
Municipal Law has given no Direction, till the Legislative can con-
veniently be assembled to provide for it. . . . Nay, 'tis fit that the
Laws themselves should in some Cases give way to the executive
Power, or rather to this fundamental Law of Nature and Government, *viz.* That as much as may be, *all* the Members of the Society
are to be preserved. For . . . many Accidents may happen, wherein a
strict and rigid Observation of the Laws may do harm, (as not to
pull down an innocent Man's House to stop the Fire, when the next
to it is a burning) and a Man may come sometimes within the reach
of the Law, which makes no Distinction of Persons, by an Action
that may deserve Reward and Pardon. . . .

   This Power to act according to Discretion for the Publick Good,
without the Prescription of the Law, and sometimes even against it,
is that which is called *Prerogative.* . . .[2]

   It is easy to conceive, that in the Infancy of Governments, when
Commonwealths differed little from Families in Number of People,
they differ'd from them too but little in Number of Laws; and the
Governors, being as the Fathers of them, watching over them for
their Good,[3] the Government was almost all *Prerogative.* A few
establish'd Laws serv'd the Turn, and the Discretion and Care of the
Ruler supply'd the rest. But when Mistake or Flattery prevail'd

---

[1] *Of Civil Government*, XIV, 159–160, 162–163, 165–167.
[2] A few paragraphs earlier Locke defined prerogative as "being nothing but a Power in
the Hands of the Prince, to provide for the publick Good in such Cases, which depending
upon unforeseen and uncertain Occurrences, certain and unalterable Laws could not
safely direct; whatsoever shall be done manifestly for the good of the People, and the
establishing the Government upon its true Foundations, is, and always will be just
Prerogative" (XII, 158).
[3] This is one of the passages in which Locke's language suggests that he believed in a
'Golden Age' (*vide supra*, pp. 163*ff.*).

¶with weak Princes to make use of this Power for private Ends of
their own, and not for the publick Good, the People were fain by
express Laws to get Prerogative determin'd in those Points wherein
they found Disadvantage from it: And thus declared *Limitationts of
Prerogative*, were by the People found necessary in Cases which they
and their Ancestors had left in the utmost Latitude to the Wisdom
of those Princes, who made no other but a Right Use of it, that is,
for the Good of the People.

And therefore they have a very wrong Notion of Government,
who say, that the People have *incroach'd upon the Prerogative*, when
they have got any Part of it to be defined by positive Laws. For in
so doing they have not pulled from the Prince any thing that of
Right belong'd to him, but only declared that that Power which
they indefinitely left in his or his Ancestors Hands, to be exercised
for their Good, was not a thing which they intended him when
he used it otherwise. For the End of Government being the
Good of the Community, whatsoever Alterations are made in it
tending to that End, cannot be an *Incroachment* upon any body,
since no body in Government can have a Right tending to any
other End. . . .

And therefore he that will look into the *History of England*, will
find, that *Prerogative* was always *largest* in the Hands of our wisest
and best Princes; because the People observing the whole Tendency
of their Actions to be the publick Good, contested not what was
done without Law to that End; or if any human Frailty or Mistake
(for Princes are but Men, made as others) appear'd in some Declina-
tions from that End; yet 'twas visible, the Main of their Conduct
tended to nothing but the Care of the Publick. . . .

. . . Upon this is founded that Saying, That the Reigns of good
Princes have always been most dangerous to the Liberties of their
People. For when their Successors managing the Government with
different Thoughts, would draw the Actions of those good Rulers
into precedent, and make them the Standard of their *Prerogative*, . . .
it has often occasion'd Contest, and sometimes publick Disorders,
before the People could recover their Original Right, and get
that to be declared not to be *Prerogative*, which truly was never
so. . . .

The Power of *calling Parliaments* in *England* as to precise Time,
Place, and Duration, is certainly a *Prerogative* of the King, but still
with this Trust, that it shall be made use of for the Good of the

¶Nation, as the Exigences of the Times, and Variety of Occasions shall require. For it being impossible to foresee which should be always the fittest Place for them to assemble in, and what the best Season; the Choice of these was left with the executive Power, as might be most subservient to the publick Good, and best suit the Ends of Parliaments.

The argument for prerogative is purely utilitarian: it will promote the end for which governments are established—*i.e.*, the general good of the whole community—if "there is a Latitude left to the executive Power, to do many things of Choice which the Laws do not prescribe."[1] Similarly it is by a utilitarian formula that Locke limits the scope and range of the executive's prerogative. This power is justified only so far as its existence actually promotes the public good. The obvious question then arises: Who is to make the utilitarian calculation? Who is to determine the nature and extent of a prerogative? Who is to decide whether, in some particular case, a certain prerogative has been violated or misused? Locke's answer is that the decision rests with the people themselves.[2]

¶ If a Controversy arise betwixt a Prince and some of the People, in a Matter, where the Law is silent, or doubtful, and the Thing be of great Consequence, I should think the proper *Umpire*, in such a Case, should be the Body of the *People*. For in Cases where the Prince hath a Trust reposed in him, and is dispensed from the common ordinary Rules of the Law; there, if any Men find themselves aggrieved, and think the Prince acts contrary to, or beyond that Trust, who so proper to *judge* as the body of the *People*, (who at first, lodg'd that Trust in him) how far they meant it should extend? . . .

Who shall be *Judge* whether the Trustee or Deputy acts well, and according to the Trust reposed in him, but he who deputes him, and must, by having deputed him, have still a Power to discard him when he fails in his Trust? If this be reasonable in particular Cases of private Men, why should it be otherwise in that of the greatest Moment, where the Welfare of Millions is concerned, and also where the Evil, if not prevented, is greater, and the Redress very difficult, dear, and dangerous?

[1] *Of Civil Government*, XIV, 160.
[2] *Ibid.*, XIX, 240 and 242.

(d) The Dissolution of Governments

What is true in the case of the prerogative is true whenever, and for whatever reason, government fails in its function—whether externally, through conquest, or internally through usurpation or because of the incompetence of either legislature or executive. The people have reserved to themselves both the right of determining whether government is fulfilling the ends for which it was established and the right of removing an inefficient or perverted government and replacing it by another. Even the legislative power is held only on good behaviour, and the final judge of this behaviour is the people itself.[1]

¶ The Legislative being only a fiduciary Power to act for certain Ends, there remains still *in the People a supreme Power to remove or alter the Legislative*, when they find the *Legislative* act contrary to the Trust reposed in them. For all *Power given with Trust* for the attaining an *End*, being limited by that End, whenever that *End* is manifestly neglected or opposed, the *Trust* must necessarily be *forfeited*, and the Power devolve into the Hands of those that gave it, who may place it a-new where they shall think best for their Safety and Security. And thus the *Community* perpetually *retains a supreme Power* of saving themselves from the Attempts and Designs of any Body, even of their Legislators, whenever they shall be so foolish or so wicked as to lay and carry on Designs against the Liberties and Properties of the Subject. . . . Whenever any one shall go about to bring them to . . . a slavish Condition, they will always have a Right . . . to rid themselves of those who invade this fundamental, sacred, and unalterable Law of *Self-preservation*, for which they enter'd into Society. And thus the *Community* may be said in this Respect to be *always the supreme Power*, but not as consider'd under any Form of Government, because this Power of the People can never take place till the Government be dissolved.

[Specifically, governments are dissolved whenever] the *Legislative* is *altered*. . . .

This being usually brought about by such in the Commonwealth who misuse the Power they have; it is hard to consider it aright, and know at whose Door to lay it, without knowing the Form of Government in which it happens. Let us suppose then the Legislative placed in the Concurrence of three distinct Persons.

[1] *Of Civil Government*, XIII, 149; XIX, 212–217, 219–222.

¶ 1. A single hereditary Person, having the constant supreme executive Power, and with it the Power of convoking and dissolving the other two within certain Periods of Time.

2. An Assembly of Hereditary Nobility.

3. An Assembly of Representatives chosen *pro tempore* by the People: Such a Form of Government supposed, it is evident,

First, That when such a single Person or Prince sets up his own arbitrary Will in Place of the Laws, which are the Will of the Society, declared by the Legislative, then the *Legislative is changed*. . . .

Secondly, When the Prince hinders the Legislative from assembling in its due Time, or from acting freely, pursuant to those Ends for which it was constituted, the *Legislative is altered*. For 'tis not a certain Number of Men, no, nor their Meeting, unless they have also Freedom of debating, and Leisure of perfecting what is for the Good of the Society, wherein the Legislative consists; when these are taken away or altered, so as to deprive the Society of the due Exercise of their Power, the *Legislative* is truly altered. For it is not Names that constitute Governments, but the Use and Exercise of those Powers that were intended to accompany them. . . .

Thirdly, When by the arbitrary Power of the Prince, the Electors or Ways of Election are altered without the Consent, and contrary to the common Interest of the People, there also the Legislative is altered. . . .

Fourthly, The Delivery also of the People into the Subjection of foreign Power, either by the Prince, or by the Legislative, is certainly a *Change of the Legislative*, and so a *Dissolution of the Government*. . . .

There is one Way more whereby such a Government may be dissolved, and that is, when he who has the supreme executive Power, neglects and abandons that Charge, so that the Laws already made, can no longer be put in Execution. This is demonstratively to reduce all to Anarchy, and so effectually *to dissolve the Government*. . . .

In these and the like Cases, *when the Government is dissolved*, the People are at Liberty to provide for themselves, by erecting a new Legislative, differing from the other by the Change of Persons, or Form, or both, as they shall find it most for their Safety and Good. For the *Society* can never, by the Fault of another, lose the Native

¶ and Original Right it has to preserve it self, which can only be done by a settled Legislative, and a fair and impartial Execution of the Laws made by it. But the State of Mankind is not so miserable, that they are not capable of using this Remedy, till it be too late to look for any.[1] To tell *People* they *may provide for themselves* by erecting a new Legislative, when by Oppression, Artifice, or being delivered over to a foreign Power, their old one is gone, is only to tell them, they may expect Relief when it is too late, and the Evil is past Cure. This is in Effect no more, than to bid them first be Slaves, and then to take care of their Liberty, and when their Chains are on, tell them, they may act like Freemen. . . . And therefore it is, that they have not only a Right to get out of it, but to prevent it.

There is therefore Secondly, another Way whereby *Governments are dissolved*, and that is, when the Legislative, or the Prince, either of them, act contrary to their Trust.

. . . The *Legislative acts against the Trust* reposed in them when they endeavour to evade the Property of the Subject, and to make themselves or any Part of the Community, Masters, or arbitrary Disposers of the Lives, Liberties or Fortunes of the People.

The Reason why Men enter into Society, is the Preservation of their Property; and the End why they chuse and authorize a Legislative, is that there may be Laws made . . . as Guards and Fences to the Properties of all the Members of the Society. . . . Whensoever therefore the *Legislative* shall transgress this fundamental Rule of Society; and either by Ambition, Fear, Folly or Corruption, *endeavour to grasp* themselves, *or put into the Hands of any other an absolute Power* over the Lives, Liberties, and Estates of the People; by this Breach of Trust they *forfeit the Power* the People had put into their Hands for quite contrary Ends, and it devolves to the People, who have a Right to resume their Original Liberty, and by the Establishment of the new Legislative, (such as they shall think fit) provide for their own Safety and Security, which is the End for which they are in Society. What I have said here concerning the Legislative in general, holds true also concerning the supreme Executor. . . . He *acts* also *contrary to his Trust* when he either employs the Force, Treasure, and Offices of the Society, to corrupt the *Representatives*, and gain them to his Purposes; or openly

[1] This argument is, of course, directed against Hobbes.

¶ pre-engages the *Electors*, and prescribes to their Choice, such, whom
he has by Solicitations, Threats, Promises, or otherwise won to his
Designs; and employs them to bring in such, who have promised
before-hand, what to vote, and what to enact.

Thus constitutional means exist, or rather such means ought to
exist, for dissolving undesirable governments, and we may suppose
that a well-intentioned but incompetent legislature will yield readily to
the wishes of the people. But where the people's government has been
overthrown by conquest or by usurpation, it is obviously unlikely
that the tyrant will accede to their desires. In this case it remains
for the people to use force against him. "The *People* . . . have . . .
reserv'd that ultimate Determination to themselves which belongs
to all Mankind, where there lies no Appeal on Earth, *viz.*, to
judge whether they have just Cause to make their Appeal to
Heaven." [1]

By this pious phrase, an "appeal to heaven," Locke does not mean
the people passively to await the operations of divine justice on their
behalf. He means that, when no earthly judge exists before whom they
can take their case (*i.e.*, when no constitutional channels of change
exist), they must put their trust in heaven and, believing in the
rightness of their cause, appeal to arms. [2]

¶   'Tis the *unjust Use of Force then*, that *puts a Man into the state of War*
with another, and thereby he that is guilty of it, makes a Forfeiture
of his Life. For quitting Reason, which is the Rule given between
Man and Man and using Force, the Way of Beasts, he becomes
liable to be destroyed by him he uses Force against, as any savage
ravenous Beast that is dangerous to his Being. . . .

It is the brutal Force the Aggressor has used, that gives his Adver-
sary a Right to take away his Life, and destroy him if he pleases, as
a noxious Creature. . . .

He that *appeals to Heaven*, must be sure he has Right on his side:
and a Right too that is worth the Trouble and Cost of his Appeal,
as he will answer at a Tribunal that cannot be deceived, and will be
sure to retribute to every one according to the Mischiefs he hath
created. . . .

Thus to the general question, When ought government to be dissolved? Locke returns the reply that it ought to be dissolved, morally

---

[1] *Of Civil Government*, XIV, 168.   [2] *Ibid.*, XVI, 176, 181-182.

it *is* dissolved, whenever it no longer serves the purpose for which it was established. But Locke is far from being the prototype of the modern soap-box agitator, and he is therefore anxious to show that the widespread acceptance of this doctrine will not result in continuous internal strife and change of government. In the first place Locke argues that a good government has nothing to fear from the acceptance of his thesis. This seems rather optimistic, since the mere fact that a government's policies are actually directed to the people's best interests does not, unfortunately, assure us that the people will see this to be the case. More to the point, he goes on to remark that, though governments are morally dissolved as soon as they are perverted from their real purpose, they are actually dissolved only when this perversion has reached considerable proportions and affects a large number of the citizens. "Nor let any one think, this [*i.e.*, the right of dissolving unsatisfactory governments] lays a perpetual Foundation for Disorder; for this operates not, till the Inconvenience is so great that the Majority feel it, and are weary of it, and find a Necessity to have it amended." [1] In other words, though the people have a constant right to appeal to the force of arms, they do not do so actually until "they judge the cause of sufficient moment" to justify the danger and inconvenience such an appeal entails.

Moreover, there is a certain inertia in the people which tends in the same direction—towards acceptance of what government offers rather than towards constant criticism. [2]

¶ People are not so easily got out of their old Forms, as some are apt to suggest. They are hardly to be prevailed with to amend the acknowledged Faults in the Frame they have been accustomed to. And if there be any original Defects, or adventitious ones introduced by Time or Corruption; 'tis not an easy thing to get them changed, even when all the World sees there is an Opportunity for it. This Slowness and Aversion in the People to quit their old Constitutions, has in the many Revolutions which have been seen in this Kingdom, in this and former Ages, still kept us to, or, after some Interval of fruitless Attempts, still brought us back again to our old Legislative of King, Lords and Commons: And whatever Provocations have made the Crown be taken from some of our Princes Heads, they never carried the People so far, as to place it in another Line.

[1] *Of Civil Government*, XIV, 168.　　　　[2] *Ibid.*, XIX, 223.

Religion and the State

We may conclude this account of Locke's political theory with a brief survey of his view of the relation which ought to exist between the religious sects and the political authority. There are several reasons for undertaking this survey here. In the first place, Locke's conception of this relation is historically of great interest: he offered a solution to the most serious contemporary problem—one which had been distressing European society for two hundred years, since the beginning of the Protestant reformation, and which is still the formula adopted to-day in democratic countries. In the second place, considerable light is thrown on Locke's conception of the nature of sovereignty in the course of his effort to distinguish the civil power from the church. By seeing his general political principles applied in a particularly difficult and 'tricky' case, we understand better both the range of the authority which Locke assigned to his sovereign and the limitations which he set upon that power. Finally, it shows us, perhaps better than anything else could, the character and point of view of the man: Locke was certainly not a mystic; he was, even before the eighteenth century dawned, already a man of the Enlightenment. But the fact that he believed the way to truth lay through the use of human reason did not prevent his being a deeply and profoundly religious man, and this combination of level-headed common sense with a deep religious sentiment is one of the most characteristic features of Locke's mind.

When we were considering Hobbes's account of religion we saw that he regarded religious feeling and sentiment as being in reality nothing more than the merest illusion and as a dangerous fanaticism which, therefore, required to be closely controlled by the sovereign lest it get out of hand. Locke completely and directly controverts this point of view. The dangerous and seditious character of the various religious sects which Hobbes thought necessitated rigid supervision is in fact caused by that supervision. Complete toleration of all sects, complete freedom from control by the civil authority, would, Locke thinks, solve all our problems, since it is only unjust attempts at suppression which cause the suppressed sects to commit seditious acts.[1]

¶ You'll say, That *Assemblies and Meetings* [of the various sects and conventicles] *endanger the Publick Peace, and threaten the Common-*

---

[1] *A Letter concerning Toleration; Humbly Submitted, etc.* (*Works*, 1727, vol. II), pp. 252, 254. subsequent references are to the paging of this edition.

¶ wealth. . . . But if this be so, why is not the Magistrate afraid of his own Church; and why does he not forbid their Assemblies, as things dangerous to his Government? . . .

Let us therefore deal plainly. The Magistrate is afraid of other Churches, but not of his own; because he is kind and favourable to the one, but severe and cruel to the other. These he treats like Children, and indulges them even to Wantonness. Those he uses as Slaves, and how blamelessly soever they demean themselves, recompenses them no otherwise than by Gallies, Prisons, Confiscations and Death. These he cherishes and defends: Those he continually scourges and oppresses. Let him turn the Tables: Or let those Dissenters enjoy but the same Privileges in Civils as his other Subjects, and he will quickly find that these religious Meetings will be no longer dangerous. For if Men enter into seditious Conspiracies, 'tis not Religion inspires them to it in their Meetings, but their Sufferings and Oppressions that make them willing to ease themselves. Just and moderate Governments are everywhere quiet, everywhere safe. But Oppression raises Ferments and makes Men struggle to cast off an uneasy and tyrannical Yoke. . . .

Believe me,[1] the Stirs that are made, proceed not from any peculiar Temper of this or that Church or religious Society; but from the common Disposition of all Mankind, who when they groan under any heavy Burthen, endeavour naturally to shake off the Yoke that galls their Necks. Suppose this Business of Religion were let alone, and that there were some other Distinction made between Men and Men, upon account of their different Complexions, Shapes, and Features, so that those who have black Hair (for example) or grey Eyes, should not enjoy the same Privileges as other Citizens; . . . can it be doubted but these Persons, thus distinguished from others by the Colour of their Hair and Eyes, and united together by one common Persecution, would be as dangerous to the Magistrate, as any others that had associated themselves merely upon the account of Religion? . . . There is only one thing which gathers People into seditious Commotions, and that is Oppression. . . .

It is not the Diversity of Opinions, (which cannot be avoided) but the Refusal of Toleration to those that are of different Opinions, (which might have been granted) that has produced all the Bustles and Wars, that have been in the Christian World, upon account of Religion. . . .

---

[1] It should be remembered that this essay is written as a letter.

Since, in one word, Locke's diagnosis of the whole trouble is that there have been "mixed together, and confounded two Things, that are in themselves most different, the Church and the Commonwealth,"[1] his prescription is equally simple: "each of them [must] contain itself within its own Bounds, the one attending to the worldly Welfare of the Commonwealth, the other to the Salvation of Souls."[2]

This leads Locke to attempt a careful delimitation of the proper spheres of church and state. We already know, of course, the function of the civil authority. This is "to secure unto all the People . . . the just Possession of [the] Things belonging to this Life." The state, that is to say, is "a Society of Men constituted only for the procuring . . . and advancing of their own *Civil Interests*, [*i.e.*,] Life, Liberty, Health, and Indolence of Body; and the Possession of outward Things, such as Money, Lands, Houses, Furniture, and the like."[3]

On the other hand,[4] a church is

¶ a voluntary Society of Men, joining themselves together of their own accord, in order to the publick worshipping of God, in such manner as they judge acceptable to him and effectual to the Salvation of their Souls. . . . Nothing ought, nor can be transacted in this Society, relating to the Possession of civil and worldly Goods. No Force is here to be made use of upon any Occasion whatsoever: Force belongs wholly to the Civil-Magistrate, and the Possession of all outward Goods is subject to his Jurisdiction. . . . The Business of true Religion is the regulating of Men's Lives according to the Rules of Virtue and Piety. Whosoever will list himself under the Banner of Christ, must in the first place, and above all things, make War upon his own Lusts and Vices. It is in vain for any Man to usurp the Name of Christian, without Holiness of Life, Purity of Manners, Benignity and Meekness of Spirit.

Hence the sincere Christian is inevitably tolerant of others. "The Toleration of those that differ from others in Matters of Religion, is so agreeable to the Gospel of Jesus Christ, and to the genuine Reason of Mankind, that it seems monstrous for Men to be so blind as not to perceive the Necessity and Advantage of it, in so clear a Light."[5]

But toleration is not merely a part of the Christian spirit. It follows equally from a consideration of the function of religion in general

---

[1] *Letter concerning Toleration*, p. 254.   [2] *Ibid.*, p. 254.   [3] *Ibid.*, p. 234.
[4] *Ibid.*, pp. 232, 235, 237.   [5] *Ibid.*, p. 234.

that religion cannot by its very nature be *enforced*. For religion has two chief concerns, one speculative, the other practical, in character.
First, as regards the former,[1]

¶ Speculative opinions . . . and *Articles of Faith* (as they are called) which are required only to be believed, cannot be imposed on any Church by the Law of the Land. For it is absurd that Things should be enjoined by Laws, which are not in Men's Power to perform. And to believe this or that to be true, does not depend upon our Will. . . .

Farther, The Magistrate ought not to forbid the preaching or professing of any speculative Opinions of any Church, because they have no manner of relation to the Civil Rights of the Subjects. . . . The Business of Laws is not to provide for the Truth of Opinions, but for the Safety and Security of the Commonwealth, and of every particular Man's Goods and Person. And so it ought to be. For the Truth certainly would do well enough, if she were once left to shift for herself. She has seldom received . . . much Assistance from the Power of Great Men, to whom she is but rarely known, and more rarely welcome. She is not taught by Laws, nor has she any need of Force to procure her Entrance into the Minds of Men. Errors indeed prevail by the Assistance of foreign and borrowed Succours. But if Truth makes not her Way into the Understanding by her own Light, she will be but the weaker for any borrowed Force Violence can add to her. Thus much for Speculative Opinions. Let us now proceed to *Practical* ones.

. . . Moral Actions belong . . . to the Jurisdiction both of the . . . Magistrate and Conscience. Here therefore is great Danger, lest one of these Jurisdictions intrench upon the other, and Discord arise between the Keeper of the Publick Peace and the Overseers of Souls. But if what has been already said [about the purposes of government] be rightly considered, it will easily remove all Difficulty in this Matter.

[The civil magistrate is concerned after the well-being of men's temporal lives here upon earth; but] Every Man has [also] an immortal Soul . . . whose Happiness [depends] upon his believing and doing those Things in this Life, which are necessary to the obtaining of God's Favour. . . . It follows from thence, first, That the Observance of these Things is the highest Obligation that lies upon

---

[1] *Letter concerning Toleration*, pp. 248–249.

❡ Mankind, . . . because there is nothing in this World that is of any Consideration in comparison with Eternity. Secondly, That seeing one Man does not violate the Right of another, by his erroneous Opinions, and undue Manner of Worship, nor is his Perdition any Prejudice to another Man's Affairs; therefore the Care of each Man's Salvation belongs only to himself. . . . Any one may employ as many Exhortations and Arguments as he pleases, towards the promoting of another Man's Salvation. But all Force and Compulsion are to be forborn. . . . Every Man, in that, has the supreme and absolute Authority of Judging for himself. And the Reason is, because no body else is concerned in it, nor can receive any Prejudice from his Conduct therein.

In a word, since what matters in religion is not outward practices and observances but the inward state of feeling and belief, what our religion is can be of no concern to the civil magistrate: he has no business to legislate about our religion, and he cannot do so, even if he would.[1]

❡   In vain therefore do Princes compel their Subjects to come into their Church-Communion, under Pretence of saving their Souls. If they believe, they will come of their own Accord; if they believe not, their coming will nothing avail them. How great soever, in fine, may be the Pretence of Goodwill and Charity, and Concern for the Salvation of Men's Souls, Men cannot be forced to be saved whether they will or no. And therefore, when all is done, they must be left to their own Consciences.

There is but one point at which the civil authority has a right to interfere with a church's complete freedom to worship God after its own manner. When the religious practices of a sect are "things [which] are not lawful in the ordinary Course of Life . . . , neither are they so in the Worship of God." [2] The magistrate has not only a right but a duty to prohibit them.

❡   If any People congregated upon account of Religion, should be desirous to sacrifice a Calf, I deny that that ought to be prohibited by a Law. *Melibœus*, whose Calf it is, may lawfully kill his Calf at Home, and burn any Part of it that he thinks fit. For no Injury is

---

[1] *Letter concerning Toleration*, p. 243.   [2] *Ibid.*, p. 245.

¶ thereby done to any one, no Prejudice to another Man's Goods. And for the same Reason he may kill his Calf also in a religious Meeting. Whether the doing so be well-pleasing to God or no, it is their part to consider that do it. The Part of the Magistrate is only to take Care that the Commonwealth receive no Prejudice, and that there be no Injury done to any Man, either in Life or Estate. . . . But if Paradventure such were the State of Things, that the Interest of the Commonwealth required all Slaughter of Beasts should be forborn for some while, in order to the encreasing of the Stock of Cattle, that had been destroyed by some extra-ordinary Murrain; who sees not that the Magistrate, in such a Case, may forbid all his Subjects to kill any Calves for any Use what-soever? Only 'tis to be observed that, in this Case the Law is not made about a religious, but a political Matter: Nor is the Sacrifice, but the Slaughter of Calves thereby prohibited.

This, then, gives us the rule which defines the relation which ought to obtain between church and state:[1]

¶   Whatsoever is lawful in the Commonwealth, cannot be pro-hibited by the Magistrate in the Church. Whatsoever is permitted unto any of his Subjects for their ordinary Use, neither can nor ought to be forbidden by him to any Sect of People for their religious Uses. . . . But those Things that are prejudicial to the Common-weal of a People in their ordinary Use, and are therefore forbidden by Laws, those Things ought not to be permitted to Churches in their sacred Rites. . . .

If each of them [state and church] would contain itself within its own Bounds, the one attending to the worldly Welfare of the Commonwealth, the other to the Salvation of Souls, 'tis im-possible any Discord should ever have happened between them. *Sed, pudet haec opprobria, etc.* God Almighty grant I beseech him, that . . . Civil Magistrates growing more careful to conform their own Consciences to the Law of God, and less solicitous about the binding of other Men's Consciences by human Laws, may like Fathers of their Country, direct all their Counsels and Endeavours to promote universally the civil Welfare of all their Children . . .; and that all ecclesiastical Men, who boast themselves to be the Successors of the Apostles, walking peaceably and modestly in the

[1] *Letter concerning Toleration*, pp. 245, 254–255.

¶ Apostles' Steps, without intermeddling with State-Affairs, may apply themselves wholly to promote the Salvation of Souls.

The Reality of Rights

Perhaps the principal feature of Locke's theory (though it is one which is certainly by no means peculiar to him) is the conception of the state and its functions as limited and conditioned by certain moral restrictions, certain inherent human rights which ought to be implemented. It is therefore worth our while, before concluding this examination of Locke's political theory, to look a little more closely at this notion of moral rights. This is by no means a simple or easy undertaking. For most people fall into one or the other of two classes: either they accept the concept of rights as being self-evidently true, or they reject it as altogether meaningless. For the one class (to which Locke, of course, belonged) it needs no defence; for the other, it can have none. And for both classes alike, any critical examination of it is difficult, if not impossible, because the self-evident can no more be discussed and analysed than can the nonsensical.

We must, however, do what we can; and, since Locke assumed the reality of rights, we may begin by seeing what can be said in criticism of this position. To begin with, it may be asked: Even supposing that there really are rights, what good are they to anyone unless they are recognized by a sovereign who has both the power and the will to implement them? What do rights 'matter'? The only thing that really 'matters' in the world, it may be said, is force. Force can get us what we want and keep it for us, while rights, which may sound very fine, are no good to anyone unless he also possesses force, in which case the rights are quite useless and unnecessary. In other words, isn't a theory which is based upon the alleged existence of rights hopelessly idealistic and impracticable? What we want is a political theory which will tell us, for instance, how countries are actually run; we are not interested in learning how they ought to be run. Or, again, supposing that we feel ourselves suppressed, we want to know how to conduct a successful revolution, not in what sorts of circumstances revolutions are morally justifiable.

A somewhat different argument against the existence of rights can be put as follows: Supposing it be allowed that some people do, as a matter of fact, believe that they and others have rights, how do they know that what they acknowledge as rights really are rights? For it there really are any rights inherent in human nature they are obviously eternally and unchangeably rights for all men. In a word, if there are rights at all they have existed always, and they always will exist. But how can anyone be certain that what he now acknowledges and believes to be a right always has been, and eternally will be, a right? The fact that some one believes something to be a right obviously does not mean that it is one. And, indeed, when we consider the variety of different things which from time to time in the history of the world men have been convinced were rights, only subsequently to reject them, it seems foolish and short-sighted to suppose that we, and our beliefs, stand in any different and especially favoured position. Why, in the face of all the evidence to the contrary, should anyone suppose himself somehow or other to have got an insight into the nature of rights, where countless generations of men have failed?

Thus the situation is exceedingly difficult for those who assert the existence of rights. On the one hand, *every* alleged right is *prima facie* suspect, if only because so many apparently eternal and absolute rights are known by us to have been superseded. On the other hand, *no* alleged right can be proved to be really a right. In a word, since we cannot, simply on the basis of its apparent eternality and absoluteness, accept an alleged right for what it claims to be, we require to have further evidence. But, in the nature of the case, there never can be any evidence at all to support our belief in the alleged right. For how could anyone ever *prove* that what he judges to be a right is in fact one? If I believe that the earth is round, or that there is a centaur in the next room, these judgments are subject to proof (or disproof) by various more or less complicated operations. But if I disagree with some one about whether such and such a thing is a right there seems absolutely no way to settle the issue between us. And if we can never tell whether what we believe to be a right is one how can we possibly know that rights as such exist? Moreover, in what sense can there be rights which no one recognizes? Yet, certainly, if there are rights, there are some rights which no one recognizes. Thus, even if, for the sake of argument, we admit (what we have just seen can never be proved) that some rights are now correctly recognized, it must be allowed that there was a time when they were completely and utterly unknown. If, for instance, we have rights to life, liberty, and the pursuit of happiness, so does the care-free native of Polynesia, so did the mediæval serf tilling the soil of his lord, and the Carthaginian or

Celtic peasant under the heel of a Roman conqueror—so, too, presumably, did Cro-Magnon man living hundreds of thousands of years ago in his caves in Southern France. But is it not meaningless to talk about rights existing where even the concept of 'rights' is unknown and would not be understood?

These criticisms obviously vary considerably in value. Perhaps the one which is, superficially, most effective is that which attacks the reality of rights from the pragmatic position—*i.e.*, from the grounds that rights are useless and without value, and that force alone counts for anything. This type of argument is always persuasive, because, whenever we look around us in the world, the possession of force appears decisive. However, it has this appearance, often, only because we take too short a view; and many defenders of rights have therefore chosen to reply to this line of argument by pointing out that the rule of force is always conservative and static and that the world has progressed, so far as it has progressed, only because from time to time in its history there have existed men who believed sufficiently in their own and in others' rights to overturn (even if only briefly) the rule of force and thereby make a small advance. Doubtless, of course, these 'crusaders' and those whom they inspire have themselves had to use force against force, but their use of force has been successful against an already existent and militant force only because of the energy, the fortitude, and the willingness for self-sacrifice which this belief in human rights is capable of arousing. Now this reply certainly points out an important truth which the critics of rights tend either to ignore or to minimize. Unfortunately, however, it is not strictly relevant, since what it proves is the usefulness and value of a belief in rights. This argument shows only that a widespread acknowledgment of rights is valuable, and this would obviously be every bit as valuable if the belief itself was an illusion and quite unfounded.

The real reply to the pragmatic line of argument, instead of attempting to meet it on its own ground, must be simply that it is irrelevant as a criticism of the reality of rights. The fact that something is useless (supposing that it is) does not have the least bearing on whether or not the thing in question is real. Since the value which rights have is simply different in kind from the value which force has, it is impossible to compare them. When, therefore, we try to measure them in the same scale, it is not surprising to find that the value of rights seems to evaporate. But this does not mean that rights are not valuable in another way. This is not at all a surprising or unusual situation. It is, for instance, the basis of the old adage that "money cannot buy everything." Money, however, is very valuable because there are many pleasant and delightful things which one can buy with it. It is rather like force, since, like force, it is an extremely useful possession to have. Happiness, on the other hand, is not useful at all: one cannot buy anything at all with happiness. If, therefore, we try to compare these two valuable things, happiness and money, in terms of the kind of value which the latter has, it is obvious that happiness, which has none of that particular kind of value, will seem quite worthless. Yet no one would say that happiness was really without value, just because the value it has is different in kind from the value money has.

There is another point of comparison here: just as happiness is one of the things which money cannot buy, so rights are things which force cannot create. This, in fact, is precisely what people mean when they say that might cannot make right. Might cannot make right because, being different kinds of things, there is no measure common to both of them, in terms of which they can both be appraised. If what interests us in the world is, let us say, success, then it may be that force alone is relevant; but, on the other hand, if what interests us is justice, it is even more obvious that force is utterly irrelevant and that rights are the only things that matter.

It is certainly true that not everybody, by any means, recognizes the existence of rights either for himself or for others. But the fact that, say, the mediæval serf failed to recognize himself as owning the same rights which we claim for ourselves to-day should not create any difficulty for those who, like Locke, believe in the reality of rights. It should no more occasion suspicion of the reality of rights than should the same mediæval serf's ignorance that the world is round cause us to doubt either its roundness now or its roundness then. Thus it seems entirely meaningful (whether it be true is, of course, another question) to say that the serf owned rights of which he did not have even the faintest conception: this means merely that, being a man and not merely an animal, he ought to have been treated differently from the way in which he was treated. He ought, for instance, not to have had his life taken, and his property seized, by an arbitrary power without due process of law; he ought to have been able to determine for himself the character of the government which ruled over him. Because, in a word, he was a human being, he ought to have been treated humanely.

As for Cro-Magnon man, we can answer in the words which Locke applies to the rights of children.[1] For primitive man, like the modern savage, is a child—that is, he is only potentially a man. And just so far as this is the case, just so far as he has a capacity for intellectual and moral development, he has claims upon us in virtue of that capacity for being human. The answer, therefore, to the question, "What rights, if any, had Cro-Magnon man?" will depend on the information which the anthropologist can provide as to the capacities of Cro-Magnon man for development from the near animal which he was to a mature and sensitive human being. Since, in any case, he was obviously hundreds of thousands of years away from this development, if we accord him any rights which modern man has it is only, as it were, by courtesy, and in recognition of what the anthropologists tell us is the continuity of historical development between him and ourselves. In the same way, a little, new-born baby is actually only an animal, and if we accord him (as we do) the right to life, if we treat his life as an end in itself and not as a means to our advantage as we do the lives of other animals, it is not because of what he is, but because we know that this animal has it in it shortly to become a man.

But how, even if rights be admitted to exist unrecognized and unacknowledged, can any particular claim be *proved* to be really a right? It must at once be admitted that no such proof is possible. But this is not a particularly serious admission, since it is perfectly clear that there must be some things incapable of any proof. If there were not these 'ultimates' incapable of proof, if everything required to be proved, it is clear that nothing at all could be proved, for the attempt to prove *any* proposition would involve an infinite regress. That all proofs thus have to rest on unproved and unprovable propositions is doubtless distressing to the argumentatively inclined, but it is simply a fact of logic which cannot be got around. If there are, then, propositions which have to be accepted without proof, there is no reason, *a priori*, why propositions which assert the existence of rights may not be propositions of this sort.

One question, however, still remains. What are we to do if some one refuses to accept a certain alleged right as real? The answer, surely, is that we must do precisely what we do in any case in which an ultimate has been questioned. If, for instance, some one questions the cogency and validity of a theorem in geometry, we can take our analysis only so far: sooner or later we come to an ultimate, say, the postulate of parallels, on which the proof of the theorem rests and

[1] *Vide supra*, p. 158.

which is itself incapable of proof. If, then, this ultimate is questioned, all that we can do is to set out in as clear and precise language as possible what we mean and ask the questioner to "Reflect again." [1]

It is by no means easy, of course, to put clearly and unambiguously what we mean by some particular right—say, the right to life, liberty, and the pursuit of happiness. Hence it may be that the difficulty of the questioner is simply one of language. In fact, a great many, perhaps all, of the disputes and disagreements about rights may be the result of our failures to understand one another. But there seems no reason why the difficulties of some questioners may not spring from their own insensitivity to rights. There is no reason why some people may not have a blind spot for rights, just as other people are colour-blind or tone-deaf. Hence a man who honestly does not understand what is meant by a certain right and who does not feel it ought to be implemented, who does not recognize that all men have a right to life, liberty, and the pursuit of happiness need not be taken too seriously.

We do not think that tone-deaf people are good judges of symphonies, nor that colour-blind people are good art critics. On the contrary, we rightly assume that their deficiencies prohibit them from passing competent judgment on works of art. Hence it never occurs to us to think that their failure to see anything in Beethoven's Ninth Symphony or in the Sistine ceiling means that these objects are not really æsthetically valuable. We do not infer that the object is æsthetically valueless just because some one is unable to experience its value; on the contrary, we infer that that man is æsthetically insensitive because he cannot experience its value. Why, therefore, if some one is insensitive to human rights, should we suppose that this implies that those rights are not real and objective? The logical inference, surely, is rather that such a person lacks some power of cognition or feeling whose presence would enable him to see the rights which really are there.

Nor will it do to reply that the colour-blind or tone-deaf man is simply abnormal and that we have other ways of checking and testing vision and hearing, so that we can tell, independently of his failure to appreciate the work of art, that he is an incompetent judge. This is, of course, an important point. It is true that we are not warranted in calling a man an incompetent art critic merely because he is insensitive

---

[1] For an interesting discussion of this point, see H. A. Prichard, "Is Moral Philosophy founded upon a Mistake?" (*Mind*, 1912).

to the work of Michelangelo; nor can we say that a man is incompetent to pass judgments on rights merely because he fails to recognize a certain, particular right. It is also true that scientists have developed techniques by means of which vision can be tested for colour-blindness. But what this reply overlooks, and what, therefore, makes it ineffectual, is the fact that we also have an independent test in the field of sensitivity to rights. Instead of being coloured dots arranged in various patterns on a sheet of paper, it is what we might call the test of history. If we had only our own and one other man's vision as evidence we could certainly know that we differ, but we could not tell whose vision was abnormal; we could not tell which one of us was colour-blind. Similarly, if the only data available were two conflicting judgments about the existence of a certain right we should be unable to say which judgment ought to be rejected as untrustworthy. Now, certainly there have been men who simply have failed to recognize human rights or have explicitly denied their reality: Thrasymachus, Hobbes, and Nietzsche, for instance.[1] But against them can be marshalled a great array of persons who are convinced of the real existence of rights. It is important to see that this is not simply a process of counting noses (though there is little doubt what the conclusion would be if it were). What is meant is that there is something at once impertinent and pathetic about the vanity and self-assurance of a mind that puts its whole faith in its own isolated experience. It is in their opposition to this narrow attitude of mind that history and an historical tradition acquire so high a value: they give us a way of checking and verifying the scope, the depth, and the adequacy of our own private experience against the accumulated wisdom and sensitivity of the race. The kind of confirmation that rights get as a result of such an examination is the only proof of which they are capable, or which they require.

Finally, we may remark that the number of people who seriously and honestly deny the existence of rights as such is probably very small. For there is an important difference between denying that

[1] We may notice in passing another difficulty in which those who deny the reality of rights find themselves involved. Our previous discussion of Hobbes revealed that in the end he was compelled to introduce rights, after having started from a position which completely excluded them. This is also true of Thrasymachus, whose similar denial of rights led him, as Socrates pointed out, into hopeless contradiction. (See Mr Foster's volume, pp. 47–50.) The fact is that one of the greatest weaknesses of the naturalistic position is the difficulty which the naturalist always experiences in maintaining this position consistently and without lapsing into one which is incompatible with it. The reason is that naturalism is opposed to, and contradicts, whole vast ranges of human experience of which the naturalist is unable to give an adequate account without departing from his naturalism.

the word *rights* has any meaning and disagreement about what things in particular are rights. Certainly, there is a good deal of disagreement among various views in any one epoch as well as between the views of one period and those of another. We have seen that most, if not all, of this disagreement may be merely verbal. But there is no reason to suppose that people must either see a right clearly and distinctly or else not at all. Here, again, there is a useful analogy with vision: besides the kind of abnormal vision which we call colour-blindness, there are all sorts of more or less serious deviations from perfect vision—far-sightedness, short-sightedness, and so on. Moreover, there is such a thing as improving vision by training and practice. That education is important, not only in vision but in all forms of experience, is clear as soon as we observe what the expert in any field —say, the connoisseur of wines or of coffees—experiences as compared with what the ordinary layman experiences. Now, there is no reason why such differences should not exist in still other fields. Why should there not be a kind of astigmatism, for instance, in the awareness of rights which distorts our perception of them? We should, as a matter of fact, logically expect to find a more and more refined and delicate sensitivity to rights as a result of the development from youth to age —whether in the individual or the race. In a word, change, on which the critics of rights insist, may not be merely the meaningless sub-stitution of one thing for another; it may be advance, progress, development.

Whatever be the final and proper conclusion of this argument over the existence of rights (and we certainly cannot hope to settle so serious and difficult a problem here), we can at least say that the value and importance of Locke's theory rests on how this issue is decided. If there are no rights, Locke's *Treatise* must obviously be dismissed as meaningless nonsense. On the other hand, if there are rights we need not worry too much whether Locke is correct in all particulars about the list of rights which he assigns to men. What is important and valuable about his theory is that he recognizes that man is a moral being and that the state, therefore, should be a moral institution. This insight, which he expressed in the somewhat ambiguous notion of a contract between free men to form a political society for their mutual advantage and convenience, is simply the recognition that the *individual* man and his well-being are the end of the state and that this end is not merely desirable, but one that *ought* to exist. This, indeed, is the supreme value of all the contract theorists—one which far outweighs the mistaken notion into which some of them may have fallen concerning the historicity of an actual contract among primitive peoples. For in this insight, however confusedly stated, they have grasped the necessary basis of any democratic political society.

FOR FURTHER READING

Texts

See footnotes at pp. 152 and 202.

Those who are interested in Locke's general philosophical position should read his *Essay concerning Human Understanding*. A convenient abridgment of this work, together with a very useful introduction, has been edited by A. S. Pringle-Pattison (Oxford University Press, 1924).

Commentaries and General Works

AARON, R. I.: *John Locke* (Oxford University Press, 1937).
   A useful general discussion.
BOURNE, H. R. F.: *Life of John Locke* (2 vols., 1876).
   A full and readable account of Locke's life and times.
GIBSON, J.: *Locke's Theory of Knowledge and its Historical Relations* (Cambridge University Press, 1917).

Other Theories

For comparison with Locke's views, the English "Bill of Rights," vide *Select Documents of English Constitutional History* (edited by G. B. Adams and H. M. Stephens (Macmillan, 1901)), pp. 462–469, and the American "Declaration of Independence" and Constitution, vide *Documents of American History* (edited by H. S. Commager (Oxford University Press, 1937)), pp. 100–103, 138–149.

CHAPTER SIX

Charles Louis de Secondat, Baron de Montesquieu

(1689–1755)

Life

LITTLE needs to be said of Montesquieu's life beyond the fact that he was a scholar and a gentleman. Unlike most of the writers we are considering in this volume, he was the heir of an affluent and not undistinguished noble family. He was born at the family château ot La Brède, near Bordeaux, and was known as M. de la Brède, until at the age of twenty-seven he inherited the title of an uncle, together with that gentleman's fortune and office, the presidency of the parliament (law court) of Bordeaux. He had already studied law and been admitted a counsellor in the parliament. He held his presidency for ten years, during which he wrote his *Persian Letters*. These purported to be a series of letters written by visiting Persians, describing the strange customs of France to their friends at home. This scheme gave Montesquieu ample opportunity to indulge in satiric criticism of the church, the state, the king, and any of the other venerable and respected institutions of his country in which his keen eye detected a hidden flaw. The *Letters* had a great success and, though they had been published anonymously, it soon became known that Montesquieu was their author.

The attractions of life in a provincial city began to pall in comparison with the opportunities awaiting the successful author in the capital. He therefore sold his presidency and moved to Paris. After some difficulties which the *Persian Letters* caused in the minds of its more conservative members Montesquieu succeeded in securing his election to the Academy. He did not, however, linger long in Paris, but set out on an extended tour of Europe, which must

have provided much of the material for *The Spirit of the Laws*.[1] He
visited Austria, Hungary, Venice, Rome (where he was cordially
received by the Pope), Switzerland, the Rhine, Holland, and finally
England, where he stayed for nearly two years. Though there
were many traits of the English which he disliked, he was much
impressed with the degree of liberty which Englishmen enjoyed.
Indeed, one of the most important sections of *The Spirit of the Laws*[2]
is little else than a panegyric on the British Constitution, which
Montesquieu believed to be responsible for the free institutions he
found there.

When he returned to France he spent less and less time in Paris,
and was increasingly occupied in the country at La Brède with
composition. In 1734 he published his *Reflections on the Causes of the
Greatness and the Decadence of the Romans*, and in 1748, after fourteen
years of unremitting labour, *The Spirit of the Laws*. He continued
working and writing until his eyes began to fail. He died, shortly
after his sixty-sixth birthday, in February 1755.

So much for the uneventful life of this gentleman-scholar. As for
his scholarship, no series of extracts, however extensive, could give a
just idea of the immense erudition and the careful scholarship which
went into the composition of *The Spirit of the Laws*. It is certainly
true that the wealth of detail Montesquieu has accumulated sometimes
submerges the main design of the work, that it is repetitious, frequently inconsistent, and very often inaccurate, and that modern
scholarship has invalidated many of Montesquieu's conclusions by
showing that his subject is even more complex than he himself realized.
Despite all flaws, however, *The Spirit of the Laws* is a monument
to, if it is not itself an example of, sound scholarship. Montesquieu
realized that political inquiry should have an empirical basis, and
he combined this realization with the development of a technique
of investigation suited specifically to this subject, and not borrowed
from theology, logic, or mathematics. Thus Montesquieu is not so
important for the permanent value of his contributions to political
theorizing as he is for his impact on the development of methodology
in political and social studies. That is to say, that Montesquieu is not
primarily a political *philosopher*. It is true that he expressed with
clarity and vigour the liberal and humanitarian ideals of the century:
his voice shares with Locke's and Rousseau's in that rising chorus

[1] *Vide infra*, for example, pp. 242*ff*.
[2] *Vide infra*, pp. 245*ff*.

which was to break into mighty song before the century's end. It is also true that he exercised a great influence on the development of constitutional practice.[1] But the fact remains that his major contribution lies not in the field of theory, but in the field of method.

Montesquieu saw not only that human institutions, customs, and laws vary widely, but that they vary to a very considerable extent with certain physical conditions like climate and soil. Hence he realized that an investigation of all such relations will throw light both on the nature of these institutions and on the possibility of their alteration and improvement. He saw, that is, that human institutions do not descend on us ready-made from a divine source, but that they have a natural *growth*, like any plant. An institution is nothing but a certain specific set of determining relations which unites a group of individuals and which, in joining them, gives them all a certain character. Hence every individual man is moulded by, and in, the various institutions of which he is a member. He and they may be studied in their various modifications and transformations, just as the different modifications which a rose-bush or an oak-tree undergoes in different environmental conditions may be studied by the botanist.

All of this amounts to saying that, after Montesquieu, it ought to have been impossible to think any longer of politics as confined to the study of what sort of code of laws, what sort of formal constitution, is 'best.' Politics, Montesquieu saw, is an integral and organic part of the whole nexus of human relations. Formal, statute law (which Montesquieu called "positive" law) is merely the highly articulate and conscious expression of much more basic and fundamental mores. Political 'science,' or the study of government, is, therefore, meaningless in isolation from a study of these patterns, or habits, of behaviour. It is, indeed, but one aspect of a much larger study which includes psychology, physiology, anthropology, geography, religion, economics, history—a study which some people to-day dignify with the title "sociology," and of which, surely, Montesquieu is one of the most important founders. If, as we have said, Hobbes is the father of social *science*,[2] Montesquieu is the father of *social* science.

---

[1] Whether Montesquieu exerted a *direct* influence on the founding fathers at the Constitutional Convention is perhaps a moot point. But there is no doubt that the doctrine of checks and balances was 'in the air' at the time, nor that the various measures incorporated into the Constitution are closely parallel to what Montesquieu advocated.

[2] *Vide supra*, p. 91.

POLITICAL PHILOSOPHY
The Concept of Law

Law, as the title Montesquieu chose for his work suggests, is its central subject. It is the keystone which makes the whole intelligible, by tying together into unity an otherwise heterogeneous collection of essays on the most diverse subjects: education, the history of the French monarchy, economics, climate and geography, the feudal system, British parliamentary practice, and a host of others. The concept of law is at once the most important, the most interesting, and the most difficult part of the work. We must therefore first turn our attention to the task of comprehending the meaning Montesquieu gives to this term. If we succeed here the rest will be easy; if we fail we shall have missed Montesquieu's chief contribution to the development of political thought.

Let us begin by making an observation which may seem a long way from our topic. When we look at the world about us we are impressed by two things: the fact of order, sequence, regularity, in a word, the fact of *uniformity*; and the fact of change, flux, difference, and *diversity*. On the one hand, there is the regularity with which day succeeds night, summer succeeds winter, death succeeds birth. "There is nothing new," we have constant occasion to remark, "under the sun." But on the other hand, none of these things ever recurs in precisely the same way: the world is as infinitely various as the ever-changing colour of sky or ocean. Both unity and variety seem ineluctable characteristics of the world of our experience. But in man's speculation about that world he has almost always falsified his experience of it by emphasizing one of these characteristics (either one) to the exclusion of the others. Let us call those who emphasize uniformity 'absolutists'; and 'relativists' those who emphasize diversity. The dispute between absolutists and relativists appears in many aspects of life, but nowhere more crucially than in the field of moral, political, and social relations. The relativist is impressed by the great diversity of laws, customs, moral codes, and types of government which sociologists and anthropologists have found in different parts of the world, and by the apparent dependence of all these different types on varying physical and social conditions in differing parts of the world. Since he can find no common principle accepted by all men, he denies the existence of any such principle. The absolutist, on the other hand, is impressed by the unity in things. Since he cannot, of course, deny the existence of this actual diversity, he is obliged to affirm the existence of what he calls a 'real' or 'ideal' moral code and type of government which, he claims, is absolutely valid and best for all men everywhere. Thus Plato, for example, recognized that the Athenians, the Spartans, and the Persians had different customs, different kinds of government, and that each judged his own to be the best. But he maintained that there was an absolutely best "stored up in heaven," from which all these different actuals deviated and in terms of which they could be appraised.

There are difficulties, naturally, with both of these extreme positions. The chief problem the relativist has to face is his inability to make comparisons between the different moral codes or types of government. One cannot, for instance, compare two measurements of length unless the disputants can agree on some one measuring rod as being valid for this measurement. My rod may say that the room is ten feet long and yours may say that it is eleven. We clearly cannot get on until both of us accept some other rod (say the one in the Standards Department of the Board of Trade) as final and definite. The Greek thinks his way of life good, the Persian his. They differ. Which is better? The relativist cannot say, since according to him there is no standard by which both of these different moral codes may be compared. Thus, for the relativist, there can be no more disputing about morals and politics than there is about taste. Unfortunately for the relativist's position, there *is* disputing about these things—more than about anything else. No one, not even the relativist himself, really believes that it is completely idle to argue about, and impossible to compare, the relative merits of, say, the Beatitudes and *Mein Kampf*.

The absolutists, of course, have no difficulty about such comparative judgments and evaluations, since they admit, and, indeed, insist on, the existence of *one* absolute law or code which is really best. But how is the absolutist to know what this absolute code is? Various absolutists differ embarrassingly, and, as we look back in history, it seems to be the case that absolutists have often naïvely accepted the code current in their own social milieu as being final for all men everywhere.

If we were to reconcile these two extreme views (neither of which, as we have just seen, is really tenable), we might consider for a moment the reconciliation already worked out and generally accepted in the field of *natural* phenomena. Here, just as much as in the realm of

man's opinions and customs, there is a great diversity on the surface—
an infinitely various and always changing world of sight, sound, and
touch. But, beneath it, we believe to exist another world of law
—the "laws of nature," we say—by which we mean the ordered,
necessary relations in which all these natural objects really stand to
one another. Thus the relation 'to the right of,' between the lamp at
my elbow and the piece of paper on which I am writing varies from
day to day, from moment to moment, even; and seems accidental,
unordered, chaotic. But, actually, we believe it to be a *necessary* relation,
because, it follows from certain already existing factors such as the
hour of the day, the candle-power of the bulb in the lamp, the weakness of my eyes, the whiteness of the paper I am writing on. Again,
if I overturn the lamp as I write, this new relation of the lamp, to my
elbow may be an 'accident,' but it is also a necessary product of certain
conditions including the lamp's weight, its centre of gravity, the
force exerted by my elbow, etc., etc. Similarly, the fall of an apple
in an orchard and the movement of the earth round the sun seem at
first sight to be completely different and unrelated events. Actually,
however, both are manifestations of the same law—gravity. When
the various complex factors of their different environments are taken
into account we can say that the apple's relation to the earth on to
which it falls and the earth's relation to the sun round which it spins
are identically the same and expressible in terms of the law of inverse
squares.[1] Thus, in the field of natural phenomena there is real unity,
real order, in the midst of change and diversity.[2]

Why cannot the same relationship between diversity and uniformity hold in the sphere of men's moral and political behaviour as
holds, we believe, in the behaviour of inanimate bodies? Why may
there not be certain fundamental patterns of behaviour—certain basic
relations—which never appear on the surface of men's conduct, but
which nevertheless give order to otherwise chaotically diverse opinions

---

[1] Bodies attract each other directly with their masses and inversely with the squares of
their distances.

[2] Montesquieu himself points this out. "These [*i.e.*, the laws of nature] are a fixed and
invariable relation. Between bodies in relative motion, movement is received, increased,
diminished, or lost, according to the relation of the quantity of matter and velocity.
Each diversity is *uniformity*, each change is *constancy*." *De L'Esprit des Lois* (*Œuvres
Complètes de Montesquieu* (8 vols., 1799)), Book I, chapter 1. The title of this work causes
some difficulty in English.   It is usually translated as "The Spirit of the Laws." We shall
follow that precedent, though Montesquieu's meaning is probably more adequately
conveyed by rendering it "The Spirit of Law." What he means is that he is trying to display the real essence or nature of laws as such. The translation given in the following
extracts is based on that of Thomas Nugent, revised by J. V. Prichard (Bohn, 2 vols.,
1896–97), but it has been corrected and repunctuated for the present volume.

and customs? If this were the case the indefinitely various *actual* behaviour patterns, conventions, customs, types of moral code, and forms of government which we find at different times in different parts of the world might be explicable in terms of the different kinds of environment, climate, etc., in which these different societies have lived.

This is precisely what Montesquieu asserted. It is, indeed, the basic assumption of his whole work. And he set himself the tremendous dual task of (1) determining what these basic underlying uniformities are and (2) what the factors are which produce the actual, observed diversity. Finally, also, he wanted to show (3) how these differences are in fact produced, so that it would be possible for statesmen and legislators to control them in the interest of making each different type of government as complete an exemplification of the ideal as it is possible for it to be.[1]

¶ Laws, in the widest possible connotation, are any necessary relations arising from a thing's nature. In this sense all beings have their laws: the Deity His laws, the material world its laws, the intelligences superior to man their laws, the beasts their laws, man his laws. . . .

I have first of all examined mankind. My conclusion is that, despite such an infinite diversity of laws and manners, they were not solely conducted by the caprice of fancy.

I have laid down the first principles, and have found that the particular cases follow naturally from them; that the histories of all nations are only consequences of them; and that every particular law is connected with another law, or depends on some other of a more general extent.

Every nation will here find an explanation of its maxims. From this we may naturally infer that to propose alterations belongs only to those who are so happy as to be born with a genius capable of penetrating the entire constitution of a state. . . .

In other words, for Montesquieu *any* relation between one thing and some other thing is a 'law.' If this terminology seems odd and forced we must remember that Montesquieu thinks that the words 'relation' and 'law' are synonymous, because he conceives the whole world in all its parts to be, through and through, ordered and regular

[1] *Spirit of the Laws*, I, 1, and preface.

in its behaviour. Moreover, this order and regularity is not merely
accidental or arbitrary; it is, through and through, rational. That is
to say, it is the kind of order, like that of, say, the number series,
which can be grasped and understood by the rational human mind.

Men, like the rest of nature, stand in ordered, necessary relations to
one another. But law in human behaviour is more complicated
because men are self-conscious and possess will. This means (1) that
they do not always and, as it were, automatically follow the pattern
established for human behaviour, as plants, for instance, follow the
pattern established for plant behaviour. In other words, men, unlike
the rest of nature, are *free* to modify, or altogether reject, behaviour
patterns which in the lower creatures and in inanimate nature are
fixed and necessary. Hence (2), men require to be ordered by another
kind of pattern. They require another kind of restraint, and this,
being self-conscious, they are able to give themselves. In a word, the
behaviour of men is complicated by the presence of law in another,
but analogous, sense. They are also subject to 'law' in the sense, not of
fixed behaviour patterns, but of rules, given by some man or assembly
or established by custom, which they must follow, subject to certain
penalties for failure to do so. In a word, religion, ethics, and politics
appear in man alone of all creation. They appear in him because they
are necessary to compensate for the presence in him of intelligence
and will, which he alone possesses.[1]

¶   The intelligent world is far from being so well governed as the
physical. For though the former has also its laws, which of their
own nature are invariable, it does not conform so exactly as does
the physical world. This is because particular intelligent beings are
limited by their nature, and consequently are liable to error; and
also because their nature requires them to be free agents. Hence
they do not steadily conform to the laws of their nature. Indeed
they frequently infringe even those of their own instituting.

Whether brutes be governed by the general laws of motion,
or by a particular movement, we cannot determine.[2] Be that as it
may, . . . it is by the allurement of pleasure that every individual

---

[1] *Spirit of the Laws*, I, 1.
[2] Hobbes, of course, maintained (*vide supra*, pp. 90–92) that animals do not have a
"particular movement"—that is, that their behaviour is not fundamentally different from
that of an inanimate object like a falling stone. Montesquieu leaves this point open, but he
does see (what is surely the case, though Hobbes denies it) that animal behaviour—and
still more so human conduct—is more free than that of 'vegetables' or stones.

¶ preserves its own life, as it is also by the same attraction that the species is maintained. Animals have natural laws, because they are united by sensation; but they do not have positive laws, because they lack knowledge. However, they do not invariably conform to their natural laws. These are better observed by vegetables, that have neither understanding nor sense. . . .

Man, as a physical being, is, like other bodies, governed by invariable laws. As an intelligent being, he incessantly transgresses the laws established by God, and changes those of his own instituting. . . . Though a limited being, and subject, like all finite intelligences, to ignorance and error, he is left to his own direction. . . . As a sensible creature, he is subject to a thousand impetuous passions. Such a being might every instant forget his Creator. God has therefore reminded him of his duty by the laws of religion. Such a being is liable every moment to forget himself; philosophy has provided against this by the laws of morality. Formed to live in society, he might forget his fellow creatures; legislators have therefore by political and civil laws confined him to his duty.

Thus in the sphere of human affairs, we have, besides natural law, what Montesquieu calls "positive," or man-made, law. And this positive law naturally varies—just as oak-trees growing in different parts of the earth vary—among different peoples living in different regions. Thus Montesquieu differs from an absolutist like Plato, who assumed that one type of government, one code of law, suits all men in all places and at all times. He was never guilty of taking this extreme view. He recognized the differences in men's natures and capacities which made different types of law, different manners and customs, essential. But he did not, on the other hand, fall into the equally fallacious relativistic position of merely reporting and recording those differences. His view is quite compatible with a belief in an absolute criterion. Indeed, Montesquieu is constantly insisting on the difference between what law actually is and what it ought to be. This means that he believes a comparison is possible. The fact that some code has been decreed or established by an authority or become a part of a people's mores, may make this code *law*, but it does not make it right. Montesquieu states the difference between what is merely *de facto* and what is *de jure* very clearly in the chapter from which we have just been quoting.[1]

[1] *Spirit of the Laws*, I, 1.

¶ Particular intelligent beings may have laws made by themselves. But they are also subject to laws which they have not made. Before there were intelligent beings, they were possible. They therefore had possible relations, and consequently possible laws. Before laws were made, there were relations of possible justice. To say that there is nothing just or unjust but what is commanded or forbidden by positive laws, is as absurd as to say that the radii of a circle are made equal by the act of drawing the circle.[1]

We must therefore acknowledge relations of justice antecedent to the positive laws by which they are established: as for instance, if human societies existed, it would be right to conform to their laws; if there were intelligent beings that had received a benefit of another being, they ought to show their gratitude; if one intelligent being had created another intelligent being, the latter ought to continue in its original state of dependence; if one intelligent being injures another, it deserves a retaliation; and so on.

The End of Government: Liberty

Natural law, though Montesquieu does not say so very plainly, appears to be simply those relations which we can infer would exist between men who did not live in a political state. We infer them from what we know about men's nature, physical and mental. Thus we know enough about man's body to know that in any circumstances it will need nourishment. Hence we can say that to seek for nourishment is a 'law of nature.'[2] There is obviously no distinction at this level between *de facto* and *de jure* any more than there is in the animal or vegetable kingdoms. But, as we have just seen, such a distinction does exist at the level of positive law. Hence Montesquieu cannot say, simply, that positive laws are the relations which follow from men's natures as social animals. This type of law has to be distinguished as good or bad. Laws are bad which are derived from bad principles or incorrectly derived from good or 'true' principles. There is a lacuna in Montesquieu's reasoning at this point, since he does not tell us what the true principles are. But presumably they must be the laws of nature already referred to. At least, if this is the case, an otherwise obscure point becomes intelligible. We can then

---

[1] This is, of course, the Hobbesian position. The example Montesquieu gives is particularly effective against Hobbes, who admitted the absolute, and not merely relative, validity of mathematics and who had, on his own basic assumptions, no business to do so.
[2] *Spirit of the Laws*, I, 2.

say that good positive laws (*i.e.*, positive laws which are *de jure* besides being *de facto*) are those which harmonize with, supplement, and otherwise implement the various natural laws. Though natural law (the 'true' principles) is everywhere the same, positive law will, of course, vary widely among different peoples, since the same natural law requires to be implemented in very different ways depending upon the different circumstances of the various nations and races, and their different capacities.

Now according to Montesquieu, "peace [is] the first law of nature."[1] Hence it follows that the highest principle of government is security. "All states," we are told, "have the same general end, which is to maintain themselves." [2] But this end is not conceived merely negatively as the preservation of life.[3] Another and better word to describe what Montesquieu has in mind is 'liberty.' Just as men have an "innate detestation of force," so, on the other hand, is "the love of liberty natural to mankind." [4]

Over and over again Montesquieu defines Liberty, presenting now this, now that, aspect of the whole complex notion which he has in mind.[5]

¶   There is no word that has been given more varied meanings, and has evoked more varied emotions in the human heart than 'liberty.' Some have taken it as a means of deposing him on whom they had conferred a tyrannical authority; others for the power of choosing him whom they must obey; still others for the right of bearing arms, and of being able to use violence. Others again have meant by liberty the privilege of being governed by a native of their own country, or by their own laws. A certain people for a long time thought liberty consisted in the privilege of wearing a long beard.[6] Some have annexed this name to one form of government exclusively of others: those who had a republican taste applied it to this species of government; those who liked a monarchical state gave it to monarchy. Thus they have applied the name of *liberty* to the government most suited to their own customs and inclinations. Since in republics the people have not so constant and so present a

---

[1] *Spirit of the Laws*, I, 2.   [2] *Ibid.*, XI, 5.
[3] Speaking of despotism, Montesquieu says that it too aims at "tranquillity; but this tranquillity cannot be called peace. No, it is only the silence of those towns which the enemy is about to seize" (V, 14).
[4] *Ibid.*, V, 14.   [5] *Ibid.*, XI, 2-4; XI, 6; XIX, 27.
[6] In a note at this point Montesquieu reminds us that "the Russians could not bear that Czar Peter should make them cut it off."

¶ view of the causes of their misery, and since there the magistrates seem to speak less and the laws more, liberty is generally ascribed to republics rather than to monarchies. In fine, since in democracies the people seem to act almost as they please, this sort of government has been deemed the most free, and the power of the people has been mistakenly identified with their liberty.

It is true that in democracies the people seem to act as they please. Political liberty, however, does not consist in an unlimited freedom to do what one pleases. In governments, that is, in societies directed by laws, liberty can consist only in the power of doing what we ought to will, and in not being constrained to do what we ought not to will.

We must continually bear in mind the difference between independence and liberty. Liberty is a right of doing whatever the laws permit, and if a citizen could do what they forbid he would no longer be possessed of liberty, because all his fellow-citizens would have the same power. . . .

The political liberty of the subject is a tranquillity of mind arising from the opinion each person has of his safety. In order to have this liberty, it is requisite the government be so constituted that one man need not be afraid of another. . . .

As the enjoyment of liberty, and even its support and preservation, consists in every man's being allowed to speak his thoughts, and to lay open his sentiments, the citizens of a [free] state will say or write whatever the laws do not expressly forbid to be said or written.[1]

[1] In an interesting section Montesquieu points out that one of the best ways of maintaining a sense of security is to establish a fixed and just code of criminal procedure. "Knowledge . . . concerning the surest rules to be observed in criminal judgments is more interesting to mankind than any other thing in the world. Liberty can be founded on the practice of this knowledge only. In a state which had the best laws imaginable in this respect, a person tried under these laws and condemned to be hanged the next day, would nevertheless have more liberty than a pasha enjoys in Turkey" (XII, 2). Among important rules of criminal procedure, Montesquieu mentions that "those laws which condemn a man to death on the deposition of a single witness are fatal to liberty. In reason there should be two, because a witness who affirms, and the accused who denies, make an equal balance, and a third must incline the scale." Again, "It is an important maxim, that we ought to be very circumspect in the prosecution of witchcraft and heresy. The accusation of these two crimes may be vastly injurious to liberty, and productive of infinite oppression, if the legislator knows not how to set bounds to it." The same thing holds true with respect to accusation of treason. "Nothing renders the crime of high treason more arbitrary than declaring people guilty of it for indiscreet speeches. Speech is so subject to interpretation; there is so great a difference between indiscretion and malice; and frequently so little is there of the latter in the freedom of expression, that the law can hardly subject people to capital punishment for words unless it expressly declares what words they are. Words do not constitute an overt act; they remain only an idea. . . . Thus a man

Liberty, in a word, is diametrically the opposite of despotism. Despotism is the arbitrary, irregular, and lawless fiat of an individual will. The life of the individual subject under a despot is therefore chaotic, uncertain, insecure, above all, miserable. True liberty, on the other hand, is not the capacity to do whatever I happen to will now; for this would be to make of me an arbitrary despot. It is rather that freedom which has its source in the sure, regular, and rational restraint of law.

Montesquieu's whole purpose in his *Spirit of the Laws* can now be restated in terms of this ideal of liberty. It is nothing less than to give concrete practical advice, based on historical precedent and other empirical evidence, about how to achieve liberty. He saw quite clearly that different peoples could achieve liberty (in his sense of the word) only in quite different ways, and also that different peoples were capable of different degrees of liberty, and hence that it would only end in misery and misfortune if we attempted to treat all men alike. In fact, his whole problem was simply to help statesmen everywhere in achieving "the object of legislation," which, in the words of Solon, is to give a people "the best laws which they can bear." [1]

The Plan of the Work

Montesquieu begins with a few definitions.[2] "Body politic" is the "united strength of many individuals." The "sovereign" is the person or persons who wield this power. But this power which the sovereign is to wield and which has its source in the union of various individuals into a body politic, depends in its turn on a real "conjunction of the wills of all these individuals." Here we get at the heart of the matter. How is such a conjunction of wills to be attained? In the first place, obviously, through the existence of a constitution which orders men's relations to one another and therefore provides the basis for co-operation and goodwill. And, in the second place, the precise type of constitution chosen must be in harmony with the manners and customs, and with the capacities and temperaments of the people for whom it is to serve. In a word, no type of constitution is *absolutely*

who goes into a public market-place to incite the subjects to revolt incurs the guilt of high treason, because the words are joined to the action, and partake of its nature. It is not the words that are punished, but an action in which the words are employed. . . . Everything is confounded if words are construed into a capital crime. . . . In writings there is something more permanent than in words, but when they are in no way preparative to high treason they cannot amount to that charge" (*Spirit of the Laws*, XII, 3, 5, 12–13).

[1] *Spirit of the Laws*, XIX, 21.   [2] *Ibid.*, I, 3.

best. In any given case, that type is best which "best agrees with the humour and disposition of the people in whose favour it is established." In fact, the laws require to be so exactly adapted to the "manner of the people for whom they are framed that it should be a great chance if those of one nation suited another."

Montesquieu realizes, as hardly anyone before him had done, that law in the true and full sense is not an artificial code handed down to a people from above. It is rather the whole body of relations, multiple and complex, growing, developing, changing, in which the various individuals in a society stand to one another. Law, in its totality, is that which gives a society its particular and unique character, which makes it *this*, rather than some other, society. It is true, of course, that Montesquieu distinguishes between law, in the narrow sense, and customs or manners. "Laws are the particular and precise institutions of a legislator, and manners and customs the institutions of a nation in general."[1] Or, again, "Laws are established, manners are inspired."[2] This is a useful technical distinction: thus we have a law fixing speed limits or prohibiting robbery, while it is (or is not) a national custom to go to church on Sundays or to wear black for mourning. But this difference is overshadowed by the fact that law and custom are both expressions of, and relative to, the whole social mores of a given people. In this wider sense law and custom are identical, or, as Montesquieu says, "Fixed and established customs have a near resemblance to laws."[2] Laws (in the sense of the promulgations of a sovereign) and customs are alike behaviour patterns which order men's relations to one another; they are alike, again, in issuing from, and being expressive of, the character and temper of the people to whom they relate; and, finally, they are alike in serving (though in different ways) the same purpose of producing a "conjunction of wills" among the members of a community.

Thus Montesquieu sees that his inquiry into what sort of law is best for a given type of people has to extend far beyond an investigation of different types of constitution. It is equally essential to study the various educational, social, economic, and religious institutions of a people in order to see whether these harmonize with the constitution and with that people's basic character. The legislator who hopes to succeed in his task must see to it that the laws he promulgates are

---

[1] *Spirit of the Laws*, XIX, 14. Montesquieu also distinguishes between custom and manners, but this difference is unimportant here (*ibid.*, XIX, 16).
[2] *Ibid.*, XIX, 12.

relative to "the general spirit of the nation." And this is formed by "various causes: by climate, by religion, by the laws,[1] by the maxims of government,[2] by precedents, morals and customs." [3]

Hence *The Spirit of the Laws* begins with an analysis of the different types of constitution, which is intended to show what is the essence (or "principle") of each. Thus, for instance, the principle of the republican type of government is "virtue," that of the monarchical type, "honour." What Montesquieu means, apparently, is that if a republic is to be a successful government in a given state, the citizens of that state must be capable of being motivated by considerations of virtue; while, on the other hand, if considerations of honour move them, monarchy is a more suitable type of government. In this way the legislator can ascertain what kind of government is "most comformable" [4] to the people for whom he is legislating. Once this is settled he must see to it that the other, non-political, institutions of his state are adjusted to this type of government. Thus, for instance, the kind of education suitable in a republic will contradict the principle of a monarchy. For the former attempts to inculcate virtue, while the latter requires that the citizens be taught honour. This leads Montesquieu to a detailed study of what "the laws of education ought to be in relation to the Principles of Government." [5] In the same way he is led to discuss the relation to the various types of government of different codes of criminal and civil law;[6] marriage, property, and inheritance laws; taxes,[7] commerce, and exchange;[8] population;[9] various social institutions such as the relations between the two sexes;[10] parents and children, master and servant;[11] and, finally, religion.[12]

In all of these connexions we must take into account the climate, which, Montesquieu thinks, is one of the most influential factors determining a people's character and capacities. "If it be true that the temper of the mind and the passions of the heart are extremely different in different climates, the laws ought to be in relation both to the variety of those passions and to the variety of those tempers." The kind of government, the kinds of institutions, which are suitable for a Northern European people would be hopelessly out of place if

---

[1] Montesquieu refers here, of course, to the laws already existing and operating at the time the legislator begins his work.
[2] Presumably this means current political theories.
[3] *Spirit of the Laws*, XIX, 4.
[4] *Ibid.*, I, 3.   [5] *Ibid.*, IV.   [6] *Ibid.*, VI.
[7] *Ibid.*, XXII.   [8] *Ibid.*, XX–XXII.   [9] *Ibid.*, XXIII.
[10] *Ibid.*, VII; XXVI, 13–14.   [11] *Ibid.*, XVI.   [12] *Ibid.*, XXIV–XXV.

the attempt were made to set them up among the negroes in Central Africa. In a word, the general outline of Montesquieu's argument is simplicity itself: If we want certain common ends—peace, stability, prosperity, happiness—what are the various ways, depending upon the different conditions in which men find themselves, of realizing them? The institutions of a given country [1]

¶ should be in relation to the climate of that country, . . . to the quality of its soil, to its situation, to its extent, to the principal occupation of the natives, whether husbandry, huntsmen, or shepherds. They should have relation to the degree of liberty which the constitution will bear; to the religion of the inhabitants, to their inclinations, riches, numbers, commerce, manners, and customs. . . . In all of these different lights they ought to be considered. This is what I have undertaken to perform in the following work.

The Types of States

It is impossible (as it would be profitless) to follow Montesquieu in the almost infinite detail into which this project leads him. Much of what he reports is inaccurate or incorrect; and, in any case, his greatest distinction is not the conclusions which he reaches, but his empirical method and the recognition of the relativity of law to social milieu. It will, however, be worth our while to examine a few typical points in some detail. We may begin with Montesquieu's analysis of types of government. Besides the two we have already mentioned [2] he admits a third—despotism. This classification is not very satisfactory. Aristocracy appears as an ambiguous sub-type; and he is soon obliged to admit that despotism does not belong in his scheme, since (being essentially lawless) it is really not a government at all. Finally, though Montesquieu does not quite see this himself, it becomes apparent that he really has two main types of government: those that are moderate and those that are not. And immoderate governments tend to become despotisms (and so not true governments) just so far as they substitute for the rule of law, rule by arbitrary fiat—whether it be that of a single individual or a mob.

Let us begin with Montesquieu's definition of his original three types. [3]

[1] *Spirit of the Laws*, I, 3.
[2] Monarchy and republic. *Vide supra*, p. 231.
[3] *Spirit of the Laws*, II, 1.

¶ A republican government is that in which the body, or only a part of the people, is possessed of the supreme power; monarchy, that in which a single person governs by fixed and established laws; a despotic government, that in which a single person directs everything by his own will and caprice, without law and without fixed rules.

This is what I call the nature of each government. We must now inquire into those laws which follow directly from this nature, and which are, therefore, fundamental laws.

(a) Republics [1]

¶ When, in a republic, the body of the people is possessed of the supreme power, it is called a *democracy*. When the supreme power is lodged in the hands of a part of the people, it is then an *aristocracy*.

In a democracy the people are in some respects the sovereign, and in others the subject.

There can be no exercise of sovereignty but by their votes, and these votes express their own will. The sovereign's will is the sovereign himself. The laws therefore which establish the right of suffrage are fundamental to this type of government. And indeed it is as important to regulate in a republic, in what manner, by whom, to whom, and concerning what, suffrages are to be given, as it is in a monarchy to know who is the prince, and after what manner he ought to govern. . . .

The people, in whom sovereign power resides, ought themselves to do all that they can do well; what they cannot do well ought to be done by their ministers. But these cannot properly be said to be their ministers unless the people have the power of nominating them: it is, therefore, a fundamental maxim of this government, that the people should choose their ministers—that is, their magistrates. . . .

Similarly, the manner of giving this suffrage is another fundamental law of republics. Suffrage by *lot* is natural to democracy; as that by *choice* is to aristocracy. . . .

In an aristocracy sovereign power is lodged in the hands of a certain number of persons. These are invested both with the legislative and the executive authority; and the rest of the people are no

[1] *Spirit of the Laws*, II, 2-3.

¶ more, in respect to them, than are the subjects of a monarchy in respect to the monarch. . . .

When the nobility are numerous, there must be a senate to regulate the affairs which the body of the nobles are incapable of deciding. In this case it may be said that the aristocracy is in some measure in the senate, the democracy in the body of the nobles, and the people are nothing.

It would be a very happy thing in an aristocracy if the people, in some measure, could be raised from their state of annihilation. . . . The best aristocracy is that in which those who have no share in the power are so few and inconsiderable that the dominant party have no interest in oppressing them. . . . Aristocratic families ought, therefore, to be as much as possible on a level with the people. The more an aristocracy approaches to democracy, the more nearly perfect it becomes; and, in proportion as it tends towards monarchy, the more it is imperfect. But the most imperfect of all is that in which the part of the people that obeys is in a state of civil servitude to those who command, as is the case in Poland, where the peasants are slaves to the nobility.

(b) Monarchies [1]

¶   The intermediate, subordinate, and dependent powers constitute the nature of monarchical government; that is, of a government in which a single person governs by fundamental laws. . . . These fundamental laws necessarily presuppose intermediate channels through which the sovereign power flows: for if there be only the momentary and capricious will of a single person to govern the state, nothing can be fixed, and hence there is no fundamental law.

The most natural intermediate power is that of the nobility. This in some measure seems to be essential to a monarchy, whose fundamental maxim is, *no monarch, no nobility; no nobility, no monarch;* but there may be a despotic prince.

There are men who have endeavoured in some countries in Europe to suppress the jurisdiction of the nobility, not perceiving that they were driving at the very thing that was done by the parliament of England. Abolish the privileges of the lords, the clergy, and the cities in a monarchy, and you will soon have a

---

[1] *Spirit of the Laws,* II, 4.

¶ popular state, or else a despotic one. . . . Power in the hands of the clergy is just as proper to a monarchy, especially of the absolute kind, as it is dangerous to a republic. What would become of Spain and Portugal, since the subversion of their laws, were it not for this power, which is the only barrier against the incursions of arbitrary power? Any barrier is useful when there is no other: for since a despotic government is productive of the most dreadful calamities to human nature, the very evil that restrains it is beneficial to the subject. . . .

It is not enough to have intermediate powers in a monarchy. There must be also a depositary of the laws. This can only be the judges of the supreme courts of justice, who promulgate the new laws, and revive forgotten ones. The natural ignorance of the nobility, their indolence and contempt of civil government, require that there should be a body invested with the power of reviving and executing the laws, which would otherwise be buried in oblivion. The prince's council is not a proper depositary. It is naturally the depositary of the momentary will of the prince, and not of the fundamental laws. Besides, the prince's council is continually changing. It is neither permanent nor numerous. Neither has it a sufficient share of the confidence of the people. Consequently it is incapable of setting them right in difficult conjunctures or of reducing them to proper obedience.

(c) Despotisms [1]

¶   From the nature of despotic power it follows that the single person, invested with this power, delegates the execution of it also to a single person. A man whose five senses continually inform him that he himself is everything and that his subjects are nothing, is naturally lazy, voluptuous, and ignorant. In consequence of this, he neglects the management of public affairs. But were he to commit the administration to many, there would be continual disputes among them; each would form intrigues to be his first slave; and he would be obliged to take the reins into his own hands. It is, therefore, more natural for him to resign it to a vizir, and to invest him with the same power as himself. The creation of a vizir is a fundamental law of this government. . . .

[1] *Spirit of the Laws*, II, 5.

The Principles of the Three Types

So far Montesquieu has given us only the most general outlines of the constitution of each type of government. Before he fills in the details he pauses to consider what he calls the "principle" of each type. By this he means the motive which leads the citizens of the various states to conform to the law. It is all very well to establish a constitution for a people, but, as Montesquieu sees, unless this people is moved to act under it nothing has been accomplished. What sorts of consideration, then, what sorts of motives, desires, and ambitions, would move the citizens of democracies, monarchies, etc., to act under, and in accordance with, the spirit of their respective constitutions?[1]

¶ Having examined the laws in relation to the nature of each government, we must investigate those which relate to its principle. There is this difference between the nature and principle of government, that the former is that by which it is constituted, the latter that by which it is made to act. One is its particular structure, and the other the human passions which set it in motion.

(a) The Democratic Principle [2]

¶ No great share of probity is necessary to support a monarchical or despotic government. The force of laws in one, and the prince's arm in the other, are sufficient to direct and maintain the whole. But in a popular state something more is required, namely, *virtue*.

This assertion is confirmed by the unanimous testimony of history, and is extremely agreeable to the nature of things. . . . When virtue is banished, ambition invades the minds of those who are disposed to receive it, and avarice possesses the whole community. The objects of their desires are changed. . . . Formerly they were free while under the restraint of laws, but now they would fain be free to act against law. Each citizen is like a slave who has run away from his master, and that which was a rule of action he now calls restraint. . . .

Montesquieu means by virtue, political probity, patriotism, and a love of equality. It is the opposite of avarice, luxury, and selfish ambition.[3]

¹ *Spirit of the Laws*, III, 1.   ² *Ibid.*, III, 3.   ³ *Ibid.*, V, 2-3.

¶ Virtue in a republic is a most simple thing. It is a love of the republic. It is an immediate and spontaneous feeling, not a consequence of reflection and knowledge. It is a sentiment that may be felt by the meanest as well as by the highest person in the state. . . .

A love of the republic is a love of . . . equality. It is likewise a love of frugality.[1] Since all men ought here to enjoy the same happiness and the same advantages, they should consequently taste the same pleasures and form the same hopes, which cannot be expected but from a general frugality. The love of equality limits ambition to the sole desire, to the sole happiness, of doing greater services to our country than the rest of our fellow-citizens. They cannot all render her equal services, but they all ought to serve her with equal alacrity.

(b) The Monarchical Principle [2]

¶ In monarchies, policy effects great things with as little virtue as possible, just as, in the most efficient machines, we find the fewest movements, springs, and wheels. In monarchies the state subsists independently of the love of country, of the thirst for true glory, of self-denial and the sacrifice of our dearest interests, and of all those heroic virtues which we admire in the ancients and which are known to us only by tradition. . . .

If monarchy lacks one kind of motive, it is provided with another. Honour, that is, the prejudice of every person and rank, here supplies the place of political virtue and is everywhere its representative. Here honour is capable of inspiring the most glorious actions and, joined with the force of laws, may lead us to the end of government as well as virtue itself.

Thus a monarchical government presupposes pre-eminence and ranks, and likewise a noble descent. . . . Ambition is pernicious in a republic. But in a monarchy it has some good effects; it gives life to the government, and it is attended with this advantage, that it is in no way dangerous, because it may be continually checked.

It is with this kind of government as with the solar system. In each there is a power that constantly repels all bodies from the centre, and a power of gravitation that attracts them to it. Honour sets all parts of the body politic in motion, and by its very action connects

---

[1] There is a detailed discussion of how to 'inspire' the citizens of a republic with a love of equality and frugality (*Spirit of the Laws*, V, 4-7).   [2] *Ibid.*, III, 5-7.

¶them. Thus each individual advances the public good, while thinking only of promoting his own interest.

(c) The Despotic Principle [1]

¶   As virtue is necessary in a republic, and honour in a monarchy, so fear is necessary in a despotic government. Virtue is not needed there, and honour would be extremely dangerous. . . . In a despotism people capable of setting a value upon themselves would be likely to create disturbances. Fear must therefore depress their spirits and extinguish even the least sense of ambition.

A moderate government may, whenever it pleases, and with the least danger, relax its springs. It supports itself by the laws and by its own internal strength. But when a despotic prince ceases for one single moment to uplift his arm, when he cannot instantly demolish those whom he had intrusted with the first employments, all is over. . . .

Though all this is perhaps over-simple, Montesquieu has a sound point here. He does not, of course, claim to give an account of what motives are *actually* present in the citizens of a republic or the subjects of a monarchy. His only contention is that these motives ought to be present if these different governments are to be successful. Again, he does not claim that each of these motives is *exclusively* present in its respective state.[2] He merely says that the sense of honour, the desire for fame, titles and advancement, plays about the same role in a monarchy as does a public-spirited sense of duty in a republic.

If we know the kind of motive (or, better, the kind of character) a people must possess in order for a given type of government to be successful two important conclusions follow. (1) Certain types of government are at once seen to be unfeasible and inappropriate for certain peoples, and certain others feasible and appropriate. (2) It becomes important to see to it that the various institutions in the state —above all, the system of education—are directed towards developing in the people the kind of character, and towards inculcating in them the kinds of ideals, which are appropriate to that particular type of government.

---

[1] *Spirit of the Laws*, III, 9.
[2] He does say that it is difficult for men living under a monarchy to be virtuous in the political sense (*ibid.*, III, 6).

Education

Of the various social institutions which mould character, we may take as typical the discussion of education.[1]

¶ The laws of education are the first that we receive; and as they prepare us for civil life, the education which every private family gives to its children ought to be governed by the plan of that great household (*i.e.*, the state) which comprehends them all. . . . The laws of education will therefore be different in each species of government: in monarchies they will have honour for their object; in republics, virtue; in despotisms, fear.

(*a*) [2] In a republican government the whole power of education is required. The fear of despotic governments naturally arises of itself amidst threats and punishments; the honour of monarchies is favoured by the passions and favours them in its turn; but virtue is a self-renunciation, which is ever arduous and painful. This virtue may be defined as the love of the laws and of our country. It requires a constant preference of public to private interest. . . .

Everything depends on establishing this love in a republic. To inspire it ought to be the principal business of education; but the surest way of instilling it into children is for parents to set them an example.

(*b*) [3] In monarchies the principal source of education is not men's formal schooling. Their real education begins when they leave school to go out in the world. For this is the school of what we call honour, that universal preceptor which ought everywhere to be our guide.

Here it is that we constantly hear three rules or maxims, *viz.*, *that we should have a certain nobleness in our virtues, a kind of frankness in our morals, and a particular politeness in our behaviour.*

The virtues that are taught here are less what we owe to others than to ourselves. They are not so much what draws us towards society, as what distinguishes us from our fellow-citizens. . . .

Education in monarchies requires a certain politeness of behaviour. . . . Politeness . . . generally . . . arises from a desire of distinguishing ourselves. It is pride that renders us polite: we are flattered with being taken notice of for behaviour which shows that we are not of a mean condition. . . .

[1] *Spirit of the Laws*, IV, 1.   [2] *Ibid.*, IV, 5.   [3] *Ibid.*, IV, 2.

¶ There is nothing so strongly inculcated in monarchies, by the laws, by religion and honour, as submission to the prince's will. But this very honour tells us that the prince never ought to command a dishonourable action, because this would render us incapable of serving him. . . .

There is nothing that honour more strongly recommends to the nobility than to serve their prince in a military capacity. And, indeed, this is their favourite profession, because its dangers, its successes, and even its misfortunes, are the road to grandeur. . . .

Honour therefore has its supreme laws, to which education is obliged to conform. The chief of these are (1) that we are permitted to set a value upon our fortune, but are absolutely forbidden to set any upon our life; (2) that, when we are raised to a post or preferment, we should never do or permit anything which would seem to imply that we look upon ourselves as inferior to the rank we hold; and (3) that those things which honour forbids are more rigorously forbidden, when the laws do not concur in the prohibition, just as those it commands are more strongly insisted on, when they happen not to be commanded by law.

(c)[1] As education in monarchies is directed towards elevating the mind, in despotic governments its only aim is to debase it. Here education must necessarily be servile. Excessive obedience presupposes ignorance in the person that obeys. . . . In despotic states, therefore, . . . education . . . must be very much limited. All it does is to strike the heart with fear and to inculcate a few very simple principles of religion. Here learning would prove dangerous . . . and as for virtue, Aristotle cannot believe that there is any one virtue belonging to slaves. If so, education in despotic countries is confined within a very narrow compass.

Taxes

We may give one more example of the way in which, according to Montesquieu, laws and institutions have to vary in different kinds of governments, by a brief extract from Book XIII, on Taxation.[2]

¶ The *public revenues* are a portion that each subject gives of his property, in order to secure or enjoy the remainder. To fix these revenues in a proper manner, regard should be had both to the

---

[1] *Spirit of the Laws*, IV, 3.   [2] *Ibid.*, XIII, 1, 12–14.

¶necessities of the state and to those of the subject. The real wants of the people ought never to give way to the imaginary wants of the state. Imaginary wants are those which flow from the passions and weakness of the rulers, from the vain conceit of some extraordinary project, from the inordinate desire for glory, and from a certain impotence of mind incapable of withstanding the impulse of fancy.[1] Often ministers of a restless disposition have imagined that the wants of their own mean ignoble souls were those of the state.

Nothing requires more wisdom and prudence than the regulation of . . . the public revenues. They should be measured not by the people's abilities to give, but by what they ought to give. . . .

It is a general rule that taxes may be heavier in proportion to the liberty of the subject, and that there is a necessity for reducing them in proportion to the increase of slavery. This . . . is a rule derived from nature that never varies. . . . In moderate governments there is an indemnity for the weight of the taxes. This is liberty. In despotic countries there is an equivalent for liberty, which is the lightness of the taxes. . . .

Taxes may be increased in most republics, because the citizen, who thinks he is paying himself, cheerfully submits to them. . . . In a monarchy taxes may be increased, because the moderation of the government is capable of procuring opulence: it is a recompense, as it were, granted to the prince for the respect he shows to the laws. In despotic governments they cannot be increased, because there can be no increase of the extremity of slavery.

A head tax is more natural to slavery; a duty on merchandise is more natural to liberty, by reason it has not so direct a relation to the person. . . . Since the tax on merchandise is really paid by the consumer, though advanced by the merchant, it is a loan which the latter has already made to the former. . . . Just in proportion to the moderation of the government, to the prevalence of the spirit of liberty, and to the security of private fortunes, a merchant has it in his power to advance money to the state, and to pay considerable duties for individuals. In England a merchant really lends to the government fifty or sixty pounds sterling for every tun of wine he imports. Where is the merchant that would dare do any such thing in a country like Turkey? And were he so presumptuous, how could he do it with the crazy and shattered fortune which a despotism allows him?

[1] Here we may presume that Montesquieu is paying his respects to Louis XIV.

Climate

If Montesquieu's discussion of climate in its relation to law is one
of the least exact and most over-simplified sections of *The Spirit of
the Laws*, it is, historically speaking, one of the most important. It
is not too much to say that it marks the beginning of modern investigation into the physical conditions which bear upon, and at least
partially determine, the character of various human institutions.

Montesquieu begins with a quaint account of the effects of different
temperatures on the body.[1]

¶ Cold air constringes the extremities of the external fibres of the
body. This increases their elasticity, and favours the return of the
blood from the extreme parts to the heart. . . . On the contrary,
warm air relaxes and lengthens the extremes of the fibres and so
diminishes their force and elasticity. People are therefore more
vigorous in cold climates. Here the action of the heart and the
reaction of the extremities of the fibres are better performed. . . .
The blood moves more freely towards the heart, and reciprocally
the heart has more power. This superiority of strength must produce various effects: for instance, a greater boldness and courage, a
greater sense of superiority and so a greater desire for revenge; a
great opinion of security, that is more frankness, less suspicion,
polity and cunning. In short, differences in climate must be productive of very different tempers. . . .

Again, the nerves that terminate from all parts in the cutis form
each a nervous bundle. . . . In warm climates where the skin is
relaxed the ends of the nerves are expanded and laid open to the
weakest action of the smallest objects. In cold countries the cutis is
constringed and the papillæ compressed . . . so that the sensation
does not reach the brain unless it be very strong. Now, imagination,
taste, sensibility, and vivacity depend on an infinite number of small
sensations. Hence the possession of these capacities is relative to the
climate. . . .

In cold countries they have very little sensibility for pleasure;
in temperate countries more; in warm countries their sensibility is
exquisite. . . . I have been at the opera in England and in Italy,
where I have seen the same pieces and the same performers. Yet
the same music produces such different effects on the two nations:

[1] *Spirit of the Laws*, XIV, 2.

¶ one is so cold and phlegmatic, and the other so lively and enraptured, that it seems almost inconceivable. . . .

From this delicacy of organs peculiar to warm climates it follows that the soul is most sensibly moved by whatever relates to the union of the two sexes. . . . In northern climates the animal part of love has scarcely a power of making itself felt. In temperate climates love, attended by a thousand appendages, endeavours to please by things that have at first the appearance, though not the reality, of this passion. In warmer climates it is liked for its own sake; it is the only cause of happiness; it is life itself.

. . . If we travel towards the north we meet with people who have few vices, many virtues, and a great share of frankness and sincerity. If we draw near the south, we fancy ourselves entirely removed from the verge of morality. Here the strongest passions are productive of all manner of crimes, each man endeavouring, let the means be what they will, to indulge his inordinate desires. . . .

The heat of the climate may be so excessive as to deprive the body of all vigour and strength. Then the faintness is communicated to the mind. There is no curiosity, no enterprise, no generosity of sentiment. The inclinations are all passive. Indolence constitutes the highest happiness . . . and slavery is more supportable than the force and vigour of mind necessary for human conduct.

Through its effect on the body climate clearly has an important bearing on legislation. Montesquieu surveys this relation in detail and in every possible field, from laws against drunkenness to the institution of marriage. We may illustrate his general treatment of this subject by a quotation from his discussion of slavery. It is clear from what has already been said, that Montesquieu believes that peoples living in the tropics are fitted only for a despotic government. But at the same time his generous liberalism pulls him in the opposite direction, and he is torn between rejecting slavery altogether and admitting it in certain special cases.[1]

¶ We ought not to be astonished that the effeminacy of the people in hot climates has almost always rendered them slaves; and that the bravery of those in cold climates has enabled them to maintain their liberties. This is an effect which springs from a natural cause. . . .

[1] *Spirit of the Laws*, XVII, 2.

Earlier, however, we are told that [1]

¶   Slavery, properly so called, is the establishment of a right which gives to one man such a power over another as renders him absolute master of his life and fortune. The state of slavery is in its own nature bad. It is useful neither to the master nor to the slave—not to the slave, because he can do nothing through a motive of virtue; nor to the master, because by having an unlimited authority over his slaves he insensibly accustoms himself to the want of all moral virtues, and hence becomes fierce, hasty, severe, choleric, voluptuous, and cruel.

In despotic countries civil slavery is more tolerable than in other governments. . . . There are countries where the excess of heat enervates the body and renders men so slothful and dispirited that nothing but the fear of chastisement can oblige them to perform any laborious duty: slavery is there more reconcilable to reason. . . .

Natural slavery, then, is to be limited to some particular parts of the world. In all other countries, even the most servile drudgeries may be performed by freemen. . . .

I know not whether this article be dictated by my understanding or by my heart. Possibly there is not that climate upon earth where the most laborious services might not with proper encouragement be performed by freemen.

Liberalism : the Ideal of Moderation

When Montesquieu speaks from the heart, his voice carries those accents of humanitarianism which were soon to sweep over Europe in a rising tide. Again and again, as in these chapters on slavery, he speaks out against absolutism and tyranny in favour of justice, humanity, tolerance. Thus, for instance, in the chapter from which we have just been quoting, he declares, "No labour is so heavy but it may be brought to a level with the workman's strength, if it be regulated by equity and not by avarice." [2] Or, in another connexion, "The alms given to a naked man in the street do not fulfil the obligations of the state, which owes to every citizen a certain subsistence, a proper nourishment, convenient clothing, and a kind of life not incompatible with health." [3]

Montesquieu constantly recurs to the thesis that moderation is the essential condition for attaining that peace and security which is the

---

[1] *Spirit of the Laws*, XV, 1, 7-8.   [2] *Ibid.*, XV, 8.   [3] *Ibid.*, XXIII, 29.

end of all government. "I say, and methinks I have undertaken this
work with no other view than to prove this assertion, that the spirit of
a legislator ought to be that of moderation: political, like moral, good
lies always between two extremes."[1] "Lenity and moderation are
better qualifications for a good government than are roughness and
severity."[2] The very nature of a despotism makes moderation
impossible. On the other hand, though it is possible in republics,
there are other disadvantages with a republican type of government[3]
which incline Montesquieu to favour monarchy—that is, of course,
where the conditions are such as to make it feasible. Unfortunately,
not all monarchies are moderate. They tend, on the contrary, constantly to be corrupted and changed either into despotisms or into
democracies.[4] The best way to preserve a moderate monarchy and to
prevent its being usurped either by a single individual or by a multitude
is to give it a constitution in which the various components in the
government are held in balance, each one checking and being checked
by every other. This is the famous doctrine of checks and balances,
which Montesquieu mistakenly believed to be the essence of the
British constitution and which was in fact subsequently introduced
into the American Constitution.[5]

¶   In every government there are three sorts of power: the legislative, the executive, and ... the judiciary.... When the legislative
and executive powers are united in the same person, or in the same
body of magistrates, there can be no liberty.... Again, there is no
liberty if the judiciary power be not separated from the legislative
and executive. Were it joined with the legislative, the life and
liberty of the subject would be exposed to arbitrary control, for
the judge would then be legislator. Were it joined to the executive,
the judge might behave with violence and oppression.
    There would be an end of everything were the same men or the
same body (whether of nobles or of the people) to exercise all three
powers. ...
    The legislative power should reside in the whole body of the
people. But since this is impossible in large states, and in small ones
is subject to many inconveniences, the people should transact by

---

[1] *Spirit of the Laws*, XXIX, 1.   [2] *Ibid.*, VII, 17. *Cf.* III, 4; V, 8; V, 11, etc.
[3] Republican governments are possible only in small states, where the citizens are content to lead a simple and abstemious life. Even so, a monarchical government has one
great advantage over a republican: it is able to act with greater expedition. *Cf. ibid.*, V, 10.
[4] *Cf. ibid.*, VIII, 6.   [5] *Ibid.*, XI, 6–7.

¶ their representative what they cannot transact by themselves. . . . It is not necessary that these members of the legislative be chosen from the general body of the nation. It is satisfactory if, in every considerable town, a representative be elected by the inhabitants. The great advantage of representatives is their capacity for discussing public affairs. For this the people collectively are extremely unfit, which is one of the chief inconveniences of a democracy. . . .

The nobility ought to be hereditary. In the first place, it is so in its own nature; and in the second, it must have a considerable interest in preserving its privileges—privileges that in themselves are obnoxious to popular envy, and so in a free state always in danger. But a hereditary power might be tempted to pursue its own particular interests and to forget those of the people. Hence in matters like the laws relating to taxation, where a very singular advantage might be gained through corrupting the nobility, this must be guarded against by allowing them no other share in the legislation than the power of veto. . . .

The executive power ought to be in the hands of a monarch, because this branch of government, having need of despatch, is better administered by one than by many. . . . The executive power ought to be given a share in the legislation . . ., otherwise it would soon be stripped of its prerogative. . . . This share must consist in the power of veto. . . .

Here, then, is the fundamental constitution of the government we are treating of. The legislative body is composed of two parts which check one another by the mutual privilege of veto. They are both restrained by the executive as the executive, in turn, is restrained by them. These three powers should naturally form a state of repose or inaction. But as there is a necessity for movement in the course of human affairs, they are forced to move, but still in concert. . . .

The monarchies we are acquainted with, unlike the [British] constitution which we have just described, do not have liberty for their immediate and primary end. Their only aim is rather the glory of the subject, of the state, or of the sovereign. . . . Though they do not distribute the three powers in accordance with the model we have just described, they do achieve some kind of partial distribution. In the degree to which this partial distribution is attained, they also realize political liberty in greater or lesser degree.

¶If they did not achieve it at all, their monarchy would degenerate into despotic government.

These last paragraphs reveal very plainly the special character of Montesquieu's mind. Here we have what is certainly a great and noble ideal—an ideal, moreover, not conceived *ab novo*, but growing out of the whole culture and tradition of the Western world. But this ideal is not asserted with the utopian fervour of the pure visionary or reformer. It is stated with a profound sense of its relativity to the actual political, social, and physical structure of a given people at a given time. We cannot, Montesquieu says, hope to achieve this ideal universally, or immediately, or independently of a complex milieu of institutions of all kinds. And not only this: we not only have to recognize that the ideal of political liberty is dependent on the attainment of certain specific institutions: we have also to recognize that these institutions themselves, however desirable, cannot be imposed on a people willy-nilly. They can only grow out of that people's nature and capacities. Political wisdom consists in knowing enough about their nature to help them to grow.

FOR FURTHER READING

Translations

See footnote, p. 222.

Commentaries and General Works

BECKER, C.: *The Heavenly City of the Eighteenth-century Philosophers* (Oxford University Press, 1932).
An entertaining and stimulating book on the period as a whole.
FLETCHER, F. T. H.: *Montesquieu and English Politics* (E. Arnold, 1939).
An attempt to trace Montesquieu's 'influence' in England.
SOREL, A.: *Montesquieu* (translated by M. B. and E. P. Anderson (McClurg, 1888)).

Other Theories

HAMILTON, A., JAY, J., and MADISON, J.: *The Federalist* (Everyman Library, 1911).

CHAPTER SEVEN

Jean Jacques Rousseau

(1712–78)

LIFE

PHILOSOPHERS seldom lead exciting lives or do anything of interest to anyone save their biographers. Their works, not their adventures, cause them to be remembered. To this rule Rousseau is a startling exception. His life and personality epitomize one of the great turning-points in the history of the Western mind. This is the transformation that occurred towards the end of the eighteenth century, from the cold, clear alpine atmosphere of the Enlightenment, to the dark and shadowy light characteristic of the Romantic reaction. We have only to compare the impartial and deliberate, the sceptical and objective, intellect of Montesquieu with Rousseau's "feeling heart" in order to sense the change that was coming over Europe. It was nothing less than the change from the bleak and disinfectant air of a hospital to the passionately vibrating warmth of a mediæval cathedral.

Rousseau was born in Geneva on June 28, 1712. Calvin's spirit still brooded over his city almost a hundred and fifty years after his death. The Genevans were still dominated by the purest, the strictest, and the narrowest church in Protestant Europe; and it is not fanciful, surely, to attribute something of Rousseau's interest in morality, his profound and passionate desire to improve the condition of mankind, to this Genevan background. To the same source may be traced Rousseau's violent disapproval of 'modern' culture, as he saw it later displayed in the Parisian salons of his aristocratic friends.

But if Rousseau was too much of a Genevan to stomach Paris, he was also too much of a Frenchman to be happy in Calvin's city. When his Huguenot ancestors fled to Geneva from France in the middle of the sixteenth century they seem to have brought with them some unstable, effervescent strain which accorded ill with the Geneva atmosphere. His maternal grandfather died of dissipation at the age of thirty-two, and his mother had some mild 'affair' (harmless enough anywhere but in puritanical Geneva, but shocking and unheard of there) before her marriage. His father, Isaac, started life in the respectable trade of watchmaker, but abandoned it to become a dancing-master. Shortly after his marriage to Rousseau's mother he left her to go to Constantinople.[1] "She urged him to return," Rousseau tells us in his *Confessions*.[2] "He abandoned everything and came home. I was the sad fruit of this reunion. Ten months afterwards I was born, ill and weak; I cost my mother her life, and my birth was the first of my misfortunes."

He was not unnaturally spoiled by his widowed father ("No one ever forced me; no one ever crossed my will"), who kept him awake all night reading aloud romances and adventure stories. Looking back on this early period, Rousseau says, "In a short time I had acquired, by this method, not only a tremendous ease in reading and comprehending, but also an insight into the passions quite unique in one of my age. . . . I understood nothing—I felt everything. All of the obscure emotions which I underwent, one after another . . . formed in me intelligence of a peculiar character and gave me wonderful and romantic impressions of life of which experience and reflection have never quite been able to cure me."

This is profoundly true, perhaps more so even than Rousseau himself realized. He was never capable of rational, sustained, and disciplined thought. He felt deeply, sensitively, passionately; at times beautifully, at other times morbidly, almost pathologically. Nothing could be more characteristic of his mind than the Preface with which he begins his *Confessions*.[3]

¶ Here is an enterprise without a precedent, one which will never have an imitator: I propose to show to my fellows a man in the whole truth of his nature. And that man is myself.

I, and no one else. I feel my heart within me, and I know other men. I am not made like any one that I have seen. I dare believe

---

[1] *Wanderlust* was, therefore, in Rousseau's blood. When his father signed an agreement with some other dancing-masters he included a clause to the effect "qu'il lui sera permis de faire un voyage, lorsque bon lui semblera" (quoted in Gerhard Gran, *Jean Jacques Rousseau* (translated by M. H. Janson, Blackwood, 1912), p. 39). Like father, like son. Rousseau, too, never hesitated to put aside whatever he was doing, to cast off all obligations in order to make a voyage, when it seemed good to him to do so.

[2] Quoted in Gran, *op. cit.*, p. 45.

[3] J. J. Rousseau, *Œuvres Complètes* (13 vols., Hachette, 1911), *Les Confessions*, vol. VIII, p. 1. The extracts from this edition have been translated especially for this volume.

¶ that no one like myself exists; and, if I am not better, at least I am different. As to whether nature has done well or ill in breaking the mould within which I was cast, you may judge after you have read what I have written here.

Let the trump of the Last Judgment sound when it will. I shall come with this book in hand, to present myself before the Sovereign Judge. And I shall say aloud, "Here is written what I have done, what I have thought, what I have been. I have put down the good and the bad with the same honesty. I have not tried to minimize what is bad, nor to add to what is good. . . . I have shown myself just as I was: vile and contemptible when I was; and good, generous, sublime when I was that. . . . Assemble about me, Eternal Being, the innumerable crowd of my fellow-men. Let them hear my confessions, let them lament my sins and blush at my unworthiness. But let each of them uncover himself before Your Throne with the same sincerity; and let a single one say, if he dare, *I was better than that man.*"

Here the type of all romantic genius speaks: insolent vanity, utter self-absorption, surrender to feeling, melodramatic bombast, unpleasant exhibitionism—all the symptoms are here. And Rousseau's life is the faithful mirror of his soul. He stole, and put the blame on a helpless, ignorant girl; he deserted a sick friend because the task of looking after him was irksome; he lived off a succession of women who fell in love with him because they wanted to mother him; he took up a whole series of different professions, only to fail in each in turn, because he lacked the perseverance and the patience to keep at them; he became a Catholic when the support of an elderly admirer seemed to depend on it, and later abandoned Catholicism when Protestantism was made a condition of his using the proud title, "Citizen of Geneva"; he lived with a stupid and uneducated woman for twenty years without marriage and had five children by her whom he placed in a foundling home because it was too much trouble to take care of them.

This is not a pretty picture; but it has another side, like Romanticism itself. In the autumn of 1749, while on his way to visit Diderot, then imprisoned at Vincennes, he had an experience akin to the kind of religious conversion which some mystics have known. As he walked along the road reading a newspaper, he chanced to see the announcement of an essay contest, conducted by the Dijon Academy, on the subject, *Has the Revival of the Sciences and the Arts helped to Purify or to Corrupt Morals?* "Instantly I saw the universe, and I became *another man.*" [1]

¶ If ever anything has resembled a sudden inspiration, it was the movement which occurred in me when I read these words. All at once, my mind was dazzled by a thousand lights, by a crowd of ideas presenting themselves together with such force and in such confusion that I was thrown into inexpressible agitation. I was overcome by a giddiness like that of drunkenness and such a violent palpitation oppressed me that . . . I flung myself under a tree where I lay for half an hour in such emotion that, on rising, I found my coat soaked with tears which I had not been aware of shedding. If only I had been able to write down a quarter of what I felt under that tree, with what clarity I would have pointed out all of the contradictions of our social system! With what force I would have exposed all the abuses of our institutions! With what simplicity I would have demonstrated that man is naturally good and that it is only through these institutions that he becomes wicked!

Here is another Rousseau: the man who first and most powerfully asserted the modern democratic belief in the infinite capacities of the ordinary man for development and improvement. Believing, on the one hand, in the innate goodness of man and, on the other hand, in the viciousness of contemporary society, Rousseau was in a position to offer a penetrating criticism of the social and political institutions of the *ancien régime*, on the grounds that they stifled human nature and prevented men from becoming what they have it in them, potentially, to be. Here, then, is the author of *The Social Contract*, of *Émile*, of *The New Héloise*: the impassioned defender of the rights of man against the usurpations of tyranny, not only in his attack on the old order, but in his programme for the kind of government and the kind of education which would make man free by the full development of his personality through a suitable environment. This is the man who was persecuted for his views, who was hounded from city

---

[1] *Confessions*, Part II, Book VIII (*Œuvres Complètes*, vol. VIII, p. 249).
  There are extant several accounts of this incident—three by Rousseau himself, all (naturally) different. The passage which follows is from the account given in a letter to Malesherbes, dated January 12, 1762 (*vide* Rousseau, *op. cit.*, *Correspondence*, X, 301). The difficult question as to which version most nearly corresponds to the actual facts of the case is discussed in detail by Gran, *op. cit.*, chapter 18.

to city in Europe as a dangerous character, whose books were banned
and burned by the public executioner, and who finally was permitted
to return to France, to die a broken and despondent old man, perhaps
by his own hand, on July 2, 1778, only two or three days after his
sixty-sixth birthday and a few short years before the Revolution of
which he was in large measure the inspiration and the prophet.

POLITICAL PHILOSOPHY

Background of Rousseau's Thought

It is no mere accident that Rousseau called his principal essay on
politics *The Social Contract*.[1] It was natural, and indeed inevitable,
that his thought should move within that general pattern of concepts
which takes the basis of political organization to be a compact between
free and independent men. The notion of a contract served to express
the growing sense of the relatively superior importance of the individual citizens of the state as opposed to the government which controls
them, and the new recognition of the value of every human individual
simply because he is a man and not because of the station in life to
which he happens to have been born. It provides a way of saying
that these individuals and their happiness and well-being are the end
to which the various agencies of the executive, even the king himself,
are but the means.

The notion of a contract, though capable of ingenious distortion
by Hobbes, more naturally accords with a theory like Locke's. It is,
indeed, central to such a theory. It serves to connect the two theses
which such theories regard as crucially important: the proposition that
there are certain absolute, moral rights possessed by all men; and the
proposition that the government's existence is conditioned upon its
willingness and ability to implement these rights. If the contract
theorists incidentally asserted the actual historical occurrence of a
contract between men, this, as we have seen, is a secondary matter
and logically irrelevant to their main purpose, which was that of

[1] The text of the *Contrat Social*, which was used as a basis for the extracts which follow,
is that printed by C. E. Vaughan in *The Political Writings of Jean Jacques Rousseau* (2 vols.,
Cambridge University Press, 1915), vol. II, pp. 21–134. References in the notes are to the
books and chapters of the *Contrat Social*, with the paging of Vaughan's edition given in
parentheses. The translation has been made by the present author especially for the present
volume.

defining the kind of state and the kind of relations between sovereign and subjects which they thought ought to exist.

This, generally speaking, is the position from which Rousseau begins; and, in this sense of the word, we may say that he was profoundly influenced by Locke. But, while Rousseau starts like Locke, he ends by reaching a very different conclusion. Thus his political philosophy has none of the simplicity and clarity of Locke's. It is confused and puzzling, ambiguous and contradictory, an almost hopeless maze of impassioned and violent assertions leading off in various directions, no one of which is pursued to its logical conclusion. The Social Contract is, indeed, a reflection of the multiple and diverse interests and attitudes of its author, just as Locke's Treatise, in its turn, is a reflection of the simplicity and straightforwardness of his life. It is not, however, merely the case that Locke's mind is more logical and consistent than Rousseau's: a part of Rousseau's difficulty results from his attempt to settle some of the problems which Locke's view involves, but which Locke himself does not altogether recognize.

Of these, by far the most crucial is the problem of consent. Consent, of course, was no problem for Locke—it was the basis of the state. It is that which, when given, makes a state moral, legitimate, and just; and which, when withheld, makes a ruler either a tyrant or a usurper. At the inception of the modern period, during the sixteenth and seventeenth centuries, the great problem had been to authorize and to ensure the authority of the national sovereign against lesser forces, such as the feudal nobility, within the state. This was how the problem appeared to Bodin and Hobbes. But when the battle for sovereign authority had been won Locke and others began to realize that the danger had now reversed itself. So far from the sovereign not being powerful enough, the problems which political theorists now faced resulted from the sovereign's having become too powerful. The sovereign had come to be regarded (or at least to think of himself) as a separate and distinct entity, having a life of his own, and having an end and purpose of his own—his own well-being—to which everything else in the state could and should be subordinated.

It was historically inevitable, therefore, and entirely correct for Locke to insist on the requirement of the subject's consent. What Locke has to say on this topic is both true and important. But unfortunately he does not go far enough. In particular, he does not see two things: (1) mere initial consent at the time of a formal contract is not sufficient, since the sovereign's acts are morally justifiable only if they are continually consented to; and (2) a majority is just as capable of exercising force against a minority in a democracy, as is one man against all of the people. In a word, Locke does not see that consent is just as much a problem in a democratic state as it is in the most absolute of tyrannies founded on the ruthless exercise of force. In fact, of all tyrants, a majority, unenlightened by any sense of the whole public good, is the most brutal, the most ruthless, and the most powerful.

It is precisely this that Rousseau saw, and the attempt to solve this problem is his chief preoccupation in The Social Contract. This attempt, we can say at once, is not entirely successful. Indeed, it leads him to a view which subsequent thinkers have developed into a position utterly at variance from Rousseau's Lockian foundation— that is, the conception of the totalitarian state.[1]

Rousseau himself was far from reaching this extreme conclusion, nor would he have accepted it had he seen that it might be derived from his own position. But the view, even only as far as he carried it himself, marks a sufficiently radical break with the Lockian concepts from which he began. This explains the striking disparity between some of Rousseau's earlier writings, like the Discourse on Inequality, and The Social Contract. One of Rousseau's recent editors has re- marked on this difference and has shown that the same disparity exists between an earlier draft of The Social Contract and the final published version.[2] This earlier draft and the Discourse agree in describing the state of nature as a utopian condition. Here Rousseau goes far beyond Locke in the idealistic picture he draws of individual human nature. In comparison with such a state of affairs, communal and social living and the political organization which it necessitates are a distinctly inferior mode of life. In the state man inevitably acquires certain vices and diseases, which have caused a marked degeneration from the perfect condition which was once his. Indeed, Rousseau looks upon social and political man as a fallen angel, and the biblical story of the expulsion from Eden might easily be a poetical account by Rousseau of man's fall from the paradise of a separate and individual existence into the state.

In the final draft of The Social Contract, all of this is changed. One reason for this change is obvious. Rousseau is no longer simply a reformer crying out against the evils of the society in which he lives; he has now addressed himself to the task of justifying the existence of

[1] Vide infra, pp. 322ff.   [2] Cf. Vaughan, op cit., I, 7ff.

the state and its organization, and he could hardly succeed in doing so if he continued to take as his starting-point a position which maintained *any* communal living to be degenerate and bad. But even more important than this change in purpose and in point of view is the change which appears to have been caused by his reflection on the problem of consent. The need he felt to improve on Locke's solution led Rousseau to the concept of a general will, which, in its turn, profoundly altered his conception of the relation of individuals to one another. Thus there resulted a doctrine of social living which directly contradicts the extreme individualism and separatism which we find in the earlier works.

According to this new conception *there is a common good into the creation of which all men can, and must, enter*, since in it they find the best good for themselves as individuals. Just so far as men live separate lives—whether actually separate in a physical sense, or only morally distinct because they refuse to subordinate their own private ends to the good of the whole group—their lives are incomplete and imperfect, and they fail to attain the mode of life best for themselves as individuals. This is obviously the complete reversal of his original position. The state of nature, so far from being an ideal from which man has departed, now becomes merely the notion of a more or less neutral condition in which men (though they are not positively bad) fail to realize all they have it in them to be, because they are leading relatively separate and independent lives. In other words, Rousseau has reached a conception of man and his relation to his fellows essentially identical with that of Plato and Aristotle. These Greek philosophers held that this relation is *organic*. That is, just as each of the various organs of, say, the human body lives its best life only in fruitful, harmonious, and co-operative functioning with all the other organs of the body, so the individual man's life is good and happy only in and through his various associations (including the state, as the highest and most perfect) with his fellows. The relations between individuals are *organic* because men are so made that they are organs in a whole whose life is a kind of rhythm pervading the lives of all its constituent elements.

This Greek view is the antithesis of the conception underlying Christian monasticism. The monk believed that only in solitary communion with his God can he attain the supreme good of life— the salvation of his soul. The Greeks, on the other hand, taking the end of life to be the fullest development of the individual's own

character and personality in all their varied aspects, came to the conclusion that a man can realize his highest good only in close and
intimate association with his fellows. Men may do for one another what
no man can entirely do for himself; hence every association (including
the state) is a mutual and co-operative undertaking for self-realization.[1]
Thus when Aristotle called man a political animal he meant that man
is so constituted as to depend on association with his fellows for
living to the fullest. And when he added that the political state is
natural, he meant, not that men necessarily live in societies, but that
it is good for them to do so, because they are so constituted as to find
this their best and most fruitful environment.

With all of this, Rousseau's position in *The Social Contract* would
entirely agree if only it were developed consistently. Unfortunately,
Rousseau is far from abandoning his earlier view and continues to
talk about a state of nature in which men were free and independent.
If Rousseau had clearly recognized the implications of his new view
of the contract, he would have seen that, from this point of view, the
state of nature is really something 'unnatural' in the same sense that we
give to the word when we talk of an unnatural vice, or an unnatural
child. Solitude, in a word, is unnatural, or abnormal, because it occurs
relatively seldom and because, when it does occur, it is bad or leads to
bad results. Thus, though Rousseau actually calls *solitude* 'natural,'
he ought to have followed Aristotle in calling *association* 'natural.'
For what Rousseau ought to mean is identical with what Aristotle
actually says: in *The Social Contract* he agrees with Aristotle in thinking
that the solitary life is inadequate, incomplete, and, in this sense, abnormal and immoral. But Rousseau has completely inverted the
meaning assigned to the term *nature*. If it be asked why Rousseau uses
the word 'natural' to mean what Aristotle would have called 'unnatural,' the answer can only be that Rousseau's terminology was
already fixed by his earlier thought on the subject, when he held that
solitude was the good and proper state for men—*i.e.*, when he originally
held that solitude was natural he meant by 'natural' what the term

---

[1] It will be recalled that both Plato and Aristotle took contemplation as the highest good
of all, since reason, according to their view, is the most valuable single element in the
human personality. It might be thought that contemplation is something that one can do
alone, indeed, that it can be done better in solitude than in company. Anyone, however,
who has experienced the stimulation which *discussion* affords will see the truth of the Greek
conception of association, even in this field. One not only gets (and gives) valuable criticism in the course of discussion, but new ideas emerge which one had not even thought
of before. These are a product of the association of minds, not merely a contribution which
one particular mind makes to some other mind.

means for Aristotle. Then, in spite of the fact that he concluded that solitude is bad, he continued to call it natural.

It is impossible indeed not to find Rousseau guilty of inconsistency in his thought as well as in his terminology, since, not seeing at all clearly the great difference between his earlier and later conceptions of the contract, he has allowed them to lie side by side to the almost hopeless confusion of the reader. In this sort of situation, the critic who is not disposed tediously to retrace the intricate and slippery path of Rousseau's actual reasoning—an undertaking hardly calculated to improve anyone's grasp of Rousseau's theory—can only ignore Rousseau's frequent deviations from consistency and concentrate on the passages in which Rousseau develops the implications of his new conception of the contract. To do so is not to add anything to what Rousseau himself said or to carry his argument beyond the point where he left it; it only frees Rousseau's important new doctrine from the tangle of irrelevancies in which he has hidden it. This procedure can do no harm so long as we remember that the course of Rousseau's own thought is much more devious. Otherwise we are likely to end with a more favourable estimate of *The Social Contract* than that document actually deserves. But, after all, what is of primary concern to us is not to make a critical evaluation of the consistency of *The Social Contract*; it is rather to understand the new notion of the contract which this work contains.

Freedom and the Contract

If we now consider the famous opening sentence of *The Social Contract*—"Man is born free; however he is everywhere in chains" [1] —it is clear that the meaning attached to these words in the first draft has to undergo a complete transformation before it can be made compatible with the position Rousseau takes in the final version. In the first draft it means that man ought to be free, independent, and solitary (because this is the best life for him); but that the conventions and customs of society, the various regulations and restrictions which political and economic institutions involve, enslave him and cause his fall from his original and blessed state of freedom. "Shades of the prison house"—Rousseau might have anticipated Wordsworth— "begin to close about the growing boy." For Rousseau, the prison

---

[1] *Contrat Social*, I, 1 (23). In the first draft this is the first sentence of the third chapter. *Vide* Vaughan, *op. cit.*, I, 454.

is the social type of living which, in this modern world, it seems impossible to escape. Thus, as it stands, this sentence is entirely in the spirit of the *Discourse*: it expresses an attitude of mind which we might call "romantic primitivism"—a nostalgia for a life of genuineness and simplicity, for that Golden Age from which the complexity of modern life has separated us.

But, when we bring the sentence into harmony with the point of view adopted in the final version, the notion that man is born free but is actually in chains becomes simply the assertion (1) that man *ought* to be free (not in the sense of being able to do just whatever he wants, but in the sense of being an element in a general will, of whose common life his own is a part), and (2) that he seldom *actually* is free (because most states are actually founded on force, instead of on a general will, as they ought to be). Thus the freedom that Rousseau is talking about is no longer licence; it is no longer the unrestricted conduct of a separate and independent individual. On the contrary, the term now describes the kind of participation in a larger life which all the various bodily organs share in when they are functioning harmoniously in a healthy body.

At first sight this is a somewhat unusual notion of freedom. It is not at all that physical freedom to do whatever we can, as Hobbes would have understood this assertion. It is not even the moral autonomy of the individual man to judge and decide for himself, which Locke would have meant. Neither of these two conceptions is compatible with any kind of restraint. Hobbes's natural freedom and Locke's moral freedom are both licence—Hobbes's, the physical licence to do whatever we have the force and power to get away with; Locke's, the moral licence to make decisions for ourselves. For licence in either of these doubtless fundamentally different senses, Rousseau substitutes the conception of a freedom not only compatible with, but actually implying, a certain kind of restraint. It is freedom in much the same sense as the term is used by Kant—"What else can freedom of the will be but autonomy, that is, the property of the will to be a law to itself? . . . A free will and a will subject to moral laws are one and the same." [1] In a long and honourable tradition the term freedom has been frequently used as implying or involving some kind of restraint. For instance, it is natural to speak of a man who gives himself up utterly to some particular desire or passion, as being a slave to that

---

[1] *Grundlegung der Metaphysik der Sitten* (translated by T. K. Abbott, in *Kant's Theory of Ethics*, Longmans, 1927, pp. 65–66).

desire or passion—say, a slave to narcotics. And similarly we speak of a man as being free when, and if, his behaviour conforms to some pattern or model which he has set himself, even if this conformity involves considerable restraint of impulses and desires tending to lead him in opposite directions.

What is the nature of that law, the willing in conformity to which makes men free, even if restraint be also involved? It must not be one imposed from without. It is rather, as Kant says, a law which men spontaneously accept. Hence they identify themselves with it, without feeling compelled or restrained to do so. In Rousseau's phrase, it issues from the general will, and the individual can identify himself with it, because his particular will is an organic part of that larger will.

So far we have considered only the opening sentence of the first chapter of *The Social Contract*. Rousseau now proceeds:[1]

¶ How has this change been brought about [*i.e.*, the change from a state of freedom to a condition in which man is bound by chains]? I shall ignore this question. What can justify it? I believe that I can answer this question.

If I considered only force, and the effects which derive from it, I would say, "So far as a people is constrained to obey, and so far as it does obey, it does well. Whenever it can shake off its yoke, and does so, it does better; because, recovering its freedom by precisely the same right which took that liberty away, either it is justified in doing so, or those were not justified who took the people's freedom away in the first instance." But the social order is a sacred right which serves as the basis for all other rights. However, the source of this right is not nature; it is founded on conventions. We require to know what these conventions are. Before coming to that, I must establish what I have just asserted.

And, before we can follow Rousseau any further, we must observe that the concept of a free individual as participating in a general will (implied, as we have just seen, in the first sentence of the chapter) really contradicts the notion of a contract with which the chapter ends. This is the case because the notion of a contract is really based, as we found to be the case in Locke's theory, on a view of human nature which takes man to be fundamentally autonomous and

[1] *Contrat Social*, I, 1 (23-24).

independent. Indeed, a contract is required to bring men together, just because they are basically independent entities. Unfortunately, the whole conception of human nature to which Rousseau's idea of a general will commits him, is incompatible with the view that men are really and basically independent of each other. The organic view, on the contrary, implies that they are basically (*i.e.*, in Aristotle's language, 'naturally') dependent on each other, since they require the society of their fellows for their own complete individual development. In a word, though Rousseau does not realize it, the new notion of a general will (to which the difficulties he felt with Locke's concept of 'consent' had led him) is thus opposed to the Lockian contract with which he had started. Or, rather, for the by now traditional original contract to accept for all time the action of the majority, Rousseau has substituted the new notion of a continuous share in a general will.

There is, however, at least one characteristic shared by this new notion of a general will and the old notion of a contract, which is also brought out in this chapter. Both conceptions equally emphasize the need for a *moral justification* for the existence of the state and its exercise of restraint, and both attempt to give that justification. A contract theorist like Locke, starting from the assumption that men are basically independent and autonomous, has to conclude that the state's exercise of restraint is justified only when these independent individuals have freely agreed and consented to the exercise of force by a majority. Rousseau, too, started from this same position, but the difficulties involved in this solution caused him to develop the concept of a general will. And this, in its turn, occasioned a radical modification of the original notion of men and their relations to one another. But the new solution, like the old one, still requires the exercise of force to be justified morally; and this is now accomplished in the notion of consent defined as a continuous participation in that organism which the state has now turned out to be. In a word, for Rousseau, just as much as for Locke, the mere exercise of force justifies nothing. Doubtless it is prudent for a people to obey when threatened with a superior force; but, since force does not create a right, a people has no reason to obey a moment beyond the time when that threat exists. It always has a right to rebel as soon as prudence and safety warrant.

This thesis is argued very effectively, and in more detail, in the following chapter.[1]

---

[1] *Contrat Social*, I, 3 (26–27).

¶ Force is physical power; I do not see that its effects can ever be moral. To yield to force is an act of necessity, not of will. It is nothing more than an act of prudence. In what sense can that be a duty?

Let us assume for the sake of argument that might does make right. This only results in utter nonsense. For, if might makes right, then the effect changes with the cause: any force which overcomes the first acquires its right. As soon as one can disobey with impunity, one disobeys legitimately; and, since might is always right, only one thing matters: manage to become the most powerful. But what sort of a right is it which perishes as soon as force ceases? If one is forced to obey, one has no duty to obey; and, if one is no longer forced to obey, one is no longer obliged. It is clear from this that the word 'right' adds nothing to force; coupled with force, it means nothing at all.

Obey those who wield the power. If this means "Yield to force," the advice is good, but superfluous. I respond that it will never be violated. . . .

Let us agree that might never makes right, and that we have a duty to obey only legitimate powers. . . .

Rousseau's point is that right and might are simply different in kind. To say that something is right (that it ought to be) is to make a *moral* assertion, while an assertion about force, on the other hand, is simply a statement of physical fact. The actual existence of force can never, therefore, be used to prove or to disprove the reality of right.[1]

¶ Grotius denies that all human authority should be exercised in the interests of those who are governed; and he cites the fact of slavery as an example. His constant method of reasoning is to establish a right by citing a fact. One could find a more logical method, but none which would be more favourable to tyrants.

It is doubtful, according to Grotius, whether the human race belongs to, say, a hundred men, or whether that hundred men belong to the human race. Throughout his book he appears to incline towards the former view. This is also the opinion of Hobbes; and amounts to saying that mankind is divided into so many herds of cattle, each of which has a master, watching over his cattle that he may devour them.

[1] *Contrat Social*, I, 2 (25–26).

¶   As a shepherd has a nature superior to that of his flock, so the
     shepherds of men—that is, their masters—have a nature superior to
that of their subjects. So reasoned the emperor Caligula, according
to Philo, it being equally possible to conclude from this analogy,
either that kings were gods, or that subjects were beasts.

Caligula's reasoning agrees with that of Hobbes and of Grotius.
But, earlier than any of them, Aristotle had said the same thing,
that is, that men are not by nature equal, but that some are born
for slavery and others for mastery.

Aristotle was right; but he took the effect for the cause. Nothing
is more certain than that every man born in slavery is born for
slavery. Slaves lose everything in their chains, even the desire to
be free of them. They come to love their servitude, just as the
companions of Ulysses came to love their sottishness. If, then,
there are now natural slaves, it is because formerly there were
slaves against nature. Force made the first slaves; their baseness has
kept them slaves.

Here Rousseau continues his argument that what *ought to be* is
different in kind from what *is*. The fact that men *are* slaves, and that
they are fit for, and even desire, nothing better, does not justify their
being enslaved. They may, in a word, be slaves, not only in fact (by,
say, law); they may even be natural slaves, for a servile condition can
destroy the moral fibre of a free man—all this may, unfortunately, be
only too true, yet it is completely irrelevant. Their condition *ought
to be* other than it is.

If, then, might never makes right, if the exercise of restraint in any
form can never be justified by force alone, what is required to make the
state a moral institution? How, in a word, *ought* force to be exercised?
Rousseau's answer, as we have already seen, is that consent is required
to justify the exercise of force—not merely (it appears gradually,
as Rousseau's thought takes shape) a consent given once and for all
on the occasion of an original contract, but consent embodied in,
and expressed in, a continuous general will.[1]

¶   Since no man has [2] a natural authority over other men, and since
     might never makes right, it follows that agreements are the basis
     for all legitimate authority among men. . . .

[1] *Contrat Social*, I, 4 (27); I, 6 (32-33).
[2] Rousseau means, of course, ' ought to have.'

¶ I assume men to have reached a condition in which the obstacles in the way of their conservation in a state of nature outweigh, by reason of their resistance, the forces which each individual has at his disposal to maintain himself in that state. Hence this primitive condition can no longer be continued and mankind would perish if it would not change its mode of life.

But, since men cannot create new forces, but only unite and direct already existing ones, they have no other way of saving themselves except to join together and so form a sum of forces capable of overcoming that resistance. . . .

This sum of forces can issue only from the co-ordinated action of a number of men. But how can a man pledge his strength and his liberty of action, together the chief instruments of his own pre-servation, without harming himself and without neglecting those duties which he owes to himself? This difficulty, stated in terms of our present problem, can be formulated as follows:

"To find a form of association capable of defending and pro-tecting with the total common force, the person and the property of each associate, and by means of which, each one, uniting himself with all the others, nevertheless obeys only himself and remains as free as ever before." Such is the fundamental problem of which the social contract gives the solution.

The clauses of this contract are so determined by the nature of the act that their least modification renders them null and void; so that, although they may well never have been formally stated, they are always the same, always tacitly admitted and recognized, until such time as, the social pact having been violated, each indi-vidual acquires again his original rights and regains that natural liberty which he had earlier renounced for the sake of a liberty based upon convention.

In these paragraphs, as so often, Rousseau still retains the language of the Lockian type of contract theory which he had really abandoned. He writes as if the kind of contract which he had in mind was a single agreement formally entered into, like a convention to form a business partnership, which continued in force until some one of the partners violated some one of its conditions. This, of course, entails the con-sent of the parties; but it is not the kind of consent implied by the conception of the general will. It is, indeed, not the kind of consent, not the kind of association, in which every individual "obeys only himself and remains as free as ever before." For the rest, as Rousseau is careful to point out, the contract he is talking about need not ever have been an historical fact. It is rather a moral fact—a kind of relationship which ought to exist and into which men from time to time do in fact enter. Rousseau is perhaps a little optimistic in suggesting that this moral order is always recognized by men, even when they do not act in accordance with it. His own remarks on Aristotle's doctrine of natural slavery, however, furnish a useful correction: men may, indeed, become so debased that they do not even recognize this order. Nevertheless, they ought to be participants in it.

The General Will and the Contract

What in detail is the character of this moral order? Rousseau gives this answer, as the passage continues.[1]

¶   These clauses [of the contract], rightly understood, may be reduced to one: the total alienation, to the whole community, of each associate, together with all of his rights. This follows, in the first place, because each individual giving himself up wholly, the circumstances are equal for all; and, in the second place, because, the circumstances being equal for all, no one has any interest in rendering them burdensome for the others.

Moreover, this alienation being made without reserve, the union which results is as perfect as it is possible to be; and no associate has any special claims. For, if there remained any special rights to any particular individuals, the result would be that each one, being in this point his own judge (for there would be no common superior who could pronounce between him and the public), would soon claim to be his own judge in all cases. Thus the state of nature would continue and the association would either be useless or result in tyranny.

Finally, each one, in giving himself up to all, gives himself up to no one. And, as there is no associate over whom one does not acquire the same rights which one gives to him over oneself, it follows that one receives the equivalence of all that one loses, and acquires in addition the force to preserve what one has.

If, then, one reduces the social compact to its essence, it amounts to this: "Each of us puts his person and all his power to the common

[1] *Contrat Social*, I, 6 (33–34).

¶ use under the supreme direction of the general will; and as a body we receive each member as an indivisible part of the whole."

Immediately, in place of the private person of each contractant, this act of association produces a moral and collective Body, composed of as many elements as the assembly has voices, and which receives from this same act its unity, its common identity, its life, and its will. This public person, which is thus formed by the union of all the particular individuals, was formerly given the name *City*, and is now called a *Republic* or *Body Politic*. Its members refer to it as the *State* when it is passive; the *Sovereign* when it is active; a *Power*, when they compare it with similar institutions. With regard to the associates, they are collectively called the *people*. When they are thought of as participating in the sovereign authority, they are called *citizens*; when they are thought of as submitting to the laws of the State, they are called *subjects*. In actual practice, however, these terms are often used very loosely and one is often taken for another. It is sufficient to know how to distinguish them, when they are employed with precision.

The relationship which thus, according to Rousseau, *ought* to exist between men (whether it does in fact exist is another question) is not merely an association which, once entered into, must not be changed, and which remains in force only so long as it is unchanged. The relationship is rather a continuous, free, spontaneous, and growing participation in something conceived of as the real good of all the associates. This kind of association is, clearly, not merely legal—not merely a contract with certain definite and stipulated conditions agreed to by both sides for the sake of certain mutual benefits to be derived from this association. It is a common life, like that of a tree, or any growing thing. And just as the various organs of the tree—roots, leaves, branches—contribute to the life of the tree, just as their individual lives would be meaningless and, indeed, altogether impossible unless they shared in this common life, so individual men, too, only develop the full, rich, and moral personality which they have it in them to be, through participating in a common life with their fellows.[1]

¶ This passage from a state of nature to a civil state produces a very remarkable change in man: it substitutes in his conduct a rule of justice for a rule of instinct and it gives to his actions a moral

[1] *Contrat Social*, I, 8 (36–37); II, 4 (46).

¶ character which theretofore they had lacked. Now, for the first time, appetite gives place to right, a merely physical impulsion to the voice of duty; and man, who before had had regard only for his own interests, finds it necessary to act on other principles, and to consult reason before hearkening to his desires. However much he deprives himself in this state of certain natural advantages, he acquires others so great, his faculties are so exercised and developed, his ideas so extended, his sentiments so ennobled, his whole soul elevated to such a point that, were it not for abuses which often degrade this new state to a condition lower than that of the state of nature, he ought ceaselessly to bless the happy moment which snatched him from that earlier state and which changed him from a stupid and limited animal into an intelligent creature and a man.

Let us reduce the items lost and gained in this transaction to terms easily compared. What man loses by the social contract is his natural liberty and an unlimited right to whatever he can get and hold on to. What he gains is civil liberty and the ownership of all that he possesses. In order not to be misled about the nature of these compensations, it is necessary to distinguish (1) natural liberty, whose limits are determined only by the power of the individual, from civil liberty, which is limited by the general will, and (2) possession, which is only the effect of force, or the right of the first occupant, from ownership, which has to be founded on a positive title.

One could also add, to what has already been said, moral liberty as one of the benefits acquired in the civil state. Moral liberty makes a man truly master of himself, for to be moved solely by appetites is slavery, and obedience to a law which one gives oneself is liberty. But I have already said too much on this subject, and the philosophical meaning of the word 'liberty' lies outside the field of my present inquiry. . . .

. . . It is . . . false that there is any real renunciation on the part of any members to the contract. . . . [So far from this being the case,] their condition as a result of the contract is better than it was before. Instead of having given anything up, they have only exchanged a precarious and uncertain mode of life for one which is better and surer; a natural independence for a real liberty; a power by which they might harm others for their own security; and their own private strength (which others might be able to overcome) for a right rendered invincible by the social union.

Here again, while the argument still has a Lockeian basis, and while the terminology is still Locke's, Rousseau has developed a point of view which, taken as a whole, differs profoundly from that of his master. For instance, the argument still has a utilitarian tone: the appeal is still, as it was for Locke, to the greater advantages which result from the contract. There are some losses, doubtless, some sacrifices, but there is a very considerable *net* gain. This implies, as we have seen in both Locke and Hobbes, a view of man as essentially a rational creature, capable of sitting down in a cool hour to calculate the profits and losses, capable of taking a long view and of acting in accordance with his best interests in the long run.[1]

But Rousseau (and this shows how far away from the simple notion of a contract his concept of a general will was leading him) denies all this in the same sentences in which, by implication, he asserts it, when he says that the contract (*i.e.*, the participation in a general will and towards a common good) makes man an intelligent being capable of acting on a plan, instead of a merely brutish animal, whose behaviour is determined by every fleeting impulse and desire. In other words, the contract makes man the kind of creature to whom the argument in favour of the contract could appeal. Only association with his fellows in pursuit of a common good makes him capable of acting on a plan and in consideration of his long run interests.

Moreover, it appears that the contract (*i.e.*, participation in a general will) not only makes man a rational creature, also it makes him *moral*. At this point, too, Rousseau has diverged strikingly from the position taken by Locke. According to Locke, man is already moral, before the contract is accepted as the basis of the state. It is, indeed, just because he is a complete moral and rational individual that he can make a contract at all. And, being already complete, the contract does nothing to him as a person; it merely furnishes him with certain important conveniences such as the ownership of property. In Rousseau's theory the concept of these conveniences which the contract brings is retained, and he writes about property in language which might be Locke's own. But for him, the chief benefit which participation in the general will bestows on man is undoubtedly the bringing out and developing of his full personality, which theretofore was only partial and incomplete.

On this point Rousseau is actually nearer to Hobbes than he is to

[1] In Hobbes's case, of course, this conception of human nature contradicts his basic attitude towards man. *Vide supra*, pp. 129*ff*.

Locke, though with an important difference. His view of human nature, as it is worked out here in *The Social Contract*, conceives of man as a mere animal before the contract, and therefore as living by force and requiring to be kept in order by force. Unlike Hobbes, however, he thinks that the contract, conceived of as participation in the general will, profoundly alters man's nature and makes him into a moral being who knows (and sometimes heeds) another law than that of force. This conception would be quite fantastic if the contract were a specific, single occurrence. Conceived of in this way, it would be open to the criticism we have already made in connexion with our examination of Hobbes's theory—namely, it is impossible to conceive of men of this kind ever joining together in a contract. It would also be open to the further objection that the mere act of putting one's name to a contract could hardly alter one's nature so completely as Rousseau supposes. Both these difficulties vanish as soon as we recall that Rousseau is here thinking of the contract as a continuous participation in a general will. Since the contract is a process, we can think of the alteration in human nature as being also gradual, not instantaneous. And similarly, there is no longer any difficulty about how brutish men can ever contract together, since we now see that this contract is but their slow and increasing recognition of a general will, a general good, in which they all can share. In other words, what we have here is the notion of a gradual development and evolution of man's moral sensibilities and intellectual powers, which proceed *pari passu* with the widening and deepening of his social relations. And these aspects of his life are mutually cause and effect of each other: an increasing association with his fellows adds to his intellectual and moral development, while this, in its turn, enables him to see his own good as tied up with the good of an ever more inclusive social group. Thus, as man passes from primitive barbarism to higher and higher stages of civilization, he also passes from social groups composed of a family or clan to those constituted by vast nations and (eventually, one can hope) the whole of mankind.

Historicity of the Contract

This brings us to the much disputed question of the historicity of the contract, which, it should now be obvious, has to be entirely restated in terms of Rousseau's conception of the general will. In fact, it is clear that if we now ask whether there has ever been an actual contract we have to answer, "Both yes and no." *No*, in the sense that participation in the general will is never complete and perfect. It is never, or at least not yet, totally inclusive and general; and certainly, as Rousseau pointed out, in all societies we know anything about, there are frequent lapses from it, on the part of various individuals, into narrowly selfish conduct. But, on the other hand, *yes*, in the sense that participation is *always* partially present and partially actual. All associations are more or less organic. Those theorists are, therefore, wrong who conceive of the possibility of associations based *entirely* on force. As we saw in our discussion of Hobbes, no group can be held together unless, in *some* sense, its members want it to hold together. There is always, in *some* sense, consent, even if it be only the consent of those whom Rousseau calls "natural slaves." Thus it is certainly true that the Nazis maintained themselves in power only by the use of force; but it is a mistake to suppose that they accomplished this *merely* by the exercise and threat of force. There is no doubt, of course, that a large part of the population actively approved of the programme and policies of the regime from the start; but there is also no doubt that some Germans, who originally opposed the Nazis, came to accept, and so to consent to, their degraded state. That this state of mind was produced by despair and hopelessness, by terror of force, by propaganda and other forms of pressure, is doubtless true; but this is all irrelevant to the fact that consent, however produced, did in fact exist.

Similarly, since every association is organic and based on consent, it follows that those theorists are also wrong who try, as Locke did, to find a source of association in merely legal action. Of course, legal associations may, and do, exist, just as associations resting on force exist. But legal associations, like associations based upon force, survive only so long as the parties to the contract consent to it. Indeed, unlike associations brought about by force, legal associations, since they are moral, would never come into existence at all unless there was consent.

What is true of associations founded on force or on legal agreement is true of all associations, at whatever stage in human history. Doubtless it is possible that some anthropologist may find in some sufficiently remote period an anthropoid creature, who lived in solitude, separated from his fellows. But Rousseau's reply would be that such a creature simply is not man at all. Even those half-men, the apes, live some sort of communal life in a family or tribe; and, in Rousseau's view, here we have the first signs of intelligence, just at the same time as, and because, we also have the first unconscious feeling of a general good in which all the members of this family or tribe share.

On this interpretation, the historicity of the contract, so far from being an absurd illusion, becomes undeniable fact. Unfortunately, however, Rousseau did not see this with sufficient clarity. His thought being still clothed in the language of the earlier contract theory, he could not altogether free himself from some of the conceptual encumbrances with which that notion had come to be embroidered.[1] Thus, at times, he clearly sees that the concept of the contract as a specific historic transaction is only a convenient fiction for describing that continuous participation in a general will which we have been discussing; while, at other times, he lapses, just as we have seen that Locke and Hobbes sometimes do, into thinking of the contract as a specific event which really did occur in the remote past.

The General Will and the Will of All

We may now continue Rousseau's description of the general will by contrasting it with what he calls the will of all.[2]

¶ It follows from what has been said that the general will is always just and always aims at the public good; but it does not follow that the deliberations of the people are always right. Man always aims at his good, but he does not always know what it is. The people are never corrupted, but they are often led astray; and it is only that which they seem to desire which is bad.

There is often a considerable difference between the general will and the will of all:[3] the former aims at the common interest; the latter aims at private interests and is only a sum of particular wills. But if we take away from these wills the various particular interests which conflict with each other, what remains as the sum of the differences is the general will.

If the people held its deliberations only after the citizens had been sufficiently informed about the issues involved, and then without there having been any communication between them, the general will would always result from the great number of small differences and the deliberation would always be good. But when factions and parties are allowed to be formed at the expense of the whole asso-

---

[1] *Vide supra*, pp. 256–257.   [2] *Contrat Social*, II, 3 (42–43); II, 4 (44–46).
[3] In the first draft this reads, "The general will is rarely that of all."

¶ciation, the whole general will breaks up into a number of lesser wills, each one of which is general in respect of its party-members, but particular in respect of the state as a whole. It is no longer possible to say that there are as many voters as men, but only that there are as many as there are parties. As the differences become less numerous, the result produced is less general. Finally, when one of the factions becomes strong enough to dominate all the others, the result is no longer a sum of small differences; it is simply one difference. When this occurs, there is no longer a general will, and the opinion which dominates is only a particular opinion. . . .

The commitments which bind us to the social organ are obligations only because they are mutual; and their nature is such that, in fulfilling them, one cannot work for others without also working for oneself. Why is the general will always just, and why does every one constantly aim at the happiness of each one of the whole group, if it is not because each one appropriates to himself this word 'each,' and so thinks of himself as he votes for all? . . .

We can see, from what has been said, that what generalizes the will is less the number of men participating in it than it is the common interest which unites them. The reason is that in this association each necessarily submits himself to the same condition which he imposes on the others—an admirable union of interest and of justice. . . .

However one looks at the principle of the social contract, we reach the same conclusion, *viz.*, that the social contract establishes a real equality among the citizens, all of whom have the same duties under it and ought to enjoy the same rights. . . .

This description is a strange mixture of utopian idealism and plain common sense which we must now try to distinguish. To begin with, what does Rousseau mean by saying that the general will is always just? At first sight this appears to be nonsense. Certainly the facts of history seem to contradict this claim only too frequently. There is no doubt that in many associations men consent to, and actively participate in, acts which are extremely unjust. Any mob setting out to lynch a negro, or the policy of the Nazi Government towards the Jews, is a case in point. Rousseau himself in effect admits this obvious fact when he says that the people are often misled or deceived about what they ought to do.[1] We should, therefore, before we hasten to

[1] Cf. *Contrat Social*, I, 7. A part of this passage is quoted *infra*, p. 282.

accuse Rousseau of inconsistency, ask ourselves whether Rousseau ever intended to assert anything so fantastic as that all men always do what is objectively just. What he appears to have had in mind is, rather, a distinction which many philosophers have drawn between a man's intention or motive, on the one hand, and the state of affairs or objective situation which he produces, on the other. The person who tries as hard as he can to do what is right, and who fails because of ignorance of the circumstances or some features of the environment over which he has no control, is obviously in some sense a good man, even though he may actually have done a harmful (and so bad) act. The mediæval inquisitors, for instance, certainly produced what seems to us a great deal of unnecessary pain and suffering, but most of them did so from the best of motives—an altruistic desire to serve the best interests of those on whom they inflicted the pain. We cannot, therefore, condemn them morally just because they had (as we now think) a mistaken estimate of relative values or a false concept of how to attain the supreme good of life.

It is this distinction between motive and overt result which Rousseau seems to have had in mind. Thus what Rousseau appears to be maintaining is that every man always as a matter of fact does aim at what he thinks will be good for the whole group of men of which he is a part, and it is because of this alleged characteristic of men's motives that he calls the general will good. But does Rousseau mean this as a statement of fact or simply as a definition? That is, does he mean to assert that, as a matter of fact, men do always aim at something which they believe (whether mistakenly or not) is good for all of their group, or does he mean merely that whenever they do so he proposes to speak of them as having, or sharing in, a general will? Certainly the former appears to be the sense of the assertion that "the general will is always just and always aims at the public good." But, on the other hand, there are two objections to taking this to be Rousseau's meaning. The first is that it is obviously and palpably false, for the members of even the smallest and most intimate of groups—the family—often aim at their private individual good, instead of aiming at what is best for the group as a whole. And the second objection is that Rousseau himself points out this plain fact. When he says, a few lines farther on, that "there is often a considerable difference between the general will and the will of all," this certainly implies that men's wills are *sometimes* not general; and this, in its turn, contradicts the assertion (if this be what Rousseau meant) that men "always aim at the public good." What Rousseau meant here may be somewhat clarified by comparing it with a later passage in which the same subject is under discussion.[1] After once more asserting that the general will "is always constant, unalterable, and pure" he admits the obvious fact that it is sometimes subordinated to lesser wills which ought to be contained within it. He explains this apparent contradiction by pointing out that

¶ Every one who distinguishes his own private interest from the common interest on some particular point nevertheless sees that he cannot separate his interest *completely* from that common interest. It is merely the case that in this particular matter, the harm to the public, which will result from his action, seems insignificant in comparison with the private good which it will bring him. Apart from this particular case, therefore, he wills the general good for the sake of his own private interests, just as strongly as anyone else.

If this be what Rousseau really means, no one would want to disagree with him. Indeed, to get a universally acceptable thesis, we have only to add the proviso (certainly acceptable to Rousseau himself[2]) that when enough men make exceptions for themselves the state will be destroyed. But, certainly, the statement that the general will is "always constant, unalterable, and pure" is hardly the best way of conveying this meaning.

In any case, whatever Rousseau may have meant to assert, the facts certainly are that men do not always aim at the public good, even supposing there really be some one thing or state of affairs which is best for every individual member of the group.[3] Rousseau gets himself into this difficulty because he tends here to assume men to be natively good and naturally enlightened. Therefore he supposes, in the first place, that if they are left alone they will see their best private interest to be identical with the interest of the group as a whole; and, in the second place, that they will act in accordance with this view of the good.[4] In a word, men's wills would always be general if they were left alone. Doubtless men are led astray by demagogues, just as

---

[1] *Contrat Social*, IV, 1 (103–104).   [2] *Vide infra*, p. 315.
[3] For a detailed discussion and criticism of this basic assumption, *vide infra*, p. 318*ff*.
[4] Here, it should be noted, Rousseau lapses into Locke's way of thinking, which is really inconsistent, as we have seen, with his own final position. But Rousseau is not even consistent in this lapse, since later on he takes the view that the people are so weak and fallible in their judgment as to require a 'legislative' to set up their state for them before they reach political maturity.

Rousseau suggests. Certainly, also, when men join parties or factions they can only too easily identify themselves and their good with that of the party, instead of with that of the whole group of which the party itself is only a part. The situation in France during the years immediately before the collapse in 1940 is a good example of what Rousseau had in mind. Frenchmen were Socialists, or Communists, or Republicans, first; and only afterwards, if at all, Frenchmen. Thus the national unity was destroyed, and individual Frenchmen sacrificed their own particular good and well-being, because, being misled by the passions engendered by factional strife, they could not see that their own best interests were dependent, not on the triumph of the particular parties of which they chanced to be members, but on the security and well-being of France as a whole.

All that Rousseau says here is true; but surely it is a mistake to suppose that the activities of party politicians are the *sole* cause of the disintegration of the general will. To assume that all men always act from good (and altruistic) motives and that they do wrong only when they are misled or deceived, is mere utopian idealism, as far, in its own way, from the facts of human nature as Hobbes's black view of man. If men are misled by sinister demagogues it is because there is a streak of selfishness and narrowness in them upon which the arts of propaganda can freely play. Rousseau supposes that a general will exists except on the infrequent occasions when men are persuaded into taking a lesser for a greater good. The facts are rather that a completely general will is attained only very rarely and for very brief periods of time. Perhaps, during some moment of great national peril or strain, the vast majority of citizens really do think and feel together, forgetting their individual interests and the selfish interests of their parties and factions, in a common cause in which they all share. They come then to act together in concert because they believe themselves (whether correctly or not is beside the point here) to have a common interest transcending in importance all those other and more individual aims which usually separate them.[1]

The smaller the group, the more frequent and the more durable, obviously, are these moments of common thinking and common feeling. In the family, the club, the college, we may see they occur relatively often; but when a group attains the size even of the smallest of the modern national states this unity of wills is immensely difficult to attain, and, when attained (unless engendered artificially), it is a

[1] Cf. *Contrat Social*, II, 1; but Rousseau does not see this with sufficient clarity.

sign of men's political, moral, and intellectual maturity. For the ability to conceive of so large, indirect, and distant a good as that of the whole state, and the ability to sacrifice more immediate and pressing private goods in its interest imply in those who have these capacities both intellectual breadth and vision and emotional sensitivity and stability.

Before we pass on we must examine one further ambiguity in the passage which we have been discussing. So far we have been considering the general will as a state of affairs produced whenever all the individual members of a group, sacrificing their own private interests, unite in aiming at some one object believed by them to be the good of the group as a whole. When, however, Rousseau says that the general will is that "sum of differences" which results when we "take away from these [individual] wills the various particular interests which conflict with each other," this seems to imply a rather different conception of the nature of the general will. Here we have the notion that, even if men aim at their own particular and private goods, the result will be a general will, because the individual differences will cancel each other, and thus the policy finally voted and decided on will be fair to all persons concerned. There is one obvious, but important, condition here: the result will be a general will *only if* every man who continues to aim at his own individual good does so good-naturedly and in a spirit of tolerance for the private aims of the other men in his group.

It makes all the difference in the world—it makes, indeed, the difference whether or not there is a general will—if "the citizen says by his vote, *It is to the advantage of the state that this measure be passed*, instead of saying, *It is to the advantage of this or that individual or of this or that party that it be passed*."[1] If the citizens vote in this frame of mind, the general will continues to survive, even where the citizens disagree sharply about what in particular is the measure which is to the advantage of the state. For in these circumstances,[2]

¶ Every citizen gives his consent to all of the laws passed, even to those whose passage he opposed, even to those which punish him when he dares to break one of them. The constant will of every citizen of the state is the general will: this is what makes them citizens and free. When a measure is proposed in the assembly of the citizens what one asks is not that they all approve it or that they all reject it,

[1] *Contrat Social*, IV, 1 (104).   [2] *Ibid.*, IV, 2 (105-106).

❡ but that they vote for or against it because they believe it will be to the advantage (or the disadvantage, as the case may be) of the state as a whole. If there is to be a general will all the citizens must vote from this motive. The result will then be an expression of the will of the whole body of the citizens; for, when the decision goes against the vote of some members, this only proves that they were mistaken about what was actually to the advantage of the state as a whole. In any case, *every* citizen always gets what he really wants (and this is what makes the will truly general), since what every citizen votes for is not some particular measure *per se*, but for this measure as a means to the good of the state. In a word, since the good of the state is the end which every citizen seeks, no one is denied what he wants. The fact that the vote goes against me proves that I was wrong about what is the correct means to the common good; hence, if my opinion had carried the day neither I nor anyone else would have got the good of the whole really aimed at by us all, and so none of us would have been free.[1]

There appear to be two distinct points involved in this contention, one of which is probably true, the other of which is almost certainly false. In the first place, Rousseau argues that all the citizens ought to try to decide what is good for the state as a whole, and vote accordingly; in the second place, he says that, if they do so, a majority will always vote in favour of what is in fact best, so that where the citizens are moved by this kind of consideration the best course of action is always voted.

Now there can be no doubt that it would be better in every way if the citizens were moved by the kind of consideration Rousseau advocates. If the citizens, that is to say, really conscientiously tried to put the public interest first, there is little doubt that the state in which they lived would be juster and stronger for their doing so. But is it plausible to argue that, in these circumstances, the best policy would *always* be followed? Even with the best will in the world, men make mistakes; and there seems no reason to suppose that a majority of the citizens through ignorance and incompetence (even where all of the citizens are trying to discover what is best for the group as a whole) may not hit on what as a matter of fact is worst, instead of what is best. A good motive, in other words, is no guarantee of a wise choice. But there is at least one important way in which this

---

[1] This passage has been rather freely translated.

kind of motive can significantly influence choice. It is a fact generally admitted that the prejudices which arise whenever our own interests are involved are one of the chief factors which prevent us from reaching objectively valid conclusions. One has only to listen to the different arguments of, say, bankers and unemployed men about the merits of the capitalistic system to see how easy it is for the mind to become blinded to certain objective facts, if these facts happen not to be sympathetic to what one takes to be one's own interests. If, then, men *could* take a completely disinterested view one of the chief factors which prevents their reaching correct conclusions would thus be removed. Hence there really is a greater probability of correct decisions being made if the citizens all adopt a disinterested attitude; but we surely cannot expect the sound policy always to get the most votes, even under these favourable conditions.

If, then, we reject the dubious claim that the majority is always right,[1] what remains is a very much more plausible assertion. And it becomes still more plausible when we see that this attitude of mind, insisted on by Rousseau as desirable because it makes a general will possible, involves no very extreme or unusual act of self-sacrifice. It does not demand an almost impossible altruism; it does not exclude attention to one's own interests. All that it asks is not so narrow and immediate an attention to one's own interests as to make any consideration for others impossible. What it asks, in fact, is nothing more than the kind of attitude the good sportsman has to his opponents in the games he plays. He plays to win, but, since the game is more important than victory, he plays it according to the rules—*i.e.*, though he wants to win, and though he tries to win, he has consideration for the rights of the other parties to the game. In a word, the possibility of a general will does not depend on any hopelessly exalted conditions, but on the development of a point of view which most men, certainly, are not altogether incapable of attaining.

The position which Rousseau is working towards in this passage is similar to that which Aristotle reached when he was considering the question whether the 'many' ought to rule or the superior 'few'—that is, the question whether what we to-day would call a democracy is a better form of government than an oligarchy or an aristocracy.[2]

[1] *Vide infra*, p. 325.
[2] *Politics* (translated by Benjamin Jowett, Oxford University Press, 1921), Book III, chapter 11 (1281a 40*ff*.).

¶   The principle that the multitude ought to be supreme rather than
the few best . . . contain[s] an element of truth. For the many, of
whom each individual is but an ordinary person, when they meet
together, may very likely be better than the few good, . . . just as a
feast to which many contribute is better than a dinner provided out
of a single purse. For each individual among the many has a share
of virtue and prudence, and when they meet together . . . some
understand one part and some another, and among them they understand the whole. . . . When [the many] meet together their perceptions are quite good enough, and, combined with the better
class, they are useful enough to the state (just as impure food when
mixed with what is pure sometimes makes the entire mass more
wholesome than a small quantity of the pure would be). . . . If
the people are not utterly degraded, although individually they may
be worse judges than those who have special knowledge—as a body
they are as good or better.

What Aristotle means is that in a free and open meeting of different
minds, each one of which is short-sightedly intent on its own narrow
interests, a middle position will be hammered out. This will be the
best on the whole for all the individuals concerned. Each individual
will have to make concessions, and all will make concessions about
equally. The result will be a programme which is fair and just to all,
because, being adapted to the different circumstances and interests of
all concerned, it does the best for all of them that, in these circumstances, can be done. Or, in Rousseau's words, it constitutes "an
admirable union of interest and of justice." In a word, what both
Aristotle and Rousseau have in mind is a government which functions
like such a group as the British Parliament or the American Congress,
in which a large number of different and diverging interests participate.
These normally succeed in amending and modifying any proposal, so
that before it becomes law it expresses, not merely the will of some
individual or faction, but the common and united interests of the whole.[1]

The fact that it is thus possible to have a general will without
unanimity,[2] the fact that the presence of a general will is compatible

[1] Neither Rousseau nor Aristotle, of course, was thinking of a representative government; but the example is valid so far as we think of the members of Parliament and of
Congress, not as representatives of larger groups, but simply as individuals who together
compose an actual group.

[2] "For a will to be general it is not always necessary that it be unanimous; but it is
necessary that all the votes be counted. Any such arbitrary exclusion destroys the generality" (*Contrat Social*, II, 1, note, (40)). *Vide infra*, also, p. 310.

with the existence of a dissatisfied (but not disaffected) minority, points back once more to the importance in Rousseau's concept of *motive*. There can be a general will in these circumstances only if, and so far as, all the individuals of the group are moved, even in their pursuit of their own private interests, by the thought of themselves as members of a group, *all* of whose members have interests deserving respect and consideration. In other words, the majority must be moved by the thought of not going too far in the furtherance of its own interests at the expense of those of the minority, even if only because it knows that it will sometime itself be a minority. And the minority, on the other hand, if only because it can look forward to the day when it becomes a majority, must give its consent to, and loyally fall in with, measures which, before their passage, it strenuously opposed. So far, in a word, as every member of the group is moved by a sense of fair play, by the sense that he is only one member of a group composed of many members each one of whom has a right to a share in the life of the group—so far as this is the case, we have a general and corporate will which is not in the least incompatible with differences of opinion among its constituent elements. The reason is that we have the *consent*, in an entirely intelligible sense, of all the members of the group; the consent, even, of those who oppose the measure.

The general will, thus understood as the attitude of mind of a group whose members have agreed to differ, is clearly a much more frequent occurrence than when it is conceived of as a real unity of minds. For, in the present sense, the general will hardly depends on any considerable intellectual or moral maturity. It is quite compatible with a relatively narrow and selfish pursuit of private interests so long as this be accompanied by a sense of tolerance and of fair play. These two meanings of the general will—as a cancellation of individual differences and as a real unanimity of thought and feeling—are connected, it should be noticed, by the importance in each of the element of motive. There is no doubt of the truth of the general proposition that the kind of motive from which one habitually or usually acts has a considerable bearing on what is produced by one's actions. Thus, for instance, a contribution of a hundred pounds to the relief of the poor involves the same amount of money whether one gives it because of one's sympathy for distress or because of one's desire for prestige. Though these different motives may on occasion lead to exactly the same conduct, there is no doubt that the man who is habitually moved by charity and sympathy is much more likely to do good in the world than is the man who thinks habitually of his reputation for good deeds. If we apply this general proposition to the realm of political activity we get at the heart of Rousseau's conception of the general will. Doubtless it is *possible* that good government, and the passage of sound legislation, may result from conduct motivated in all sorts of ways, good, bad, and indifferent. But Rousseau's point is that the kind of motive which is most likely to issue in these results and to produce a permanently (and not merely accidentally) good government is a desire, felt by all the citizens, for the general good. Whether this results in their all desiring exactly the same thing—a state of affairs which, certainly, occurs only infrequently—or whether it results in their continuing to desire different things but being prepared to consent to a compromise solution in which every one secures about the same amount of benefit as every one else and makes about the same sacrifices—this is immaterial. The important thing is that in both cases our government is just, because it is based upon consent, not upon force.[1]

Sovereignty

(a) *Unlimited.* If this be what Rousseau means by his general will it remains to be seen how he applies this concept in working out the details of his political theory. To begin with, in Rousseau's state the general will is sovereign.[2]

¶ Every act of sovereignty, that is, every authentic act of the general will, restricts or works to the advantage of all citizens, equally. . . . What, then, is an act of sovereignty, exactly? It is not a convention made by a superior with an inferior; it is a convention made by the whole Body with each of its members—a convention which is just, because it rests on the social contract;[3] equitable, because it is common to all; useful, because it has no other object than the general

---

[1] In an interesting article which expresses the alarm many people felt at the intense partisanship which the 'third term' issue raised during the 1940 presidential campaign in the United States, the editors of *Life* magazine appealed to the American people to adopt an attitude of mind which they described in terms strikingly similar to Rousseau's. Whether they knew it or not they were arguing in favour of Rousseau's conception of a general will. Vide *Life*, October 18, 1940.

[2] *Contrat Social*, II, 4 (45, 43).

[3] It is just, that is, because it rests on the continuously given consent (in the sense we have just defined) of all the citizens.

¶ good; and permanent, because it is guaranteed by the public force and the supreme power. . . .

If the State or the City is a moral person whose life consists in the union of its members, and if its self-preservation be the greatest of its needs, it requires a universal and compelling force to move and dispose each one of its particular elements in the interests of all. Just as nature gives each man an absolute power over all his parts, so the social contract gives an absolute power to the Body Politic over all of its parts. It is this power which, as I have said, is called 'sovereignty' when it is directed by the general will. . . .

Rousseau gives his sovereign just as absolute and supreme a power as Hobbes assigned to his. But, in Rousseau's case, this power is not based upon an historically dubious and psychologically implausible original contract; it is based upon consent, in the sense of a free acceptance by every individual of the exercise of force by the whole group of which he is a part, in the preservation of the common life of the group in which he has a part. Since the 'contract' on which Rousseau's sovereign rests is of this kind, since it rests on a perpetually renewed and living consent, it follows that there can be no restrictions or conditions on the sovereign of the kind which might exist if sovereignty were the product of a business agreement entered into for mutual benefit. At any time, the sovereign has (or, rather, is) precisely that power which the citizens consent to. It is, in fact, a variable, growing, and dynamic thing.[1]

¶   It is against the nature of the Body Politic for the sovereign to impose on itself a law which it cannot alter. . . . The sovereign being in the position of an individual person who makes a contract with himself, it follows that there neither is nor can be any kind of fundamental law which binds the people taken as a whole, not even the social contract. . . .

The sovereign, being nothing more than the totality of individuals who compose it, neither has, nor can have, any interest contrary to theirs. Consequently, there is never any need for the sovereign to give guarantees to the subjects, for it is impossible that the whole body should wish to do harm to all of its members. . . . It follows simply from its nature that the sovereign is always what it should be.

[1] *Contrat Social*, I, 7 (34–35).

What, in Rousseau's eyes, justifies giving the sovereign this absolute and unlimited power? It is justified only by the fact that the
people have consented to it. What would otherwise be merely the
brutal and vicious exercise of force becomes moral, because it is a
condition freely accepted by those on whom it is placed. In a word,
the exercise of force which sovereignty entails is justified because it is
a restraint which men put upon themselves; because, in Rousseau's
state, it is the people who are at once the subjects over whom force
is exercised, and the sovereign who exercises it.

But if sovereignty be justified by the people's consent why, we must
ask, do they give their consent? Only because (and here, once more,
the familiar utilitarian argument reappears) it is to their advantage to
do so. If all individuals were equally rational and enlightened, government would not be necessary, for men would live together in peace
and harmony, without requiring any force to keep them in order;
just as the members of a family, all of whom love and trust one
another, live together peaceably without requiring the exercise of
paternal authority to keep them in order. Unfortunately, not all
individuals are sufficiently rational to see that their own best interests
can in the long run be attained only by sacrificing immediate private
goods. Since they are not intelligent enough of their own accord
to choose a greater, but distant, good, when it is opposed to a lesser
good which is, however, nearer at hand, these individuals must be
forced to make this choice.[1]

¶   Every individual, as a man, can, indeed, have a particular will
which contradicts, or at least is dissimilar to, the will which he has
as a citizen. His particular interest can speak to him in a voice
altogether different from that of the general interest. Thinking of
himself as self-sufficient and naturally independent, he can conclude
that what he contributes to the common cause is a free gift, which
is more burdensome to the donor than it is advantageous to the
recipients. Regarding the moral person which constitutes the State
as a merely fictitious entity, because it is not a man, he enjoys the
rights of citizenship, without wishing to fulfil the duties of the
subject. . . .
If the social contract be not merely an empty formula, it tacitly
implies a clause which alone gives force to the others, that any
individual who refuses to obey the general will may be constrained

[1] *Contrat Social*, I, 7 (35–36).

¶ by the whole body of citizens.[1] This means nothing more than that such an individual will be forced to be free. This is the condition which . . . alone justifies the exercise of civil authority in ways which, without it, would be absurd, tyrannical, and subject to hopeless abuses.

Even if we take this statement at its face value it seems badly confused.[2] At one point, certainly, it does go beyond Locke, since Rousseau's argument makes much more clear, what was only vaguely implied in Locke's, that the individual is subjected to restraint, not merely for the good of the whole group, but also for his own private good. But, though this is doubtless a more *moral* justification for the exercise of force (since it is made to rest on the good of the very individual upon whom the force is exercised), it is easy to see that it would not appeal very strongly to a man who was facing imprisonment or execution. And the criminal, surely, would be correct in not finding the argument plausible. That is (quite apart from the difficulty of convincing the criminal himself), it really does not promote his best interests to have his life or liberty taken from him.

There is a difference, Rousseau might reply, between those occasional lapses into a narrowly selfish point of view of which an enlightened citizen might now and then be guilty, and the habitually anti-social conduct of a member of the criminal classes; and it is only with the first type of man that this theory is primarily concerned. We really can, Rousseau might urge with considerable plausibility, be said to have the consent of the first type of man to the exercise of force upon him when it is necessary. Knowing, as he does, that socially cohesive conduct in the long run best promotes his own interests, and knowing also that he will occasionally find the attractions of some more immediate selfish good too strong to resist, he may very well consent to the use of restraint whenever he yields to the temptation. Thus, we consent to (*i.e.*, approve of) the establishment of a speed limit and of a penalty for travelling at excessive speeds; and, though we may complain when we ourselves are fined, nevertheless we consent, in a perfectly intelligible sense, to being penalized. We approve the existence of this law, because, in the first place, we are sufficiently enlightened to see that excessive speeds are in fact dangerous to ourselves and contrary to the public good; and because, in the

---

[1] Compare Locke's position on this point; *vide supra*, pp. 171–172.
[2] For criticisms of a more basic character, *vide infra*, pp. 324–325.

second place, we know enough about ourselves and our fellow-citizens to be sure that without some sort of penalty we would yield to the desire to get to our destination rapidly, even though all the while aware of the fact that this speed is endangering both ourselves and the public. It is therefore reasonable, in this sort of case, for Rousseau to talk about our giving our consent to being restrained, and about our being "forced to be free." We can be forced to be free, in Rousseau's sense of freedom as meaning conformity to a law of our own choosing, because we really do choose the law which, for instance, sets an upper speed limit. We can be forced to do what is in the public interest, because the public interest is, after all, what we really want.

But what of the habitual and hardened criminal? He clearly stands outside of this whole scheme. And he stands outside of it because his good really is not involved in the good of the whole group. On the contrary, he can attain his good only at the expense of the group's good. It is impossible, therefore, to pretend that the criminal consents to *his* punishment; it is impossible to say that he is forced to be free: the law which he is being forced to obey is not a law of his choosing. And it is not of his choosing, because, being the kind of man he is, obedience to this law, so far from promoting his own best interests, actually destroys those interests.

There is, of course, no reason why Rousseau should not exclude criminals from the operation of his general will. Logically, indeed, he should exclude them, because what makes them criminals is their failure, or inability, to share in the general will. But what he should also see, and what one suspects he does not see, is that in any society the number of criminals—*i.e.*, of persons who do not participate in the general will—is very considerable. In other words, the notion of a *completely* general will is, as we have already seen, only an ideal; and there still remains the problem (which Rousseau tends to pass over) of what to do about the large number of men who are either unable, or unwilling, to share in the common good of the group to which they happen to belong. Doubtless, in the ideal state, there will be no problem, because there will be no criminals: every one will have the kind of status which makes his good *really* dependent upon, and involved in, the good of all the other members of his group. This is very fine, but it does not throw any light on what to do in a society like our own, where the social and economic structure is such that the interests of various individuals and classes really do seem to be mutually incompatible. Criminals, in this sense of the word, really are justified in disobedience, and the exercise of force upon them is, on Rousseau's own account, unjustified and immoral.

(b) *Inalienable*. So far we have seen that the sovereign power is absolutely unlimited. It is also, according to Rousseau, inalienable and indivisible.[1]

¶   I say that sovereignty, being merely the exercise of the general will, can never be alienated; and the sovereign, since it is only a collective being, can be represented only by itself. Power, certainly, can be transferred; but not will. . . .

For the same reason that sovereignty is inalienable, it is indivisible. For will is either general or it is not, either the will of the whole body of the people or that of a part only. In the first case, the expressed will is an act of sovereignty and constitutes a law; in the second case, it is only a particular will or an act of magistracy —a decree at the most.

But our politicians, unable to divide sovereignty on principle, divide it according to its object: they divide it into force and into will; into the legislative power and into the executive power; into the rights of taxation, of justice, and of war; into powers of internal administration and those of foreign affairs. Sometimes they confuse all these parts together, sometimes they separate them. . . .

These errors result from not having an exact conception of the nature of sovereignty, and from taking as parts of the sovereign what are only emanations from it. Thus, for example, it is customary to suppose that the acts of declaring war and of making peace are acts of sovereignty; but this is not the case. For neither of these acts is a law; each is only the application of a law. That both are merely particular acts which determine the application of the law in specific cases will be obvious to anyone who clearly sees what the word 'law' means. . . .

In every case . . . the rights, which are supposed to be parts into which the sovereign power is divided, turn out on examination to be all subordinate. Every one of them presupposes a supreme will of which these rights are nothing but the channels of execution.

This may seem at first sight mere subtlety and sophistication, but Rousseau actually has a sound point to make here. If tradition or

---

[1] *Contrat Social*, II, 1 (40), and II, 2 (40–41).

written constitutions seem to 'separate' powers, giving some—say, the right to levy taxes—to Parliament or Congress, and reserving others, as the case may be, to the King or to the States of the American Union, this may be a convenient mode of expression. But, in Rousseau's opinion, we should never allow ourselves to forget the fact that ultimately *all* of the power is in the hands of the people as a whole; that such separations, divisions, reservations, and other existent arrangements are only convenient channels or devices used by the sovereign people in the exercise of its power; and that, as a corollary, such arrangements exist only as long as the real sovereign, which lies behind them and sanctions them, regards them as expedient. In a word, what Rousseau says here is but a generalization of Locke's dictum on the subject of the royal prerogative, formulated in terms of the new theory of the general will.[1]

(c) *The Source of Law*. Finally, the sovereign is the source of all law.[2]

¶   But what then is a law? . . .

When the whole people decrees for the whole people, it considers only itself. If a relation then be formed, precisely the same object (but seen from two points of view) forms the two terms of the relation.[3] When this happens, the object of the decree made is general, like the will which decrees it. Such an act is what I call a law.

When I say that the object of laws is always general, I mean that the Law considers the subjects collectively and their actions in the abstract; it never has for its object an individual man or a particular action. Thus it is quite possible for the Law to decree that there shall be such and such privileges; but it can not grant them specifically to certain individuals. Again, several classes of citizenship, and the conditions for admission to each, can be established; but the Law cannot specify such and such individuals as being admitted to such and such classes. Similarly, the Law can establish a monarchical type of government and an hereditary succession, but it cannot designate who shall be king or name a royal family. In a word, no function which refers in any way to an individual can belong to the legislative power.

Since law has been defined as an act of the general will, there is

[1] *Vide supra*, pp. 194*ff.*   [2] *Contrat Social*, II, 6 (49–50).
[3] One term is the whole people as sovereign, the other as subjects.

¶obviously no need of asking who has the right of making the laws; nor is there any need of asking whether the prince be above the laws, since he is but a member of the State; nor whether a law can be unjust, since no one is ever unjust towards himself;[1] nor how it is that one can be free even while one is submitting to the authority of laws, since they are nothing but the expression of our own will.

It follows, moreover, that, just as the Law issues from a general will, so it is directed to an object which is general. Hence, on the one hand, nothing which an individual, whoever he may be, orders on his own initiative can ever be law, while, on the other hand, what the sovereign itself orders is not law if it be directed to a particular object. In such a case it is rather a decree; not an act of sovereignty, but an act of magistracy.

I call a *Republic*, then, every state governed by laws, whatever may be the actual form of its administration, because in a republic only the public interest governs: that is what the word 'republic' means. Every legitimate government is republican. . . .[2]

A republic, or state governed by laws, is thus one which is so organized, whatever be its specific form, that the people are sovereign. It is a government so organized that the people consent to its actions because those actions are what the people want done. It is a government, in a word, designed to translate the people's will into political action, to achieve whatever ends the people have in view. A shorter way of putting all of this is to say that a republic is a government in which there is a general will and it is sovereign.

(d) *Ideal and Actuality.* It follows that a republic, as Rousseau defines it, is simply the ideal type of state. At this point a familiar question is bound to arise: is it *merely* an ideal, or are there republican governments actually in existence? By his assertion that "the general will is sovereign" does he mean that it actually is sovereign or only that it ought to be sovereign? Is this proposition a factual or a moral assertion? This

---

[1] This would have been clearer if Rousseau had said that laws as he defines them are never unjust, since he calls 'law' only that which, being an expression of the general will, has been consented to by all those over whom it has authority.

[2] At this point Rousseau has added the following note: "I understand by this term, not merely an Aristocracy or a Democracy, but generally any Government which is directed by the general will and so by law. It is not necessary for a government to be legitimate that it be identical with the sovereign. It is enough that it be directed by, and be the minister of, the sovereign. Hence a Monarchy may be a Republic."

means (since we have already seen in what sense general wills are, or may be, actual) asking whether or not such actual general wills are, or ever have been, sovereign. It does not follow, just because a general will exists, that it is sovereign. Indeed, as Rousseau points out, the problem of making the general will sovereign, the problem of creating channels of expression by means of which the general will can be translated into action, is precisely the chief task which confronts any constitutional assembly.

Although, therefore, a general will may exist and, nevertheless, be rendered relatively powerless by the type of political structure existing in that state, we may say that a general will always *tends* to be sovereign. Other things being equal, the more general a will, the more powerful and nearly sovereign it is. Again, no actual sovereign, whatever its form be, can for long withstand a general will which is opposed to that sovereign and its policies. In practice the policies of all actual sovereigns are constantly being modified by pressure, even from wills which are far from being completely general. How much the sovereign's policies are thus modified depends, of course, on what the strength of the sovereign is *vis à vis* the articulateness of the will which is opposed to it. A more fashionable modern way of putting all this is to say that in any state there exist pressure groups of all sorts to which the sovereign is subject. The pressure exerted by any group is a variable determined by such factors as its size, cohesion, degree of organization, and the like. Rousseau would simply add to this that, if and when we have a group which includes *all* the citizens of the state, organized into a coherent and articulate body, we then have a will which is really general and which is also the actual sovereign in that state. Thus the whole problem of a state organization becomes for him the problem of finding that form of government in which the executive, whatever its form—whether king, council, or parliament—is but the servant of, and the minister to, the collective will of the whole body of citizens.

It follows from all of this that the answer to our question about the ideality of the general will's sovereignty must be both 'yes' and 'no.' *Yes*, the sovereignty of the general will is merely an ideal, in the sense that no general will is completely (or at least for long) sovereign in the full sense. In no actual state organization is the executive *completely and fully* responsive to the general will, even supposing such a will always to exist. The channels through which the general will is meant to express itself are never perfectly open and unrestricted. In other words, in every actual state the executive is never merely the minister of the people, but always has some power in its own right and is, therefore, at least partially sovereign. On the other hand, the answer must also be *no*. The sovereignty of the general will is not merely an ideal, in the sense that in every actual state the sovereign has to take the general will into account, just so far as there is one. No actual sovereign, not even the most complete despot, is altogether independent of the will of his subjects, nor immune from influence by them, even if this influence be only that of custom and tradition. Thus there may be states too primitive or too despotic for the subjects to be organized into articulate pressure groups; but even here there is a customary way of doing things to which the actual sovereign has to conform and within whose limitations he has to work. And these customs and traditions are nothing but the expression of the people's will fixed and embodied in behaviour patterns before that will is sufficiently conscious and articulate to express itself in written law.

The Legislator

Before we begin our consideration of the various types of government in which the sovereignty of the general will can best express itself we must pause briefly on Rousseau's concept of what he calls a "legislator." This concept is introduced in the following way: Rousseau points out that what we are aiming at is a government by law. It is a government in which, whatever its form, the people really rule themselves. The laws obeyed by them, being the expression of their own wishes and desires, are freely consented to by them. In other words, the precise form of the government is unimportant, if the government is truly of, for, and by the people. But, human nature being, as it is, weak and fallible, we cannot hope that a people can hit, unaided, on a form of government which will enable it to rule itself.[1] A young and politically immature people is much more likely, even with the best will in the world, to set up a government which defeats the ends for which it is established. It ends by issuing commands by force, instead of serving as an instrument for executing the general will. This being the case, a people who is about to set up a government requires the expert assistance of a legislator who can work out a form of government suitable to their particular needs and requirements.[2]

[1] *Vide supra*, p. 273, *n.* 4.
[2] *Contrat Social*, II, 6 (50–51); II, 7 (51*ff.*).

❡   The people who are subject to a law ought to be its author; the conditions of association ought to be regulated by those who form the association. But how are they to regulate them? Will it be a common accord, or a sudden inspiration? Does the Body Politic have an organ for expressing its desires? ... How can a blind and ignorant multitude, which seldom knows what it wants (because it seldom knows what is good for itself) work out for itself so huge and so difficult a problem as a system of legislation which will provide such an organ? The people of itself always aims at what is good; but, unaided, it does not always know what is good. The general will is always just, but the judgment which directs it is not always enlightened. ... Individual men are sufficiently enlightened to know what is good; but they sometimes reject it in favour of what is less good, though more enticing. The people, on the other hand, taken as a whole, aim at the good, without always knowing what it is.[1] All are equally in need of direction. Individual men need to have their wills made to conform to what their reason tells them is good; the people as a whole needs to be enlightened about what is really good for it.[2] With this knowledge there results a union of the reason and the will of the social body; from that, in its turn, the harmonious association of all elements; and, finally, the greatest possible amount of power. This explains why a legislator is necessary.

To find what rules are best suited to political societies would require an intelligence which could understand all human passions without experiencing any of them, which, without having any relation to our nature, nevertheless comprehended it completely.... It would take gods to provide men with laws. ...

He who dares to undertake the institution of a political society must feel himself capable of changing human nature, so to speak; of transforming the individual, who by himself is a perfect and solitary whole, into a part of a greater whole; ... of substituting for an independent and merely physical existence, one which is dependent and moral. He must, in a word, take away from man certain natural forces, and give to him forces foreign to his nature

---

[1] Here Rousseau recurs to, and, indeed, goes beyond, the Aristotelian position which we have already examined (*vide supra*, p. 278). It is not so much, as Aristotle maintained, that the 'many' manage to hit on a compromise policy which is best for all; rather, Rousseau thinks, the individual selfish *intentions* somehow cancel each other out, leaving a combined intention which is not selfish at all.

[2] These sentences have been very freely rendered in an effort to clarify Rousseau's thought, which is exceedingly compressed in the original.

¶ which he cannot use without the association of his fellows.[1] The more that these natural forces are annihilated, the more strong and durable become the acquired forces. The more, too, the institution itself becomes permanent and perfect. In fact, we can say that a legislation reaches the highest point of perfection it can possibly attain at precisely that point where the individual citizen is nothing, and can do nothing, without the association of his fellows, where the acquired force of the whole people is equal, or superior, to the sum of the natural forces of all the individuals.

From every point of view, the legislator is an extraordinary man in a state. . . . Though he institutes the government, he has no place in the constitution which he instituted. His particular and superior function has nothing in common with the administration of human affairs. For if the magistrate, who has command over men, has no power over laws, so the legislator, who has direction over laws, has no power to command men. Otherwise the laws instituted by him would be the ministers of his private desires and would only serve to perpetuate his injustices. He could never avoid adopting a private point of view and would thus destroy the holiness of his work. . . .

Thus we find in the legislator's work, at one and the same time, two apparently incompatible aspects: a programme above any human power, and an authority, for carrying it out, which is absolutely nil.

Another difficulty deserves mention. The learned will not be understood if they speak to the plain man in their own language, instead of using his. Many ideas cannot possibly be translated into the language of the plain man: some views are too general, and some objects too remote, for his comprehension. Every individual is interested only in that plan of government which seems to serve his own immediate needs, and sees only with difficulty the great advantages consequent upon those restrictions which good laws entail. For a young and immature people to appreciate sound political maxims and to follow the fundamental rules of political science, it would be necessary for cause and effect to be inverted. Social sense and feeling, whose development is actually a product of the institution, would have to inaugurate the institution itself; and men would have to be, before there are any laws, what they can

[1] All of this, it should be observed, is a reversion to a Lockian view of human nature before the contract.

¶become only as a result of the existence of laws. Thus, since the legislator can employ neither force nor reasoning, he is obliged to have recourse to a different kind of authority—one which compels without the exercise of force, which persuades without convincing.

This is what has compelled the founders of states, in every age, to have recourse to the intervention of heaven and to attribute to the gods their own wisdom, to the end that their peoples, submitting to the laws of the state as if they were laws of nature and recognizing the same power at work in forming the city that works in the creation of man, might freely obey and docilely carry the yoke of public happiness.

This sublime reason is altogether above the comprehension of plain men. Its decisions the legislator puts into the mouths of the gods, in order to discipline those whom considerations of human prudence could not move. But not every man can make the gods speak, nor will every one be believed when he declares himself their interpreter. The great soul of the legislator is the real miracle which proves his mission. . . .

Here, again, as so often in Rousseau, we have a curious mixture of penetrating insights and fabulous nonsense. First, as regards the existence of a 'legislator,' there is no lack of historical support for Rousseau's assertions. He obviously has in mind the custom which the Greek city-states had of inviting distinguished citizens or foreigners to compose constitutions for their use. And, for that matter, Rousseau himself was invited, on two occasions, by Corsica and by Poland, to serve as a constitution-maker. If these proposals were never realized, it was no fault of Rousseau's, who in his enthusiasm saw himself as a modern Solon or Lycurgus, and who made in each case a careful study of the situation of the country in order to be able to determine what particular kind of constitution it should have.

To take a modern example, in the American Constitution we find a body of laws 'given' to a people by a legislator, for there is no reason why Rousseau's legislator need be a single individual. He may just as well be a group of men united in a constitutional convention. Certainly, again, such an individual or convention does have, as Rousseau maintains, an anomalous and extra-constitutional position. Since its function is merely to work out a constitution, it is not itself included in the constitution which it produces; and, though it has the authority to frame such a constitution and to propose it to the people for approval, it has no power to enforce its acceptance. But to describe this plain and simple fact in such far-fetched and rhetorical language as Rousseau uses is misleading and, therefore, dangerous. There is neither reason nor need to characterize the legislator as 'holy' and 'superhuman,' simply because this man, or group of men, is designated by the people to submit a constitution for approval. It seems that Rousseau is here himself guilty of a curious naïveté: he appears to be taking literally and at their face value his own remarks on divine inspiration and sanction, though, in the same breath, he himself tells us that these expressions have no real validity and are merely designed to appeal to the simplicity of the plain man.

Nevertheless, under all this ecstatic verbiage about the grandeur of the legislator and his mission, one can detect a core of plain common sense. It is, certainly, no easy matter to work out a kind of constitution, or political organization, in and through which the general will can freely express itself; and Rousseau is quite correct in emphasizing this difficulty and the requirement of expert knowledge, if the problem is to be solved satisfactorily. But the resolution of this difficulty is not primarily contained in the notion of a spontaneous and arbitrary fiat on the part of some invited legislator. Such a legislator may occasionally solve the problem; but, even where he does, a high degree of political maturity is required of the people as a whole, both, in the first place, to invite the expert to frame their constitution, and, in the second place, to accept it when it is presented. As Rousseau himself points out, the acceptance of a good constitution requires a kind of political maturity and wisdom in the people which is itself only the product of living under such a constitution. The real answer to Rousseau's problem, therefore, is not that a young and politically immature (or, indeed, any) people can have a good constitution made overnight and out of whole cloth by an expert legislator; it is rather that the framing of a good constitution is a slow and painful process of development, of trial and error, of gradual growth. A legislator is not a demigod, descending from Sinai with a ready-made code of laws; being as much a product of his social milieu as are the men and women whom he serves, he is limited in every way by the level of political maturity which they happen to have reached. As he and they grow in political maturity, they are the better able to frame sound constitutions; and, as these sounder constitutions succeed one another, he and they develop still further that political sense and social feeling which are at once the basis and the final result of all good government. Thus we are not faced with a vicious circle from which the only exit is an appeal to a divinely inspired superman. The political sense of a people and the form of government under which it lives rather mutually condition one another in a spiral of development so as to result in ever more efficient and stable democratic forms.

Forms of Government

In order to follow Rousseau's account of the various possible forms of government we must recall that, for him, government is merely an intermediary agency between the people as sovereign and the people as subject. It is merely the organ through which the sovereign people expresses its will and brings about changes in the external world. It thus stands to the general will in precisely the relation in which the hand or foot stands to the will of an individual man: it is the instrument by which the will is executed.[1]

¶ We have seen that the legislative power belongs to the people exclusively. . . .

This public power, however, requires its own agent to keep it united and to put it to work under the direction of the general will, to serve as a channel of communication between the State and the sovereign, to do for the public person what the union of body and soul, so to speak, does for the individual man. In this lies the justification of government—often unfortunately confused with the sovereign whose minister it is.

What, exactly, is government? An intermediary body, established between the subjects and the sovereign in order to secure their mutual communication and charged with the execution of the laws and with the maintenance of liberty, civil as well as political.

The members of this body are called magistrates or *kings*, that is, governors; and the whole body is called *prince*.[2] Thus those are altogether correct who maintain that it is not by means of a contract that the people submit themselves to their rulers. It is nothing more than a commission, or an employment. The rulers, as simple officers of the sovereign, exercise in its name the power of which it has made them the depositaries. It follows that the sovereign can

---

[1] *Contrat Social*, III, 1 (64–65).
[2] In a note at this point Rousseau remarks that "in Venice the college is called *Most serene Prince*, even when the Doge himself is not present."

¶ limit, modify, or recover this power as it chooses, that its alienation in inconsistent with the nature of a political society and contradicts the ends of association.

Thus, in my terminology, *government*, or supreme administration, is the legitimate exercise of the executive power; and *prince* or *magistrate*, the individual or group charged with this administration.

In a word, just as a man can *do* nothing, no matter what he *wills*, unless he has arms, legs, and other organs, so the general will can do nothing unless it has an agent which acts for it and in its name. It follows that, for Rousseau, the criterion for assessing the relative values of the different possible types of government is simply their efficiency in translating the general will into action, just as my arm is a good arm if it does expertly, easily, and efficiently all the things which I want it to do. It follows also that, since general wills vary, depending upon the size and character of the group of people composing it, no *one* form of government is absolutely best. "As a thousand different things can change the circumstances of a people, it is not only the case that different governments can be good for different peoples, but the same people can require different governments at different times." [1] The kind of government which is best for a maritime people, and which most effectively translates their will into political reality, might become bad and tyrannical if it were applied to an agricultural people. A large and populous country and a sparsely settled country will obviously require dissimilar forms of government. A politically mature people can best express its will in a very different political structure from the kind most suited to a young and politically in-experienced people. Hence the science of politics is the study of those principles and laws by which we determine exactly what kind of government is suitable for a given people. This is an extremely difficult task, and cannot, therefore, as we have seen, be left to the people themselves. It requires an expert—one not only well versed in the general principles of political science, but competent to make a careful and empirical study of the customs, the character, and the environment of the people for whom he is preparing a constitution. [2]

¶ Just as an architect, before beginning the construction of a huge building, makes soundings on the site to see whether it can carry

[1] *Contrat Social*, III, 1 (66).
[2] *Ibid.*, II, 8 (54–56); II, 10 (60–61); II, 11 (61–63).

¶ the weight, so the wise legislator does not begin by establishing laws which are good in themselves; but first he attempts to discover whether the people for whom he intends them is capable of supporting such laws. This is why Plato refused to prepare constitutions for the Arcadians and for the Cyrenians. He knew that these two peoples were wealthy and could not, therefore, endure equality. And, again, this is why in Crete there were good laws and bad men: Minos had only disciplined a people already encumbered with vice.

A thousand nations have had their place in the sun, which have never been capable of living under good laws. And even those who might have been capable maintained this state of maturity during only a fraction of their whole political life. For most peoples, like most men, are docile only in youth. As they grow old they become incorrigible. As soon as customs become established and prejudices become deeply rooted, it is both dangerous and impossible to reform them. . . .

On the other hand, youth is not infancy. For nations, as for men, there is a period of youth (or, if one prefers, of maturity) for which we must wait before giving a constitution to a people. Unfortunately, it is not easy to recognize a people's maturity, and if the legislator anticipates it his whole work is lost. One people will be politically mature from birth; another will not be at the end of ten centuries. The Russians will never be really mature politically, because the attempt to make them so was undertaken too early. . . . Some of the things which Peter did were sound, but for the most part they were out of place. He saw that his people were barbarous. He did not see that they were not ripe for civilization. He wished to make them polished, when what they really needed was discipline. . . .

What people, then, is fit for legislation? One which, although already bound together by ties of common origin, interest, or convention, has never yet felt the yoke of law; one whose customs and superstitions are not too deeply rooted; one which does not fear destruction by foreign invasion; . . . one in which each member may be known to all the others and in which it is not necessary to lay on a man heavier burdens than he can bear; one which is independent of other peoples, but on which they are dependent; one which is neither rich nor poor, but which has a sufficiency for its purposes; one which, finally, combines the consistency of an old people with

¶ the docility of a new people. . . . All these conditions being difficult to find realized, it follows that few states have good constitutions.

There is, however, still one country in Europe which is capable of being given a constitution. It is Corsica. The courage and the constancy with which this noble people has recovered and defended its liberties deserve some wise man who can teach it how to preserve them.[1] I have a premonition that some day this little island will astonish Europe.

If we inquire in what, precisely, consists the greatest good of all, the attainment of which must be the end of every system of legislation, we find that it reduces to two main objects: *liberty* and *equality*. Liberty, because every particular dependence is so much force taken from the body of the state; equality, because liberty cannot exist without it.

I have already defined civil liberty.[2] As for equality, there is no need to take this word to imply that all the citizens have absolutely identical amounts of power and property. I mean, rather, as regards power, that no man should have enough to use it violently, and that its exercise should be limited by one's rank in the state and by the laws; and, as regards property, that no one be rich enough to buy another or poor enough to be forced to sell himself. This involves, on the part of the great, moderation in profits and authority and, on the part of the poor, moderation of avarice and covetousness.

This equality, it will be said, is only an ideal for speculation. It cannot exist in practice. But, even if abuse is inevitable, does it follow that we should not at least try to regulate it? Just because the natural sequence of events always tends to destroy equality, the authority of law should always intervene to maintain it.

But these general objects of all good legislation must be modified in each country in terms of its particular circumstances as determined by the local situation and the character of the inhabitants. On the basis of these circumstances one then assigns to each people a system of law and a type of constitution which will be best, not perhaps in itself absolutely, but relatively to the state destined to receive them. If, for example, the legislator is confronted with an

---

[1] *Vide supra*, p. 292. On the whole, however, Rousseau seems to be disposed to give up Europe as hopeless, and to look towards the new world as a more fruitful ground for the establishment of good governments.

[2] By civil liberty Rousseau means, of course, the condition of a man who, as a part of the sovereign, gives himself the laws to which he is subject.

¶ over-populated country whose soil is poor and sterile, he should work out a constitution calculated to turn the people towards industry and the arts. Then they will be able to exchange their surplus manufactures for the commodities which they lack. On the other hand, is the country rich and fertile, but lacking in inhabitants? In this kind of case the legislator should devote all of his attention to agriculture, which causes men to multiply. He should exclude industry, since it would serve only to depopulate the country still further by collecting the few inhabitants in one or two places. Or, again, if the country has an extended and commodious shore line, it is well to cover the sea with ships and cultivate commerce and navigation. This country will have a brilliant career but a short one. . . . In a word, beyond the general principles common to all, each people has some peculiarities which require that its laws and constitution be different from those of every other people. . . . The author of *The Spirit of the Laws* has shown in innumerable examples how the art of the legislator suits the constitution to the special objects of each people.

The constitution of a state is truly solid and permanent only when the laws are suitable to, and harmonious with, the natural circumstances of a people, so that the laws and these circumstances are in agreement on the same points, and so that the laws, so to speak, only support, accompany, and rectify them. But, if the legislator mistakes the nature of a people and works out for them a principle opposed to its natural tendencies; if, for instance, his principle is directed towards the increase of wealth, while the natural tendencies of the people are towards an increase in population; if the former be towards servitude and the latter towards liberty, or if the former towards peace and the latter towards war—if any of these things happens the laws will gradually lose their authority, the constitution will be altered, and the state will not cease to be a prey to disturbances until it be finally destroyed or changed, and invincible nature assert itself once again.

Governments are classified by Rousseau according to the number of individuals who compose them.[1]

¶   The sovereign can, in the first place, commit the executive power to the whole people, or to a majority. In this case there are more

[1] *Contrat Social*, III, 3 (71-72).

¶ citizens who are magistrates than there are merely private citizens. This type of government is called a *democracy*.

Or the sovereign may put the government into the hands of a small number, in which case there are more private citizens than there are magistrates. This type is called an *aristocracy*.

Finally, the sovereign may concentrate the government in the hands of a single magistrate from whom all others hold their power. This third type, which is the most common, is called *monarchy*, or royal government.

It should be noted that all of these types, or at least the first two, may exist in varying degrees. Thus, democracy may embrace the whole people or it may be reserved to the majority; and an aristocracy, in its turn, can include either a very small, or a very considerable, number of individuals. . . . Thus there is a point at which each type of government flows over into the next type; and thus we see that, within these three general types, government is really capable of taking as many diverse forms as the state has citizens.

Are governments composed of many members, or governments composed of few members, better? It is impossible to lay down an absolute rule that democracy is better or worse than monarchy. "It has always been disputed which type is the better, without considering that each one is better in some situations and worst in others."[1] Rousseau does hold, however, that it is possible to draw up some maxims or principles by which may be determined the size of government best suited to each particular state. For instance, a large government (a democracy) is preferable in some types of states because of certain advantages it possesses, but it also has disadvantages which make a monarchy, or government by a single individual, preferable in others. It is clear, indeed, that[2]

¶ the total force of the government, being always identical with the force of that state itself, never varies. It follows from this that the more it is obliged to use its force to restrain its own members, the less remains to it to control the people as a whole.

The consequence of this is that the more numerous the magistrates, the weaker the government. Since this maxim is fundamental, we must make it as clear as possible.

Let us observe, then, that it is possible to distinguish three

[1] *Contrat Social*, III, 3 (72).   [2] *Ibid.*, III, 2 (69).

❡ essentially different wills in the person of the magistrate. In the first place, there is his own will as a distinct, private individual. It aims, naturally, at his own private interests. Secondly, he has a will which he shares with all the other magistrates. It aims at the common interest of the prince. And, since it aims at the private good of the government, taken as a separate body, this will is general, so far as the government is concerned, but particular with respect to the whole state of which the government is, after all, but a part. Finally, every member of the government, being also a part of the sovereign, has a will which aims at the good of the whole people. This will, finally, is therefore general both in respect of the state, taken as the whole, and the government, taken as part of that whole.

In other words, every individual not only has his own interests as a particular individual, but also the interests shared with the other members of each group to which he belongs. If these interests interlock and supplement each other, they mutually reinforce one another, but, if they are (or seem to be) opposed, they pull the individual in different directions and perhaps end by being self-defeating. Thus the individual magistrate has his own interests to look out for as Tom Jones or John Smith; he also has to look out for his interests as a magistrate, shared by him, of course, with the other members of that group; and, finally, he has a set of interests, transcending all these, which he shares with all other citizens of the state. Just as the individual can satisfy all his different interests only if these interests can be made to harmonize and mutually reinforce one another, so the state itself can survive only if the various particular wills composing it can be subordinated in varying degrees, depending on the degree of their particularity, to the general interest of the whole. It follows that [1]

❡ under a perfect constitution, the particular wills of all the various individual men would be entirely subordinate and vanish, and the private will of the government would be very much subordinate.[2] Hence, under a perfect constitution, the general will or sovereign is always dominant and serves as the rule determining all the lesser wills.

[1] *Contrat Social*, III, 2 (69–71); III, 3 (72).
[2] What Rousseau says here about the government, considered as a lesser group within the state, applies equally well, of course, to any such group, like a trust or trade union. Rousseau has the government chiefly in mind, because, since in his day it was the most powerful minority group, it was the chief offender by setting up its own private interests in opposition to the general interest.

¶ But, in actual practice, human nature is such that these different wills all become more active as they are more concentrated, so that actually, the general will is the weakest; the common will of the magistrates, next; and the particular will of the individual, strongest of all. Thus every member of the government is first of all his own individual self; next, a magistrate; and only finally a citizen: a scale directly opposed to what the social order requires.

This much established, it follows, if the government be placed in the hands of a single man, that the private will and the group will are identical, since the ruler can have no interests as an individual which are different from his interests as a magistrate. Hence the governmental will, in these circumstances, is as strong as it may be, since there are within it no lesser, private wills to oppose it.... Thus the most active government is that of a single individual—*i.e.*, monarchy.[1]

On the other hand, suppose we unite the government and the legislative authority, that is, suppose we make the sovereign to be also the executive, so that all the citizens are also magistrates. Then the governmental will, being confounded with the general will, has no more power than the latter; and all the various particular wills are left, unrestrained, in full force. Hence such a government will . . . have a minimum of force or activity.

These relations are incontestable, and there are other considerations which serve to confirm them. . . .

It is certain that the execution of any business becomes slower and less efficient as more and more people are concerned with its direction: in putting too much emphasis on prudence, we do not know how to seize fortune when it comes; we let the occasion slip, and, by thinking too deeply on the event, we may lose the fruits of our own deliberation.

I have just proved the government to become slack in proportion as the number of magistrates increases. I have already proved that the greater the number of citizens, the more powerful the repressive force required.[2] Consequently, the relation of the magistrates to the government should vary inversely with the relation of the

---

[1] As the government's will becomes unified and so more powerful, it also becomes more dangerous, since this government, being very definitely a minority, may find its own private interest opposed to the general interest, and, being strong, may be able to have its own way.

[2] It is not clear what precise passage Rousseau has in mind here; but in any case his point is likely to be generally accepted as not requiring a detailed proof.

¶subjects to the sovereign. That is to say, as the state expands, the government should contract, so that as the number of inhabitants increases, the number of magistrates should decrease.

So far, I have been speaking merely of the relative strengths of different governments, without regard to their rectitude. When we turn to this consideration, we find the situation reversed: the more numerous the magistrates, the more the collective will of the government approaches identity with the general will, while, under a monarchical government, the will of the magistracy is simply the will of a particular individual man. Thus what one loses in one direction, one gains in another; and the art of the legislator is to know how to determine the point at which the government's strength and its will, which are always in inverse proportion, can be combined to result in the greatest advantage to the state. . . .

If, in the different states, the number of supreme magistrates should be in inverse proportion to the number of citizens, it follows that, generally speaking, a democratic type of government is best suited to small states; an aristocratic type, to middle-sized states; and a monarchy, to great states. This general rule is derived directly from the principle we have laid down; but how can we ever take into account all the multitude of particular circumstances which might furnish exceptions?

(a) Democracy [1]

¶   It is not good for those who make the laws to execute them, nor for the whole body of the people to turn away from taking a general view of things in order to give its attention to particular concerns. Nothing is more dangerous than the influence of private interest on public affairs; and the abuse of the laws by the government is a less serious evil than the corruption of legislators, which is the inevitable consequence of their becoming concerned with particular things. In this way the state becomes altered in substance and reform is impossible. A people who could possess the governmental authority without sometimes abusing it would not require that authority to restrain them; a people who could always govern themselves well would not need to be governed.

Indeed, if we speak exactly, there never has been, and there never will be, a true democracy. . . . It is impossible to expect a whole

[1] *Contrat Social*, III, 4 (72–74).

¶ people to remain constantly assembled together in order to devote itself to the business of government; and it is easy to see that commissions could not be established to take over the direction of public affairs without the form of government being changed.

I believe it possible, in fact, to lay down the following principle: when the functions of government are divided among several tribunals, the smaller ones sooner or later become the most powerful, if for no other reason than because the ease with which smaller groups expedite business naturally brings the power into their hands.

Besides, nothing is more unlikely than to find together the various conditions which this kind of government presupposes. In the first place, the state must be small, so that the people can easily be assembled and so that every citizen may know all the others. Secondly, the pattern of social behaviour must be simple, so that there will be little business that requires the citizens' attention and no need at all for complicated debates. Again, all the citizens must be about equal in rank and in fortune, without which equality of rights and authority will not long continue. And, finally, there must be little or no luxury. For luxurious living is either the consequence of wealth or else renders wealth necessary. In either case, it corrupts both the rich and the poor: the rich by their possession of it, the poor by their covetousness of it. Luxury gives a nation over to indolence and vanity; it takes away from a state all of its citizens, to make them slaves to one another and all of them slaves to opinion. . . .

If there were a people of gods, they could govern themselves democratically. But so perfect a government is not suitable for men.

(b) Aristocracy [1]

¶ In an aristocracy there are two distinct moral persons; *viz.*, the government and the sovereign. Consequently there are two general wills, one which is truly general, because it is the will of all the citizens; the other only relatively to the members of the administration, whose common purpose it expresses. Thus, although the government may determine its private policy as it pleases, it may never speak to the people save in the name of the sovereign, that is, in the name of the people itself. This is something which must never be forgotten.

[1] *Contrat Social*, III, 5 (74–75).

❡ Primitive societies were governed aristocratically. The heads of families deliberated among themselves over the affairs of the whole group, and the younger men followed the authority of age and experience without question. Hence are derived such terms as *priests, elders, senators, gerontes*. Even in our own day, the natives of North America are admirably governed in this way.

But, as natural inequality gives place to the kind of inequality which results from social institutions, riches and power come to be preferred to age and experience; and the aristocracy becomes elective. Finally, as power comes to be transferred by a father to his sons, along with property, and as some families become patrician, the government develops into an hereditary aristocracy, and we find senators who are but twenty.

There are thus three types of aristocracy: natural, elective, and hereditary. The first is suitable only for primitive peoples; the third is the worst of all forms of government; the second is the best. It is aristocracy properly so called.

Besides the advantage which results to it from the distinction of the two powers, aristocracy has a further advantage in the choice of the members of the governing body. In a democracy all of the citizens are born magistrates; but in an aristocracy the number of magistrates is limited and citizens become magistrates only by an election. In this way honesty, intelligence, experience, and all the other grounds on which some citizens are preferred and stand higher in the public esteem become so many additional guarantees that the people will be wisely governed.[1]

Moreover, in an aristocracy assemblies are held more easily, the public business is better discussed and more thoroughly and systematically carried out, and the reputation of the state abroad is better maintained by venerable senators than by an unknown and contemptible multitude.

In a word, the best and most natural order is that in which the wisest govern the many, providing that we can be sure that they will govern the many for its profit and not for their own. There is no need uselessly to multiply the means of government, nor to do with twenty thousand men what a hundred carefully chosen ones can do still better.

---

[1] It may be felt that Rousseau is a little too optimistic in supposing that "honesty, intelligence, and experience" are attributes universally esteemed by the public, and that possession of these qualities will therefore ensure election to the governing body of the state.

(c) Monarchy [1]

¶ So far we have conceived the prince as a moral and collective person united by the force of the laws and as the depositary of executive power in the State. Now we have to consider this power as gathered together in the hands of a natural person, a real individual man, who alone has the right of disposing it in accordance with the laws. Such an individual is called a monarch or king.

In the other forms of government a collective entity represents an individual. Here, on the contrary, we find that an individual represents a collective entity; so that the moral unity which constitutes the prince is here at the same time a physical unity, and all those faculties, which in other governments the Law only succeeds in uniting together with so great efforts, are here found naturally combined.

. . . Here all the springs of the machine are in the same hand; everything is directed towards the same end. There are no conflicting movements tending to destroy one another; and it is impossible to conceive any kind of constitution in which less effort produces a more considerable action. . . .

But, if no other government has more vigour, in none, also, can a particular will more easily come to dominate all the others. Everything is directed to the same end, it is true; but this end is never the happiness of the public; and the government's power constantly works to the detriment of the state.

Kings desire to be absolute. . . . Even the best kings want the power to do evil, if they please, without ceasing to be masters. It is all very well for political sermonizers to say to them that, the people's power being their own power, their own greatest interest is to have a people which is flourishing, numerous, and strong.[2] Kings know very well that this is not true. It is to their personal interest that the people should be weak and miserable, so that it is in no position to resist the king's will. . . .

One inevitable and essential weakness of monarchy makes it always inferior to a republican [3] government: in the latter the voice of the people hardly ever raises to the highest places any but enlightened and capable men, who fill their posts with distinction,

---

[1] *Contrat Social*, III, 6 (76–81).
[2] This argument was put forth by Hobbes.
[3] In accordance with the terminology he is using Rousseau should have written 'democratic' here, instead of 'republican.' *Vide supra*, p. 299.

¶ while in monarchical governments, on the other hand, those who reach the top are most often only petty bunglers, rogues, and schemers. Their small talents may get them great places at court, but serve only to display their incompetence to the public as soon as they are established in them. The people is not so often mistaken in its judgment of men as is a king: and a man of real worth is almost as rare as a royal minister as a fool is as the head of a republican government. . . .

For a monarchy to be well governed, its size or extent would have to be proportionate to the capacities of those who govern. . . . However small a state may be, its ruler is almost always too small for it. When, however, as rarely happens, the state is too small for its ruler, it is still badly governed, since now the ruler, hearkening only to the grandeur of his ambitions, forgets the interest of his people. . . . We might say, therefore, that a kingdom ought to expand or contract with each new reign, according to the abilities of the king. . . .

The most obvious difficulty about a monarchical government is the lack of that continuous succession which in both of the other types maintains an uninterrupted connexion. When one king dies, another is needed; elections are stormy and in any case involve dangerous intervals, and unless the citizens have an integrity and probity which this kind of government scarcely admits of, bribery will be joined to corruption. . . .

What has been done to prevent these evils? The crown has been made hereditary in certain families; and an order of succession has been established which prevents any dispute at the death of a king. That is to say, the inconvenience of regencies has been substituted for the inconvenience of elections; an apparent tranquillity has been preferred to a wise administration; and it has been decided to risk having rulers who are children, monsters, or imbeciles, rather than to dispute over the election of a good king. . . .

Everything conspires together to deprive a man elevated to rule over others of both justice and reason. We are told that much trouble is taken to instruct young princes in the art of ruling; but it does not appear that they learn much from this education. One would do much better to begin by teaching them the art of obedience. The greatest kings celebrated in history have been those who were never brought up to reign. In fact, this is a science mastery of which one loses by becoming too well acquainted with

¶ it, and which one more easily acquires by obeying rather than by commanding. . . .

One consequence of this lack of coherence is the inconstancy of a royal government, which is ruled first according to this plan and then according to that, depending on the character of the reigning prince or of those who rule in his name. The result is that a monarchy lacks both a fixed object and a consistent policy, but floats from maxim to maxim and from project to project, as other governments do not in which the prince is always the same. . . .

If, as Plato says, a natural king is rare, how often do nature and fortune combine to crown him? And if a royal education necessarily corrupts those who receive it, what can one hope from a succession of men who have been brought up to rule? One simply deceives oneself if one identifies royal government as such with government by a good king. To see what this kind of government is in itself, one must think of it under shallow or wicked princes; for those who ascend the throne are either already shallow and wicked, or, if they are not, the throne will soon make them so.

These difficulties have not escaped the attention of royalist political writers. The remedy, they tell us, is to obey without complaint. God sends us bad kings in His wrath, and we must endure them as divine punishments. This kind of talk is doubtless edifying, but it suits the pulpit better than it does a book on politics. What would one say of a doctor who promised miracles and whose whole art consisted in exhorting the sick to have patience? We do not need to be told that we have to put up with a bad government when we have one; the question is rather how to find a good one.

(d) Mixed Governments [1]

¶ Strictly speaking, no government is simply of one or the other of these types. The solitary ruler of a monarchy requires subordinate magistrates, while a popular government has to have a head. Thus, in the distribution of executive power, there is always a gradation from a greater number to a lesser, with this difference, that sometimes the greater number depends on the lesser and sometimes the lesser on the greater. . . .

Which is better, a simple government or a mixed government? . . .

[1] *Contrat Social*, III, 7 (81–82).

¶ In itself a simple government is better, just because it is simple. But when the executive power is not sufficiently dependent on the legislative, . . . this lack of balance must be rectified by dividing the government. The sum of the divided parts has no less power over the subjects but their division renders the whole executive less strong *vis à vis* the sovereign.

The same difficulty can be prevented by establishing intermediary magistrates who, the government being left undivided, serve simply to balance the two powers one against the other, and to maintain their respective rights. In this case the government is not so much mixed as it is moderated.

Similar means can be used to correct the opposite fault. When the government is too weak, tribunals of magistrates may be set up to strengthen it. This has to be done in all democracies. In the former case, government is divided to reduce its power; in the latter, to augment it. This follows because the maximum of strength as well as the maximum of weakness is equally to be found in simple governments. Mixed governments, on the other hand, tend towards a mean position in respect of the power they can dispose.

The Maintenance of Sovereignty

If government is merely the agency by which the sovereign people translates its will into politically efficacious action it follows that the people's task is not done when a particular type of government is selected and particular men are chosen to fill the various governmental posts. The sovereign people must remain in being, or at least subject to periodic call, to ratify the actions of its government, to appraise its performance, and, if necessary, to recall it and find another to take its place.[1]

¶ It does not suffice that the assembly of the people should have on one occasion settled the constitution of the state by sanctioning a certain constitution. Nor is it sufficient for the people to have established a perpetual government or to have set up a rule for all subsequent elections of magistrates. Besides the extraordinary assemblies which unforeseen circumstances may require, it is necessary to set regular assemblies at certain fixed intervals, which may in no circumstances be cancelled or prorogued, and such

[1] *Contrat Social*, III, 13 (93–94); III, 14 (94–95); III, 18 (100–102).

¶ that on these days the people come together legitimately by law, without the need of any special, formal convocation. . . .

It is impossible to set down any exact rule as to how frequently these assemblies should occur, since there are so many different factors which have to be considered in each state. But we can at least say that, generally speaking, the greater the strength of the government, the more frequent should be the assemblies. . . .

As soon as the people is legitimately assembled as sovereign, the whole jurisdiction of the government ends, the executive power is suspended, and the person of the least citizen becomes as sacred and as inviolable as that of the chief magistrate, for the representative loses his function in the presence of those whom he represents. . . .

These intervals during which the prince's power is suspended and in which he recognizes, or ought to recognize, an actual superior, have always been regarded by him as dangerous. These assemblies of the people which are the bulwark of the state and a curb on the government have always been a horror to the rulers, who therefore spare no pains, nor objections, nor threats, nor promises in efforts to prevent the citizens from assembling. And if the citizens are greedy, cowardly, and pusillanimous, if they prefer their ease to their freedom, they will not be able long to withstand the redoubled efforts of the government. . . .

It follows . . . that the act by which a government is set up is never in any circumstances a contract, but a law ; that the depositaries of the executive power are not the masters of the people, but its officers; that the people can set them up and remove them as it pleases; that for these officers there is no question of rights under a contract, but simply a question of carrying out the people's instructions; that in carrying out the tasks which the people assigns to them they are merely fulfilling their duty as citizens, without acquiring any right to argue about the conditions.

Thus, for instance, if the people happens to institute an hereditary government . . . , it by no means engages itself permanently to this form of government. The administration is only provisional and lasts only until the people is pleased to order it otherwise.

It is true that these changes are always dangerous and that an established government should never be altered until it has become incompatible with the public interest; but this circumspection is merely a political maxim and not a rule of right. . . .

It is also true that in all such cases one cannot be too careful to

¶observe all the requisite forms for distinguishing a regular and legal act from a seditious tumult, and an act of the general will from the clamour of a faction. . . .

[This being the nature and the purpose of the periodic assemblies of the people, it follows that] two propositions must always be put to the people at the opening of every assembly . . . to be voted on separately.

The first: *Does it please the sovereign to continue with the present form of government?*

The second: *Does it please the people to leave the administration in the hands of those who are at present charged with it? . . .*

It is not necessary, when the people vote on these or other questions, that unanimity be attained. "There is but one law which, by its nature, requires unanimous consent: it is the social pact itself, for the act of forming a civil association is the most voluntary act in the world."[1] But beyond this contract (which is usually tacit, since continued residence in an already established state implies consent), the vote of the majority "always obliges all the others." Nevertheless, it is not always the case that a simple majority is decisive.[2]

¶   A difference of one vote destroys equality; a single opponent destroys unanimity. But between unanimity and equality there are a number of stages, and each of these corresponds to a declaration of the general will, depending on the condition of, and the needs of, the Body Politic at a particular time.

Two general maxims will serve to determine the nature of this correspondence. The first is that the result of the vote should approach nearer to unanimity as the issues debated are more serious and important. The second is that the more the matter requires speed and expedition, the more it is possible to reduce the size of the majority required, so that in an affair which requires an immediate decision, a majority of one is sufficient. The first of these maxims seems more consonant with the laws; the latter better suited to practical affairs. In any case, it is their combination which most satisfactorily determines what the size of the majority should be.

If we can now suppose a people assembled together to determine what kind of government it wants, we may ask what considerations should govern its choice.

[1] *Contrat Social*, IV, 2 (105).   [2] *Ibid.*, IV, 2 (106).

The Influence of Climate on Government

Though, as we have seen, Rousseau is prepared to offer general criticisms of the different forms of government, he does not think it is possible to say that some one form is absolutely best, another absolutely worst. He is too much persuaded of the truth of Montesquieu's contention, that variations in climate profoundly alter men's characters and capacities, to suppose that some one form of government will be equally suitable for all peoples everywhere. Hardly anyone to-day would deny the general thesis that different peoples require different forms of government. We have only to look at the failure of the republic set up in Germany after the First World War to recognize the truth of this observation. It is clear now that the German people was not ready for the Weimar constitution and that, given conditions as they were in Germany in 1919, a stable and permanent government must have had some different form. But these conditions which caused the collapse of the republic were not so simple as Rousseau and Montesquieu would have us believe. On the contrary, they were many and various—economic, social, psychological—and it is absurd to attempt to trace them all to climatic roots, or to suppose that, had the climate of Germany only been different, the Weimar constitution would have been a success.[1]

❡   To ask, What is the best form of government absolutely? is to raise a question which is too indeterminate to be answered; or, if one prefers, it is a question which is as capable of as many good answers as there are possible combinations in the absolute and relative positions of a people. . . .

Liberty, not being a fruit of all climates, is not within the reach of every people. The more one considers Montesquieu's principle, the more one recognizes its truth; the more it is contested, the more occasions there are for establishing it by means of new proofs.

In every government in the world, the public person is a consumer who produces nothing. From where comes the substance which it consumes? From the labour of its members. The necessities of the public person are supplied from the superfluities of the individuals in the state. It follows that a civil state can be maintained only where the products of men's labours exceed what is required to meet their own needs.

[1] *Contrat Social*, III, 9 (86–87); III, 8 (82–86).

¶   But this excess varies from country to country. . . . What it is depends on the fertility of the climate, on the kind of work which the soil demands, on the nature of its products, on the energy of the inhabitants, on the higher or lower rate of consumption which they require, and on several other similar factors which altogether determine the result. . . .

Inhospitable and barren regions, in which the product would not be worth the labour, should remain uncultivated and desert, or at the most, inhabited only by savages; regions in which men's labours return barely enough for subsistence should be inhabited by barbarous peoples: in such lands any form of political society would be quite impossible. On the other hand, lands where the excess of the product over the work is moderate are suitable for a free people. And those whose rich and fertile soil requires little work to reap an abundant harvest should be governed by a monarchy, so that the luxury of the prince may consume the superfluities of his subjects, it being far better that this excess should be absorbed by the government than that it be dissipated by the individual citizens. There are, I know, exceptions to what I have said; but they only serve to confirm the rule, since sooner or later they end in revolutions which restore the natural order of things. . . .

Because of the effect of climate despotism suits hot countries; barbarism, cold ones; and good governments, countries located in the temperate zone. . . .

To all of these various considerations, I can add one more which depends on them and which strengthens them. It is that hot countries need fewer, and can support more, inhabitants than can cold countries. This produces a double superfluity, which works to the advantage of despotisms. The greater the territory over which a given number of inhabitants is spread, the more difficult revolutions become, because it is hard for men to join together quickly and secretly and it is always easy for the government to learn of their intentions and to interrupt their lines of communication. On the other hand, the smaller the territory in which a numerous people dwells, the more difficult it is for the government to usurp the sovereignty. The people's leaders can meet together as safely in their homes as the prince in the council of his ministers, and the crowd can assemble as quickly in the public squares as the prince's troops can in their barracks. . . . Sparsely populated countries are thus most suitable for tyrannies: wild beasts rule only in the desert.

The Best Size for a Country

Since tyranny is the least satisfactory of all forms of government for the people concerned, and since a successful tyranny becomes increasingly difficult as the size of a country decreases, we can expect Rousseau to favour small, rather than great, states. There are other reasons, as well, for this preference. Rousseau is opposed, as we shall see, to representation for many reasons, and only small nations can live under a direct democracy. Again, it is clear that the realization of a general will is easiest in small nations and becomes more and more unlikely as the size of the state and the number and complexity of the citizens' interests increase.[1]

❡ As nature has set limits to the size of the well-made man, which are only violated in the shape of giants and dwarfs, so there are natural limits to the size of a good state: it must not be too large to be well-governed, it must not be too small to defend itself. For every state there is a maximum limit to the force which it can possess and which it often fails to attain to by attempting to become too large. The greater the extent over which a social bond is required to hold, the weaker its strength, and, generally speaking, a small nation is proportionally stronger than a large one.

There are a thousand reasons for the truth of this proposition. In the first place, the task of administration becomes more difficult at greater distances, just as a weight becomes heavier at the end of a longer lever. Again, administration necessarily becomes more burdensome as the number of different administrative units increases. Each city has a government of its own which is paid for by the people of that city; each district has a separate government which must also be paid for by the same people, next each province, then the various higher governmental bodies, satrapies, and viceroyalties, which cost more and more the higher we mount and all of whose expenses must be borne by the same unhappy people, and so on, until we reach the supreme administration, whose costs are overwhelming. So many surcharges keep the subjects exhausted; and, far from being better governed under all these different orders, they are less well-governed than if there were but one. . . .

And this is not all. It is not only the case that such a government has less ability to enforce laws vigorously and quickly, to prevent

[1] *Contrat Social*, II, 9 (56–58).

¶nuisances, to correct abuses, and to stifle seditious movements in out-of-the-way places; it is also the case that the people living in such a country have less affection for leaders whom they never see, for their country, which seems to them to be the whole world, and for their fellow citizens, who are for the most part strangers to them. The same laws will not be suitable to all the various provinces of a great country, which, having different customs and living under different climatic conditions, will require different forms of government. But different codes of laws only create trouble and confusion when applied in the same country to men living under the same rulers and in constant communication with each other. . . . The rulers, for their parts, weighed down by the multiplicity of affairs, see nothing for themselves, and the country is actually run by clerks in government offices. Finally, officers in distant provinces constantly tend to usurp the central authority, and the various measures which have to be taken against them to maintain it absorb all of the public funds; nothing remains to be devoted to promoting the happiness and well-being of the people. Indeed, scarcely enough remains to them to serve for their defence. Thus it is that a building too big for its foundations gives way and collapses under its own weight.

Representation

In a great state which attempts to live under a democratic government the functions which are performed in a monarchy by royal ministries fall upon the shoulders of representatives chosen by the people, since in so large a state the tasks of administration are too complex and too time-consuming to be borne by the people themselves. This is the greatest objection to attempting to run a great state on democratic lines, since it means that the people have to surrender their greatest right and most important duty.[1]

¶ As soon as the public service ceases to be the chief concern of the citizens, as soon as they prefer to serve with their purses rather than in their own persons, the state is near ruin. Is their country at war? They hire soldiers to fight for them and remain at home. Is public business pressing? They name deputies to attend to it and concern themselves with their own private affairs. Thanks to their laziness

[1] *Contrat Social*, III, 15 (94–98).

¶ and their wealth, they end by hiring soldiers to enslave their country and representatives to sell it.

It is the turmoil of commerce and industry, it is the avid desire for profits and love of softness and luxury which cause men to substitute money service for personal service. . . .

The better the state is constituted, the more public affairs, as opposed to private business, occupy the minds of the citizens. In fact, there is far less private business because, since every individual shares in the sum of common happiness, there is less reason for him to occupy himself with private affairs. . . . As soon as men say of the public business: *What does it matter to me?* we can count the state as lost. . . .

Sovereignty cannot be represented for precisely the same reason that it cannot be alienated. It consists, we have seen, in the general will, and will is not something that can be represented. It is either the same or it is different; there is no other alternative. The people's deputies are not, cannot be, its representatives. They are only commissioners appointed by the people, who have no power to conclude anything definitely.[1] For unless the people in person ratifies a law, it is not law. The English people thinks itself free, but it is badly mistaken. It is free only during a general parliamentary election: as soon as a parliament has been elected the people is again enslaved, it is nothing. The use which this people makes of the brief moments of its liberty shows that it deserves to lose it.

The idea of representation is modern. It is derived from feudal government, that iniquitous and absurd government in which the human species is degraded and the name of man is held in dishonour. . . .

Everything considered, I do not see how the people can preserve its rights as sovereign unless the state be very small. . . .

The Degeneration and Death of States

It is clear from what Rousseau says here and elsewhere that he does not expect his state to endure for ever. Just as the body can endure as a

[1] Here Rousseau in effect admits everything for which supporters of representative government could contend. It is not the fact of representation as such which is evil; it is bad only when the representatives illegally seize the power or when the people become indifferent and give up their sovereignty. But either of these things may happen under *any* form of government and is much less likely to happen in a representative democracy than in, say, a monarchy. This is a good example of the way in which Rousseau allows his emotion to get the better of his common sense and so to commit him to absurd and indefensible assertions.

living organism only so long as all the elements within it are function-ing together in harmony and living a common life, so the state can survive only as long as there exists a general will among all the citizens. When the general will is destroyed or weakened, when the citizens begin to put their own private interests or the interests of the parties or factions to which they belong before the national interest as a whole, the state is doomed. It falls a prey either to internal convulsions or to pressure from without.

Ideally, since actual political experience is the best, and, indeed, the only, training for political maturity, we might expect a republican state to grow stronger and stronger, the older it gets and the greater the citizens' experience in the art of self-government. This is, of course, a favourite thesis of Rousseau, but it is not really contradicted by what he says here. It *is* true up to a point that a republic grows stronger as its citizens mature in political wisdom. Unfortunately, as the state grows stronger, luxuries creep in, and the moral fibre of the people weakens. The sense of value of the citizens becomes dis-torted, and they come to prefer a life of ease to one of active political endeavour, and their own immediate private interests to those of the group as a whole. When this happens the general will is destroyed.

On this point, too, there is a perfect analogy between the state and the living body. Since we learn how to live well only by practice and experience, it might be supposed that the older we grow, the more vigorous and skilled our bodies become; and this is true up to a point. But decay inevitably sets in; tissues degenerate and grow flabby; here or there an organ ceases to function perfectly or fails to maintain the same rhythm which pervades the others, and so the whole body is weakened and becomes an easy prey to disease. Even an Aristotle could not put more emphatically the concept of the state as a natural organism.[1]

¶ Generally speaking, there are two ways in which governments can degenerate—*viz.*, when they are contracted and when the state is dissolved.

A government undergoes contraction when it passes from the hands of a larger number into the hands of a smaller number, that is, when it changes from a democracy to an aristocracy or from an aristocracy to monarchy. This is the natural tendency of all govern-

[1] *Contrat Social*, III, 10 (88–91); III, 11 (91–92).

¶ ments. If it ever passed from the hands of a smaller number to those of a greater, we could say that it was undergoing relaxation; but this inverse process is impossible. . . .

The dissolution of states can occur in two ways.

First, when the prince no longer administers the state according to law and usurps the sovereign power. When this happens a remarkable change occurs. It is not so much the government, but the state itself which undergoes contraction. I mean that the former, relatively large state is dissolved and that within it, another and smaller state is formed, which is composed solely of the members of the government. To the rest of the people this new state is nothing but a master and tyrant, so that the moment the government usurps the sovereignty, the social contract is broken and all the plain citizens acquire their original, natural right. This means that now the government forces them and that they have no moral obligation to obey its commands.

The same thing happens when the members of the government separately usurp the power which they ought only to exercise together as a body. This is no less an infraction of the law and actually produces even greater disorder. For, in these circumstances, we have, as it were, as many princes as there are magistrates; and the state, no less divided than the government, either perishes or changes its form. . . .

Such is the natural and inevitable tendency of even the best constituted governments. If Sparta and Rome have perished, what state can hope to survive for ever? If we wish to set up a durable establishment let us not dream of making it eternal. We shall fail altogether if we attempt the impossible and flatter ourselves that human creations can be given a permanence which does not belong to the works of man.

The Body Politic, just as well as the human body, begins to die at birth and carries in itself the seeds of its own destruction. But the constitutions of states, like those of men, can vary, and both may be preserved a longer or shorter time, depending on how robust they are. The constitution of a man is the work of nature; that of the state is a work of art. Since men are born with the kind of constitution they happen to have, there is nothing they can do to prolong their lives; but they have it in their power to lengthen the life of the state by giving it the best possible constitution. Even the best of constitutions will not endure for ever; but it will outlive any

¶other, if unforeseen accidents do not cause its death before its time.

The source of political life is the sovereign authority. The legislative power is the heart of the state; the executive is the brain, which directs the movements of the other parts. The brain may be paralysed and the victim still live: a man does not necessarily die when he becomes an imbecile; but life ends the moment the heart ceases its functions.

The General Will

The notion of the general will is not only the most central concept of Rousseau's theory; it is also the most original, the most interesting, and historically the most important contribution which he made to political theory. We cannot, therefore, conclude our examination of Rousseau without attempting an evaluation of this concept. In particular, we must look at two major objections to the idea of a general will, either of which, if it were valid, would materially lessen any permanent value which Rousseau's theory might be thought to have. The first of these concerns the applicability of the general will doctrine to large states; the second, certain instable elements in the doctrine which cause it to tend to shift from a basically democratic, to a more totalitarian, point of view.

We have said all along that there is no reason to reject the general will as being *merely* utopian; but it has also been pointed out that in most states a really general will does not occur very often or last very long. And the larger the state, the less frequent and the less permanent the general will, so that it may be doubted whether a general will in countries the size of the modern Great Powers, and having their economic and social diversity, can occur at all. It is not mere chance that the frequency of a general will varies inversely with the size and diversity of the state. A general will is possible in a given group, if, and only if, there is a good common to all the members of that group. It does not follow, of course, that a general will exists as soon as such a common good exists (for it is also necessary that the various members *recognize* this good), but it is clear that no general will can be real or effective unless that good exists. Now, although only the most extreme and individualistic of egoists would deny the possibility of any goods which are common to more than one person, it seems obvious that the larger the group, the less likely there is to be a good which is common to all its members. This is because a common good is not just an object large enough to be shared by a number of people, like a supply of chocolate ice cream big enough to 'go round' at a children's party; it is something which grows out of deeply rooted *organic* relations between the members of a group, like the common life and the common interests that may develop between husband and wife in a happy marriage. Unfortunately, the larger the group, the more difficult it becomes to establish organic relations binding together the various members of the group and the less plausible it is, therefore, to argue that all the members have a good in common; or, to put the matter another way, the more vague, tenuous, and abstract becomes the good which unites them.

Thus we can accept the Greek premise that man develops his full and best self only by living in communities with other men and that the solitary life is bad, since man needs some associates, without having to conclude that he must be associated with all, or even with a very large number of men. As a matter of fact, neither Plato nor Aristotle, both of whom started from this premise, reached this conclusion. On the contrary, both of them carefully limited the size of the state in which man was to associate with his fellows and so lead the good life. And Aristotle, at least, went counter to the dominant political current of his day, when he insisted that the state be kept small.[1] Moreover, not only must the state be restricted to a single city, as regards size; only a small and select minority of the inhabitants were thought to have, or to be capable of sharing in, a common good. The vast majority—slaves, artisans, mechanics, and the like—were denied citizenship as being incapable of effective participation in those organic relationships on which the state is based.

Rousseau recognized the same limiting condition on the organic state which Plato and Aristotle felt; and like Aristotle he was obliged, in order to preserve it, to set himself against the characteristic type of political organization of his own day, since by the eighteenth century the modern national and territorial state had already been developed. Rousseau's modern disciples, however, have not followed their master

---

[1] Aristotle's life was almost exactly contemporaneous with the growth of the empire. His father was a boyhood friend of King Philip of Macedon; Aristotle himself was Alexander's tutor and died shortly after Alexander's own death. Modern critics of Aristotle are puzzled to know why, with so striking an example before him, Aristotle should altogether have ignored the possibility of a state larger than a city. Perhaps the answer is that Aristotle disapproved of the new unit of organization and, fearing to criticize it openly, preferred to ignore it completely. In any case, there is little doubt about his attitude.

in observing this restriction.[1] They have swum with the current and attempted to adapt the doctrine of the general will to the great modern state. And this has created a very serious problem, for, when the restriction on size is removed, it is really difficult to see how this concept can any longer serve as the basis for a democratic political organization. The problem which thus confronts these modern followers of Rousseau (one which they do not always see) is how to set up a representative democracy without destroying the general will, or transforming it into something which is the antithesis of democracy. May it not be necessary to found a great representative democracy on some other concept than that of the general will? Since Rousseau did not think that there was any other possible basis for democracy, and since he did not think that representation was compatible with the existence of a general will, he was obliged (since it is obvious that democracy cannot be direct in a large state [2]) to exclude large states and to insist on keeping the state small enough to have a direct, non-representative democracy. Unfortunately the modern democratic theorist cannot take this course. It is even more evident now than it was in Rousseau's time that the day of the completely autonomous small state is over. Areas which have a common economic life require to have some sort of common political organization; and, since the world is increasingly becoming an economic unit, it follows that some sort of world-wide political structure is necessary. It seems safe to say that the lack of adequate organizations of this kind was one of the principal causes of the First World War, as it was of the Second. The League of Nations was an abortive attempt to set up this kind of political structure. The Nazi scheme to dominate Europe, and, indeed, the whole world, was a more thoroughgoing attempt to accomplish the same end by fundamentally different means. The defeat of the Nazis has ended, it is to be hoped, the attempt to organize the world on totalitarian lines. But the need for some all-inclusive entity is now generally recognized, even though it is also obvious that the development of any democratically organized unit of this magnitude is likely to be a slow and painful task. If, then, Rousseau's simple solution in terms of the small state has to be abandoned it is obviously a question of some importance to determine

---

[1] For instance, T. H. Green (*vide* his *Lectures on the Principles of Political Obligation* (Longmans, 1931)). However much Green may have read his Rousseau through Hegelian spectacles, the basis of his theory is essentially Rousseau's doctrine of the general will.

[2] The initiative and referendum are two attempts of somewhat dubious value to make direct democracy work in large states.

whether Rousseau's type of democracy based upon a general will can be adapted to large states, or whether some new basis for democratic institutions must be worked out.

This question breaks down into two separate, though connected, points. In the first place, is it possible for organic relations to develop between the diverse members of large groups? In the second place, is Rousseau correct in asserting that a general will cannot be represented? To put a complex and debatable matter briefly, we would say that large groups can have a really common end, *if* the members of these groups are not too different in outlook and point of view, and if their interests are not too various. This does not mean that the members of a given group *must* be formed in precisely the same mould (though this is *one* way of attaining unity, as the Nazi methods show); what it does mean is rather that the various members of the group understand one another and have sympathy for each other's different wants and aspirations. If this sympathy and understanding exist (and the two mutually condition one another), the various members of the group may have very different tastes, amusements, and activities without excluding the possibility of an organic state. The development of sympathy and understanding depends, partly, on education and on facilities for communication; and, partly, on there not being too great diversity of interests within the group. Where there are, for instance, enormous differences in the financial position of the members of the group, where the group is divided into workers who labour long hours for small pay, and capitalists who live on the income from their investments, there is a *prima facie* difficulty in achieving that kind of harmony of interests which is a condition of the organic state. It does seem at least questionable whether the capitalistic system in its present form is compatible with the existence of a general will in large industrial states; but, on the other hand, we should not exclude the possibility of modifications in the economic structure of society which (together with the kind of understanding of one's fellow citizens afforded by travel, the cinema, the radio, and various other modern means of communication) might result in the creation of a real general will in communities larger than any that Rousseau dreamed of.

Similarly as regards representation. Here, again, it may be that Rousseau takes too narrow a view. There seems no reason to suppose that universal education, and the increased capacities for a grasp of larger issues which that may be supposed to produce, may eventually make it possible for a general will to express itself through representatives. Political groups and organizations serve a useful purpose in keeping the citizens actively and intelligently interested in what their representatives are doing, and prevent their adopting an attitude of dull indifference, while the existence of local self-government means that all the citizens, no matter how large the state, participate directly in some of the functions of government. Again, it seems possible to develop a system of representation which is worked out, not merely on a geographical basis, but on the basis of the major economic interests and pursuits of the various citizens. In a word, the major difficulty with indirect democracy is the tendency of the representative (whether deliberately or not) to usurp the sovereignty and of the people to accept uncritically whatever their representatives propose. And this difficulty may be minimized or removed by devices of the kind we have just mentioned. If the citizens are alive to what their representatives are about, if these deputies represent their basic interests rather than their arbitrarily chosen places of residence, we may expect that a general will can be kept alive even in a great state with many millions of inhabitants and occupying hundreds of thousands of square miles of territory.

But what is important is that political philosophers, political scientists, and, above all, practical politicians recognize the problem which great states create and that they devise techniques to remove it, instead of taking it for granted that a general will can exist in a large state as well as in a small one. It seems safe to say, for instance, that one of the most serious problems that the United States has to face to-day is the direct consequence of the failure of the founding fathers (and of successive generations of politicians) to realize this and to incorporate in the Constitution the necessary measures for making the general will effective.[1]

This brings us to the second [2] main objection which the doctrine of the general will has to meet. The chief danger of applying the concept of the general will *as such*, and without devices of the kind we have been discussing, to large states is the tendency the state develops, in such circumstances, to become totalitarian—*i.e.*, to become a dictatorship by, and in the interests of, a small government

---

[1] As a matter of fact, since Hamilton and other members of the constitutional convention feared the influence which public opinion might exercise on government ("The people, sir, is a great beast"), various so-called *safeguards* were introduced to mitigate the effective expression of the general will.

[2] *Vide supra*, p. 318.

or clique. Moreover, when this happens the government finds (whether consciously or not) in the concept of a general will a useful formula for giving itself the appearance of a moral justification and for disguising the fact that it, and not the people, rules.

Let us put in the first place, then, a tendency of the concept of the general will to become totalitarian by distinguishing the state from the individuals who, rightly considered, compose it. This process has two stages: first the state is hypothetized as a separate entity, and then, in actual practice, this entity is identified with the government in power. Men have a natural tendency, it would seem, to attribute more unity to some things than they actually possess and, in particular, to treat what are actually only collections of individual things or elements as if they themselves were real individuals. There is no end of illustrations of this general tendency. For instance, a well-ordered collection of distinct qualities, say, red, spherical, and sweet, is rightly called an 'apple,' and we tend to think of there being a thing, 'apple,' somehow distinct from, though doubtless connected with, this pattern of related qualities. Or, again, a corporation, which is actually only a collection of individuals related in certain specific and definable ways, is often thought of and treated as if it were somehow itself an individual, different from, though connected with, the individual stockholders who compose it.

This tendency of thought naturally affects men's attitude towards the state. They tend to take the whole organism, which Rousseau defines the state to be, as if it were another distinct and separate individual, having a life of its own; and then, because it is so much larger than any real individual person, to treat it as if it were the end for which they exist. In other words, there is a tendency to forget the organic nature of the whole, to forget, that is, that the whole is nothing more than a number of individuals between whom certain organic relations exist. The result is that the value and worth of the constituent individuals is lost sight of, and the basic relation between man and the state is completely altered from what Rousseau conceived it to be. For him the whole is *nothing* but the individuals in their various organic relations, and this whole thus conceived is properly a means to the happiness and well-being of all the particular individuals who together constitute it. That is to say, properly conceived, the state is nothing but the various individuals in their organic relations instead of isolated and separated; and they, for their part, develop these relations only because by doing so they can live better, richer, and more fruitful lives for themselves. It is false, therefore, to say that the individuals may be sacrificed for the sake of the state.[1] This would be true only if the state were somehow a super-individual over and above all the real men and women who, in point of actual fact, are it. And since, of course, no such super-individual ever exists, what inevitably happens when this kind of view is adopted is that the government identifies itself with this mythological being. Hence in practice, the majority of individual members of the state, whose happiness ought to be the end and reason for its existence, are merely means to the well-being and happiness of those few individuals who compose the government.

This conflict between the point of view which regards every individual as being supremely important and valuable, but which sees that his importance and value can be properly and fully realized only in the society of others like himself, and the point of view which submerges the various individuals in some hypothetical super-entity, the state, conceived of as being somehow greater than the individuals who compose it, is absolutely fundamental to modern society. Though there is no doubt on which side Rousseau himself belongs, it is easy to see why the theory of the general will can be turned into a valuable weapon in the hands of those who hold the contrary point of view. We have only to consider Rousseau's famous dictum that a man may be forced to be free, in order to see how this can happen. Rousseau meant, of course, that a man may be forced to do something by the sovereign of which he is a part. If he and all the other members of the sovereign will to do that which is to the best interest of the state as a whole, and if the majority decide that it is to the state's best interest that he be punished for, say, speeding, then there is a perfectly intelligible sense in which he can be said to have willed his own punishment.[2] Ideally, therefore, every individual forces himself to be free. Actually, however, the individual is forced by the executive, or by its agents, the police; and if the executive does not truly represent the sovereign, or if it has usurped the sovereignty, the exercise of force upon the individual is altogether incompatible with his being free. Thus in large states (or, for that matter, even in small ones) where the executive often does not express the general will, Rousseau's dictum becomes a convenient way of giving lip

---

[1] It is not absurd, of course, to say that some particular individual may not, on occasion, have to be sacrificed, or punished, either for his own good, or even for the good of the other individuals in the state.

[2] *Vide supra*, pp. 283*ff*.

service to the principle of freedom, while maintaining a tyranny as ruthless as that of any dictator.

Again, there is, as we have seen,[1] a tendency in Rousseau to attribute superior powers of wisdom to the majority, and to suppose that its verdict is always correct. It is one thing to say that, as a matter of simple expediency, it is right always to follow the majority, even when it is wrong. It is quite another to claim a mystical insight for the majority which somehow always enables it to know what is best. We have, indeed, only to add a few flourishes to this latter notion—to conceive of the general will as a separate and distinct entity (instead of simply as a consensus), say, as the Aryan or the German 'soul,' and to think of this soul as welling up in, and speaking with the voice of, some particular individual who is the representative of the majority—in order to get the so-called *Führerprinzip* on which National Socialism was based.

There is a third aspect of Rousseau's doctrine which has a tendency to develop into totalitarianism, particularly when the theory is applied to large states containing diverse populations. As we have pointed out, in such states there may well be no general, or common, good. If this is the case, and if, nevertheless, it be assumed that there always must be some common good, what happens is that the good of some dominant group is identified with this supposed general good, and the various goods of the other individuals and groups, whose interests cannot be fitted into a single harmonious pattern, are sacrificed for its sake. Thus, once again, Rousseau's doctrine becomes a cloak (and not always, by any means, deliberately) for a point of view fundamentally different from his own.

There is one final twist which the theory of a general will can be given. The appearance of a really general will can be produced and maintained artificially by means of propaganda and other devices which a shrewd and sufficiently unscrupulous government will know how to employ. For Rousseau, of course, each member of the assembly which was to express the general will determined how to vote by a free and open consideration of all the various possible alternatives; and he believed that if men approached this inquiry in the right spirit, with the right motive, and with a reasonable degree of intelligence a majority would always be found to have voted correctly. And for Rousseau, education, in the broadest sense, is simply an instrument for assisting the voters to reach a reasonable and unprejudiced

[1] *Vide supra*, pp. 273*ff.*

decision. In the hands of totalitarian politicians, however, who see the value of a general will for strengthening and stabilizing the state, all of this is inverted. And the general will is not achieved at the end of a process of free and rational inquiry, as Rousseau expected, but during a process in which the citizens' minds are shut off from any but the particular alternative which the government wishes. What is produced in these circumstances is not in the least a general will, but something akin to an hypnotic state, whose really sinister nature is once more disguised by appropriating to it the fair terminology of Rousseau. This is perhaps the most complete inversion of Rousseau's own theory. Instead of there being a real meeting of minds, which is the directive force and energy within the state, there is an artificial agreement actually produced and maintained by the government. Instead of the general will being the source of government, the reverse is the case. Instead of schools, Press, radio, and cinema being used to educate the citizens and so to enable them to reach a true consensus, these agencies are used to keep them ignorant and to prevent their achieving anything but an apparent unanimity. And at the same time this is the most dangerous perversion of Rousseau's theory, since it is the one most difficult, even for the best-intentioned governments, to avoid falling into.

But on the other hand, there seems to be no reason why the general will should necessarily become perverted in this, or any other, way. Though the objections we have been raising are serious, they need not be fatal. After all, perhaps the greatest danger is a failure to recognize and to appreciate the difficulties in Rousseau's conception. If this is done, proper steps will be taken, especially in complex modern states, to insure the existence of a really common good, and to make it possible for the general will which results from it to be effectively expressed by its representative, the executive. But none of this is possible unless the nature of a general will is understood. Above everything else, therefore, it is essential not to let our thought on this subject be influenced by a false and insidious metaphysics. We must not allow ourselves to hypothetize or objectify the state as a super-entity distinct from the individuals who compose it, for at the end of this road lies totalitarianism. We must, in a word, remain true to the essential vision which Rousseau shared with Locke and some of the other early modern theorists, that the state, however we conceive its origin or its form of organization, exists only to make the good life possible for *all* the men and women who live in it.

FOR FURTHER READING

Translations

See footnotes, pp. 249 and 252.
Those who are interested in other works by Rousseau might begin with his *Émile* (Everyman Library, 1911), or his *Confessions*.

Commentaries and General Works

BABBITT, I.: *Rousseau and Romanticism* (Constable, 1919).
  A bitter attack on Rousseau's basic ideas.
GRAN, G.: *Jean Jacques Rousseau* (translated by M. H. Janson (1912)).
  A useful and complete biography.
JOSEPHSON, M.: *Jean Jacques Rousseau* (Gollancz, 1932).
MORLEY, J.: *Rousseau* (Macmillan, 2 vols., 1915).
  A somewhat prejudiced account.
OSBORN, A. M.: *Rousseau and Burke* (Oxford University Press, 1940).
  An attempt to show that Burke and Rousseau are, basically, not so far apart.
VAUGHAN, C. E.: *The Political Writings of Jean Jacques Rousseau* (Cambridge University Press, 2 vols., 1915).
  The introductions to the French texts are very useful.

Other Theories

For comparison with Rousseau's view, the French "Declaration of the Rights of Man," printed in Thomas Paine's *Rights of Man* (Everyman Library, 1915).

CHAPTER EIGHT

Edmund Burke

(1729–97)

LIFE

ALMOST all of the political philosophers examined in this volume had some connexion with, and experience of, the course of politics. Few of them were the purely academic, armchair kind of thinkers we sometimes like to pretend philosophers are. But only two of our thinkers were primarily men of political action. What we found to be true of Machiavelli is equally true of Burke. Neither of them anywhere sets out explicitly, formally, or systematically the principles on which his conception of the state rests: we do not find, for instance, the elaborate psychological analysis of human nature that Hobbes thought necessary as a basis for his political theory, or the carefully formulated moral principle with which Bentham begins. Nevertheless, the principles are there, embedded, as it were, in the actual concrete problems being dealt with. It is this fact—the fact that they are not merely opportunists, nor merely glib and unreflecting activists—which warrants their inclusion in this volume. But we must not suppose ourselves to be condescending to them by admitting them to this company.

Indeed, Burke is a fine example—a far better one than Machiavelli—of what is perhaps the best of all kinds of thinking—a happy and fruitful compromise between a too narrow devotion to immediate facts and a too exalted and transcendent soaring above them. Most minds tend in varying degree towards one or the other of these extremes. Neither is satisfactory. The trouble with the former is that it fails to see the forest for the trees. It becomes lost in relativism and particularism, and fails to look for what *should*, or *might*, be, being too absorbed in what is. Again, since no one can get on for a moment without some sort of guiding principles, this type of thinker is not without them. But for the most part he is unaware of the assumptions he makes and so is uncritical of them, even though their unsoundness may vitiate and infect what he does in the realm of practice.

On the other hand, the opposite extreme is equally fatal. Here we have a tendency either to distort facts through over-simplification or, still worse, to ignore the fact which cannot be reconciled with theory. A concern for what William James called "the stubborn and irreducible facts" of daily experience will alone bring flights of fancy down to earth; but a mere concern for facts, unillumined by a larger view, is likely to issue in a narrow cynicism.

The really sound mind lies in a mean position between these two extremes. It may be defined as a *realistic* mind, one in which theory illumines practice and practice tempers theory. This is the kind of mind Aristotle had; it is, as we shall see, the kind of mind Burke had. Hence, in studying Burke, we ought to be interested not merely in what he says (though this is certainly not without interest to us), but also in how he says it—*i.e.*, in the way in which his mind works.

If Burke and Machiavelli are alike in being active politicians, they differ in almost every other way. As we have seen, Machiavelli was typical, both in his strength and weakness, of the age in which he lived. On the other hand, the currents of Burke's mind ran counter to the dominant movements of thought and feeling in the century in which he lived. He was an opposition member, not only of Parliament where he sat for many years, but of the age.

When he entered Parliament in 1765 he was still largely unknown. Born in Ireland and educated at Trinity College, Dublin, he went to London in 1750 to seek his fortune, first in the law and, when that profession proved not to his liking, in letters. Though he had written an essay on *The Sublime and Beautiful* which attracted some attention, he cannot be said to have achieved any great success, and his only political experience had been an unhappy tour of duty in Ireland under the Irish secretary, "Single Speech" Hamilton. He lacked both the fortune and the family, either of which might have automatically assured him a career,[1] and he was too honest and independent to rise, as others in his condition did, by servilely doing the bidding of some

---

[1] Late in life he said of himself, "I was not ... swaddled and rocked and dandled into a legislator. *Nitor in adversum* is the motto of a man like me. I possessed not one of the qualities nor cultivated one of the arts that recommend men to the favour and protection of the great. I was not made for a minion or a tool. ... At every step of my progress in life (for in every step I was traversed and opposed), and at every turnpike I met, I was obliged to show my passport. Otherwise no rank, no toleration, even, for me." (*Letter to a Noble Lord, Writings and Speeches of Edmund Burke* (12 vols., 1901–6), V, 193. All references in this chapter are to the paging of this edition.)

great man.[1] Yet from his first speech in the House he was felt to be a rising man.

At that time the Government of England was in transition. Since 1688 the country had been ruled by the great Whig families of the Revolution. In the face of danger from the Stuart pretenders, the Crown had not been disposed to contend for power with those who had established it in the first instance, and the fact of the succession after Anne of a German prince, ignorant of the English language and of English customs, had only perpetuated the power of the Whigs. However, by 1760, when George III came to the throne, their power had begun to decline. In part this was the consequence of a weakening of their own sense of social responsibility and of party loyalty. The younger generation, as Burke never ceases to point out, hardly had the strength of character owned by the Whigs of Lord Somers's day. At the same time the new king determined not merely to reign but to rule. This meant completely reorienting the direction of Government. Since the settlement of 1688 the king had chosen for his Ministers men acceptable to Parliament. Now an effort was made to choose only "King's men" as ministers and to bend Parliament to the King's will as transmitted through his Ministers. This was to be accomplished by persuasion, bribery, or any other means available. Unfortunately, it appeared that Parliament was only too willing to be won over to the King's cause and, what was perhaps worse, was prepared to use the same high-handed methods in its dealings with the people that the King used towards it.[2]

This is the situation into which Burke was plunged on entering Parliament. From his point of view the constitution was being undermined. A revolution was being accomplished no less serious and

---

[1] Thus he broke with Hamilton after their return from Ireland, and surrendered a comfortable pension, rather than accept a dishonourable dependence.

[2] Burke had in mind, among other matters, the case of John Wilkes. In 1763 Wilkes, who was then a Member of Parliament, published a series of attacks on the King's favourite, Lord Bute, and on the speech from the throne. Action was brought against him, he was expelled from the House and sentenced to imprisonment. Since he was abroad at the time and did not return for his sentence he was outlawed. Meanwhile, in 1768, Parliament was dissolved, Wilkes returned to England, secured a reversal of his outlawry and was elected to a seat in the new Parliament from Middlesex. He was expelled once more and duly re-elected by the voters of Middlesex. There followed a series of expulsions and re-elections, until finally, on the fourth occasion, he received 1143 votes, as against 296, in spite of the fact that the full weight of the Crown was exerted against him. Nevertheless, the House of Commons rejected him and declared his opponent elected. Here, Burke felt, the House of Commons was departing from its original and constitutional function as a body of the people's representatives and was, instead, taking to itself the character of an oligarchical assembly, co-opting its own members in opposition to the wishes of the people.

dangerous because it was unaccompanied by violence and bloodshed. It must be allowed that Burke did not see the situation altogether as we would to-day. Others of the opposition, recognizing, as he did, the danger, advocated extension of the franchise, more frequent elections, and abolition of the King's extensive patronage. But these remedies seemed to Burke almost as fatal as the disease they were intended to cure. He believed, as against his opponents, that the Government should exist for the whole people; but he did not, as we to-day might, hold that the way to accomplish this was by putting the final power in the people's hands. He maintained rather, that the people's representatives in Parliament should do, not what the people want, but what they from their superior wisdom and experience think is best. They should not conceive themselves merely as the instruments for making effective somebody else's will—whether that of the King or that of the electorate. Rather, as enlightened, prudent, and responsible statesmen, they should rule *for* the people. Hence Burke's objection to the attempt of the "King's men" to rule was not that they were taking the direction of affairs away from its rightful owners, the people; but that men of this stamp, under the dominion of the king and dependent upon his favour, would not, and could not, rule for the best interests of the country as a whole.

Another great contemporary issue in which Burke took an active part was the conduct of affairs in America. Matters in the colonies there, which had been going from bad to worse for some years, came to a head in open rebellion in 1775. Burke had as little sympathy as any man with the abstract metaphysical arguments (the "rights of man") by which the colonists sought to justify their conduct; but this did not distract him from what seemed to him the reason of their cause. He could detect injustice and oppression in America as well as in England, and he also recognized incompetence, bungling, and stupidity when he saw them. Again and again he points out to the Government the folly of its policies in language which is a striking example of his ability to combine moral fervour with practical common sense. In these speeches, as always, Burke never forgets the immediate issues, but he invariably sees beyond them. Thus in the course of his attacks on the North administration he lays the basis for a sound colonial policy.

Of equal importance is Burke's attack on the corruption and incompetence of the British rule in India. This came to a head in the famous and long-drawn-out impeachment proceedings against Warren

Hastings, but for the purposes of illustrating this phase of Burke's thought, we give an extract from an earlier episode—the speech on the debts of the Nabob of Arcot. A word or two is necessary to explain the background of this speech.

The British were not the first Europeans to reach India, but they came increasingly to dominate the peninsula. Though their interest was wholly commercial, their contests with the other traders caused the enterprise to take on an increasingly military and political tone, and this was continued and deepened by the need for maintaining order among the native rulers. One thing led to another, Indian rulers unfavourable to British interests were removed and replaced by men who were, and soon the British found themselves the virtual rulers of the country. Nevertheless the direction of policy continued in the hands of a private stock company with its head office in London. In actual fact, however, since it required the best part of a year for the directors to communicate with their agents, the real management of affairs was in the hands of the company's servants in India. An organization which had worked fairly well for a private trading association was quite incapable of the efficient conduct of a vast political administration. The company's servants, finding themselves in possession of great power and completely uncontrolled by any responsible officials, busied themselves in extorting huge fortunes from the unhappy country. The directors did their best to regulate their practices and, among other measures, forbade their employees to accept gifts from the Indian rulers. Unfortunately it was easy to circumvent this prohibition by 'lending' money to the princes at exorbitant interest rates. As a matter of fact, since the persons involved were often only penniless adventurers, the money seldom changed hands in the first place, but in one way or another enormous obligations were contracted which in the long run had to be paid by the native population.

The debts of the Nabob of Arcot were contracted in this way. When their dimensions became known in England the company was ordered by Parliament to institute an investigation, but before this was completed the government changed its mind, moved to close the whole matter, and to authorize payment in full. It was at this point in the affair that Burke's speech was delivered.

Burke's last years were clouded by many disappointments. Both private and public events conspired against him. It was not enough that he himself never attained office at all commensurate with his abilities. In 1794, just as his own life was drawing to a close, he was shattered by the loss of his son, on whom all of his hopes had been concentrated.[1] Nor could he find any cheer in the situation of his own country or that of Europe. From the first Burke had looked upon the Revolution in France with the deepest suspicion—a judgment which seemed to him more than confirmed by the execution of the king and queen and by the Terror. If the French chose to destroy themselves, that was, doubtless, their own affair. Unfortunately, as Burke clearly saw, this could not be accomplished without serious repercussions in every country in Europe. He saw with alarm that there were not lacking in his own country admirers and would-be emulators of the events occurring across the Channel. But the liberty aimed at by the revolutionists, and so enticing to some Englishmen, seemed to Burke only a caricature of real freedom. It was, he thought, only licence, a kind of anarchy which would degenerate into the vilest of tyrannies. In fact, both in its violent course and in its lawless outcome, the Revolution seemed to Burke the antithesis of everything important in the sphere of politics. Though, in these circumstances it is hardly surprising that he should have fallen into certain excesses of sentiment and certain extremes of disapproval, it is none the less unfortunate, since it makes Burke sound at times (as he seemed to the surprised and delighted English court) like a die-hard Tory. If he had not been so near to the Revolution, if his beloved constitution had not seemed in such imminent danger, he would have seen that his chief difference with the revolutionists was not so much on the question of *aims* as on the question of *means*. Thus it is not liberty that Burke disapproves of; it is the attempt to achieve liberty without considering either the condition of the institutions through which it is to be attained, or the various other ends (*e.g.*, security, peace, prosperity) which are also desirable. In other words, Burke's real thesis against the Revolution (one which seems to have been amply borne out) is that, however noble their aims, disaster can be the only outcome of a sudden and violent overthrow of existing institutions and of age-old traditions by a group of visionary and impractical idealists without any political experience.

[1] "Had it pleased God to continue to me the hope of succession, I might have been, according to my mediocrity . . . , a sort of founder of a family. . . . But a Disposer whose power we are little able to resist, and whose wisdom it behoves us not to dispute, has ordained it in another manner, and (whatever my querulous weakness might suggest) a far better. The storm has gone over me; and I lie like one of those old oaks which the late hurricane has scattered about me. . . ." (*Letter to a Noble Lord*, V, 207–208.)

POLITICAL PHILOSOPHY

The Constitution [1]

¶ Nobody, I believe, will consider it merely as the language of spleen or disappointment, if I say, that there is something particularly alarming in the present conjuncture. There is hardly a man, in or out of power, who holds any other language. That government is at once dreaded and contemned; that the laws are despoiled of all their respected and salutary terrors; that their inaction is a subject of ridicule, and their exertion of abhorrence; that rank, and office and title, and all the solemn plausibilities of the world, have lost their reverence and effect; that our foreign politics are as much deranged as our domestic economy; that our dependencies are slackened in their affection, and loosened from their obedience; that we know neither how to yield nor how to enforce; that hardly anything above or below, abroad or at home, is sound and entire; but that disconnexion and confusion, in offices, in parties, in families, in Parliament, in the nation, prevail beyond the disorders of any former time: these are facts universally admitted and lamented. . . .

It is impossible that the cause of this strange distemper should not sometimes become a subject of discourse. . . . Our Ministers are of opinion, that the increase of . . . wealth in the hands of . . . the people, has rendered them universally proud, ferocious, and ungovernable; . . . so that they have trampled upon all subordination, and violently borne down the unarmed laws of a free government; barriers too feeble against the fury of a populace so fierce and licentious as ours. . . .

I am not one of those who think that the people are never in the wrong. They have been so, frequently and outrageously, both in other countries and in this. But I do say, that in all disputes between them and their rulers, the presumption is at least upon a par in favour of the people. Experience may perhaps justify me in going further. When popular discontents have been very prevalent, it may well be affirmed and supported, that there has been generally something found amiss in the constitution, or in the conduct of government. The people have no interest in disorder. When they do wrong, it is their error, and not their crime. But with the governing part of the state, it is far otherwise. They certainly may act ill by design, as well as by mistake. . . .

---

[1] *Thoughts on the Cause of the Present Discontents, op. cit.*, I, 433*ff*.

¶ [The fact is rather that] a great change has taken place in the affairs of this country. For in the silent lapse of events as material alterations have been insensibly brought about in the policy and character of governments and nations, as those which have been marked by the tumult of public revolutions. . . .

The power of the Crown, almost dead and rotten as Prerogative, has grown up anew, with much more strength, and far less odium, under the name of Influence. . . .

At the Revolution, the Crown, deprived, for the ends of the Revolution itself, of many prerogatives, was found too weak to struggle against all the difficulties which pressed so new and un-settled a government. The court was obliged therefore to delegate a part of its powers to men of such interest as could support, and of such fidelity as would adhere to, its establishment. Such men were able to draw in a greater number to a concurrence in the common defence. This connexion, necessary at first, continued long after convenient; and properly conducted might indeed, in all situations, be an useful instrument of government. At the same time, through the intervention of men of popular weight and character, the people possessed a security for their just proportion of import-ance in the state. But as the title to the Crown grew stronger by long possession, and by the constant increase of its influence, these helps have of late seemed to certain persons no better than incumbrances. . . .

To get rid of all this intermediate and independent importance, and *to secure to the court the unlimited and uncontrolled use of its own vast influence, under the sole direction of its own private favour,* has for some years past been the great object of policy. If this were compassed, . . . government might then be carried on without any concurrence on the part of the people; without any attention to the dignity of the greater, or to the affections of the lower sorts. A new project was therefore devised by a certain set of intriguing men, totally different from the system of administration which had prevailed since the accession of the House of Brunswick. . . .

[This was] the idea . . . of forming a regular party . . . under the name of *King's men.* To recommend this system to the people, a perspective view of the court, gorgeously painted, and finely illuminated from within, was exhibited to the gaping multitude. . . .

[While, on the one hand, the Crown was being thus exalted, it was necessary, on the other hand, to attack the old Parliamentary

¶ Government in the hands of the Whig nobility.] One of the principal topics which was then, and has been since, much employed by that political school, is an affected terror of the growth of an aristocratic power, prejudicial to the rights of the Crown, and the balance of the constitution. . . .

It is true, that the peers have a great influence in the kingdom, and in every part of the public concerns. While they are men of property, it is impossible to prevent it, except by such means as must prevent all property from its natural operation: an event not easily to be compassed, while property is power; nor by any means to be wished, while the least notion exists of the method by which the spirit of liberty acts, and of the means by which it is preserved. . . .

I am no friend to aristocracy, in the sense at least in which that word is usually understood. . . . But, whatever my dislikes may be, my fears are not upon that quarter. The question, on the influence of a court, and of a peerage, is not, which of the two dangers is the more eligible, but which is the more imminent. He is but a poor observer, who has not seen, that the generality of peers, far from supporting themselves in a state of independent greatness, are but too apt to fall into an oblivion of their proper dignity, and to run headlong into an abject servitude. . . .

Thus much of the topics chosen by the courtiers to recommend their system; it will be necessary to open a little more at large the nature of that party which was formed for its support. . . .

It must be remembered, that since the Revolution, until the period we are speaking of, the influence of the Crown had been always employed in supporting the Ministers of State, and in carrying on the public business according to their opinions. But the party now in question is formed upon a very different idea. It is to intercept the favour, protection, and confidence of the Crown in the passage to its Ministers; it is to come between them and their importance in Parliament; it is to separate them from all their natural and acquired dependencies; it is intended as the control, not the support, of administration. . . .

It is this unnatural infusion of a *system of favouritism* into a government which in a great part of its constitution is popular, that has raised the present ferment in the nation. . . .

A plan of favouritism for our executory government is essentially at variance with the plan of our legislature. One great end un-

¶doubtedly of a mixed Government like ours, composed of monarchy, and of controls, on the part of the higher people and the lower, is that the prince shall not be able to violate the laws. This is useful indeed and fundamental. But this, even at first view, is no more than a negative advantage; an armour merely defensive. It is therefore next in order, and equal in importance, *that the discretionary powers which are necessarily vested in the monarch . . . should all be exercised upon public principles and national grounds, and not on the likings or prejudices, the intrigues or policies, of a court.* This, I said, is equal in importance to the securing a government according to law. The laws reach but a very little way. Constitute government how you please, infinitely the greater part of it must depend upon the exercise of the powers which are left at large to the prudence and uprightness of Ministers of State. Even all the use and potency of the laws depends upon them. Without them, your commonwealth is no better than a scheme upon paper; and not a living, active, effective constitution. . . .

It had always, until of late, been held the first duty of Parliament *to refuse to support government, until power was in the hands of persons who were acceptable to the people, or while factions predominated in the court in which the nation had no confidence.* . . .

That man who before he comes into power has no friends, or who coming into power is obliged to desert his friends, or who losing it has no friends to sympathize with him; he who has no sway among any part of the landed or commercial interest, but whose whole importance has begun with his office, and is sure to end with it, is a person who ought never to be suffered by a controlling Parliament to continue in any of those situations which confer the lead and direction of all our public affairs; because such a man *has no connexion with the interest of the people.*

Those knots or cabals of men who have got together, avowedly without any public principle, in order to sell their conjunct iniquity at the higher rate, and are therefore universally odious, ought never to be suffered to domineer in the state; because they have *no connexion with the sentiments and opinions of the people.*

These are considerations which in my opinion enforce the necessity of having some better reason, in a free country, and a free Parliament, for supporting the Ministers of the Crown, than that short one, *That the King has thought proper to appoint them.* . . .

Parliament was indeed the great object of all these politics, the

¶end at which they aimed, as well as the instrument by which they were to operate. But, before Parliament could be made subservient to a system, by which it was to be degraded from the dignity of a national council into a mere member of the court, it must be greatly changed from its original character. . . .

The House of Commons was supposed originally to be . . . a *control* issuing *immediately* from the people. . . . It was hoped that, being of a middle nature between subject and Government, they would feel with a more tender and a nearer interest everything that concerned the people, than the other remoter and more permanent parts of legislature. . . .

Whatever alterations time and the necessary accommodation of business may have introduced, this character can never be sustained, unless the House of Commons shall be made to bear some stamp of the actual disposition of the people at large. . . . For it is not the derivation of the power of that House from the people, which makes it in a distinct sense their representative. The king is the representative of the people; so are the lords; so are the judges. They all are trustees for the people, as well as the Commons; because no power is given for the sole sake of the holder; and although government certainly is an institution of divine authority, yet its forms, and the persons who administer it, all originate from the people.

A popular origin cannot therefore be the characteristical distinction of a popular representative. This belongs equally to all parts of government and in all forms. The virtue, spirit, and essence of a House of Commons consists in its being the express image of the feelings of the nation. It was not instituted to be a control *upon* the people, as of late it has been taught, by a doctrine of the most pernicious tendency. It was designed as a control *for* the people. Other institutions have been formed for the purpose of checking popular excesses; and they are, I apprehend, fully adequate to their object. If not, they ought to be made so. . . .

For my part, I shall be compelled to conclude the principle ot Parliament to be totally corrupted, and therefore its end entirely defeated, when I see two symptoms: first, a rule of indiscriminate support to all Ministers; because this destroys the very end of Parliament as a control, and is a general, previous sanction to misgovernment: and secondly, the setting up any claims adverse to the right of free election; for this tends to subvert the legal authority by which the House of Commons sits. . . .

¶ For a considerable time this separation of the representatives from their constituents went on with a silent progress. . . . In the last session, the corps called the *King's friends* made a hardy attempt, all at once, *to alter the right of election itself*; . . . to disable any person disagreeable to them from sitting in Parliament, without any other rule than their own pleasure; . . . and to take into [Parliament], persons who avowedly had never been chosen by the majority of legal electors, nor agreeably to any known rule of law. . . .

A violent rage for the punishment of Mr Wilkes was the pretence of the whole. . . .

I will not believe, what no other man living believes, that Mr Wilkes was punished for the indecency of his publications, or the impiety of his ransacked closet. If he had fallen in a common slaughter of libellers and blasphemers, I could well believe that nothing more was meant than was pretended. But when I see, that, for years together full as impious, and perhaps more dangerous writings to religion, and virtue, and order, have not been punished, nor their authors discountenanced; that the most audacious libels on royal majesty have passed without notice; that the most treasonable invectives against the laws, liberties, and constitution of the country, have not met with the slightest animadversion; I must consider this as a shocking and shameless pretence. . . .

It behoves the people of England to consider how the House of Commons, under the operation of these examples, must of necessity be constituted. . . . The power of the people, within the laws, must show itself sufficient to protect every representative in the animated performance of his duty, or that duty cannot be performed. The House of Commons can never be a control on other parts of government, unless they are controlled themselves by their constituents; and unless these constituents possess some right in the choice of that House, which it is not in the power of that House to take away. If they suffer this power of arbitrary incapacitation to stand, they have utterly perverted every other power of the House of Commons. . . .

But we must purposely shut our eyes, if we consider this matter merely as a contest between the House of Commons and the electors. The true contest is between the electors of the kingdom and the Crown; the Crown acting by an instrumental House of Commons. It is precisely the same, whether the Ministers of the Crown can disqualify by a dependent House of Commons, or by

¶a dependent Court of *Star Chamber*, or by a dependent Court of King's Bench. If once members of Parliament can be practically convinced that they do not depend on the affection or opinion of the people for their political being, they will give themselves over, without even an appearance of reserve, to the influence of the court.

Indeed, a Parliament unconnected with the people is essential to a Ministry unconnected with the people; and therefore those who saw through what mighty difficulties the interior Ministry waded, and the exterior were dragged, in this business, will conceive or what prodigious importance, the new corps of *King's men* held this principle of occasional and personal incapacitation, to the whole body of their design. . . .

The first ideas which generally suggest themselves, for the cure of Parliamentary disorders, are, to shorten the duration of Parliaments; and to disqualify all, or a great number of place-men, from a seat in the House of Commons. . . .

If I wrote merely to please the popular palate, it would indeed be as little troublesome to me as to another, to extol these remedies, so famous in speculation, but to which their greatest admirers have never attempted seriously to resort in practice. I confess, then, that I have no sort of reliance upon either a triennial Parliament, or a place-bill. With regard to the former, perhaps it might rather serve to counteract, than to promote the ends that are proposed by it. To say nothing of the horrible disorders among the people attending frequent elections, I should be fearful of committing, every three years, the independent gentlemen of the country into a contest with the treasury. It is easy to see which of the contending parties would be ruined first. Whoever has taken a careful view of public proceedings, so as to endeavour to ground his speculations on his experience, must have observed how prodigiously greater the power of ministry is in the first and last session of a Parliament, than it is in the intermediate period, when members sit a little firm on their seats. . . .

The next favourite remedy is a place-bill. The same principle guides in both; I mean, the opinion which is entertained by many, of the infallibility of laws and regulations, in the cure of public distempers. . . . It is not easy to foresee, what the effect would be, of disconnecting with Parliament the greatest part of those who hold civil employments, and of such mighty and important bodies as the

¶ military and naval establishments. It were better, perhaps, that they should have a corrupt interest in the forms of the constitution, than that they should have none at all. . . . This is not a thing to be trifled with; nor is it every well-meaning man that is fit to put his hands to it. Many other serious considerations occur. I do not open them here, because they are not directly to my purpose; proposing only to give the reader some taste of the difficulties that attend all capital changes in the constitution; just to hint the uncertainty, to say no worse, of being able to prevent the court, as long as it has the means of influence abundantly in its power, of applying that influence to Parliament; and perhaps, if the public method were precluded, of doing it in some worse and more dangerous method. Underhand and oblique ways would be studied. The science of evasion, already tolerably understood, would then be brought to the greatest perfection. It is no inconsiderable part of wisdom, to know how much of an evil ought to be tolerated; lest, by attempting a degree of purity impracticable in degenerate times and manners, instead of cutting off the subsisting ill-practices, new corruptions might be produced for the concealment and security of the old. It were better, undoubtedly, that no influence at all could affect the mind of a member of Parliament. But of all modes of influence, in my opinion, a place under the Government is the least disgraceful to the man who holds it, and by far the most safe to the country. I would not shut out that sort of influence which is open and visible, which is connected with the dignity and the service of the state, when it is not in my power to prevent the influence of contracts, of subscriptions, of direct bribery, and those innumerable methods of clandestine corruption, which are abundantly in the hands of the court, and which will be applied as long as these means of corruption, and the disposition to be corrupted, have existence amongst us. Our constitution stands on a nice equipoise, with steep precipices and deep waters upon all sides of it. In removing it from a dangerous leaning towards one side, there may be a risk of oversetting it on the other. Every project of a material change in a government so complicated as ours, combined at the same time with external circumstances still more complicated, is a matter full of difficulties: in which a considerate man will not be too ready to decide; a prudent man too ready to undertake; or an honest man too ready to promise.

India [1]

¶ Fraud, injustice, oppression, peculation, engendered in India, are crimes of the same blood, family, and cast with those that are born and bred in England. . . . The difference [between peculation in Westminster and in Madras] is . . . in our attention to the one and our total neglect of the other. Had this attention and neglect been regulated by the value of the several objects, there would be nothing to complain of. But the reverse of that supposition is true. The scene of the Indian abuse is distant, indeed; but we must not infer that the value of our interest in it is decreased in proportion as it recedes from our view. In our politics, as in our common conduct, we shall be worse than infants if we do not put our senses under the tuition of our judgment, and effectually cure ourselves of that optical illusion which makes a brier at our nose of greater magnitude than an oak at five hundred yards' distance. . . .

When this gigantic phantom of debt first appeared . . . it naturally would have justified some degree of doubt and apprehension. Such a prodigy would have filled any common man with superstitious fears. He would exercise that shapeless, nameless form, and by everything sacred would have adjured it to tell by what means a small number of slight individuals, of no consequence or situation, possessed of no lucrative offices, without the command of armies or the known administration of revenues, without profession of any kind, without any sort of trade sufficient to employ a peddler, could have, in a few years, (as to some, even in a few months,) amassed treasures equal to the revenues of a respectable kingdom? Was it not enough to put [the Ministers] . . . on their guard, and to call upon them for a strict inquiry, (if not to justify them in a reprobation of those demands without any inquiry at all,) that, when all England, Scotland, and Ireland had for years been witness to the immense sums laid out by the servants of the Company in stocks of all denominations, in the purchase of lands, in the buying and building of houses, in the securing quiet seats in Parliament or in the tumultuous riot of contested elections, in wandering throughout the whole range of those variegated modes of inventive prodigality which sometimes have excited our wonder, sometimes roused our indignation, that after all, India was four millions still in debt to *them*? India in debt to *them*! For what? Every debt, for which an

[1] *Speech on the Nabob of Arcot's Debts, op. cit.,* III, 11*ff.*

¶ equivalent of some kind or other is not given, is, on the face of it, a fraud. What is the equivalent they have given? What equivalent had they to give? What are the articles of commerce, or the branches of manufacture, which those gentlemen have carried hence to enrich India? What are the sciences they beamed out to enlighten it? What are the arts they introduced to cheer and to adorn it? What are the religious, what the moral institutions they have taught among that people, as a guide to life, or as a consolation when life is to be no more, that there is an eternal debt, a debt "still paying, still to owe," which must be bound on the present generation in India, and entailed on their mortgaged posterity for ever? A debt of millions, in favour of a set of men whose names, with few exceptions, are either buried in the obscurity of their origin and talents or dragged into light by the enormity of their crimes! . . .

If this body of private claims of debt, real or devised, were a question, as it is falsely pretended, between the Nabob of Arcot, as debtor, and Paul Benfield and his associates, as creditors, I am sure I should give myself but little trouble about it. . . . But the gentlemen on the other side of the House know as well as I do, and they dare not contradict me, that the Nabob of Arcot and his creditors are not adversaries, but collusive parties, and that the whole transaction is under a false colour and false names. The litigation is not, nor ever has been, between their rapacity and his hoarded riches. No: it is between him and them combining and confederating, on one side, and the public revenues, and the miserable inhabitants of a ruined country, on the other. These are the real plaintiffs and the real defendants in the suit. Refusing a shilling from his hoards for the satisfaction of any demand, the Nabob of Arcot is always ready, nay, he earnestly, and with eagerness and passion, contends for delivering up to these pretended creditors his territory and his subjects. It is, therefore, not from treasuries and mines, but from the food of your unpaid armies, from the blood withheld from the veins and whipped out of the backs of the most miserable of men, that we are to pamper extortion, usury, and peculation, under the false names of debtors and creditors of state.

[As an example of the way in which the debts have been accumulated, we have the evidence of] a letter written from one of undoubted information in Madras to Sir John Clavering, describing the practice that prevailed there, whilst the Company's allies

¶were under sale, during the time of Governor Winch's administration.

"One mode," says Clavering's correspondent, "of amassing
money at the Nabob's cost is curious. He is generally in arrears to
the Company. Here the Governor, being cash-keeper, is generally
on good terms with the banker, who manages matters thus. The
Governor presses the Nabob for the balance due from him; the
Nabob flies to his banker for relief; the banker engages to pay the
money, and grants his notes accordingly, which he puts in the
cash-book as ready money; the Nabob pays him an interest for it
at two and three per cent. *per mensem*, till the tunkaws he grants
on the particular districts for it are paid. Matters in the meantime
are so managed that there is no call for this money for the Company's service till the tunkaws become due. By this means not a
cash is advanced by the banker, though he receives a heavy interest
from the Nabob, which is divided as lawful spoil."

Here, Mr Speaker, you have the whole art and mystery, the
true free-mason secret, of the profession of *soucaring*;[1] by which a
few innocent, inexperienced young Englishmen, such as Mr Paul
Benfield, for instance, without property upon which anyone would
lend to themselves a single shilling, are enabled at once to take
provinces in mortgage, to make princes their debtors, and to
become creditors for millions. . . .

That you may judge what chance any honourable and useful end
of government has for a provision that comes in for the leavings
of these gluttonous demands, I must take it on myself to bring
before you the real condition of that abused, insulted, racked, and
ruined country; though in truth my mind revolts from it, though
you will hear it with horror, and I confess I tremble when I think
on these awful and confounding dispensations of Providence. I
shall first trouble you with a few words as to the cause.

The great fortunes made in India, in the beginnings of conquest,
naturally excited an emulation in all the parts and through the
whole succession of the Company's service. But in the Company it
gave rise to other sentiments. They did not find the new channels
of acquisition flow with equal riches to them. On the contrary,
the high flood-tide of private emolument was generally in the
lowest ebb of their affairs. They began also to fear that the fortune
of war might take away what the fortune of war had given. Wars

---

[1] That is, money-lending.

¶ were accordingly discouraged by repeated injunctions and menaces: and that the servants might not be bribed into them by the native princes, they were strictly forbidden to take any money whatsoever from their hands. But vehement passion is ingenious in resources. The Company's servants were not only stimulated, but better instructed by the prohibition. They soon fell upon a contrivance which answered their purposes far better than the methods which were forbidden: though in this also they violated an ancient, but, they thought, an abrogated order. They reversed their proceedings. Instead of receiving presents, they made loans. Instead of carrying on wars in their own name, they contrived an authority, at once irresistible and irresponsible, in whose name they might ravage at pleasure; and being thus freed from all restraint, they indulged themselves in the most extravagant speculations of plunder. . . .

On this scheme of their servants, the Company was to appear in the Carnatic in no other light than as a contractor for the provision of armies, and the hire of mercenaries for his use and under his direction. . . .

In consequence of this double game, all the territorial revenues have at one time or other been covered by those locusts, the English soucars. Not one single foot of the Carnatic has escaped them: a territory as large as England. During these operations what a scene has that country presented! The usurious European assignee . . . flies to the Nabob's presence to claim his bargain; whilst his servants murmur for wages, and his soldiers mutiny for pay. . . . Every man of rank and landed fortune being long since extinguished, the remaining miserable last cultivator, who grows to the soil, after having his back scored by the farmer,[1] has it again flayed by the whip of the assignee, and is thus, by a ravenous, because a short-lived succession of claimants, lashed from oppressor to oppressor, whilst a single drop of blood is left as the means of extorting a single grain of corn. Do not think I paint. Far, very far, from it: I do not reach the fact, nor approach to it. Men of respectable condition, men equal to your substantial English yeomen, are daily tied up and scourged to answer the multiplied demands of various contending and contradictory titles, all issuing from one and the same source. Tyrannous exaction brings on servile concealment; and that again calls forth tyrannous coercion. They move in a circle, mutually producing and produced; till at length nothing of humanity is

[1] Collector of revenue.

¶left in the government, no trace of integrity, spirit, or manliness in the people, who drag out a precarious and degraded existence under this system of outrage upon human nature. Such is the effect of the establishment of a debt to the Company, as it has hitherto been managed, and as it ever will remain, until ideas are adopted totally different from those which prevail at this time.

. . . Let us do what we please to put India from our thoughts, we can do nothing to separate it from our public interest and our national reputation. . . . A government has been fabricated for that great province; the right honourable gentleman says that therefore you ought not to examine into its conduct. Heavens! what an argument is this! We are not to examine into the conduct of the Direction, because it is an old government; we are not to examine into this Board of Control, because it is a new one. Then we are only to examine into the conduct of those who have no conduct to account for. Unfortunately, the basis of this new government has been laid on old, condemned delinquents, and its superstructure is raised out of prosecutors turned into protectors. The event has been such as might be expected. . . . For one, the worst event of this day, though it may deject, shall not break or subdue me. The call upon us is authoritative. Let who will shrink back, I shall be found at my post. Baffled, discountenanced, subdued, discredited, as the cause of justice and humanity is, it will be only the dearer to me. Whoever, therefore, shall at any time bring before you anything towards the relief of our distressed fellow-citizens in India, and towards a subversion of the present most corrupt and oppressive system for its government, in me shall find a weak, I am afraid, but a steady, earnest, and faithful assistant.

France [1]

¶ DEAR SIR,

You are pleased to call again, and with some earnestness, for my thoughts on the late proceedings in France. . . .

You see, Sir, by the long letter I have transmitted to you, that, though I do most heartily wish that France may be animated by a spirit of rational liberty, and that I think you bound, in all honest policy, to provide a permanent body in which that spirit may reside, and an effectual organ by which it may act, it is my mis-

---

[1] *Reflections on the Revolution in France, op. cit.*, III, 235ff.

¶ fortune to entertain great doubts concerning several material points in your late transactions. . . .

I flatter myself that I love a manly, moral, regulated liberty as well as any gentleman . . . and perhaps I have given as good proofs of my attachment to that cause, in the whole course of my public conduct. . . . But I cannot stand forward, and give praise or blame to anything which relates to human actions and human concerns on a simple view of the object, as it stands stripped of every relation, in all the nakedness and solitude of metaphysical abstraction. Circumstances (which with some gentlemen pass for nothing) give in reality to every political principle its distinguishing colour and discriminating effect. The circumstances are what render every civil and political scheme beneficial or · noxious to mankind. Abstractedly speaking, government, as well as liberty, is good; yet could I, in common sense, ten years ago, have felicitated France on her enjoyment of a government, (for she then had a government,) without inquiry what the nature of that government was, or how it was administered? Can I now congratulate the same nation upon its freedom? Is it because liberty in the abstract may be classed amongst the blessings of mankind, that I am seriously to felicitate a madman who has escaped from the protecting restraint and whole-some darkness of his cell on his restoration to the enjoyment of light and liberty? Am I to congratulate a highwayman and murderer who has broke prison upon the recovery of his natural rights? This would be to act over again the scene of the criminals condemned to the galleys, and their heroic deliverer, the metaphysic Knight of the Sorrowful Countenance.

When I see the spirit of liberty in action, I see a strong principle at work; and this, for a while, is all I can possibly know of it. The wild gas, the fixed air, is plainly broke loose: but we ought to suspend our judgment until the first effervescence is a little subsided, till the liquor is cleared, and until we see something deeper than the agitation of a troubled and frothy surface. I must be tolerably sure, before I venture publicly to congratulate men upon a blessing, that they have really received one. . . . I should therefore suspend my congratulations on the new liberty of France, until I was informed how it had been combined with government, with public force, with the discipline and obedience of armies, with the collection of an effective and well-distributed revenue, with morality and religion, with solidity and property, with peace and order, with

¶ civil and social manners. All these (in their way) are good things, too; and without them, liberty is not a benefit whilst it lasts, and is not likely to continue long. The effect of liberty to individuals is, that they may do what they please: we ought to see what it will please them to do, before we risk congratulations, which may be soon turned into complaints. Prudence would dictate this in the case of separate, insulated, private men. But liberty, when men act in bodies, is *power*. Considerate people, before they declare themselves, will observe the use which is made of *power*—and particularly of so trying a thing as *new* power in *new* persons, of whose principles, tempers, and dispositions they have little or no experience, and in situations where those who appear the most stirring in the scene may possibly not be the real movers. . . .

The dislike I feel to revolutions, the signals for which have so often been given from pulpits,—the spirit of change that is gone abroad,—the total contempt which prevails with you, and may come to prevail with us, of all ancient institutions, when set in opposition to a present sense of convenience, or to the bent of a present inclination,—all these considerations make it not unadvisable, in my opinion, to call back our attention to the true principles of our own domestic laws, that you, my French friend, should begin to know, and that we should continue to cherish them. . . .

[The fact of the matter is that here in England] the very idea of the fabrication of a new government is enough to fill us with disgust and horror. We wished at the period of the Revolution, and do now wish, to derive all we possess as *an inheritance from our forefathers*. . . .

You will observe, that, from Magna Charta to the Declaration of Right, it has been the uniform policy of our Constitution to claim and assert our liberties as an *entailed inheritance* derived to us from our forefathers, and to be transmitted to our posterity—as an estate specially belonging to the people of this kingdom, without any reference whatever to any other more general or prior right. . . .

By a constitutional policy working after the pattern of Nature, we receive, we hold, we transmit our government and our privileges, in the same manner in which we enjoy and transmit our property and our lives. The institutions of policy, the goods of fortune, the gifts of Providence, are handed down to us, and from us, in the same course and order. Our political system is placed in a just

¶ correspondence and symmetry with the order of the world, and with the mode of existence decreed to a permanent body composed of transitory parts, wherein, by the disposition of a stupendous wisdom, moulding together the great mysterious incorporation of the human race, the whole, at one time, is never old or middle-aged or young, but, in a condition of unchangeable constancy, moves on through the varied tenor of perpetual decay, fall, renovation, and progression. Thus, by preserving the method of Nature in the conduct of the state, in what we improve we are never wholly new, in what we retain we are never wholly obsolete. . . .

Through the same plan of a conformity to Nature in our artificial institutions, and by calling in the aid of her unerring and powerful instincts to fortify the fallible and feeble contrivances of our reason, we have derived several other, and those no small benefits, from considering our liberties in the light of an inheritance. Always acting as if in the presence of canonized forefathers, the spirit of freedom, leading in itself to misrule and excess, is tempered with an awful gravity. This idea of a liberal descent inspires us with a sense of habitual native dignity, which prevents that upstart insolence almost inevitably adhering to and disgracing those who are the first acquirers of any distinction. By this means our liberty becomes a noble freedom. It carries an imposing and majestic aspect. It has a pedigree and illustrating ancestors. It has its bearing and its ensigns armorial. It has its gallery of portraits, its monumental inscriptions, its records, evidences, and titles. We procure reverence to our civil institutions on the principle upon which Nature teaches us to revere individual men: on account of their age, and on account of those from whom they are descended. All your sophisters cannot produce anything better adapted to preserve a rational and manly freedom than the course that we have pursued, who have chosen our nature rather than our speculations, our breasts rather than our inventions, for the great conservatories and magazines of our rights and privileges. . . .

You had all these advantages in your ancient states; but you chose to act as if you had never been moulded into civil society, and had everything to begin anew. You began ill, because you began by despising everything that belonged to you. . . .

This unforced choice, this fond election of evil, would appear perfectly unaccountable, if we did not consider the composition of the National Assembly: I do not mean its formal constitution, which,

¶ as it now stands, is exceptional enough, but the materials of which in a great measure it is composed, which is of ten thousand times greater consequence than all the formalities in the world. . . .

After I had read over the list of the persons and descriptions elected into the *Tiers État*, nothing which they afterwards did could appear astonishing. Among them, indeed, I saw some of known rank, some of shining talents; but of any practical experience in the state not one man was to be found. The best were only men of theory. . . .

Whilst I revere men in the functions which belong to them, and would do as much as one man can do to prevent their exclusion from any, I cannot, to flatter them, give the lie to Nature. . . . Their very excellence in their peculiar functions may be far from a qualification for others. It cannot escape observation, that, when men are too much confined to professional and faculty habits, and, as it were, inveterate in the recurrent employment of that narrow circle, they are rather disabled than qualified for whatever depends on the knowledge of mankind, on experience in mixed affairs, on a comprehensive, connected view of the various, complicated, external, and internal interests which go to the formation of that multifarious thing called a State. . . .

[What is worse, this Assembly, so constituted, is absolutely supreme. It] has no fundamental law, no strict convention, no respected usage to restrain it. Instead of finding themselves obliged to conform to a fixed constitution, they have a power to make a constitution which shall conform to their designs. Nothing in heaven or upon earth can serve as a control on them. What ought to be the heads, the hearts, the dispositions, that are qualified, or that dare, not only to make laws under a fixed constitution, but at one heat to strike out a totally new constitution for a great kingdom, and in every part of it, from the monarch on the throne to the vestry of a parish? But "Fools rush in where angels fear to tread." In such a state of unbounded power, for undefined and undefinable purposes, the evil of a moral and almost physical inaptitude of the man to the function must be the greatest we can conceive to happen in the management of human affairs. . . .

It is no wonder, therefore, that . . . it is vain to talk to them of the practice of their ancestors, the fundamental laws of their country, the fixed form of a Constitution whose merits are confirmed by the solid test of long experience and an increasing public strength and

¶ national prosperity. They despise experience as the wisdom of unlettered men; and as for the rest, they have wrought underground a mine that will blow up, at one grand explosion, all examples of antiquity, all precedents, charters, and Acts of Parliament. They have "the rights of men." Against these there can be no prescription; against these no argument is binding: these admit no temperament and no compromise: anything withheld from their full demand is so much of fraud and injustice. Against these their rights of men let no government look for security in the length of its continuance, or in the justice and lenity of its administration. The objections of these speculatists, if its forms do not quadrate with their theories, are as valid against such an old and beneficent government as against the most violent tyranny or the greenest usurpation. They are always at issue with governments, not on a question of abuse, but a question of competency and a question of title. . . .

Far am I from denying in theory, full as far is my heart from withholding in practice, (if I were of power to give or to withhold,) the *real* rights of men. In denying their false claims of right, I do not mean to injure those which are real, and are such as their pretended rights would totally destroy. If civil society be made for the advantage of man, all the advantages for which it is made become his right. It is an institution of beneficence; and law itself is only beneficence acting by a rule. Men have a right to live by that rule; they have a right to justice, as between their fellows, whether their fellows are in politic function or in ordinary occupation. They have a right to the fruits of their industry, and to the means of making their industry fruitful. They have a right to the acquisitions of their parents, to the nourishment and improvement of their offspring, to instruction in life and to consolation in death. Whatever each man can separately do, without trespassing upon others, he has a right to do for himself; and he has a right to a fair portion of all which society, with all its combinations of skill and force, can do in his favour. . . .

Government is a contrivance of human wisdom to provide for human *wants*. . . . Society requires not only that the passions of individuals should be subjected, but that even in the mass and body, as well as in the individuals, the inclinations of men should frequently be thwarted, their will controlled, and their passions brought into subjection. This can only be done *by a power out of themselves,* and not, in the exercise of its function, subject to that will and to

¶ those passions which it is its office to bridle and subdue. In this sense the restraints on men, as well as their liberties, are to be reckoned among their rights. But as the liberties and the restrictions vary with times and circumstances, and admit of infinite modifications, they cannot be settled upon any abstract rule; and nothing is so foolish as to discuss them upon that principle. . . .

What is the use of discussing a man's abstract right to food or medicine? The question is upon the method of procuring and administering them. In that deliberation I shall always advise to call in the aid of the farmer and the physician, rather than the professor of metaphysics.

The science of constructing a commonwealth, or renovating it, or reforming it, is, like every other experimental science, not to be taught *a priori*. Nor is it a short experience that can instruct us in that practical science; because the real effects of moral causes are not always immediate, but that which in the first instance is prejudicial may be excellent in its remoter operation, and its excellence may arise even from the ill effects it produces in the beginning. The reverse also happens; and very plausible schemes, with very pleasing commencements, have often shameful and lamentable conclusions. In states there are often some obscure and almost latent causes, things which appear at first view of little moment, on which a very great part of its prosperity or adversity may most essentially depend. The science of government being, therefore, so practical in itself, and intended for such practical purposes, a matter which requires experience, and even more experience than any person can gain in his whole life, however sagacious and observing he may be, it is with infinite caution that any man ought to venture upon pulling down an edifice which has answered in any tolerable degree for ages the common purposes of society, or on building it up again without having models and patterns of approved utility before his eyes.

These metaphysic rights entering into common life, like rays of light which pierce into a dense medium, are, by the laws of Nature, refracted from their straight line. Indeed, in the gross and complicated mass of human passions and concerns, the primitive rights of men undergo such a variety of refractions and reflections that it becomes absurd to talk of them as if they continued in the simplicity of their original direction. The nature of man is intricate; the objects of society are of the greatest possible complexity: and therefore no

¶simple disposition or direction of power can be suitable either to man's nature or to the quality of his affairs. . . . If you were to contemplate society in but one point of view, all these simple modes of polity are infinitely captivating. In effect each would answer its single end much more perfectly than the more complex is able to attain all its complex purposes. But it is better that the whole should be imperfectly and anomalously answered than that while some parts are provided for with great exactness, others might be totally neglected, or perhaps materially injured, by the over-care of a favourite member.

The pretended rights of these theorists are all extremes; and in proportion as they are metaphysically true, they are morally and politically false. The rights of men are in a sort of *middle*, incapable of definition, but not impossible to be discerned. The rights of men in governments are their advantages; and these are often in balances between differences of good—in compromises sometimes between good and evil, and sometimes between evil and evil. . . .

[In destroying the monarchy the French have removed one of the chief motives for public order.] All the pleasing illusions which made power gentle and obedience liberal, which harmonized the different shades of life, and which by a bland assimilation incorporated into politics the sentiments which beautify and soften private society, are to be dissolved by this new conquering empire of light and reason. All the decent drapery of life is to be rudely torn off. All the superadded ideas, furnished from the wardrobe of a moral imagination, which the heart owns and the understanding ratifies, as necessary to cover the defects of our naked, shivering nature, and to raise it to dignity in our own estimation, are to be exploded, as a ridiculous, absurd, and antiquated fashion. . . .

On the scheme of this barbarous philosophy, which is the off-spring of cold hearts and muddy understandings, and which is as void of solid wisdom as it is destitute of all taste and elegance, laws are to be supported only by their own terrors, and by the concern which each individual may find in them from his own private speculations, or can spare to them from his own private interests. In the groves of *their* academy, at the end of every vista, you see nothing but the gallows. Nothing is left which engages the affections on the part of the commonwealth. On the principles of this mechanic philosophy, our institutions can never be embodied, if I may use the expression, in persons—so as to create in us love

¶ veneration, admiration, or attachment. But that sort of reason which banishes the affections is incapable of filling their place. . . .

But power, of some kind or other, will survive the shock in which manners and opinions perish; and it will find other and worse means for its support. . . .

When ancient opinions and rules of life are taken away, the loss cannot possibly be estimated. From that moment we have no compass to govern us, nor can we know distinctly to what port we steer. . . .

You see, Sir, that in this enlightened age I am bold enough to confess that we are generally men of untaught feelings: that, instead of casting away all our old prejudices, we cherish them to a very considerable degree; and, to take more shame to ourselves, we cherish them because they are prejudices; and the longer they have lasted, and the more generally they have prevailed, the more we cherish them. We are afraid to put men to live and trade each on his own private stock of reason; because we suspect that the stock in each man is small, and that the individuals would do better to avail themselves of the general bank and capital of nations and of ages. Many of our men of speculation, instead of exploding general prejudices, employ their sagacity to discover the latent wisdom which prevails in them. If they find what they seek, (and they seldom fail) they think it more wise to continue the prejudice, with the reason involved, than to cast away the coat of prejudice, and to leave nothing but the naked reason; because prejudice, with its reason, has a motive to give action to that reason, and an affection which will give it permanence. Prejudice is of ready application in the emergency; it previously engages the mind in a steady course of wisdom and virtue, and does not leave the man hesitating in the moment of decision, sceptical, puzzled, and unresolved. Prejudice renders a man's virtue his habit, and not a series of unconnected acts. Through just prejudice, his duty becomes a part of his nature. . . .

To avoid, therefore, the evils of inconstancy and versatility, ten thousand times worse than those of obstinacy and the blindest prejudice, we have consecrated the state, that no man should approach to look into its defects or corruptions but with due caution; that he should never dream of beginning its reformation by its subversion; that he should approach to the faults of the state as to the wounds of a father, with pious awe and trembling solicitude. By this wise prejudice we are taught to look with horror on those

¶ children of their country who are prompt rashly to hack that aged parent in pieces and put him into the kettle of magicians, in hopes that by their poisonous weeds and wild incantations they may regenerate the paternal constitution and renovate their father's life.

Society is, indeed, a contract. Subordinate contracts for objects of mere occasional interest may be dissolved at pleasure; but the state ought not to be considered as nothing better than a partnership agreement in a trade of pepper and coffee, calico or tobacco, or some other such low concern, to be taken up for a little temporary interest, and to be dissolved by the fancy of the parties. It is to be looked on with other reverence; because it is not a partnership in things subservient only to the gross animal existence of a temporary and perishable nature. It is a partnership in all science, a partnership in all art, a partnership in every virtue and in all perfection. As the ends of such a partnership cannot be obtained in many generations, it becomes a partnership not only between those who are living, but between those who are living, those who are dead, and those who are to be born. Each contract of each particular state is but a clause in the great primeval contract of eternal society, linking the lower with the higher natures, connecting the visible and invisible world, according to a fixed compact sanctioned by the inviolable oath which holds all physical and all moral natures each in their appointed place. . . .

In this, as in most questions of state, there is a middle. There is something else than the mere alternative of absolute destruction or unreformed existence. . . . I cannot conceive how any man can have brought himself to that pitch of presumption, to consider his country as nothing but *carte blanche*, upon which he may scribble whatever he pleases. A man full of warm, speculative benevolence may wish his society otherwise constituted than he finds it; but a good patriot, and a true politician, always considers how he shall make the most of the existing materials of his country. A disposition to preserve, and an ability to improve, taken together, would be my standard of a statesman. Everything else is vulgar in the conception, perilous in the execution. . . .

I am convinced that there are men of considerable parts among the popular leaders in the National Assembly. Some of them display eloquence in their speeches and their writings. This cannot be without powerful and cultivated talents. But eloquence may exist

¶ without a proportionable degree of wisdom. . . . I confess myself unable to find out anything which displays, in a single instance, the work of a comprehensive and disposing mind, or even the provisions of a vulgar prudence. Their purpose everywhere seems to have been to evade and slip aside from *difficulty*. . . . Difficulty is a severe instructor. . . . [But] amicable conflict with difficulty obliges us to an intimate acquaintance with our object, and compels us to consider it in all its relations. It will not suffer us to be superficial. It is the want of nerves of understanding for such a task, it is the degenerate fondness for tricking short-cuts and little fallacious facilities, that has in so many parts of the world created governments with arbitrary powers. . . .

It is this inability to wrestle with difficulty which has obliged the arbitrary Assembly of France to commence their schemes of reform with abolition and total destruction. But is it in destroying and pulling down that skill is displayed? Your mob can do this as well at least as your assemblies. The shallowest understanding, the rudest hand, is more than equal to that task. . . .

The errors and defects of old establishments are visible and palpable. It calls for little ability to point them out; and where absolute power is given, it requires but a word wholly to abolish the vice and the establishment together. The same lazy, but restless disposition, which loves sloth and hates quiet, directs these politicians, when they come to work for supplying the place of what they have destroyed. To make everything the reverse of what they have seen is quite as easy as to destroy. No difficulties occur in what has never been tried. . . .

At once to preserve and to reform is quite another thing. When the useful parts of an old establishment are kept, and what is superadded is to be fitted to what is retained, a vigorous mind, steady, persevering attention, various powers of comparison and combination, and the resources of an understanding fruitful in expedients are to be exercised; they are to be exercised in a continued conflict with the combined force of opposite vices, with the obstinacy that rejects all improvement, and the levity that is fatigued and disgusted with everything of which it is in possession. But you may object, "A process of this kind is slow. It is not fit for an Assembly which glories in performing in a few months the work of ages. Such a mode of reforming, possibly, might take up many years." Without question it might; and it ought. It is one of the excellences of a

¶ method in which time is amongst the assistants, that its operation is slow, and in some cases almost imperceptible. If circumspection and caution are a part of wisdom, when we work only upon inanimate matter, surely they become a part of duty too, when the subject of our demolition and construction is not brick and timber, but sentient beings, by the sudden alteration of whose state, condition, and habits, multitudes may be rendered miserable. . . . Political arrangement, as it is a work for social ends, is to be only wrought by social means. There mind must conspire with mind. Time is required to produce that union of minds which alone can produce all the good we aim at. Our patience will achieve more than our force. If I might venture to appeal to what is so much out of fashion in Paris—I mean to experience—I should tell you, that in my course I have known, and, according to my measure, have co-operated with great men; and I have never yet seen any plan which has not been mended by the observations of those who were much inferior in understanding to the person who took the lead in the business. By a slow but well-sustained progress, the effect of each step is watched; the good or ill success of the first gives light to us in the second; and so, from light to light, we are conducted with safety through the whole series. We see that the parts of the system do not clash. The evils latent in the most promising contrivances are provided for as they arise. One advantage is as little as possible sacrificed to another. We compensate, we reconcile, we balance. We are enabled to unite into a consistent whole the various anomalies and contending principles that are found in the minds and affairs of men. From hence arises, not an excellence in simplicity, but one far superior, an excellence in composition. Where the great interests of mankind are concerned through a long succession of generations, that succession ought to be admitted into some share in the councils which are so deeply to affect them. If justice requires this, the work itself requires the aid of more minds than one age can furnish. It is from this view of things that the best legislators have been often satisfied with the establishment of some sure, solid, and ruling principle in government—a power like that which some of the philosophers have called a plastic Nature; and having fixed the principle, they have left it afterwards to its own operation. . . .

In old establishments various correctives have been found for their aberrations from theory. Indeed, they are the results of various necessities and expediences. They are not often constructed after

¶ any theory: theories are rather drawn from them. In them we often see the end best obtained, where the means seem not perfectly reconcilable to what we may fancy was the original scheme. The means taught by experience may be better suited to political ends than those contrived in the original project. They again react upon the primitive constitution, and sometimes improve the design itself, from which they seem to have departed. I think all this might be curiously exemplified in the British Constitution. At worst, the errors and deviations of every kind in reckoning are found and computed, and the ship proceeds in her course. This is the case of old establishments; but in a new and merely theoretic system, it is expected that every contrivance shall appear, on the face of it, to answer its ends, especially where the projectors are no way embarrassed with an endeavour to accommodate the new building to an old one, either in the walls or on the foundations. . . .

The effects of the incapacity shown by the popular leaders . . . are to be covered with the "all-atoning name" of Liberty. In some people I see great liberty, indeed; in many, if not in the most, an oppressive, degrading servitude. But what is liberty without wisdom and without virtue? It is the greatest of all possible evils; for it is folly, vice, and madness, without tuition or restraint. Those who know what virtuous liberty is cannot bear to see it disgraced by incapable heads, on account of their having high-sounding words in their mouths. Grand, swelling sentiments of liberty I am sure I do not despise. They warm the heart; they enlarge and liberalize our minds; they animate our courage in a time of conflict. Old as I am, I read the fine raptures of Lucan and Corneille with pleasure. Neither do I wholly condemn the little arts and devices of popularity. They facilitate the carrying of many points of moment; they keep the people together; they refresh the mind in its exertions; and they diffuse occasional gayety over the severe brow of moral freedom. Every politician ought to sacrifice to the Graces, and to join compliance with reason. But in such an undertaking as that in France all these subsidiary sentiments and artifices are of little avail. To make a government requires no great prudence. Settle the seat of power, teach obedience, and the work is done. To give freedom is still more easy. It is not necessary to guide; it only requires to let go the rein. But to form a *free government*, that is, to temper together these opposite elements of liberty and restraint in one consistent work, requires much thought, deep reflection, a sagacious, power-

¶ ful, and combining mind. This I do not find in those who take the lead in the National Assembly.

Detailed comments on Burke's views are unnecessary and out of place. Unnecessary, because Burke speaks, not to the technical philosopher but to the plain man, and so requires no exegesis to make his meaning clear. Out of place, because it is not our function to try to decide whether Burke was correct in attacking triennial parliaments or payment of the Nabob of Arcot's debts. Such matters—which comprise much of the specific content of Burke's writings—are long since only so much water over the dam, and in any case our concern, as political theorists, is not with this kind of problem.

Burke's value as a political philosopher does not rest on anybody's decision about such detailed points. It rests, in the first place, as we have already suggested, on the kind of mind he had, with its rare combination of qualities. We have given such extensive extracts from his writings because only in action can that mind reveal its nature. We understand it only when we see it at work organizing the facts of political experience, yet constantly ascending above them to take a larger view.

When Burke takes this larger view it is always worth our while to listen to his report of what he sees. Thus he may be violently prejudiced against the National Assembly and its new constitution for France. And though this may partially invalidate some of his specific recommendations and judgments, it does not in the least destroy the permanent value of his conception of human nature and the various subsidiary conclusions he draws from it.

This conception of human nature is never stated explicitly; yet it underlies everything he says. It grows out of his observations of mankind; and in turn it colours those observations. It is the agent which draws all of his most diverse assertions into significant and intelligible order; it is the lens that brings everything he wrote into sharp, clear focus.

For Burke, man is complex, like the world he lives in. This world is a vast nexus of interlocking, mutually dependent events. Things may indeed happen everywhere in an orderly fashion; but, for practical purposes, this is a matter of belief or faith, rather than of knowledge. Thousands upon thousands of factors condition even the simplest causal sequence. Hence the sciences, especially those dealing with human nature and conduct, are only rough approximations, not in the least those mathematically exact disciplines in which, as we have seen, Hobbes so fondly believed. There are too many "latent and intricate" causes, Burke says, for us ever to know with any precision what the final outcome of any act will be, even for the individual agent himself, still less in its impact upon the other members of society.

Since this is a failure of human intelligence, we can infer another property of human nature from the fact of man's uncertainty about himself and his world. Man is doubtless reasonable, but he is not so reasonable as he believes himself to be. He is not merely, or even chiefly, intellect. He is also passion, prejudice, and habit. What a man does is not so much the result of a careful, logical plan; it is rather built up of habits which are themselves determined by the society of which he is a member and into which he was born. He is more likely moved by some sentiment, desire, or feeling, than by a clear-sighted vision of some eternal verity. There is, in fact, a fundamental disparity between the world as reason reveals it and the world as it really is. For reason, the world falls into beautifully distinct groups of entities, between which simple well-defined relations hold. For reason there are, for instance, 'dogs' and 'cats,' or 'animate' and 'inanimate' things. For reason, all dogs have a dog-quality which distinguishes them from cats; living things are the exact opposite of things which are not living. Everything is clear, simple, and easy. But in actual fact dogs differ among themselves about as much as they differ from cats; what being 'animate' consists in is practically impossible to define; and there are things which do not fall simply and obviously into either the animate class or the inanimate class.

What is true at the level of knowledge, holds equally at the level of conduct. For reason, 'good' and 'bad' seem as completely and absolutely distinct as do animate and inanimate. But, when we face the actual alternatives of conduct, the sharp lines become wavy, the clear profiles, cloudy. Reason tells us that "everything is what it is and not another thing"; experience gives the lie to this. What anything is depends on how it stands to other things, so that nothing is just itself absolutely. A thing, for instance, does not own its properties absolutely; the properties it happens to have depend on the relations in which it stands to other things. Thus 'white' is not the colour that this piece of cloth owns; white is the colour it happens to have now, in this light, for these eyes, and so on. Similarly, a certain line of conduct, a certain goal or ideal, is not absolutely good or bad. An action may be very noble, or prudent, or altruistic in one set of circumstances;

and in different circumstances the same action may be cowardly, fool-hardy, and selfish. We oversimplify and so falsify the real nature of the world and ourselves if we think that the distinct schema, the fixed and immutable concepts, the well-ordered laws, as revealed by reason, correspond to experience as it really is.

This criticism of reason, this exaltation of experience, may all seem a long way from Burke; certainly we cannot find any passage in which he says as much. Actually, however, this notion of the world and of man determines all the main lines of his thought. This it is that makes him, for instance, a defender of what is old, what is conventional, what is long established. Since man is essentially a creature of habit, it is foolish and dangerous to try to abolish his habits. He will act, at best, only erratically and arbitrarily, if we take away the old channels which human nature has gradually fashioned for itself and through which it flows easily and spontaneously. Doubtless reason can discover many faults in these old patterns; doubtless they are far from ideal. But they are still much better than anything we are likely to get in their place. We may see some 'crying evil' in existing conditions and desire to do something about it. What we do not see is that any fundamental change in this single respect will have repercussions—such is the mutually dependent nature of the world—all along the line. And even if we understand this our minds are not big enough to cope with all the complex matters which would have to be considered before the scheme could safely be put into operation. But even if, *per impossibile*, we could work out such a vast scheme on paper, it would fail in application because it could not adjust to the subtle and intricate nuances of actual conditions. And, in any case, however perfect the scheme, however suitable to all possible conditions, its novelty would be a fatal stumbling block. It does not stir the affections, it cannot rest on the habitual responses, of the population. Contemplation of the alleged (or real) improvement which the scheme will bring may serve as a sufficient motive for the academicians who constructed it, but the plain man requires something nearer to his heart. Hence the scheme will inevitably fail, and, the old institutions under which men lived being destroyed, nothing remains to preserve order but the use of force or terror. This explains Burke's distrust of the French Revolu-tion; he hates and fears it, as he does any large scheme of reform, however noble in motive, because it involves a radical alteration of existing institutions and of customary patterns of behaviour. Like all reformers, the authors of the Revolution have made two serious mistakes. They have supposed themselves and the French people alike to be more reasonable than they are. They themselves are not, as they impertinently suppose, reasonable enough to work out a better scheme than the existing one; and the French people require for the smooth working of the society of which they are a part all those old sanctions, enthusiasms, loyalties, and fears which the new order has begun by abolishing and in whose stead it has none to offer.

It is not, Burke thinks, that the liberty sought by the revolutionists is valueless. Liberty is a noble ideal; but it is dangerous if it is not practical. Of course, liberty is valuable; but so are other things as well: security and property, for instance. It may be that the institutions of the *ancien régime* were deficient in liberty; but in a slow, gradual growth by trial and error, by adaptation to circumstances, a form of government had developed which, if not perfect, at least took account of, and in a measure achieved, a variety of goods. And this is better than so to insist on achieving some one good (it does not matter what) that all others are lost. For goods are not good in abstraction and isolation, but only so far as they fit harmoniously into a full and complete life.

In all of this Burke was doubtless reacting not only against the specific events of the revolution in France, but against a climate of opinion widespread in his contemporary world. Pope spoke for the century when he facilely characterized the world as "A mighty maze! but not without a plan."[1] Burke had little of the optimism with which the eighteenth century faced the problems of knowledge and of conduct. He did not believe that it was a simple matter either to know what we ought to do, or, knowing it, to do it. The world, he thought, is too complex to lay down a few simple rules which will hold absolutely in all cases; and our natures are too complex, our motives too various and conflicting, for us to be able rationally to follow such rules even if they exist.

These conclusions are strikingly modern in tone. Psychological, sociological, and anthropological investigation has shown that the world is not so simple, nor man's motives so logical, as we once supposed. This judgment has not been without its effect on modern political theory. If man is not primarily rational, it is idle, many have concluded, to appeal to his 'reason.' If man is essentially an animal, moved by animal loves and fears, we can best control him by playing

---

[1] Professor Whitehead has remarked on this. Vide *Science and the Modern World* (Cambridge University Press, 1925), p. 118.

upon these passions. Such Hobbesian conclusions seem inevitable to many, who, like Burke, see that the eighteenth-century exaggeration of the role of reason over-simplified the problems of knowledge and of conduct.

But Burke, unlike these contemporary thinkers, was saved from such cynical conclusions by his sense of the past. If the individual man has only a "small store of reason" there is a larger stock in society as a whole. There is nothing mystical or Hegelian in this notion—nothing that smacks of the concept of the state as a super-individual. What Burke means is simply that the result of a slow growth through the centuries, a long process of trial and error, has been to condense into our social institutions an immense store of wisdom which is thus available for every individual to draw upon so long as he lives in, and under, those institutions.

In place of the individual reason of the individual man, which was the primary political motive for Locke, Rousseau, and other 'enlightened' thinkers, Burke does not substitute brute force and propaganda, as did Hobbes and as do some modern writers. He conceives rather of society as an organism: its parts held together not as members of a joint stock company are, by a sense of mutual benefit, nor as slaves obedient to some Eastern despot, but as organs which have grown together, sharing a common life and following a customary pattern of behaviour whose smooth working is the product of a long period of unconscious growth. The heart does not browbeat the stomach, nor does it appeal to the stomach's sense of advantage to be gained by co-operation. Heart, stomach, and other organs have grown into this kind of arrangement, a mutual give and take which may, doubtless, not be ideal, but which is better than anything we could invent for them—better, indeed, than any arrangement they can reach except as a result of another long process of gradual growth.

This doctrine comes out clearly in Burke's notion of 'prejudice.' For a man of the Enlightenment, a prejudice is a judgment made on insufficient evidence. As such it is probably false, certainly inadequate. It should, therefore, be uprooted and replaced by a judgment which is certainly true, because it rests on good and sufficient grounds. For the Hobbesian sovereign and for some of our contemporary totalitarians, a prejudice is a sign of man's essential irrationality. Men are inevitably prejudiced. To uproot one prejudice is only to substitute for it another. But this weakness is a convenience that may be played upon to induce in men a desired line of conduct.

For Burke, a prejudice is a basic and inevitable part of human nature. Its function is to provide a powerful motive for action. In all this he agrees with the Hobbesian school. But for him this motive is not imposed from without. It is contained within. A prejudice contains a "latent wisdom" which has, as it were, grown up within the prejudice. How otherwise could it have survived long enough to become the prejudice that it is, but for the fact that it serves a useful purpose to society, even if that use be quite unrecognized by those who share the prejudice and act on it? Hence our prejudices should not be eradicated. They actually impel us to socially significant and valuable conduct. Without them we should want a sufficient motive, since nothing would be left us but "naked reason." And prejudice has a "motive to give action to that reason, and an affection which will give it permanence." [1]

Certainly this doctrine is not without its difficulties and dangers. Prejudice can contain evil as well as good. How are we to distinguish? A veneration for the past may induce a hatred of even the slightest change. A wise dislike of wild schemes of reform may result in a dogged refusal to allow any improvement. In fact, what Burke has to say may sometimes sound like a philosophical defence of die-hard Toryism. But because a concept can be misused, because it can be pushed to a false extreme, does not mean that it is without value. Burke himself, on the whole, maintained a just and reasonable mean. He was certainly at heart no more a die-hard Tory than he was an extreme radical. What name we attach to Burke's politics—whether we call him a "true conservative" or a "real liberal"—does not matter much, if we understand the quality of mind that these terms attempt to label. In many respects he does not differ so much from the revolutionists: he has as elevated a moral sense, as true a sense of justice, as profound a hatred of force, as has Rousseau or any of the other protagonists of the Revolution. But with Burke these noble ideals are tempered (though not annulled) by his realism. He knows how to make them effective instruments of progress, instead of dangerous weapons of anarchy, because he sees that these abstract ideals can have specific concrete meaning at any given point in time only in terms of what human nature is capable of at that time; and because he sees that human capacities are not absolutely and for ever fixed, but determined by the complex maze of institutions which form man's total social milieu. These institutions in which human nature is rooted have a slow, natural growth of their own, which can be

[1] *Vide supra*, p. 354.

interrupted, altered, or accelerated only with peril to the whole structure. It is like the human body which has a natural growth from the fœtus to adult man. We can assist this in some small ways; we can treat specific diseases as they occur, by specific remedies; we can supervise diet and exercise in the interest of general health. But if we try any radical acceleration of the body's growth, we are likely to get into serious trouble; we may even cause its death. Too much concern with its well-being may destroy it. Doubtless it would be better if things were simpler, more logical, less dependent on time and on history, more easily manipulated by human foresight and ingenuity. But they are not; and we must make the best that we can of it. This is the way the body is; this is the way the world is. The lesson, above all, to learn from Burke is this: we must start with the world as it is, not as we should like it to be.

For Further Reading

Texts

See footnote, p. 329.

Commentaries and General Works

COBBAN, A.: *Edmund Burke and the Revolt against the Eighteenth Century* (Allen and Unwin, 1929).
MORLEY, J.: *Edmund Burke* (Macmillan, 1928).
  Morley is also the author of the excellent article on Burke in the *Encyclopædia Britannica*, 11th edition.
OSBORN, A. M.: *Rousseau and Burke* (Oxford University Press, 1940).
PAINE, THOMAS: *The Rights of Man* (Everyman Library, 1915).
  A passionate reply to Burke's *Reflections*.

CHAPTER NINE

Jeremy Bentham

(1748–1832)

LIFE

THE juxtaposition of Burke and Bentham, as we have it in this book, is instructive. It should make us wary of generalizations about 'national character' and the 'temper of an age' into whose pleasant vagueness we are always tempted to fall. For here are two nearly contemporary Englishmen who are as little alike as any two men could be. Or, if it be pointed out that Burke, after all, was born an Irishman, we have only to compare Bentham with Montesquieu in order to see how misleading such generalizations can be. Like Burke, Montesquieu has all the characteristics which we usually associate with an 'English' mind—he is essentially conservative and empirical. He has a sense of the continuity of the present with the past; a veneration for the historical process by which institutions have been formed; a recognition that this is a natural development which human ingenuity may assist, but which it cannot radically alter. Bentham, on the other hand, is typically 'French': like the revolutionists across the Channel, he is a rationalist in thought and a radical in conduct. He feels that the historical process is not an orderly growth; it is only a meaningless wilderness. Hence the present is not continuous, but only contiguous, with the past. At any moment we can break with what has gone before and reorganize the world *ab initio* in accordance with our enlightened, carefully thought-out plan.

Whatever may be true about the qualities of Bentham's mind, the details of his life are prosaically English. His official biography managed to fill two volumes; but it is possible for us to be shorter, since Bentham's life—like Kant's—was as uneventful as the most regular of regular verbs. From the very beginning Bentham was retired, scholarly, and pedantic. He never really came into contact with that world whose complexities, disorders, and irregularities offended him. As a child, instead of playing games, he read the classics (he began learning Latin at the age of three). The result of this precocity was that his formal education at Westminster School and later at Queen's College, Oxford, was largely a waste of time. It was also a period of unhappiness, since he found his teachers stupid and his contemporaries, and their interests, unsympathetic to his tastes.

Bentham came of a family of well-to-do lawyers, and in 1763 he entered Lincoln's Inn himself to begin the study which was to be his life-long pursuit. Since he was not obliged to earn his living by competition for clients, he characteristically turned away from the practice of law to devote himself to theory. In this airy and abstract atmosphere he throve mightily, writing prolifically but publishing little and bringing to completion less. Most of what did see the light of day appeared only as 'fragments' and 'introductions'—parts of larger projects whose realization Bentham never achieved, since each difficulty which developed in the course of writing expanded itself into a separate treatise. Each of these in turn developed difficulties which required further treatises, and so on endlessly. Bentham was quite incapable of dealing effectively with the problems created by this expanding universe of treatises. But he was fortunate in finding a friend, a Genevan named Dumont, who took his manuscripts in hand, condensing, simplifying, and also translating them into French. This work has subsequently been done into English.[1] Though this is thus Bentham twice removed, the reader who seeks a short and relatively painless introduction to our author will do well to devote himself to it, rather than to plunge into the twenty-two volumes of his collected works.[2]

Bentham's interests were infinitely various: he wrote on economics, on logic, on psychology, on penology, on theology, on ethics—being led into each of these fields in the course of some other inquiry. But his main interest, to which he constantly recurs, is the law. Naturally this interest is not historical or expository: it is critical, or, as Bentham calls it,[3] 'censorial'—he tells us what he thinks the law ought to be.

[1] Bentham's *Theory of Legislation*, translated from the French of Étienne Dumont by Charles Milner Atkinson (Oxford University Press, 2 vols., 1914). The reader who wishes to acquire some sense of Bentham's own prolixity might consult his *Fragment on Government* (see note 1, page 4). It runs to 150 pages and consists of a minute and often captious criticism of a couple of paragraphs of Blackstone's *Commentaries*.

[2] *The Works of Jeremy Bentham* (edited by John Bowring, William Tait, 22 vols., 1843 *et seq.*).

[3] *Fragment on Government* (edited by F. C. Montague, Oxford University Press, 1931, p. 120).

The law ought to be reformed; and this reformation ought to be dual in nature. In the first place, Bentham never wearies of criticizing the content of existing laws on the ground that they fail to achieve the purpose for which they were (or ought to have been) promulgated. In the second place, he finds the arrangement of laws, or rather the lack of any systematic arrangement, indefensible. Bentham's views on the nature of sovereignty, on the organization of government and its relation to subjects and other political problems, are really determined by his desires for legal reform. Thus Bentham is in fact no more a political philosopher than he is an economist, a psychologist, or a moralist. He is, of course, all these things, but only indirectly and accidentally. First, last, and always he is a reformer. But we must remember that he is a curious kind of reformer. Most reformers are, perhaps, too practical, too shortsighted: they cannot see the woods for the trees. But Bentham was so much preoccupied with his own definition of 'forest' and with various deductions from it, that he did not see how little real woods are like his conception of them.

POLITICAL PHILOSOPHY

The Principle of Utility

Although none of our philosophers has written so voluminously as has Bentham, we can give a fair idea of his theory more shortly than was possible in any other case. This is so because the schema of Bentham's thought is simple and straightforward: he states a single principle (which he takes to be so clear and self-evident as to require no proof) and proceeds to apply it in exhaustive detail to every department of political activity. Our discussion of Bentham can follow his own programme. We shall first state the principle in question and venture to offer some criticisms of it, and then give one or two illustrations of the way the principle is applied.[1]

Bentham's principle is shortly stated. It is that, of the various possibilities open to us in any given case, we ought to choose that which will produce the greatest happiness (*i.e.*, pleasure) to the greatest number.[2]

[1] This may be thought to treat Bentham too cavalierly. If so, we may remind the reader that the plan of this series includes a more extensive treatment of Bentham in the third volume.

[2] *Theory of Legislation*, pp. 1-5, 28, 42-43, 37-39.

¶ The end and aim of a legislator should be the HAPPINESS of the people. In matters of legislation, GENERAL UTILITY should be his guiding principle. The science of legislation consists, therefore, in determining what makes for the good of the particular community whose interests are at stake, while its art consists in contriving some means of realization. . . . To apply [this principle] with complete efficiency, that is, to make it the very foundation of a system of reasoning, three conditions must be fulfilled.

First, we must attach to the word *Utility* a clear and precise connotation. . . .

Second, we must assert the supreme and undivided sovereignty of this principle by rigorously discarding every other. . . . No exception to its applicability can, in any circumstances, be allowed.

Thirdly, we must discover some calculus or process of 'moral arithmetic' by means of which we may arrive at uniform results. . . .

Nature has placed mankind under the governance of two sovereign masters, *Pleasure* and *Pain*. To them . . . we refer all our decisions, every resolve that we make in life. The man who affects to have withdrawn himself from their despotic sway does not know what he is talking about. To seek pleasure and to shun pain is his sole aim, even at the moment when he is denying himself the greatest enjoyment or courting penalties the most severe. This maxim, unchangeable and irresistible as it is, should become the chief study of the Moralist and of the Legislator. To these two motives the *principle of utility* subjects everything.

Utility is an abstract term. It means the property or tendency of any particular thing to shield from some evil or to secure some good. *Evil* means pain, suffering or the cause of suffering. *Good* means pleasure, or the cause of pleasure. . . .

The *Principle of Utility*, accordingly, consists in taking as our starting-point, in every process of ordered reasoning, the calculus of comparative estimate of pains and pleasures, and in not allowing any other idea to intervene.

I am an adherent of the *Principle of Utility* when I measure my approval or disapproval of any act, public or private, by its tendency to produce pains and pleasures; when I use the terms *just, unjust, moral, immoral, good, bad*, as comprehensive terms which embrace the idea of certain pains and certain pleasures, and have no other meaning whatsoever. And it must always be understood that I use these words *Pain* and *Pleasure* in their ordinary signification,

¶ without having recourse to arbitrary definitions for the purpose of ruling out certain forms of pleasure, or denying the existence of certain pains. . . .

An adherent to the *Principle of Utility* holds virtue to be a good thing by reason only of the pleasures which result from the practice of it: he esteems vice to be a bad thing by reason only of the pains which follow in its train. Moral good is *good* only on account of its tendency to secure physical benefits: moral evil is *evil* only on account of its tendency to induce physical mischief. But when I say 'physical,' I refer to pains and pleasures of the heart and mind as well as to the pains and pleasures of sense: I have in view man, just as he is, in his actual constitution.

Should an adherent of this principle find, in the commonly accepted list of virtues, some action from which more pain than pleasure would ensue, he would not shrink from treating the alleged virtue as a vice; he would not allow himself to be deceived by a vulgar error, nor would he readily believe that we must rely on the practice of sham virtues to afford support for genuine ones. Moreover, should he find in the ordinary list of stock offences some trivial act, some harmless form of pleasure, he would not shrink from transferring the alleged offence into the category of lawful acts: he would feel sympathy with the alleged criminals, and reserve his indignation for the unctuous worthies who seek to harass them. . . .

We daily experience a variety of perceptions which give us no concern at all: which are, so to speak, constantly gliding over us without engaging our attention. In this way we find that most everyday familiar objects no longer produce sensations lively enough to cause us either pleasure or pain. The names 'pleasure' and 'pain' can, indeed, be properly applied only to what may be called 'interesting perceptions'; that is to say, perceptions which force themselves into notice amidst the crowd, and are such as we desire either to prolong or to make an end of, as the case may be.

Interesting perceptions are either simple or complex: simple when they cannot, in any instance, be resolved into more than one: complex when they are composed of several simple pains or simple pleasures, or, perhaps, of a mixture of pleasures and pains. It is the nature of the exciting cause which determines us to regard several pleasures as a complex pleasure, and not as divers simple ones. When pleasures are excited at the same time and by the action of the same cause, we are apt to treat them all as constituting a single

¶ complex pleasure. Thus, a theatrical display, which gratifies several of our senses at once by the beauty of the scenery, the dresses, the action of the players, the music, and the society, constitutes such a complex pleasure. . . .[1]

The diffusion of Pleasures and the avoidance of Pains are the only ends which a legislator should have in view. It behoves him, then, to acquire a just and precise appreciation of their respective values. Seeing that Pleasures and Pains are the *instruments* he has to work with, he ought to make a very careful study of their magnitude and strength, which, indeed, from another point of view, constitute their value.

Now, if we examine the *value* of a pleasure, considered by itself and in relation to a single individual, we shall find that it depends on four circumstances: (1) *Its Intensity*; (2) *its Duration*; (3) *its Certainty*; (4) *its Proximity*.

The value of a pain depends upon like considerations.

But, in dealing with Pains and Pleasures, it is not enough to assess their value as though they were, necessarily, isolated and independent. Pains and pleasures may have as *consequences* other pains and pleasures. If, therefore, we wish to estimate the *tendency* of any act from which pain or pleasure directly results, we must take into account two other circumstances: These are (5) *its Fecundity* or *Productiveness*; (6) *its Purity*. A *productive pleasure* is one which is likely to be followed by other pleasures of the same kind. A *productive pain* is one which is likely to be followed by other pains of the same kind. A *pure pleasure* is one which is not likely to produce pain. A *pure pain* is one which is not likely to produce pleasure.

When the calculation is to be made in relation to a number of individuals, yet another circumstance is to be taken into account— (7) *its Extent*. That is, the number of persons who are likely to be affected by this particular pleasure or pain, as the case may be.

Suppose we wish to take exact account of the value of a certain action. We must follow, in detail, the various operations which have just been indicated. These provide the elements of a moral calculus, and Legislation may thus become a mere matter of

---

[1] Bentham finds fifteen simple pleasures and only eleven (it is comforting to note) simple pains. They are: *Pleasures* of sense, wealth, skill, amity, good character or repute, power, piety, benevolence, malevolence, intellect, memory, imagination, hope, association, and relief; and *Pains* of privation, sense, awkwardness, enmity, ill-repute, piety, benevolence, malevolence, memory, imagination, and anticipation.

¶Arithmetic. The *evil*, or *pain*, inflicted is the expenditure; the *good*, or *pleasure*, engendered is the income.

The rules of such a calculus are the same as those of any other. . . .

The will cannot be influenced except by motives; and to speak of a *motive* is to speak of Pain or Pleasure. A being, in whom we were powerless to excite an emotion either of pain or of pleasure, would, so far as we are concerned, be utterly independent.

The pain or the pleasure, which is attached to the observance of a law, forms what is called the *sanction* of the law. The laws of one State are not laws in another; and for this reason, that they have there no sanction, no obligatory force. Now, we find four distinguishable sources from which pleasures and pains are wont to flow: the *Physical*, the *Moral or Popular*, the *Political*, the *Religious*.

Regarding pains and pleasures in the character of punishment and reward attached to certain rules of conduct, we may, therefore, distinguish four sanctions:

1. The *physical or natural* sanction comprises the pains and pleasures which we may experience, or expect, in the ordinary course of nature, not purposely modified by any human interposition.

2. The *moral* sanction comprises such pains and pleasures as we experience, or expect, at the hands of our fellows, prompted by feelings of hatred or goodwill, or contempt or regard: in a word, according to the spontaneous disposition of each individual. This sanction may also be styled *popular*; the sanction of *public opinion*, or of *honour*; or the sanction of the *pains and pleasures of* sympathy.

3. The *political* sanction comprises such pains and pleasures as we may experience, or expect, at the hands of the magistracy, acting under law. This might, with equal propriety, be termed the *legal* sanction.

4. The *religious* sanction comprises such pains and pleasures as we may experience, or expect, in virtue of the forebodings and promises of religion.

A man's house is destroyed by fire. Is it by reason of his own imprudence? If so, it is a punishment of the *natural* sanction. Is it by direction of the magistrate? If so, it is a punishment of the *political* sanction. Is it owing to the ill-will of his neighbours who withheld assistance? If so, it is a punishment of the *popular* sanction. Is it supposed to have been occasioned by the immediate act of some offended Divinity? If so, it will be a punishment of the *religious* sanction, or, in vulgar parlance, a judgment of God. This

¶illustration shows that the same sorts of pain belong to all the sanctions: the difference lies only in the circumstances which bring them into operation.

Our classification of the sanctions will be found very useful in the course of this work. It affords a simple and uniform nomenclature, absolutely necessary to the discrimination and correct labelling of the various kinds of moral force, which, as intellectual levers, constitute the machinery of the human heart. They do not, of course, act upon all men in the same way or with the same effect; and, indeed, the four sanctions are sometimes found as allies, at other times as rivals, or even as open enemies. When they act together, they operate with irresistible force; when they are in direct conflict, they mutually enfeeble each other; while, even if they be rivals, they can hardly fail to lead men into hesitating and confused actions.

We might readily conceive four distinct bodies, or codes, of law which would correspond respectively to the four sanctions; though the highest point of perfection would, manifestly, be reached could they be consolidated or merged in a single code. This goal is, as yet, far distant; but, after all, it may be impossible to attain it. . . .

It will be recalled that Bentham set up three "conditions" which his principle had to fulfil: It must be "clear and precise"; it must be the single and sufficient account of motivation; it must be applicable by means of a "moral calculus." In the passages we have quoted Bentham has attempted to meet these conditions. We must now point out that in no case was he successful. The principle is, in fact,

(a) *Ambiguous*. When Bentham urges us to produce the greatest happiness for the greatest number, he implies that in any given case there is *one* alternative which (if we knew it) would be the correct course of action to pursue. But suppose two possible actions, x and y. Suppose x to be capable of producing 25 units of happiness for each of 5 people ($25 \times 5 = 125$); and y, 4 units of happiness for each of 25 people ($4 \times 25 = 100$). Which is the correct course to follow? If we are ruled by the recommendation to produce the greatest happiness, we shall do x; if by the recommendation to serve the greatest number, we shall do y. In other words, what appears on the surface to be a single, self-evident exhortation is really two separate exhortations which (more often than not) contradict each other.

(b) *Insufficient*. Bentham not only argues that we *ought* always to aim at pleasure, but that as a matter of fact everybody does always aim at pleasure. This is an over-simplification of human motives. Even allowing that men ought to seek nothing but pleasure, it is clear that they are often moved by other considerations. It is not the case, as Bentham supposes, that we all act from a single motive, desire for pleasure; that we differ, if at all, only in the objects which produce pleasure for us; and that the whole problem of conduct is simply a matter of determining what objects will produce the most pleasure. It is characteristic of Bentham, for instance, to identify duty and interest—*i.e.*, to claim that we have but one duty, which is to seek the greatest possible pleasure. If Bentham were correct, no one would ever feel a conflict between duty and interest; but as a matter of fact such a conflict is a matter of common experience.[1] Suppose we are faced with the alternative of telling the truth or escaping a concentration camp. If we conceive the former to be our duty, we may do it, despite the suffering we bring down upon ourselves. To deny that men sometimes do in fact choose this kind of alternative is to fly in the face of experience; but it is folly to claim (as Bentham is obliged to) that the man who chooses this alternative does so because it gives him an excess of pleasure.

The fact seems to be that men are not moved by one motive, but by many diverse ones; that there is not one satisfaction, pleasure, present in varying amounts, but many qualitatively different satisfactions.

Bentham supposes there to be but one end, pleasure, and the only variation of satisfaction is in quantity—whether more or less pleasure. It seems rather to be the case that there are many qualitatively different satisfactions, which are only too often incapable of comparison simply in terms of more or less. This fact about human motivation is hidden from Bentham by his concentration upon the word pleasure. And this is only an empty abstraction. If we must use the word at all, we had best talk about pleasure*s*; but it would be safer to avoid it altogether. Bentham, however, appears to suppose the existence of an identical object corresponding to the word—*i.e.*, he supposes that there exists an entity, pleasure, like a physical object, which may be added to, divided, parcelled out, like a plate of cakes at a tea party. Unfortunately for Bentham, there is no simple, self-identical entity pleasure

---

[1] It is not argued here that men are *correct* in detecting such a conflict, but merely that they do feel conflicts of this kind and that these conflicts are sometimes expressed in their conduct. If Bentham were correct in maintaining that men seek nothing but pleasure, it is obvious that nobody could ever experience a conflict between duty and interest.

corresponding to the term, and attaching itself in greater or less amount to various objects and activities. There are, rather, many various and qualitatively diverse satisfactions, each coloured through and through by the object or activity which bears it. Bentham supposes that there is a lump of pleasure of a certain mass (like a cake of a certain weight) attached to going for a walk and so much more or less of the same lump attached to staying at home. But we have only to take leave of theory for the sake of introspection in order to see that there is a going-for-a-walk satisfaction qualitatively distinct from the attractions of staying at home, because each is characterized by all the peculiar flavours which make up each activity.

(c) *Inapplicable*. Bentham's moral calculus presupposes the view of pleasure we have just been criticizing. It is not, indeed, very satisfactory even then, for he does not give any scale for weighing his various factors against each other. It is all very well, for instance, to say that we must consider both intensity and duration. If we had two pleasures of equal intensity, we would know enough to choose the more durable. But suppose they vary both in intensity and duration, what then? How much intensity weighs against how long duration? Since Bentham does not tell us, his calculus is not of much use. And the fact is, of course, that he cannot tell us. Satisfactions are not the sorts of things which can be measured. Or, rather, though we can perhaps make some sort of estimate of, say, duration and proximity, these calculations are of little significance in choosing between two qualitatively different satisfactions—*e.g.*, doing one's duty and avoiding punishment.

The last three factors in the calculus (*i.e.*, productiveness, purity, and extent) create another kind of problem. Any calculation of pleasures and pains is a calculation about the future. Now, quite apart from the impossibility of comparing qualitatively distinct satisfactions, there is a difficulty about the future course of events. We have not only to choose between x and y on the basis of their immediate consequences in the way of pleasure and pain, but on the basis of their consequences into an indefinitely remote future and (presumably) for generations yet unborn. We may want to draw back from this conclusion and to set a limit to the future which has to come into the legislator's considerations. But where, and on what basis, are we to set the limit? And in any case it is clear that, however short-range the view we require of him, that future is too uncertain for his estimates to possess the precision Bentham requires and expects.

Reform

The principle is supposed to give us an absolutely precise criterion for testing every existing institution, every proposed piece of legislation. Existing practices, however, are the product of a slow, haphazard process, partly natural growth, partly trial and error, partly adaptation to circumstances, partly compromise between opposite pressures. Few if any of them may be supposed to satisfy the requirements of utility. It would be natural, therefore, to expect Bentham to be a radical reformer. Eventually Bentham did, indeed, call for a basic reform of the British Government, since he decided that rule by a democratic majority was most likely to produce the greatest pleasure for the greatest number.[1] But this can hardly be said to be extreme radicalism; and as a matter of fact Bentham is often as conservative as any Tory. The reasons for this apparent paradox are not far to seek. In the first place, the principle of utility, being only pseudo-scientific, does not give objectively valid results. When an engineer calculates the stresses for a bridge he is building, the results he reaches are not significantly affected by his temperament or emotional biases. But the principle of utility is so subjective that one's conclusions are always weighed in certain directions rather than in others. Thus Bentham's native caution determines him to favour security and the *status quo*.

Again, Bentham is a devoted adherent of *laissez-faire*. He thinks that governmental regulation and 'interference' ought to be kept at a minimum, and that when it is necessary it should be only negative: it may restrict certain practices, but it may not enforce others. He reaches this conclusion not only because he believes that we all aim at pleasure, but because he also believes that we are sufficiently rational to see that in the long run our well-being is best promoted by that of others.

In the third place, Bentham considers that men's expectations are relevant to his calculus. This inevitably leads him to favour the *status quo*. For men expect to continue in the possession of the goods they already own, and they will be pained by the disappointment of this expectation. If we take this distress seriously, as Bentham does, we shall not advocate any very extensive reform of existing institutions. All of this can be seen in more detail in the passages which follow.[2]

[1] In some respects Bentham's conclusions about the form of government are like those of the French revolutionists, though he bitterly opposed the reasons by which they reached this position. It is not, of course, that he is really any less doctrinaire than they; for, if they argue from abstract 'rights of man,' Bentham argues from an equally abstract 'pleasure'. But he *thinks* that they are talking metaphysical nonsense, while he is purely scientific.

[2] *Theory of Legislation*, pp. 65, 119–129.

¶ It is, then, with government as it is with medicine; its only business is the choice of evils. Every law is an evil, because every law is a violation of liberty; so that government, I say again, can only choose between evils. What should be the aim of the legislator when making this choice? He should satisfy himself of two things: *First*, that in all cases the events which he strives to prevent are really evils; and, *secondly*, that these evils are greater than those he is about to employ as the means of prevention. . . .

The legislator ought to confer rights with alacrity, because they are in themselves a benefit; he ought to impose obligations with reluctance, because they are in themselves an evil. The principle of Utility requires that he should never impose a burden except for the purpose of conferring a benefit of greater value. . . .

Now, every curtailment of liberty is, in the nature of things, likely to be followed by a feeling of pain, more or less great; and this, quite independently of such suffering and inconvenience as may be occasioned by the form of restraint resorted to in the particular case. It follows, therefore, that no restriction ought to be imposed, no power conferred, no coercive law sanctioned, save on some specific and sufficient grounds. . . .

[For the same reason] the care of providing enjoyments should be left almost entirely to the individual himself, the principal function of government being to protect him from suffering. . . .

In prescribing and distributing rights and obligations, the legislator should, as we have pointed out, seek as his end and aim the happiness of the body politic. Inquiring more particularly wherein this happiness consists, we find four subordinate objects: 'Subsistence,' 'Abundance,' 'Equality,' 'Security.' . . . All the functions of law may be referred to one or other of these four heads: to provide subsistence, to aim at abundance, to encourage equality, and to maintain security. . . . 'Subsistence' . . . is included in 'abundance': and yet it is very necessary to consider it separately; inasmuch as the law ought to approve many things with a view of providing subsistence, which it should by no means suffer for the mere purpose of promoting abundance. . . .

I have ranked 'equality' among the objects of the law. In any arrangement contrived to give to all men the greatest possible sum of happiness, there is no reason why the law should cast about to give more to one man than to another. . . . But herein lies the peril:

¶a single mistake [in extending equality too far] may overthrow the social order and dissolve the bonds of society.

Some persons may be surprised to find that 'Liberty' is not ranked among the principal objects of the law. But, if we would avoid confusion we must regard it as a branch of 'security.' 'Personal liberty' is security against a certain class of wrongs which affect the person; while what is called 'political liberty' is also a branch of security—security against injustice at the hand of the persons intrusted with government. . . .

. . . What is done in the interests of 'security' may, at the same time, promote 'subsistence' and 'abundance.' But, on the other hand, circumstances occur in which it is not possible to reconcile these objects, and a measure suggested by one principle will be condemned by another. For example, 'equality' might require such a distribution of property as would be incompatible with 'security.' When, between two of these ends, conflict, in fact, occurs, we must needs determine which is to prevail. . . .

Now, at the first glance, it is plain that 'subsistence' and 'security' rise together to the same height;[1] while 'abundance' and 'equality' manifestly stand at a lower level. Indeed, without security, equality could not endure for a day; and without subsistence, abundance would obviously be an impossibility. The first two objects are life itself; the last two serve, so to speak, as the embellishments of life. . . .

Equality ought not to be favoured, except when it does not injuriously affect security, nor disappoint expectations aroused by the law itself, nor disturb a distribution already actually settled and determined.

Property [2]

¶ That we may more fully appreciate the advantages of law, let us endeavour to form a clear conception of 'property.' We shall find that there is no such thing as natural property; it is entirely the creature of law.

Property is nothing more than the basis of a certain expectation; namely, the expectation of deriving hereafter certain advantages from a thing (which we are already said to possess) by reason of the relation in which we stand towards it. . . .

[1] Two pages earlier we were informed that "'security' is the principal, indeed the paramount, object."

[2] *Theory of Legislation*, pp. 145, 147, 148, 157.

¶ As regards property, 'security' consists in there being no shock or disturbance occasioned to the expectation, founded on the laws, of enjoying such and such a portion of wealth. The legislator owes the greatest respect to such expectations, for they are expectations which he himself has brought into being: it is essential to the happiness of society that he should not defeat them; and, whenever his edicts clash with them in any degree, those edicts give rise to a proportionate measure of positive evil. . . .

Anxious to act with due regard to this great principle of Security, what should be the ordinance of the legislator in respect to the mass of property already in existence? He ought to maintain the distribution as it is actually established. . . .

How is it possible to make a fresh distribution without taking from somebody what he already possesses? How can you despoil one man without assailing the security of all? . . . What becomes . . . of security, industry, happiness? . . .

But, perhaps, it may be objected that the laws of property, while good for those who have great possessions, press hardly on those who have none: that the poor man is really poorer and more unhappy than he would be without any such laws.

Now, by creating property, the laws have created wealth; while, so far as poverty is concerned, it is not the work of the laws at all—it is the original condition of mankind. The man who lives only from hand to mouth is exactly in the position of man in the state of nature—the savage. In an artificial state of society, the poor man, I admit, gains nothing save by painful toil; but, even in a state of nature, what could he obtain save by the sweat of his brow? . . . The work of our peasants is more monotonous [than that of savages], but their reward is better assured: the lot of their womankind is not so hard: there are more expedients for support, in case of infancy or old age:[1] the rate of increase in population is infinitely

---

[1] Bentham argues very effectively in favour of state support of the indigent. After painting a vivid picture of the pains of destitution (which, he says, is the "saddest aspect of social life"), he points out that, apart from action by a governmental agency, there are but two means of relief. These are savings and voluntary contributions, and neither is at all adequate.

"In view of these reflections [he goes on], we may, as it seems to me, lay it down as a general principle of legislation that a regular system of contribution should be established for the relief of the poor; it being clearly understood that those only are to be regarded as poor who lack the necessaries of life. . . . As to the scale of legal—that is to say, compulsory—contribution, it should not be in excess of simple necessaries; to go beyond this would be to tax industry for the benefit of sloth. . . ." (*Theory of Legislation*, pp. 174–175.)

¶ greater—and this circumstance alone would suffice to show on which side superiority of happiness lies.

This is a characteristic Benthamite argument! The fact (if it is a fact) that modern workers are happier than savages does not prove that they are as happy as they might be. The fact that we should all be more unhappy than we are at present were there no property laws at all, does not prove that we might not be more happy were there different property laws. The fact that a condition in which some own property is preferable to a condition of savagery does not prove that the former condition is preferable to one in which there is public ownership of property. Nor, once again, is it obvious that the disappointment of the wealthy will outweigh the joy of the poor, supposing that a redistribution of property occurs. In fact, any argument based, as Bentham's is, on expectations is extremely precarious. For expectations are variable, and if they change enough the argument may vanish. What percentage of his income does a man expect to have left after he has paid his taxes? Bentham's generation would suffer a shock of incalculable proportions by what is accepted with equanimity to-day. In a word, the arguments from utility, even if they were valid in other respects, break down because they assume that human nature in the second half of the eighteenth century is the final and ultimate form of man. Bentham's neglect of the past makes him fasten all the more firmly on the present. Because he fails to see that the present has grown out of the past he fails to see that the present will eventually grow into the future. Hence he fails to see the relativity of his own argument to conditions as they happen to exist when he wrote.

Bentham and Ourselves

In some respects we are very close to Bentham; in others we are farther from him than from Machiavelli. In some respects, again, he belongs in the century of his birth;[1] in others he points the way that

---

[1] Montague has put this very well. He says that "Bentham's writings . . . are highly characteristic of that remarkable age of thought which is commonly styled the eighteenth century, but which really extended from the cessation of the wars of religion to the outbreak of the French Revolution. They display all its most striking attributes; its immense hopefulness of the future joined with the extravagant contempt for the past; its generous humanity alloyed with a somewhat sordid conception of human nature; its venturous scientific spirit suffused with the most arrogant dogmatism; its grotesque pedantry blended with the shrewdest common sense " (*op. cit.*, p. 57).

political philosophy was to take in the nineteenth and twentieth centuries. This is why a chapter on Bentham fittingly stands both at the end of this volume in the series and at the beginning of the next.

If we compare Bentham with Locke, for instance, we find two entirely different modes of argument. They may agree that one of the State's most important functions is the protection of private property. But Locke argues this because he recognizes that all men have a natural right to "life, liberty, and estate." Bentham, on the other hand, thinks it sufficient to show that the protection of private property is conducive to "the general happiness." We may phrase this differently by saying that Locke's justification of the State is primarily moral, while Bentham's is primarily hedonistic. Locke's argument moves almost entirely in the domain of certain allegedly self-evident axioms about human nature and conduct. He is chiefly interested in pointing out what these axioms are and in showing what implications they ought to have in the sphere of political relations. He urges that these axioms ought to be implemented in the actual political structure, but he is not concerned to show how this can be accomplished. With Bentham the political problem is radically simplified. According to him we have one clear and indubitable end—pleasure. Everything else is merely a calculation of how this end can be produced. All political problems are therefore problems about ways and means. Their solution depends on a sound knowledge of the actual political, social, and economic process. Thus Bentham makes political *theory* insignificant in comparison with political *science*, for every political problem is automatically reduced to a form which requires an immediate empirical investigation.

Now, though there certainly were political theorists in the nineteenth century, it is fair to say that this interest in practice has become more and more dominant. There is no doubt that to-day Bentham's type of argument is more sympathetic than is Locke's. Even though the latter's thesis is embedded in the American Constitution, we have only to read a newspaper editorial, listen to a debate in Congress, or study a decision of the Supreme Court in order to see how pervasive Bentham's point of view is. It is not fashionable to-day to argue in favour of a piece of legislation that it is 'right'—*i.e.*, in agreement with some intuitively recognized moral principle. We rather support the proposal by urging that it is 'good'—*i.e.*, that it will produce more happiness than the alternative. And even if we do hold the action to be right, it is usually only on the ground that it is productive of some good. In a word, like Bentham, we are more interested in results than we are in principles. In this broad sense Bentham may be said to have been a harbinger of the ever increasingly pragmatic temper of the modern mind.

But, if we find Bentham's conception of the end and method of politics congenial, the same cannot be said for the means. Here we differ widely from Bentham and find ourselves more at home with, say, Burke or Montesquieu. The fact is that, just as Bentham simplified the political problem by reducing everything to a calculation of the means to one end, so he also simplified it by reducing the calculation itself to an easy hedonistic appraisal. And this latter simplification, whatever we feel about the former, would be universally rejected to-day. For one thing, few people think that human motivation is as uniquely directed as Bentham conceived it to be. Men do not seem to aim at a single abstraction, 'pleasure,' so much as at an almost infinitely various and diverse group of specific things. Again, to-day most people would say that Bentham's notion of human nature is too optimistic. Even if all men do aim at the same thing, pleasure, it is not so easy for them to "sit down in a cool hour" [1] and determine what action will produce the greatest amount of pleasure. In a word, Bentham's view seems to us naïve, because we know (or think we know) more about psychology. Machiavelli seems to us to know more about human nature than all of Bentham's scientific apparatus could teach him. We may not agree with all that Machiavelli says, but like him we find man to be an exceedingly complex creature, sometimes enlightened, but often perverse, irrational, and inconsistent.

We also find Bentham's calculation of means naïve because we have (or think we have) a keener sense both of man's dependence on the institutions in which he lives and of their growth through an historical process. Like Bodin and Montesquieu we are very much aware of our relation to our physical environment; like Montesquieu and Burke we are very much aware of our relation to our past; like all three of these thinkers we are highly conscious of the extent to which a complex social and physical milieu determines the kind of people we are. In this respect, therefore, we are much closer to them than to Bentham, who almost entirely ignored these factors and conceived men to be self-enclosed individuals, as independent of each other and their environment as are the bricks which together form a wall.

Thus the interesting thing for us about Bentham is not his specific

---

[1] The phrase is Bishop Butler's.

recommendations, though these certainly had an impact on the course of events through the intermediation of his disciples. It is rather the fact that he is a transitional figure. In the *way* in which he conceives human nature and the play of political forces, he is as intellectualistic and rationalistic as the most eighteenth-century of philosophers. But in his conception of the political problem as essentially a practical one, in his interest in reform, in his concern for physical well-being, he is much more nearly our contemporary than the dates of his birth and death suggest.

FOR FURTHER READING

Texts

See footnotes, p. 367.

Commentaries and General Works

MacCunn, J.: *Six Radical Thinkers* (Arnold, 1907).
      Contains a useful but short chapter on Bentham.
Mill, J. S.: *Utilitarianism* (Everyman Library, 1910).
      This is the classic statement and defence of the Benthamite thesis.
Stephen, L.: *English Utilitarians* (Duckworth, 3 vols., 1900).
      The first volume is devoted to Bentham.

Index